The Unruly New Territories

The Unruly New Territories

Small Houses, Ancestral Estates, Illegal Structures, and Other Customary Land Practices of Rural Hong Kong

Malcolm Merry

HKU PRESS
香港大學出版社

Hong Kong University Press
The University of Hong Kong
Pok Fu Lam Road
Hong Kong
https://hkupress.hku.hk

ISBN 978-988-8528-32-5 (*Hardback*)

British Library Cataloguing-in-Publication Data
A catalogue record for this book is available from the British Library.

Digitally printed

Contents

1

An Unruly Territory

Ever since incorporation into Hong Kong at the end of the nineteenth century, the New Territories have been causing trouble. Initially that was in the form of armed resistance to the British takeover of April 1899. This was followed by reluctance to co-operate with, and occasional misleading of, the surveyors who mapped and recorded the land and its ownership on behalf of the new authorities. Then it turned out that most of the land had two owners and some of the population tried to convince the new government that they owned land which was not theirs. A pattern was set for the future.

The truculent attitude and independent spirit of the rural population was referred to by Sir Frederick Lugard, Hong Kong's governor, a few years after the takeover. 'The people are not lambs in the Territory!' he declared to Legislative Council approval.[1] The spirit has been noted by one familiar with rural life in the mid-twentieth century. Dr James Hayes, who served as a District Officer in various, largely poorer, parts of the New Territories, became aware that the past was still influencing thinking and behaviour: 'For centuries, circumstances had obliged them to be self-managing and independent-minded, and their robustness and tenacity, tinged with a strong dose of pragmatism, was still very much in evidence.'[2]

This spirit must have been one of the factors behind the population's careful and considerate treatment by Hong Kong administrators during that century. Traditional attitudes and customs were indulged and protected by colonial officers, especially in regard to land and houses. Care and consideration was also advisable because of the organizational capacity and solidarity of the indigenous community evident in rural committees and the Heung Yee Kuk.

Contrary to their original intention of simply using the existing Ching land register, the new authorities imposed upon rural landowners a fundamental change in the method of holding land. They were forced to do so by circumstances. The change, which is explored later in this book, was not as great as has been claimed

1. Quoted in James Hayes, 'The Great Difference, The Great Rift, and The Great Need: The New Territories of Hong Kong and Its People, Past and Present' (2008) 30 *Asia Pacific Journal of Public Administration* 139, 143 ('The Great Difference' (article)).
2. Hayes, 'The Great Difference' (article) 160.

from time to time by indigenous spokesmen, but the perception that it was has fuelled rural discontent for generations. So has the conviction that the incoming government reneged on promises made in 1899 not to interfere with the people's customs. In fact the government instituted a statute specifically preserving customary law in land matters and recognizing family landholding institutions and other traditional practices. Most of that statute, the New Territories Ordinance, survives today. Its background and content are dealt with in six of the chapters that follow.

As if in compensation for such perceived wrongs, government officials embarked on an approach of mollifying and indulging the indigenous community and their practices. The policy was to keep things much the same, so the territory was shielded from developments elsewhere. The way of life in rural parts in the 1950s and 1960s, with their quaint villages, ancient ways and preserved culture, was in marked contrast to that in urban Hong Kong and on the mainland. The whole place seemed out of time, a museum piece, more Chinese than China itself. Even in those days the contrast and the privileges led to New Territories people being described as 'China's spoilt children'.[3]

The Kuk

Partly spurred by perceived grievances against their treatment by the New Territories administration, in 1926 wealthier members of the local population established a representative body out of which emerged the Heung Yee Kuk, or Rural Representative Council. This association's original aim was to promote the welfare of the people of the New Territories not just in respect of agricultural land and housing, but also in commerce and industry. Within a generation of the absorption of the area into the vibrant Western-style colony of Hong Kong, native leaders had resolved to exploit the opportunities it created. They have been doing so ever since. Making difficulties for the government has been part of their method, and a successful one.

The kuk has become a well-organized and effective modern interest group with influence well beyond what might be expected given the numbers of the people that it represents. Consisting as it does of people with roots in the New Territories, it has not been without internal disputes. Factionalism and machinations in the 1950s led to withdrawal of official recognition, followed by the kuk's reform in November 1959 with the enactment of its own ordinance.[4] The object was, according to the ordinance's long title, 'to ensure that it will as far as possible be truly representative of informed and responsible opinion' in the New Territories. Its governing body is made up of representatives elected by the various rural committees, themselves elected by indigenes and other villagers.

---

3. Austin Coates, *Myself a Mandarin: Memoirs of a Special Magistrate* (Hong Kong: Heinemann Asia, 1975), p 62.
4. Ordinance No 45 of 1959 (11 November 1959), now Cap 1097.

The kuk represents 'the people of the New Territories', a phrase repeatedly used, but not defined, in its ordinance. Since some villages came into existence after 1898 and are represented on rural committees, the people referred to are not confined to aboriginals, but the majority of the population in the modern New Territories, those who live in suburbs and new towns, are certainly not regarded as being represented by the kuk. Here, therefore, 'the New Territories' is largely synonymous with the rural areas.

The statutory functions of the kuk are full of high-sounding generalizations: to promote and develop mutual co-operation between the people of the New Territories and understanding between those people and the government; to advise the government on social and economic development in the interests of the welfare and prosperity of those people; and to encourage observance of such of their customs and traditional usages as are conducive to their welfare. The focus is upon their relationship with each other and with the administration, without regard for the wider Hong Kong community. The ordinance remains redolent of the era in which it was first enacted: of paternal concern for the rural poor and advancement of the under-privileged.

The well-meaning aims of the colonial government were hardly reciprocated by the kuk's leaders. Rather, they dwelt upon perceived injustices, particularly in relation to land, and composed a narrative of victimhood that quite ignored both historical fact and the good fortune of their incorporation into twentieth-century Hong Kong. This statement of one of the kuk's chairmen indicates the attitude: 'Without the consent of the New Territories landowners the Hong Kong Government unilaterally drew up the Block Crown Lease in 1905 in order to control the use of private land'.[5] These assertions disregard the principal purpose of the leases, which was to raise government revenue, ignore the exclusive rights bestowed by the leases upon the leaseholders (who under the imperial Chinese system had to share ownership with landlords), assume a pre-colonial freedom to use land that probably never existed and overlook the modern reality that control of the use of land is a widespread and legitimate power of government. In similar vein is this exaggerated and vaguely-threatening extract from a press release by the kuk in 1981: 'New Territories people loathe colonialism and there is a limit to their toleration of the unfair measures taken by the Hong Kong Government towards the New Territories'. In reality, as we shall see, rural people soon learnt to exploit and enjoy the benefits of being part of a free-enterprise economy. The more thoughtful among them must occasionally have reflected upon what their fate would have been had they remained within imperial China.

The kuk as a body has naturally shown the attributes of those it represents and of whom it is composed. It has been vociferous and tenacious in furthering their interests, attaching itself determinedly to those in authority, in latter years

5. Chan Yat-san, Heung Yee Kuk chairman, 1968–1978.

under the leadership of a superb political operator, its long-serving chairman the late Lau Wong Fat. But long before Mr Lau's chairmanship the practice had arisen of the government directing rural affairs in consultation with the kuk, as if the country areas were no business of the rest of Hong Kong. This unofficial condominium may be said to have worked. When land was needed for the factories and other undertakings which transformed the colony into an industrial powerhouse soon after the Second World War, farmers in the affected areas were persuaded to swap country for town. When continuation of British rule came under threat from mainland-inspired agitation in 1967, the majority of the kuk's leaders and of the rural population rallied to the government's side. They may or may not have loathed the colonialism that had brought so many changes to their lives, but most feared the available alternative even more. When, a few years later, land was needed for housing Hong Kong's rising population, country landowners acquiesced in providing it and were eventually well rewarded for doing so.

The acquiescence may have been reluctant but the kuk's wealth, organization, skilled negotiation and successful lobbying ensured that exceedingly generous compensation was offered to the owners whose lands were taken. At about the same time, it secured exorbitant privileges with regard to village houses. During the Sino-British negotiations on the future of Hong Kong in the 1980s, the kuk pressed the governments of both countries to heed its concerns. Later, further favourable terms were extracted from those who drafted the Basic Law of the Hong Kong Special Administrative Region (HKSAR). When functional constituencies were introduced into the Legislative Council in 1988, one (with the smallest electorate) was allocated to the kuk. Successive Chief Executives of the HKSAR have invited an individual from the kuk to join their Executive Council. In the twenty-first century, despite greatly changed circumstances, the kuk and the rural committees have been strident in asserting and advancing the sectional interests of the indigenous community.

They continued to be successful in doing so after the territory was handed back to China. The HKSAR's government has treated the indigenous with indulgence similar to that of its predecessor. In 1997 the government attempted to curb the sale of indigenous building rights to developers by insisting that applicants for small house grants make solemn declarations that they had not sold their rights to anyone and that they were the owners of the land on which the small house was to be built, a subversion of the Small House Policy that had been rife for years. When prosecutions for making false declarations followed, the kuk vehemently protested and the government eventually backed down, saving face by substituting criminalization of the conduct with an ineffective condition forbidding the practice in the house grant. In 2011 the proliferation of illegal extensions to village houses as a result of decades of failure to enforce building controls at last led to an announcement that action would be taken against them. Again, the rural reaction was sharp and again the administration backed off, substituting a voluntary register of such extensions for honest offenders in place of enforcement of the law. The kuk celebrated its continued dominion over the New Territories by building itself a palace-like headquarters at Shatin.

Certainly the Heung Yee Kuk's greatest achievement has been ensuring the continuation of rural privileges by entrenchment of indigenous traditional rights and interests, in Article 40 of the Basic Law. Those rights and interests are to be protected by the HKSAR, so the article declares. The provision is opaque: nobody knows exactly what rights and interests are referred to. This may be deliberate, the result of political compromise. Judges have so far largely avoided having fully to define the phrase. But it must refer to something and the doubt has given the kuk enough traction to intimidate administrators and challenge those who seek to curb indigenous privileges. The kuk believes that the article sets the Small House Policy in stone. This will be examined later in the book when an account will be given of the background to and content of the policy and an attempt will be made to give more meaning to Article 40.

Forged by Land and Climate

In fact, the attitudes that characterize the rural population go back to well before they were incorporated into the colony of Hong Kong. Survival in the largely rugged terrain and harsh summer climate of Po An Hsien (later San On or Xin'an), the imperial Chinese administrative district or county out of which the New Territories were later to be carved, demanded self-reliance and inventiveness of its villagers. In the seventeenth century the population had suffered the dislocation and trauma of forced evacuation. Only the hardy survived and returned. They were largely Cantonese, or Punti. Later they were joined by industrious peasant farmers from elsewhere. Under Ching rule, San On had enjoyed a large amount of autonomy.[6] The mountains were indeed high and the emperor far away. County magistrates were starved of resources and their staff corrupt. They relied upon local leaders to run the villages and markets. By the time of the British takeover, a large proportion of the people were descended from Hakka immigrants originating from northern and central China, people who had had the initiative to start a new life in an unpromising environment. The population's lives were remote from the regional capital, Canton, and little touched by the light and ineffective local government of the magistrate. At the end of the nineteenthth century their way of life had hardly changed for more than two hundred years.

During those centuries not only had the inhabitants of San On acquired some independence from central government, they had also evolved a system of landholding and transfer that was flexible and inventive—and illegal. Both the independence and the system were swept away by the reforms of land and administration introduced during the early years following the British takeover. However, incorporation

6. Hayes, 'The Great Difference' (article)143.

into Hong Kong hardly affected the attitudes of the people. They remained suspicious of authority. Writing thirty years after the takeover, S. H. Peplow, who had experience of rural parts from his service as Land Bailiff and as a District Officer, observed that life there little differed from that in other parts of China, nor had it altered much during the years of British occupation:

> The average villager does not set great store by cleanliness, or better housing. He finds himself unable to understand our aims and ideas . . . He frankly dislikes our iconoclastic spirit, our want of imagination, and our blindness to the forces of nature. He fears the inquisitions of the Police, or for that matter any other officer of the government service.

Peplow went on to recount how, if he asked a group of villagers for a certain person, they would enquire what the man was wanted for and Peplow would be forced into a long explanation before, if it was not a serious matter, one of them would step forward and reveal that he was the one sought.[7]

The people were conservative as well as suspicious. They were set in their ways, resisted innovation and adhered to custom and superstition. Veneration of ancestors and continuation of the male line were important, as was respect for age and experience. Lineage, clan, village and land were the essence of their identity. They were protective of their traditions and privileges. Traces of these attitudes can be detected in several aspects of the New Territories' twentieth-century story.

Housing Privileges

The most prominent example of continuing rural indulgence has been the Small House Policy, instituted towards the end of 1972, the main feature of which is the making of land available at preferential prices to male villagers so that they can exercise their custom of building a house for their families. Originally those houses were truly small but rural disdain for restrictions upon size and colonial accommodation of indigenous demands led to their becoming progressively larger. The policy has resulted in Hong Kong's village areas being dominated by uniform rectangular three-storey houses. These buildings proliferated during the final three decades of the last century and the early decades of the present one. The houses have usually been built by developers, nominally on behalf of indigenous villagers. The houses are rarely occupied by an aboriginal family, for they have been sold to others by the developer with the co-operation of the villager. That co-operation has extended to misleading the authorities about the real ownership of the land upon which the house is to be built. How this came to be is explained in Chapter 12 of this book.

7. S. H. Peplow, *Hong Kong About and Around* (Hong Kong: Commercial Press, 1930), extracted in John Strickland (ed), *Southern District Officer Reports: Islands and Villages in Rural Hong Kong, 1910–60* (Hong Kong: Hong Kong University Press, 2010), pp 8 and 11.

The exploitation and continuation of the Small House Policy are controversial matters. They have had the effect of pitting the minority and largely rustic indigenous population against the urban majority. The policy has become the primary exhibit for those who charge that villagers are privileged, selfish and grasping. Aboriginal exemptions from payments of rates and increases in government rent are similarly resented. The sympathy that indigenous minorities attract elsewhere is notably lacking in Hong Kong.

Yet from the rural point of view these privileges are not simply justified by traditional practices and promises from long ago. They have been earned by a vital contribution to Hong Kong's twentieth-century success, namely the provision of land for the expansion of the colony and the SAR. Villagers have been uprooted to make way for reservoirs and roads. Their land has been compulsorily taken to be covered by new towns. They have seen housing, much of it subsidized, provided for millions of people both on what was once their land and in the urban areas. Hong Kong has prospered beyond the wildest imaginings of 1898 or even 1948. Why should they be denied a share of the wealth?

To indigenous minds, the turning of the small house right into money is a form of compensation for the losses that they have suffered in the last seventy years or so. In that time, little more than the span of two generations and within living memory, their communities have been turned upside down by change. A stable life, centred on village, family, tradition and land, has given way to a hectic, more commercial existence.

According to the indigenous narrative, this started when their ancestors were incorporated against their will into a colony run by foreigners. At first there was not a great deal of change; they could use their land much as before and the new rulers actually brought some benefits. But then came the Japanese, followed by squatters, immigrants and severance from the rest of China. The government took their cherished soil for this and that project. They were not given replacement farms, nor paid compensation that fully reflected the fact that the fields were to be developed. Farming had ceased to be a viable occupation. The government told them that they could not build on what ground they retained, nor use it for anything except agriculture. At the same time they saw the rest of the population prospering in a reformed economy, living in better housing in the new towns and the high-quality estates on what used to be their land, and the property market booming.

Against that background it was only natural that the rural community should regard the sale of their traditional housing rights as a way of tapping into that prosperity. To them, it is simply unfair that the rest of Hong Kong should enjoy the benefits of the transformation made possible by the development of the New Territories yet at the same time resent villagers' desire to share in those benefits. It appears to them inconsistent of the Hong Kong government to proclaim its belief in the free market yet try to prevent them from selling their rights and their property to the highest bidder.

Ruined Environment

Prosperity has led to the conversion of what was once agricultural land into a variety of unsightly 'brown field' uses. The decline of rice farming in the middle of the twentieth century was rapid, spurred by migration of agricultural workers to more remunerative employment in the city and abroad. The industrialization of Hong Kong, followed by the opening of China and consequent growth in cross-border trade, provided economic impetus for new uses. Absence of legal controls and improvement in roads laid disused agricultural lots open to exploitation. The administration's hands-off attitude meant that building controls were not applied to the New Territories (except in northern Kowloon) until 1961. Even then, there was an exemption for village-type houses. Planning controls, regulating other uses, took longer to arrive, being extended to the New Territories only in 1991. Prior to these statutory restrictions upon land use, the administration had relied for control upon the terms of Crown leases. These were standard-form grants made early in the twentieth century covering whole tracts, and listing in a schedule the individual lots of which they consisted. It had been thought that their terms were adequate since they prevented building without governmental permission and limited use of the land to that recorded in the schedule. As explained in Chapter 17, the limitation proved a delusion. The effect of a court decision in 1982 was that every use that did not need permanent structures was allowed. The easiest such use to arrange was open-air storage. The timing of the legal clarification was financially fortunate for rural landholders in that roads to and within the New Territories were being improved and cross-border trade was prospering. But it was unfortunate for the rural environment. In the aftermath, container yards, vehicle parking lots, building supply depots, car repair shops, scrap metal and spare parts pounds, waste tips and wrecked car dumps proliferated. Any use that could yield profit might be attempted. That is why today one also encounters restaurants, golf driving ranges, holiday camps, motor tracks, columbaria, and other odd uses of doubtful legality under environmental and planning legislation.

In turning their property to such uses, indigenous landholders are of course taking advantage of commercial opportunities. There is nothing shameful or illegal in that, although the contrast with their professed concern for and reliance upon tradition where that leads to advantage is striking.

Degradation of rural areas is not solely the result of the absence of planning restrictions during a vital period in Hong Kong's development. The building of so many village houses, almost all to be sold to the non-indigenous, has produced construction waste, much of it simply dumped, as well as flooding and pollution consequent upon site formation and the construction of vehicular access routes (some unauthorized) and parking spaces. The deliberate piling of refuse of all descriptions upon vacant land has more recently come to the fore. Owners allow these unsightly and dangerous 'waste mountains' in order to improve the chances of the land being re-zoned for housing use.

A Vanished Life

Following the closure of 'New China' to the world after 1949, the rural New Territories was one of the few places in which traditional China survived and was available to be observed. Consequently, the villages attracted more than their share of attention from historians, anthropologists, and social scientists from Western centres of learning. They marvelled at the close-knit, family-based nature of the villages, the veneration of ancestors, the role of custom, and the rice-growing economy. They were intrigued by the place of collectively owned ancestral estates in the way of life. But their investigations revealed an uncomfortable truth for those who value the old ways: the population was quite willing to discard subsistence agriculture for something less arduous and better remunerated and the younger ones at least did not mind at all giving up their land provided that the money was right. The people were ready to disregard their customs and exploit their heritage if that was to their material advantage. So the customary right to build a small house in the village for the family was transformed into the sale of that right to a developer who would construct and sell the house to an incomer. The practice of passing from generation to generation shared ancestral estates held by customary institutions (t'so and t'ong) was found to be subject to the collective wish of the generation currently enjoying the estate to sell it. The moral bar upon an individual selling inherited land and houses was revealed to be similarly flexible.

Even into the 1980s guide books advocated a visit to rural Hong Kong for a taste of traditional China. Visitors would be rewarded with walled villages, venerable halls, ancient temples and the occasional water buffalo. If they came at festival time, they would witness rituals, processions and feasts. But beneath the appearance, attitudes had altered. Social trends and commercial pressures meant that the old world was vanishing. Not the least of these was the change in the make-up of the rural population. Indigenous people had become a minority. Immigrants from other parts of China had moved in.

Rural Squatting

Rapid expansion of the population of Hong Kong after the Second World War inevitably led to strains upon housing and infrastructure. In urban parts this manifested itself in the appearance of dense areas of squatter huts. In the New Territories there were squatters too, although fewer in number. They took over both government and private land. Those who settled on private land tended to be squatters of a different sort, immigrant farmers taking over unused fields or staying on after renting them from owners who later died, emigrated or lost interest. This was followed by the acquisition by developers of swathes of erstwhile agricultural terrain which they kept vacant for long periods in 'land banks' for future construction, thereby presenting further opportunities to squatters. Deficiencies in the system contributed to the opportunities for taking over others' property—lot boundaries were imprecisely identified and there was no scheme of registered title with plans. The upshot was an outbreak of litigation in which land was alleged to have been acquired by adverse possession, that is to say by a long period of exclusive control without the consent of the true owner.

The taking of land without entitlement, a sort of property theft that eventually becomes legally sanctioned, is not confined to country parts but it is prone to occur more there because of the absence of walls and owners. In the city, most properties are parts of buildings with consequent restricted access and greater security. In the country, there is simply more open space abandoned by owners to be occupied by squatters. Consequently, most instances of long unauthorized use happen in the New Territories. These are dealt with in Chapter 15.

Executive Indulgence

The peculiar history of the New Territories underlies all these phenomena. The Small House Policy built upon a custom that existed long before Hong Kong took over in 1899. For a number of reasons, colonial administrators appeased the local population. The recognition of the custom, its replacement (or perhaps extension) by the policy and their continuation since in the face of public hostility can be explained by those reasons: the promise in 1899 that good customs of the settled population would not be interfered with, the sound sense of keeping the natives content, the need for a light touch given the numbers and resources of staff in the administration, the recognition that British control was temporary, a feeling that the New Territories were culturally different from the rest of the colony, gratitude for villagers' wartime support, and interest in (bordering upon enchantment with) the indigenous way of life by administrators posted to the rural areas. More recently a less attractive factor, which was always part of the mix, has come to the fore: the political influence of rural representatives. This, and understandable reluctance by administrators to avoid controversy in a climate in which even the seemingly most straightforward issue is prone to become politicized, must explain the continued indulgence of the indigenous minority after June 1997.

The relaxed and paternalistic approach of colonial-era District Officers no doubt contributed also to the attitude of their successors towards villagers' extensions of their not-so-small houses. But the main contribution towards that attitude is that contemporary district administrations are inevitably more concerned about the problems of the populous new towns, in reality cities, which now dominate their districts. Enclosed balconies and unauthorized rooftop coverings in the villages no doubt seem of minor importance.

The 'abuse' of the Small House Policy, as it is frequently labelled, may be the greatest but is by no means the only instance of rural inhabitants' disregard for authority. Almost as grievous is their willingness to extend their houses, upwards, outwards and downwards, without the permission that is required by law. This practice of building 'illegal structures' and engaging in unauthorized building works is widespread, not only amongst the indigenous but also other inhabitants of villages and owners of other types of property in the New Territories. It would be widespread elsewhere in the SAR too, were enforcement of the law as loose as it is in rural parts.

The reasons for that lax enforcement are a matter of debate but there is no doubt that the authorities have treated the rural community more leniently than its urban counterparts. No fewer than three investigations and reports by the Ombudsman have proved this. The reaction of the administration to these reports has been cautious and muted. This has increased friction between town and country. There seems to be one law for the former and another (or rather, no) law for the latter.

Anyway, it is unclear who is responsible for forcing the removal of such structures. For many years the Buildings Ordinance did not apply to the New Territories and even now small village houses are exempt from it, so the Building Authority is out of the picture. They fall within the purview of the District Land Office. However, the responsibility and the exemption apply only to those houses' original construction within set dimensions. Extensions beyond those dimensions are a matter for the Building Authority. So the District Lands Office is in turn out of the picture.

Amid such confusion it is understandable that little was done about the growth in unauthorized building work in and around the villages. A practice of extending the house became tolerated; once tolerated, it became regarded by villagers as allowed; and once allowed, it came to be seen as a right. So when in 2012 the government announced a 'crackdown' on illegal structures in the villages, the reaction of some rural spokesmen was one of outrage and indignation. As one indigenous leader declared on a different occasion, 'villagers are not easy victims!'[8] The same leader once told the press that the police required permission to enter his village.

Integration

Rural resistance to building inspections easily grows into threats and intimidation of government officials. Such conduct can also be directed towards outsiders who occupy land near the villages. Indigenous people have been known to resort to intimidation in attempts to remove squatters or to prevent a resident exercising a right of way. Such conduct gives the villages a reputation as a source of triad membership. The separate, closed nature of the indigenous community and its tradition of self-governance perhaps explain, though do not excuse, this conduct. It certainly

8. Brian Kan of Tsung Pak Long near Sheung Shui, quoted in Hayes, 'The Great Difference' (article) 154.

encourages the impression that their villages are beyond rule by law. Incidents of corruption, for instance the buying of votes in village elections, reinforce that impression. So do incidents of extortion, as when a government building contractor's preparatory site work is accused of ruining the local fung shui which can only be repaired by a generous donation to village funds.

Piracy and smuggling, once associated with the New Territories, may have declined but the modern rural regime presents special opportunities for bribery. A village elder whose confirmation is required that an applicant for a small house is a clan member may expect some consideration from the applicant. A voter in village elections may demand of a candidate payment for his vote. An estate manager may anticipate some consideration from the tenant for his signature upon a lease of customary land. These are seen as natural dealings by an insular community with its own values and which is used to exploiting its opportunities.

The position of members of the rural community in the modern, wealthy Special Administrative Region into which they are now integrated seems anomalous. It is questionable whether they are different from the rest of the population and whether they really are indigenous. They are not distinguishable by race, language, religion or dress from the majority of Hong Kong's population. They are not homogenous in origin, being a mixture of Cantonese, Hakka, Hoklo, and Fukinese. They no longer live far from the centres of urban life; indeed many have moved to town or abroad. What distinguishes them are certain vestiges of a former way of life and the privileges bestowed upon them by government.

Despite that integration, rural leaders continue to profess their community's separateness. They declare that they and their ancestors have lived in their village for thousands of years, as if this is a special virtue and as if other Chinese had no *heung ha* (native place). The claim is anyway inaccurate since everyone was forced to leave the region by imperial edict during the seventeenth century and absence for purposes of work has been a fact of life for New Territories men for more than a century. Looking back over the past 120 years, if one were seeking a distinguishing feature of rural people who can trace their ancestors to the villages of 1898, it would not be sense of place or reverence for the past but rather disdain for the rules.

2

Treaty, Takeover, and Trouble

To understand why the New Territories are different we have to go back to the time of their creation. Under the Convention of Peking in June 1898 the area of the colony of Hong Kong was extended twelvefold by a fixed term, ninety-nine-year cession by Imperial China to the United Kingdom of 365 square miles of land in San On (Xin'an) County, the administrative district immediately next to Hong Kong.[1] It was agreed that 'the limits of British territory shall be enlarged under lease to the extent indicated generally on the annexed map'. The length of the so-called lease was to be ninety-nine years. The territory ceded, which broadly was the southern half of the county, stretched north from the existing land border of the colony at Boundary Street in Kowloon to the Shumchun (Shenzhen) River and included numerous nearby islands. One of them, Lantau, was larger than Hong Kong island. The extension soon became known within the colony as 'the New Territory'.

The 1898 convention was in fact the second Convention of Peking. It was also the third and last by which the colony was acquired by the United Kingdom. Hong Kong island had been ceded to it by China in perpetuity by the first Convention of Peking in 1843. Then by the Treaty of Nanking a slice of the mainland, the area of the Kowloon Peninsula south of Boundary Street plus Stonecutters' Island, had been ceded, also in perpetuity, in 1863. The New Territories was a much larger slice. It contained many more inhabitants than the areas which had been the subject of the earlier cessions.

Population of the New Territory

The population of the extension in 1898 numbered about 100,000 of whom between 80,000 and 90,000 resided north of the Kowloon hills.[2] They were a mixture of Punti, Hakka, Tanka, and Hoklo. The last two were boat dwellers and comprised about

1. Convention Respecting an Extension of the Hong Kong Territory signed at Peking on 4 June 1898.
2. Hugh D. R. Baker in *Sheung Shui, A Chinese Lineage Village* (London: Frank Cass & Co, 1968) (*Sheung Shui*) suggests 84,000. The 1901 census showed a population, including New Kowloon, of just over 100,000. The 1911 census showed a total New Territories population (excluding New Kowloon) of 80,662. The estimate of 100,000 by Lockhart included Shumchun.

10 per cent of the people. The Punti spoke Cantonese and had been amongst the earliest settlers in the region. The Tangs, the oldest Punti lineage, claimed to have arrived more than a thousand years earlier, although the foremost English-language historian of the region states that 'no dogmatic statements can be made about the age of any particular settlement' and the Hakka may well have arrived at about the same time as the Punti.[3] During the 1660s virtually everyone had been forced by the new emperor to abandon their homes and move inland, making claims of a thousand years of continuous settlement somewhat problematic.

In 1898 the Punti made up about half the population in southern San On. By and large, they occupied the best agricultural land, in the northern part of the territory. As their Cantonese title implies, most of the Hakka ('strangers' or 'visitors') had arrived in Hong Kong later, one to two hundred years before 1898. The Hakka had their own dialect; they tended to inhabit the higher and less fertile ground; they comprised about 40 per cent of the population.[4] The Tanka were Cantonese-speaking boat dwellers and fisherfolk, whilst the Hoklo were also boat dwellers but from Fujian and north-east Guangdong and spoke Hokkien; together they comprised slightly more than 10 per cent of the population.[5]

There were market towns and fishing ports in the new territory but most of the population lived in villages, each one dominated by one or two clans or extended families.[6] Their life was settled and traditional, being centred on family and lineage, and the economy was largely agricultural. The two main ports (which also had markets), at Tai O and Cheung Chau on the islands, each had about 7,600 people, rather more than half living on boats. The main market towns, Kowloon City, Shamshuipo, Yuen Long, and Taipo, each held about 500 inhabitants. There were smaller markets at Shek Wu Hui, Sha Tau Kok, and Sai Kung. After allowing for 8,000 Tanka and 1,000 Hoklo, the population of the villages must have totalled no more than 70,000. Given that there were at least 670 villages in the territory, the average number of people in each village would have been around one hundred.[7] There was a wide range of sizes however. The villages were distributed across the region but most of the terrain was rocky and mountainous and there were extensive marshes along the coastline. Less than a third of the land was used or occupied.[8]

There was a marked decline in the numbers of people living in Guangdong, including southern San On, during the latter half of the nineteenth century. The evidence lies in abandoned land, ruined houses and disused fishing stations, as well

3. James Hayes, *The Hong Kong Region 1850–1911: Institutions and Leadership in Town and Countryside* (Hong Kong: Hong Kong University Press, 2012), pp 25 and 28 (*The Hong Kong Region*).
4. M. J. E. Palmer, 'The Surface-Subsoil Form of Divided Ownership in Late Imperial China: Some Examples from the New Territories of Hong Kong' (1987) 21 *Modern Asian Studies* 1, 18–19, 52–53, 61 ('Surface-Subsoil').
5. The 1911 census put the number of Hoklo at 1,444.
6. Patrick H. Hase, *Custom, Land and Livelihood in Rural South China: The Traditional Land Law of Hong Kong's New Territories, 1750–1950* (Hong Kong: Hong Kong University Press, 2013), p 13 (*Custom*). Hase estimates that there were 20,000 families living in the territory (*Custom*, p 412, fn 30).
7. Other estimates of the number of villages are 700 and 800.
8. Hayes, *The Hong Kong Region*, pp 46, 56–59 and 102.

as oral accounts from elderly inhabitants.[9] The reason for the decline is obscure: it could have been war or emigration or the lure of Hong Kong, but it was probably some sort of disease. The unsanitary conditions in the villages lay them open to cholera, typhus and the like.

In his study of the villages of the Shek Pik valley in western Lantau which eventually were inundated by the waters of a reservoir, James Hayes suggests that the valley supported a much larger population in the middle of the nineteenth century than in 1898. By then the higher rice terraces had been abandoned and more than 50 acres had gone out of cultivation. In the great survey a few years later about 400 structures were recorded in the villages but 37 houses (mainly ruined) and numerous huts were unclaimed. Descendants put the decline down to bad *fung shui*.[10]

Boundaries of the New Territory

The ceded area illustrated by a map annexed to the treaty showed the land boundary as a straight line cutting through the meanders of the Shumchun (Shenzhen) River. It was agreed that the exact boundaries would be fixed later after proper surveys. James H. Stewart Lockhart, the tough little Scot who was Hong Kong's sinophile Colonial Secretary and Registrar General, had carried out extended visits to the territory in advance of British takeover. He wanted the line to be drawn to bring Shumchun into the colony since it was the market town and focal point for much of the northern part of the territory. He had some support in the British government, including from the Prime Minister, Lord Salisbury.[11]

However, China resisted and a commission consisting of Lockhart and Chinese officials settled upon the north bank of the river itself, together with the Sha Tau Kok River and the northern shores of Mirs Bay on the eastern side and of Deep Bay on the western side, as the boundary in March 1899.[12] In consequence, villages such as Sha Tau Kok were divided and branches of the same clan who happened to inhabit different villages became separated. Similarly, farmers found that they had to cross a border in order to reach their fields from their homes. Shumchun was cut off from the southern portion of the valley which was its natural hinterland.

British Motives

The Convention has been denounced subsequently as unequal, which it was, since the United Kingdom gave nothing, not even symbolic rent, in return for the grant. This does not mean that it was not consensual or valid. It has also been castigated

9. Hayes, *The Hong Kong Region*, p 46, fn 126 (p 213).
10. Hayes, *The Hong Kong Region*, pp 105 and 109–110.
11. Peter Wesley-Smith, *Unequal Treaty 1898–1997: China, Great Britain and Hong Kong's New Territories* (Hong Kong: Oxford University Press, 1980), ch 2 (*Unequal Treaty*).
12. The treaty provided that Chinese military vessels could continue to use the waters of the two bays.

as 'naked imperial expansion'.[13] This is inaccurate to the extent that it suggests that consent of the Chinese authorities was not obtained and that there were no reasons for the cession other than lust for land. As far as Britain was concerned, the area was acquired for purposes of defence: this was reflected, and apparently accepted by China, in the treaty's preamble which declared that 'it has for many years past been recognized that an extension of Hong Kong Territory is necessary for the defence and protection of the Colony'. The declaration was an exaggeration: until a few months before the Convention the British government had rejected suggestions that it seek more land for Hong Kong because it wanted to set an example for other nations not to exploit imperial weakness by indulging in a scramble for China. However, Britain also wanted to protect the trade and commerce that flowed through its prosperous little colony. Military commanders were recommending the acquisition of a buffer to protect the northern shore of the harbour.[14] Furthermore, the Hong Kong government was under pressure from local businessmen, including speculators who had bought up land near the existing boundary with the mainland, to secure more space for the expanding city.

Concern about defence had been spurred by the fact that several other powers, fearful of each other's ambitions, had been acquiring interests in China. The Japanese had recently emerged from the Sino-Japanese War of 1894–1895 victorious and with territory, including Formosa. Germany, a powerful young empire ambitious for colonies, had occupied Kiaochow near Tsingdao in Shandong and then had negotiated with the Ching (Qing) government in Peking a 'lease' of it for ninety-nine years from 1 January 1898. The Russians, who had previously expanded into north-east China, had done likewise in respect of Port Arthur (Lushun) and Dalian in the Liaoning Peninsula, for twenty-five years from 27 March 1898. In April of that year, the USA had mustered its fleet at Mirs Bay near Hong Kong for war against Spain in the Philippines. The French had colonial ambitions in south-east Asia and, having won a war with China in 1885, were now turning their attention northwards. They acquired a ninety-nine-year cession of Kwangchow-wan (or Canton Bay, modern Zhanjiang), on the south China coast opposite Hainan, also in April 1898.

These unwelcome developments caused concern that the colony with its magnificent harbour would be threatened by one of those powers. This could be ameliorated by pushing the land boundary back about 20 miles, beyond the range of contemporary artillery. So the British ambassador and plenipotentiary at Peking, Sir Claude MacDonald, was instructed to approach the imperial government with a

---

13. Steve Tsang, *A Modern History of Hong Kong: 1841–1997* (Hong Kong: Hong Kong University Press, 2003), p 38. Tsang's suggestion that Britain opened no military facilities in the New Territories after taking them over is not correct.
14. Geoffrey Robley Sayer, *Hong Kong 1862–1919: Years of Discretion* (Hong Kong: Hong Kong University Press, 1975), pp 80–81 (*Years of Discretion*).

request for a grant of more territory for Hong Kong. This resulted in the Convention in the summer of 1898.

The Convention's Terms

The treaty and its drafters referred to the convention as, or as creating, a lease. Subsequently it has been widely and habitually referred to as a lease. The description is a convenient way of emphasizing the temporary nature of the grant, thus distinguishing it from the majority of international cessions, which are permanent transfers of land. Both parties wished to have that emphasis: the Ching in order to fend off allegations that they had given away part of China; the British to fend off allegations that they were participating in the carving up of China.

However, the analogy with a lease in private domestic law is flawed. First and most importantly, the parties were two sovereign powers; accordingly what was being transferred was not just possession of land but sovereignty or jurisdiction over it too. When eventually, more than a hundred years later, it was argued in court that the convention created a lease in law comparable to that between landlord and tenant one judge accepted the submission; but in another case six years later a different judge rejected the submission and then the following year a third judge agreed with the second.[15] The last two judgments accepted that the convention was an agreement between sovereign powers for the ceding of land for a definite time, not a lease, and operated on an international, not a domestic, level. It did not create any leasehold estate in favour of the British Crown or any reversionary estate in favour of China.

The status of the convention had actually been judicially settled in the 1980s in a case in which legislation empowering the Hong Kong Government to take (resume) land compulsorily had been challenged as inconsistent with the treaty's provision about expropriation and with proclamations made by Sir Henry Blake, Hong Kong's governor at the time that Britain took possession of the extension, about ten months after the convention. There the Court of Appeal held that breaches of the convention were not justiciable by a subject in the domestic courts. Enforcement of a treaty was a matter for the states which were parties to it.[16]

The second reason that the convention could not be a lease, even if it had been a domestic agreement, is that it lacks the necessary certainty. The precise boundaries of the leased land were not defined. The annexed map only 'indicated generally' the limits of the extension. The land border was left to be agreed later by a commission. An agreement to agree, though acceptable diplomatically, would not have sufficed

15. *Chau Ka Chik Tso v Secretary for Justice*, HCA 10670/2000 (Louis Chan Dep-J, 30 December 2009) (point not argued in subsequent appeals); *Li Kwok Ching v Secretary for Justice*, HCA 1303/2010 (Godfrey Lam J, 31 March 2015); *Lam Man Lau v Secretary for Justice*, DCCJ 1682/2012 (Deputy District Judge Alfred Cheng, 25 July 2016).

16. *Winfat Enterprises (HK) Co Ltd v Attorney General* [1984] HKLR 32 (CA); confirmed [1988] 1 HKLR 5 (PC).

in a domestic lease without some principle or formula in it to give adequate guidance as to how the boundaries were to be ascertained: all the treaty said was that each government was to carry out a survey. The frontier that was eventually settled upon differed from the straight line marked upon the convention's map since it followed the course of two rivers and brought the whole of the waters of Mirs Bay and Deep Bay into British jurisdiction.

Third, no rent or other consideration was agreed for the use and enjoyment of the land. It seems that Britain contemplated that it would make some payment, probably regarding this as another detail to be settled later, and that the Chinese representatives asked about payment.[17] Whilst it is possible to have a valid domestic lease with no rent stipulated if that is what was intended, this is not so if the common intention was that there would be rent but that the fixing of its figure, or a formula for its fixing, is left for later.[18]

So the analogy with a lease of land in domestic law is limited and flawed. Indeed, the Convention is so poorly drafted that it is doubtful if any self-respecting lawyer would have approved it and whether any careful landlord or tenant would have accepted its terms. Sir Claude MacDonald, who initially drafted it and did so in a hurry and without adequate briefing, was a soldier by training and had no help from someone with a legal mind. 'In consequence', as Dr Peter Wesley-Smith, the principal scholar of the events that led to the Convention and its consequences, has observed, 'it is a vague and imprecise document allowing no easy interpretation'.

Nevertheless, the land grant was good enough for the parties. Lockhart was dispatched to inspect the extension and report upon it for the benefit of Hong Kong's incoming governor, Sir Henry Blake. By the New Territories Order in Council made at Balmoral on 20 October 1898 the extension was declared by Britain to be part of the Colony of Hong Kong and all laws in force in the colony were to take effect in the New Territories on a date to be fixed by the Governor. This was significant for it showed that, as far as Britain was concerned at least, the territory was theirs for the duration, an integral part of Hong Kong, and was not foreign territory under British rule.[19]

The fort known as the Kowloon Walled City, an imperial police and customs post, was excluded from the area granted. It was agreed that the Chinese officials stationed in the walled city were to continue to exercise jurisdiction there 'except so far as may be inconsistent with the military requirements for the defence of Hong Kong'. This proviso was intended to save face for the imperial authorities but it stored up complications for the future. A nearby granite pier, linked to the walled city by a narrow market street, was ostensibly reserved as a landing place for Chinese vessels. There was also difficulty concerning other customs posts within the ceded area. When the British minister in Peking mentioned that these would

17. Wesley-Smith, *Unequal Treaty*, Ch 2.
18. *Ashburn Anstalt v Arnold* [1989] Ch 1 (CA, Eng) (overturned on another point by HL).
19. Wesley-Smith, *Unequal Treaty*, pp 88–91.

have to close, Chinese representatives, faced with the prospect of loss of revenue, indignantly insisted that they had received assurances to the contrary.[20]

The treaty provided that there was to be no expropriation or expulsion of inhabitants of the district included within the extension. This is one of several instances of poor drafting in the text. Presumably 'no expropriation' meant that the property of those who were living in the district was not to be taken by the government. But, somewhat inconsistently, the text went on to say that if land was required for official purposes it was to be bought at a fair price. This proved to be a hostage to fortune.

Opposition

Not surprisingly, the inhabitants of the ceded area were not all content to be transferred to the government of a foreign country. The ten months between the making of the treaty and Great Britain's taking of possession of the territory was extraordinarily long. The delay was caused by the absence on leave of Lockhart, the wait for the arrival of the recently-appointed Blake, the need to discuss arrangements with Peking and a desire that American ships leave Mirs Bay before the takeover.

The delay gave those who feared the transfer an opportunity to cause trouble. Chinese resentment had arisen over the customs question. In August the Empress Dowager had seized power in Peking. Hostility had been shown to Lockhart and his party during his tour of inspection in October. At Kam Tin, one of the centres of the Tang clan, money was raised to resist the British takeover. In Ping Shan, another of their strongholds, the clan's ancestral hall at Hang Tau Tsuen became a place to plan the resistance. So difficulties were to be expected.

Rumours and Speculators

As the change in rulers approached, the natural trepidation of people in the affected territory was exploited and inflamed by rumour. The foreigners will confiscate our land; they will pull down our houses; they will impose taxes and duties and charges; they will prohibit our customs; they will impose their own barbaric practices; our way of life will be ruined; the fung shui will be destroyed; they will poison us; we will become foreigners. These were the sorts of story in circulation during the pre-handover period.

The rumours may have been put about by speculators scheming to buy land close to Kowloon and to the proposed railway cheaply from panicking villagers.[21] Equally, the activities of these speculators in buying up the land itself may have sparked resentment and inflamed feelings. The speculators were mainly from urban

20. Sayer, *Years of Discretion*, pp 83 and 108.
21. Wesley-Smith, *Unequal Treaty*, p 84.

Hong Kong but one of the major lineages was deeply involved in a large land venture at Cheung Sha Wan in anticipation of the British takeover.[22]

The rumours may also have been spread by lineage leaders. Certainly more could have been done by the Hong Kong authorities to counter the scaremongering before people became agitated. As it was, by April 1898 many peasants were fired up and ready for rebellion.[23]

Not that all the clans in all the villages were intent on armed resistance. Lineages which were not resident in southern San On, but which had landed interests there, played no part; nor did villagers from the eastern side of the territory and people from New Kowloon.[24] Hundreds of years of inter-village rivalry and clan enmity meant that unity could not be achieved. Villages kept arms to fight other villages as well as bandits and robbers. There was schism even between villages of the same lineage. Hakka villagers living a hardscrabble life in Sai Kung had no love for prosperous Cantonese lineages living off their rental payments.

Resistance

As the planned date of the ceremonial taking-over, 17 April 1899, drew near, the temporary structures made of bamboo, palm leaves and rattan (mat sheds) erected for the ceremony at a camp on a hill near the new Taipo Market were threatened, then twice destroyed, by villagers. The chief of police, Henry May, a man of 'fearless impetuosity and a grimness all his own', who had led an advance party to Taipo to prepare for the takeover ceremony, was forced into uncharacteristic retreat by the threatening attitude of the locals.[25] Blake travelled to Canton to seek the help of the viceroy who issued a proclamation exhorting the inhabitants of the territory to live in peace and sent soldiers to assist in keeping order. Nevertheless, during the period 14 to 19 April there were several incidents of armed resistance from the clans, most notably near Taipo in the centre and Kam Tin in the north-west of the territory. Both places were within the sphere of the widespread Tang clan. The eastern part of the territory, the islands and areas near Kowloon were not involved. These comprised mostly poor Hakka settlements of minor clans who made payments to the major clans of the prosperous central part of the territory which claimed seigniorial rights over much of San On.[26]

It would be an exaggeration to call the incidents a war or even an insurrection. The contests were few and brief, although bloody. They were really a small rebellion instigated by a privileged segment of the population. However, the fierceness of the

---

22. Palmer, Surface-Subsoil, pp 49–51.
23. Patrick H. Hase, *The Six-Day War of 1899: Hong Kong in the Age of Imperialism* (Hong Kong: Hong Kong University Press, 2008), p 54 (*Six-Day War*).
24. Palmer, Surface-Subsoil, 48, fn 13; 89, fn 226.
25. Sayer, *Years of Discretion*, p 112.
26. Palmer, Surface-Subsoil, 58–64; Sayer, *Years of Discretion*, p 84.

brief fighting, involving several thousand men, uniformed, trained and armed, took the British by surprise.

The ceremony for taking formal possession was brought forward to 16 April as a result of the threat. The resisters had made artillery emplacements overlooking the Lam Tsuen valley and the pass between Kam Tin and Taipo. They bombarded, then attacked, the British camp. However, their weapons were antiquated and they were no match for regular soldiers with modern weapons and better training, supported in one incident by the guns and crew of a Royal Navy destroyer, HMS *Fame*.[27]

An accurate figure for the number of resisters killed cannot be given because their comrades removed the dead and wounded from the scene. One estimate puts the number at about 500.[28] Many fled, others were arrested. Two were eventually hanged. Most of the dead were young, poor and of low status. The organizers of the rebellion were elders of the clans, wealthy landowners and so-called gentry (scholars). None of them was killed. So in that respect, the rebellion resembled wars elsewhere. It also resembled other wars in that a memorial was erected at the mass grave of the dead, although in this case in a remote place, almost as if the perpetrators wished to forget the misbegotten fighting.[29]

It seems that it was the leadership of the Tangs which had organized the uprising with elders of other large clans from the north and west of the territory. They had recruited the help of trained bands of clan members as well as irregular or mercenary Chinese soldiers.[30] Men from across the Shumchun River, an area notorious for triad connections, had also taken part. The rebels came from all the big clans there but were mainly Tangs. They were all Cantonese-speaking (Punti) and generally from flat areas with rich farmland.

The major clans had cause to fear, and to feel aggrieved by, the handing of their domains to a foreign sovereign. They had not been consulted about the change. The new border would separate the various branches of their families, one from the other. Moreover, since they owned or controlled much of the land but did not farm it, they had most to lose from any land reform. The older and wealthier clans such as the Mans and the Tangs were powerful kinship groups each of which were the effective rulers of a portion of the territory that was to be ceded. Part of that portion they had been granted by the Emperor but a larger part of it they had in effect

27. Fame, built in 1892, spent her entire operational service in the Far East and later took part in fighting surrounding the Boxer rebellion. Its landing party was led by the belligerent Lt Roger Keyes who rose to Admiral of the Fleet and first Chief of Combined Operations in the Second World War: Brian D. Wilson (former District Officer, Yuen Long) on britishempire.co.uk.
28. Hase, *Six-Day War*, pp 103–111. Other estimates are lower, although perhaps they were influenced by the desire to play down the conflict.
29. At an orchard near Fung Kat Heung in the north-west of the territory. A nunnery was later built next to the grave: Hase, *Six-Day War*, pp 103–104.
30. Wesley-Smith, *Unequal Treaty*, p 58. James L. and Rubie S. Watson, 'Self-Defence Corps, Violence and the Bachelor Sub-Culture in South China: Two Case Studies', Ch 11 in *Village Life in Hong Kong: Politics, Gender, and Ritual in the New Territories* (Hong Kong: Chinese University Press, 2004) (*Village Life*). Each village had bands of 'braves' trained by the military to assist with keeping order and fighting other villages.

seized. Their domains included some of the best agricultural land. They claimed more of this land than they had been granted, some of it classified as waste but long put under cultivation, thereby avoiding paying land tax. The surplus was let to poor peasants, members of lesser lineages and immigrants living in smaller communities nearby which were in effect appendages or satellites of the larger villages in which the wealthier clans resided. The tenants paid market rents and protection money to their subjugators. Within each area the dominant clan controlled markets, transport and schools. They enjoyed privileged access to the magistrate who needed their co-operation to maintain order and whose staff were willing to under-report the clan's landholding if suitably rewarded. The imposition of modern and efficient government in place of the weak imperial authorities threatened their status, power and prestige.

The tenant farmers living in these dependent villages would not have been similarly motivated to resist change. However, they and other villagers in the north, centre, and west of southern San On would have been used to following the leaders of the main clans who were really the governors of their district and who were not above exercising coercion upon those who did not obey. The fear and xenophobic fervour stirred up by the rumours would have convinced many to resist the change in sovereignty anyway.

Once it became clear that armed resistance was futile and that the new government wanted friendly relations, the clan elders turned from confrontation to co-operation. They blamed the fighting on aggressive elements from north of the Shumchun River and responded positively to overtures from the incoming administration.

Magnanimity

Blake used the crisis of the resistance as an opportunity to take over Kowloon City. To mark British displeasure at the conduct of the viceroy in Canton whom he suspected of quietly encouraging the opposition, Blake claimed that military requirements envisaged by the convention as an occasion for ousting Chinese jurisdiction there had arisen and sent the Hong Kong Volunteers to occupy the fort: it was turned into a police station later. On 27 December 1898 another Order in Council was made, this one at Windsor, the preamble to which noted that the exercise of jurisdiction by Chinese officials in the City of Kowloon had been found to be inconsistent with military requirements for the defence of Hong Kong, and ordered revocation of the article in the previous Order in Council by which it had been declared that Chinese jurisdiction should continue there. As far as Britain, and also the courts of Hong Kong, were concerned, that was that. British troops also seized Shum Chun to encourage the viceroy to remove officials from the customs stations within the extension. The troops were withdrawn after five months, the stations having been relocated.[31]

What was to be done with the surviving fighters? Lockhart was in favour of taking a firm line with the rebels, but Blake was more emollient. He regarded the resistance as merely a temporary civil disturbance, the product of ignorance and anger, such as he was used to from his time as a magistrate in his native Ireland. On his visit to the rebel areas in August, the uprising was not mentioned. Lockhart also visited the territory and used sterner words. Together, Lockhart and Blake performed a kind of Scots-Irish 'hard cop, soft cop' act.

Thereafter something of a veil was drawn over the incidents. They became a mutual embarrassment but they had not been forgotten. Ninety-nine years later, after Hong Kong had been handed back to China, those who died in the conflict were lauded by some as patriotic heroes.

The fighting formed part of the background to relations between the indigenous rural population and their new governors. This difficult episode caused the administration to treat rural interests with caution and respect. The unruliness of the New Territories had been established and for the native population had already started to pay dividends.

31. Sayer, *Years of Discretion*, pp 84–85; *In re Wong Hon* (1959) HKLR 601.

3

Land Survey and Settlement

Governor's Proclamation

No doubt the signs of popular resistance had been one of the reasons that at the takeover ceremony on 16 April 1899 Sir Henry Blake had assured the local population by declaration in Chinese that their 'landed interests will be safeguarded and their usages and good customs will not in any way be interfered with'. Shortly before that, the viceroy in Canton and the county magistrate had also told the local population that all would be well. The good-natured Blake had experience of handling local resentment of British rule when he had been a magistrate in Ireland. He appreciated that reassurance of the population was the key to quelling their anger. He visited the New Territories again in August 1899, first to Taipo, later to Yuen Long, to meet prominent people, explain the administration's policies and ask for support. At the Tang ancestral hall near Yuen Long pleasantries were exchanged and mutual admiration was expressed. It is doubtful that anybody mentioned that the hall had been one of the places at which the resistance had been planned.

Blake's declaration resonates even today, for one of the arguments made by indigenous representatives for the retention of their customary rights is that they had been assured that the pre-existing position would not be changed. However, Blake was forced to act in a manner inconsistent with his reassurances almost from the outset and in a fundamental way.

The Great Survey

Preparations for dealing with land titles began soon after the start of the ninety-nine-year term granted by the Convention and well before the formal taking of possession. Land ownership was important because it formed the basis of the raising of government revenue by the new rulers. Initially the plan was to register New Territories land and its owners on the Deeds Register already kept for all private land in the colony by the Land Office in Hong Kong.[1]

1. Judith Sihombing, 'The Torrens System in the New Territories' (1984) 14 HKLJ 291.

However, attempts to discover from imperial Chinese records the landed interests that Blake had referred to proved impossible. The magistrate at first resisted Lockhart's efforts to see the land register. This may have been actuated by resentment at the new arrangements but it may equally have been the result of embarrassment, for the register was out-of-date and may never have been accurate. When Lockhart did get to see and consider the register, he found it unsatisfactory, concluding that little reliance could be placed upon it. Much of the land under cultivation had never been reported to or registered by the authorities.[2]

The Hong Kong administration was under pressure from London to collect Crown rent from landowners in the new territory, so that the cost of running it could be met. Given the inadequate imperial records, reluctantly the administrators had to embark upon a survey of the entire 365 square miles to find out who owned what before they could extract rent. On the way back from leave at the end of 1898, Lockhart stopped at Columbo and consulted land officials in Ceylon. They favoured a complete survey, or at least that is what Lockhart, who had been pressing for such a survey, told the Governor. Since there was not the expertise in Hong Kong to perform such an enormous undertaking, the Ceylonese suggested that Hong Kong ask the Government of India to lend officers from its well-organized survey department. In Hong Kong the Director of Public Works and the commander of the Royal Engineers supported the suggestion.[3] In London the Secretary of State, Joseph Chamberlain, an ardent believer in the virtues of the British Empire famous for his monocle and orchid, saw settlement of titles as a priority. The securing of rights to land would be 'a great inducement to content and loyalty, and to the popularity of British rule,' he wrote.[4] Chamberlain urged that work begin as soon as possible. In March 1899 Blake ordered that a cadastral survey be carried out. Notices in Chinese were posted explaining the objects of the exercise in advance. In the autumn staff from the Survey of India arrived and began work.

The surveyors and their assistants were mainly Moslems from cooler northern India, led by two British surveyors, Messrs George P. Tate and W. J. Newland. Chinese coolies were enlisted to assist. Tate was struck by the fact that local farmers took little notice of the survey operations. The technique was labour intensive, using chains and tape to mark out lots by hand. Each village had numerous little plots to map. Every structure had to be marked. The surveyors and their helpers found conditions hostile: oppressive heat and humidity, unhealthy climate, steep terrain, few and rough roads, uncooperative population. 'The country is broken and mountainous, and the greater part is some of the most difficult country that I have ever seen,' Tate lamented. At least one inspector, one surveyor and five Indian coolies died in the process; several were sent home ill and some died on the journey back.

2. HMSO, *Report on the New Territory at Hong Kong* (London: 1900), p 8.
3. Ibid.
4. CO, Eastern No 66, Correspondence respecting the Extension of the Boundaries of the Colony, November 1900.

Village children played with the surveyors' stakes and cord. As a result, the work took longer than expected, extending from 1899 to 1904.[5]

In such inhospitable surroundings the surveyors adopted their own familiar labels for geographical features. Rivers were renamed: the large tidal estuary and its feeding waters at Sheung Shui known as the Ng Tung Ho they called the Indus. The Sheung Yu river that flows near Hang Tau before crossing what is now Long Valley (then marshes) and joining the Ng Tung, they named after a tributary of the Indus, the Sutlej. These names are no longer generally used but can be found on older English-language maps of Hong Kong and even on the government's current online English-language maps. One at least survives in popular usage: in India an informal name for the Sutlej is Bea's River; the former riding club near Hang Tau, now the country club of the Hong Kong Jockey Club, which is close to the Sheung Yu, is known as Bea's River. The surveyors also bequeathed to Hong Kong a useful word, nullah, meaning a ravine but extended in its new setting to include a deep drain.

The territory was divided into areas or blocks for purposes of the survey and recording of ownership. These were known as demarcation districts, except that in New Kowloon and Sai Kung some were called survey districts. Maps had to be drawn of each district, showing the location and boundaries of each lot of land claimed to be in separate ownership.

Notices were posted requiring those who claimed to own or occupy land to attend for claim forms to be filled in for them by clerks, but people were slow to do so. The main reason was that, despite Blake's reassurances, they were suspicious of the new regime's intentions. They feared that the government meant to take their land away and the exercise of recording and registering claims was a means to make that easier.[6] An initial deadline for submission of claims of 1 October 1900 had to be extended.

Demarcation teams were sent out to map the land. When surveyors visited a locality those who claimed a plot were invited to come forward and point it out. Its boundaries were then marked on the map with a lot number assigned to it. Claimants gave basic particulars to the officials: place name; their name and whether owner or tenant; if the latter, name of the owner; lot number; and description of the land. The area of each plot was calculated in acres to two decimal points.

The location of a plot was often difficult to describe. The name of the nearest village had to be used, or the local name of the ground. In addition, there was a fundamental difficulty: peasant farmers were not used to expressing the size of their land by Western measurements; instead they used its capacity to produce rice. Even

5. Exhibit at the Hong Kong Cultural Museum, Shatin. Different sources give different dates for completion of the survey. In *The Great Difference: Hong Kong's New Territories and Its People 1898–2004* (Hong Kong: Hong Kong University Press, 2006) (*The Great Difference* (book)). Hayes says that the work was finished in May 1903. Mills-Owens J suggested 1904 in *Tang Kai-chung v Tang Chik-shang* [1970] HKLR 276 at 287–288.

6. HMSO, *Report on the New Territory at Hong Kong*, p 7.

where measurements were given, they used Chinese units and, despite using the same name, the size of these units varied according to the locality.[7]

The particulars would be recorded in Chinese on a slip of paper or *chi chai* (literally, little paper) which carried a chop stating that it was not proof of ownership. The allocated district and lot numbers would be added. Despite the disclaimer, the *chi chai* were often treasured by villagers and treated like title deeds.[8] The Land Court would later adjudicate upon these claims.

One surprising difficulty encountered was that holders of red deeds evidencing an imperial grant could be vague about the location and boundaries of their holdings and asked for more time to investigate. These owners, who were often representatives of clan institutions, did not farm the land and might live a long distance from it. For generations they, like their forbears, had been content to collect rents, often through agents, without visiting the property itself and without knowing any particulars of it. They were, in Western terms, rentiers or absentee landlords. Control of the land was entirely in the hands of the occupier who made payment to the imperial grantee.

The occupier might regard himself as the true owner, his payments to the red deed holder being in his eyes reimbursement of imperial land tax rather than rent, in which case he would make a claim to be registered as owner under the new system. Accordingly the new authorities would have to decide which claimant to recognize, the occupier or the red deed holder. There was invariably another complication, that the areas of land asserted by the two claimants did not match. Occupiers were in the habit of extending the land which they farmed beyond the original bounds, encroaching upon neighbouring (perhaps waste) land without telling the imperial grantee; and if the latter became aware of the encroachments and even if he demanded increased rent as a result, he would not inform the magistrate for fear of incurring the expense of a further registration and of extra land tax or of the magistrate confiscating the land.

Cadastral survey sheets were drawn, initially to a scale of sixteen inches to a mile. It was soon realized that this scale was too small. There were so many little lots that a larger scale was necessary, the better to pick out details. The larger scale maps showed buildings in blocks. Only at smaller scales were individual houses discernible.[9] So the rest of the maps were drawn at thirty-two inches to a mile and a second set of survey sheets was prepared at that scale for those districts which had already been surveyed at the larger scale. The second set exposed inaccuracies on the original plans.

During demarcation, the surveyors and their field staff composed 'field area statements'. They used Survey of India sheets in common form and recorded in

---

7. HMSO, *Report on the New Territory at Hong Kong*, p 17.
8. Hayes, *The Great Difference* (book), pp 28–29; Hayes, *The Hong Kong Region*, xxix, fn 30.
9. Law Reform Commission of Hong Kong, Report on *Adverse Possession* (Hong Kong: 2014); Hase, *Custom*, p 89.

columns the lot number, its classification (quality), acreage and description. These details were to form the basis of the information in the schedules to the later block leases. Claims to ownership were recorded, then matched to the lots on the survey sheets. The results were published in villages in the vicinity of the land and objections were invited. Any alterations found necessary were then made. After verification, rent was charged and, once paid, each owner was issued with a *chap chiu* being a certified extract from the rent roll showing an owner's holdings.[10] Although these were easily lost, they became accepted as evidence of title.

In the circumstances of difficult physical conditions, inadequate scale, insufficient staff, and (by modern surveying standards) primitive technique, mistakes in the survey were inevitable. The area statements recorded, and the maps showed, more lots than were listed in the schedules. The reason for this was that no documents of title could be produced by claimants for certain lots and others were waste land. Boundaries and walls were shown out of their true position; the number of houses in a row was mistakenly stated; what was shown on the plan often was not consistent with physical features on the ground; lots situated at the margin of one sheet did not match the same lots shown at the margin on another sheet. Consequently, the survey plans were not a dependable record of boundaries. Unsurprisingly, a number of disputes have arisen as a result of inaccuracies in lot boundaries.[11]

In all, 328,639 lots in 477 demarcation districts were recorded. This was aside from house lots which took the total to about 354,000 lots.[12] Each district had a volume of papers consisting of the lease, survey sheets and the schedules particularizing the number, area, and address of the lots and their owners, use, and rent.

At the same time that the lease schedules were composed, the all-important Crown rent rolls, or A books, were drawn up.[13] Land was divided into three classes according to its perceived quality. First-class agricultural land was charged rental at the rate of HK$3 per square foot, second class at $2 per square foot and third class at $1 per square foot. The rates for houses were also in three classes. Houses occupying 0.02 of an acre (i.e. twice the size of the standard small house) or more were charged $1 per annum. Second class houses or huts were those of 0.01 of an acre or less; they were charged 50 cents per annum. Third class houses were latrines: no rent was charged for them. Slightly higher levels were charged for land in New Kowloon. Building land was charged at the rate of $50 an acre (twice that if the

10. The procedure is described by Hunter J in *Lintock Co Ltd v Attorney-General* [1985] 2 HKC 555 at 560–562, based on evidence in that case; also *To Kan Chi v Pui Man Yau*, CACV 32/1999 (3 February 2000). *Chap chiu* were not issued in New Kowloon: Roger Nissim, *Land Administration and Practice in Hong Kong* (Hong Kong: Hong Kong University Press, 4th edn, 2016), p 16 (*Land Administration*).
11. Law Reform Commission of Hong Kong, Report on *Adverse Possession*; *Lintock Co Ltd v Attorney-General*, above; *Man Kam Tong v Man Lin Tai* [1984] HKLR 181, [1985] 2 HKC 299; *Tam Mo Yin v Attorney General* [1996] 1 HKC 379; *Liu Ma Cheung v Liau Yin Fu*, HCA 181/2004 (26 October 2007); *Kwok Ping v Kwok Chau Wing*, DCCJ 2000/2007 (28 February 2013).
12. W. J. Newland, *A General Report on the Survey of the New Territories from November 1899 to April 1904* (Hong Kong: 1904).
13. *Lintock Co Ltd v Attorney-General*, above, at 563.

village was thriving) and 50 cents per annum for a house.[14] These rates may appear to be modest but they were generally much higher than those for the imperial land tax. The total rent recorded, which for the government was the object of the exercise, was HK$348,111.57; it was not to increase for years. The amount actually collected however was lower.[15]

The leases covered only a fraction of the territory. The rest, mostly remote and steep, became Crown land even though certain clans asserted an unproved interest in it. So did areas on the periphery of villages, even though the inhabitants regarded it as belonging to the village or clan.

Land Court

The survey was carried out under the auspices of a body that had been established in 1900, the New Territories Land Court. The name may suggest that it was a tribunal for the adjudication between rival claimants to a piece of land. The Land Court did do that but its remit was much wider. It was established by ordinance to investigate and adjudicate upon disputed claims.[16] The survey was part of the process of investigation, so the court also supervised the demarcation. The ordinance provided that on claims being established, titles were to be granted. A period was given for making late claims.

The court was an administrative and quasi-judicial body. Its procedure was kept simple. Claimants were invited to come forward so that details of their claims might be recorded. *Chi tsai* were issued to claimants. The imperial red and customary white deeds were accepted as proof of title. So was the *chap chui*, the receipt for payment of imperial land tax. A list of claims and claimants was posted in the nearest village to the land in case objections were made. The cadastral map was used to find the piece of land claimed. A statement was received from the survey officers as to the size of each piece and a demarcation book prepared by the demarcators stated ownership, the nature of land and amount of rent.

The court updated the rent roll so as to ensure revenue for the government. It could award compensation to those whose claims were disappointed. Once a claim had been upheld, Crown rent was assessed. Once the rent had been paid, a grant of the land would be made. The form that the grant would take was not initially decided.[17]

The court was composed of senior-level civil servants, some with legal qualifications. Its president was a lawyer, initially H. E. Pollock, an eminent local barrister, followed from 1902 by Henry Gompertz. An Oxford graduate, Gompertz

14. Nissim, *Land Administration*, p 20.
15. Orme states that HK$115,448.05 was collected in 1910.
16. Land Court (New Territories) Ordinance 1900, No 8 of 1900, soon replaced by the Land Court New Territories Ordinance, No 18 of 1900. All together there were three Land Court ordinances.
17. Judith Sihombing, 'The Torrens System in the New Territories', 293.

had served in the high-flying administrative grade (as a 'cadet') in Penang and the Straits Settlements, learning Chiu Chow, Hokkien and Cantonese before becoming Assistant Registrar General in Hong Kong, being called to the Bar and thereafter becoming Assistant Colonial Secretary. After the Land Court he was senior magistrate and editor of the law reports, then a long-serving Supreme Court judge in Hong Kong before moving back to Malaya as Chief Justice. A member of the court, J. R. Wood, was another who became a judge, as was its Registrar, Kemp. Other cadets from Hong Kong, Messrs Halligan, Messer and Clementi, were also members. Cecil Clementi, a Sinologue, went on to become Governor of Hong Kong.

The Land Court considered each holding separately. Once satisfied, the court entered details of the owners in the schedules to the block leases.

A major part of the court's task was to adjudicate between the competing claims to ownership of the imperial grantee, who was responsible for payment of land tax, and the person who paid the imperial grantee for actual use of the land and who was often the occupier or cultivator. Before doing so, a study was conducted of land tenure under the imperial Chinese system. Members of the court called imperial grantees who did not occupy their own land 'taxlords'. This signified that such claimants were absentee landlords whose main function was as an intermediary for payment of the tax.

By and large the court favoured the claims of the occupiers over those of the taxlords. This meant that most imperial grantees were eliminated from the new way of landholding, to the delight of the occupiers. The justification given for doing so was that these grantees had broken Ching law by allowing others into possession without the magistrate's permission and a change in registration. Occasionally the dispossessed imperial grantee would be compensated by an award of land elsewhere. This explains the incidence of 'taxlord lots' on the land register.

A member of the court examined each block lease and satisfied himself that the contents were correct, then signed the indenture which was later also signed by the Governor.[18] Inevitably there were inaccuracies. The information contained in the lease schedules was only as good as the information that had been given to the surveyors and to the court.

The court completed work by the end of 1904. The way was then open for the making of land grants to successful claimants. The legislation establishing the court had declared the New Territories to be the property of the government.[19] Once the Land Court had adjudicated in respect of a piece of land 'a title appropriate to the case' was to be awarded by the government.[20] The early plan to register deeds for New Territories lots at the existing Land Registry had been put into operation but had to be abandoned once it became apparent that much of the land was held

18. Hayes, *The Great Difference* (book), p 199, fn 53. Clementi claimed he must have signed his name 500,000 times.
19. A provision now in s 8 of the New Territories Ordinance (Cap 97).
20. Land Court New Territories Ordinance, No 18 of 1900, s 14.

on an informal customary basis without supporting deeds and that the holders were anyway reluctant to come forward out of suspicion of official motives. An alternative suggestion was to set up a register of titles for customary landholdings, with registration bestowing title. This was actually put into legislation in 1902 but repealed before becoming operative because it was realized that it was incompatible with the scheme already implemented whereby the Land Court would adjudicate upon and the Governor would approve the title.[21] So it was decided that new grants would be issued by the Crown. Those grants would have to be limited to the period of British sovereignty, which meant that they could be leasehold only, expiring by 30 June 1997.

Block Crown Leases

Leases, for a term of seventy-five years from 1 July 1898 with a right of renewal for a further twenty-four years less three days, were granted in 1905 and 1907 to those who were regarded as owners of lots. The reason for the curious length of these leases seems to be that shortly before the making of the Convention of Peking, Chamberlain, as Secretary of State for the Colonies, had co-incidentally directed that all government grants in British colonies should not exceed seventy-five years, or at the outside ninety-nine years. He reasoned that terms of 999 years, which the governor had been granting, were practically freehold and deprived the government of control and the advantage of any future enhanced value. A shorter term would enable colonial governments to bring ground rents up to market levels at more frequent intervals, to the benefit of their treasuries.[22] Chamberlain, one of the most prominent politicians to hold the post of Colonial Secretary, was a hard-headed businessman who had made a fortune in manufacturing in Birmingham before establishing his political name as a social and educational reformer as Lord Mayor of that great Victorian industrial city and thereafter entering national politics.[23] Presumably the civil servants in Hong Kong, rather than ask for an exemption from Chamberlain's directive for New Territories leases so that they could issue terms of ninety-nine years (less a few days), decided dutifully to obey. This left the balance of the last twenty-four years of British sovereignty hanging. To give a further lease immediately for the balance would defy their instructions that seventy-five years should be granted. Inventively, they granted the lessee an option, rather than a further term, for that balance.[24]

---

21. Sihombing, 'The Torrens System in the New Territories', pp 292–295, 297–298, 304.
22. James William Norton-Kyshe, *History of the Laws and Courts of Hong Kong* (London: Fisher Unwin, 1898), Vol 2, pp 543–544.
23. Chamberlain had been in charge of sales and accounts at the family's screw-making business, Nettlefolds (now part of GKN).
24. By legislation in 1969 the options were all deemed to be exercised unless the grantee objected.

The Crown grants were made for blocks of land rather than individual plots, one printed lease covering all the lots in a particular area set out in the schedule to the lease. The block approach had occasionally been used in the past for village areas on Hong Kong Island.[25] There was a variety in the size and class of the lots of agricultural land. The area of the house lots in almost every case was one-hundredth (0.01) of an acre.[26] A plan of the block and the lots was annexed to the lease. Each lease was signed by the Governor at the relevant time, Matthew Nathan in 1905 and Frederick Lugard in 1907.

Land granted under these block leases in the early twentieth century became known as 'old schedule lots'. Land sold by the Crown from 1900 was called 'new grants'. Both types of grant expired three days prior to the end of the cession on 30 June 1997.[27] Termination three days in advance was presumably to ensure that no Crown lease would extend beyond the end of British possession and so avoid breaking the rule of landlord and tenant law that a tenant (here, the British Crown) could not grant a term to a sub-tenant (here, the Crown lessee) longer than the tenant's own lease from the landlord (here, China). At the time, it was not realized that the analogy with domestic law was misguided since the 1898 'lease' was not really a lease.[28]

Although leases are normally contracts between landlord and tenant, in reality there was no negotiation or consensus between the government and the grantees under the block leases. The leases were more unilateral fiat of the Crown as sovereign than agreement with its new subjects. Grantees were given no real opportunity to accept or refuse the grant. If they declined to register their claims, they would lose their land to the Crown. The terms of the lease were standardized and set by the government. They included certain restrictions upon the grantee's freedom of action. They were entirely in English. The amount of rent was dictated by the classification of the land as assessed by the Indian surveyors. Lessees did not sign their lease to signify their acceptance of it. They were not issued with a copy. The original lease for each district was placed in a large bound volume followed by the all-important schedule listing the details of the lots.[29]

The contents of the body of the leases were uniform and printed. The typewriter, then in its infancy, was not used. The terms and conditions were not laid out in the numbered paragraphs familiar from modern government grants but in intense blocks of type with any variable details filled in by hand. Much of the language was old fashioned even for the time.

25. Lawrence Wai-chung Lai, Daniel Chi-wing Ho, and Hing-fung Leung, *Change in Use of Land: A Practical Guide to Development in Hong Kong* (Hong Kong: Hong Kong University Press, 3rd edn, 2017), p 8, fn 3.
26. *Lintock Co Ltd v Attorney-General* [1985] 2 HKC 555 at 557 (Hunter J).
27. Subsequently the grants were all extended to 2047 by legislation.
28. See Ch 2.
29. Secretary for the New Territories, 'The Land "Problem" in the New Territories', Memorandum for the Executive Council, 24 August 1977.

One of the printed conditions was an express term forbidding the conversion to building use without government permission of land demised as agricultural ground. This applied to the great majority of the lots.[30] To drive home the point, there was also a covenant forbidding the erection of any building or structure on the land without government permission, whether the land was demised as agricultural or otherwise. So, in order to build, the grantee would have to obtain permission in the form of a licence under the terms or an express waiver of the terms. In addition, there was a clause, common in leases of the era, banning the exercise of any 'noisy, noisome or offensive trade or business whatever' on the land.[31] Provision was made for revision of the Crown rent after ten years, although, pursuant to a promise made by Nathan in 1906, this was not in fact carried out except where a change in use from that listed in the schedule was permitted.[32] Rent for the option period of twenty-four years less three days was stipulated to be at a revised rent but as the beginning of that period approached, Chamberlain's idea was abandoned and a decision was taken for political reasons not to alter the rent. By then old schedule rents had become nominal through inflation.

The grant or demise was applicable to each lot rather than to all the lots en bloc. What was granted to an individual owner was the piece or parcel of ground set out in the schedule as 'more particularly delineated and described on the plan' attached to the lease. This was the plan of the demarcation district created by the surveyors, with all its imperfections. The schedules were laid out in printed columns. The details in the columns were completed by hand, in neat copperplate. The details were only as accurate as the information given to the civil servants who filled them in. Many of the Crown lease schedules were found to contain errors. Clementi made a number of corrections to them when issuing *chap chui*.[33]

The consequence of the grants was that the old system of dual ownership by imperial grant and perpetual customary tenure had been superseded by common law leaseholds of seventy-five years with right of renewal for another twenty-four years. This altered landholding in a fundamental way but it could hardly be otherwise given the confused imperial records, the change in sovereignty and Britain's time-limited interest in the New Territories.

30. In *Watford Construction Co Ltd v Secretary for New Territories* [1978] HKLR 410 'demised as' was interpreted as meaning demised as being land which is or is described as agricultural ground in the description in the schedule.
31. Considered in *Uni-Creation Investments Ltd v Secretary for Justice* [2018] 2 HKC 531.
32. Nathan to Elgin, No 263, 23 October 1906, CO 129/335; proclamation of 11 July 1906.
33. *Lintock Co Ltd v Attorney-General*, above, at 563.

Land Register

The New Territories Land Ordinance of 1905 instituted a register of the land, based on the block lease schedules. The register was not a register of title, merely of documents affecting title, as was the case with the urban deeds register. The previous intention had been that the new register would be one of title, reflecting changes in land registry systems that had occurred in the six decades since the urban register had been instituted in the 1840s as a register of documents, but this was incompatible with the scheme set up by the Land Court Ordinance. In any event, there were so many inaccuracies in the lease schedules and the demarcation plans and so few documents of title that title registration would probably have proved unworkable.

The Block Crown Leases were the first documents on the new register. They were entered in the district land registry which covered the area in which the land was situated. The block leases became the root of the title to all the lots which they recorded.

Registration was by means of taking a record (initially in manuscript) in the form of a memorial or summary of the instrument which was tendered for registration. The memorial contained essential matters only, such as the names of the parties, the identity of the land and the nature of the instrument. It was signed by the parties or their solicitors, numbered and kept in the archive. Payment of stamp duty was recorded. Two copies were made, one for the registry, the other for the registrant.

Four New Territories district Land Registry offices were established. The main registry at Victoria dealt with New Kowloon and the islands. New registries were opened at Taipo and Ping Shan near Yuen Long. Another, at Sai Kung, soon followed.[34] The convenience of so many offices may be contrasted with the imperial registry which offered only one office, some distance away, for the whole of San On.

It was intended that entry on the register should be a simple matter. The procedure was fairly straightforward. Nevertheless, notes for guidance of District Officers were issued in 1908. Simplicity did not mean that the record of transactions was up-to-date. Villagers often did not bother to register successions to property, divisions of property or even sales or mortgages of property. This did not cause difficulties so long as the land remained within the family. Trouble was encountered later, however, if and when the land came to be sold or resumed. Entry on the Crown rent roll was free of charge: another contrast with the imperial system under which a large fee was exacted for entries.

34. HMSO, *Report on the New Territory at Hong Kong*, pp 5–6.

Enduring Settlement

Despite occasional criticism of the terms of the block leases by representatives of indigenous interests, the New Territories land settlement has endured. No attempt was made to change it when Hong Kong reverted to Chinese sovereignty. More than 110 years after issuance of the leases, 210,000 private old schedule lots remained on the record and the imperfect old Demarcation District plans were still referred to. The system is likely to remain in use. The Hong Kong Institute of Surveyors reckons that a re-survey today would take ten years and cost HK$19 billion.

4

Profile of a Territory

The Lie of the Land

Geographically the extension of the colony could be divided into four parts. There was the relatively flat expanse of the northern section of the Kowloon peninsula, immediately abutting upon the existing British possession and extending to the foot of a range of hills running from Devil's Peak in the east to Golden Hill in the west and including Lion Rock and Fei Ngor Shan (Kowloon Peak), collectively referred to as the Kowloon Hills.[1] In 1898 this area was already urbanizing and naturally would become an extension of Kowloon town. It was accordingly named New Kowloon and treated separately from the rest of the ceded land. To its west and beyond the hills lay the area called Sai Kung, effectively two peninsulas, beautiful and mountainous, but remote, rugged and sparsely populated. The hills to the north of New Kowloon formed a natural barrier between it and the main body of the New Territories, an area of valleys, rivers, plains and hills, with a central massif of Tai Mo Shan (Big Hat Mountain). This body was separated from Sai Kung by the steep sides of Ma On Shan (Horse Saddle Mountain) and the waters of a sea inlet, known as Tolo Channel and Tolo Harbour, fed by the Shing Mun River. The main body contained the flattest and most fertile land in the extension as well as the two principal market towns, Taipo and Yuen Long.

The last major section was the island of Lantau (or Lantao) and the other 235 small islands. Lantau was large but again mountainous. Its only major settlement was the fishing town of Tai O towards its western extremity. Of the other islands, only two were of significance, Lamma because of its proximity to Hong Kong Island and Cheung Chau, between Lantau and Hong Kong Island. Cheung Chau, nick-named Dumb Bell Island because its shape, was the most intensely populated island as a result of the fishing port that occupied its central, low-lying area.

---

1. Other hills in the series are Tate's Cairn (Tai Lo Shan), Temple Hill (Tsz Wan Shan), Beacon Hill and Eagle's Nest.

New Administration

This geography suggested the administrative divisions that were to be adopted by the incoming government. New Kowloon was treated as part of the old colony. The rest of the territory was initially regarded as one administrative unit, governed from Taipo. In 1909 it was divided into two districts, each with its own District Officer. The somewhat irrationally named and composed Southern District consisted of Sai Kung in the east, Lantau in the south-west and all the other islands no matter where situate. The Northern District comprised all the rest of the mainland portions; in other words, the main body of the territory. There was to be a District Commissioner, based in Taipo, overseeing both districts.

This arrangement followed an abortive attempt to organize the administration on more local lines. Initially legislation was passed permitting division of the extension into districts.[2] The idea behind this division was to foster good relations with the population by allowing them to continue to manage their own affairs. Disputes were to be settled by committees of elders. Each village or group of villages would have representatives, 'committee men', for liaison with the administration. They could explain the object of government measures to the villagers, reflect back village views and advise the administration. This idea would have been familiar to the inhabitants since the village headman as a link between magistrate and peasantry was an institution of imperial China. There would be one such man for every 50 to 100 people: a similar proportion to that in China.[3] Circulars were issued asking for names to be recommended. The names which had been approved by the Governor were published in a list in July 1899. The following month the Governor met the nominees in two separate groups, one from the east of the territory, the other from the west. According to Lockhart, these men possessed neighbourhood influence and their advice was generally followed.[4] No doubt they included some of the instigators of the April troubles.

But the reality proved not quite as Lockhart had imagined. The districts and sub-districts did not accurately reflect local organization. The real powerbrokers in the villages turned out not to be a village's lineage elders but leaders of large patrilineage institutions from the wealthiest communities which held sway across certain areas. They dominated smaller communities within their aegis, collecting 'taxes', controlling markets and ferries and acting as arbiters in local affairs. If necessary they used violence to settle disputes and maintain and extend their privileges. They were on good terms with the imperial magistrate, or mandarin, who by the latter half of the nineteenth century was so weak that he depended upon them to keep order and rarely tried to exercise any control or become involved in the resolution of disputes. The only way in which the lesser lineages in smaller villages could

2. Local Communities Ordinance, No 11 of 1899.
3. George Jamieson, *Chinese Family and Commercial Law* (Shanghai: Kelly and Walsh, 1921), pp 63 and 71.
4. HMSO, *Report on the New Territory at Hong Kong* (London: 1900), p 5.

resist was by forming alliances with each other and playing off one powerful lineage against another. The interposition of officers of the Hong Kong government for the mandarin altered the balance of power by providing a new and effective source of authority to which the population looked for guidance. As a result, the provisions for rule by committee men were never fully implemented.[5]

The new government nevertheless set up its own institutions. Government buildings were erected on the hill overlooking Taipo market at which the flag had been raised and the ceremonial taking of possession had been held. An imposing building was put up on the brow of the hill as the District Office for the territory. A police station and a government school were also constructed on the hill. Nearby, a station for the new Kowloon-Canton Railway soon followed. A large house was built for senior government officials on an island linked by causeway to the hill; later it was to become the home of the District Commissioner, New Territories.[6] When, a few years later, the New Territories was divided into two districts, the Taipo office became that for the Northern District. The District Office for the far-flung Southern District was in a commercial building in Victoria, the central district on Hong Kong Island, convenient for the administrators if not for those they administered.

So, although the extension was legally part of Hong Kong, in administrative practice the bulk of it was treated differently from the rest of the colony. The model employed was that of District Officers used in large parts of the British Empire. In fact this suited the nature of the territory, remote and lightly populated, difficult to reach and to travel around, with predominantly native inhabitants. It suited in another way too, for the system was reminiscent of that which it replaced. The District Officer's duties were wide, comparable with those of the imperial magistrate. He supervised land matters, selling and acquiring it, collecting rent from it, certifying transactions in it and granting permission (licences) to build upon it. In addition, he sat as a judge (with both criminal and small civil jurisdiction), dealt with minor public works, liaised with the community and made recommendations to higher authorities. The difference was that, unlike the mandarin, the District Officer had the resources and the interest actually to carry out those duties and, being from outside Chinese culture, was free of the traditional influences and ugly corrupt practices that blighted the Chinese system in later years.[7]

As far as most inhabitants of the territory were concerned, the District Officer was the government. As successor to the imperial magistrate he was leimanfoo, the mother-and-father official who looked after their problems. Those who served as

---

5. Maurice Freedman, 'Shifts of Power in the Hong Kong New Territories', Ch 11 in *The Study of Chinese Society: Essays* (Stanford, CA: Stanford University Press, 1979) (*The Study of Chinese Society*).
6. The hill, called Flagstaff Hill by the British, is Wan Tau Tong; the island, Yuen Chau Tsai, is now a promontory behind a large housing estate; and the house is Island House, now a declared monument used as an education and studies centre of the World Wide Fund for Nature.
7. Steve Tsang, *Governing Hong Kong: Administrative Officers from the Nineteenth Century to the Handover to China, 1862–1997* (Hong Kong: Hong Kong University Press, 2007), p 41 (*Governing Hong Kong*); David Akers-Jones, *Feeling the Stones: Reminiscences by David Akers-Jones* (Hong Kong: Hong Kong University Press, 2004), Ch 2 (*Feeling the Stones*).

District Officers were generally impressive people, well-educated and well-behaved, with a sense of purpose, propriety and duty. The district office was an early posting for many of the elite 'cadets' recruited from private schools and universities in Britain to become meritocratic generalists in the Hong Kong civil service. Several took a deep interest in the culture and history of the people they supervised and wrote about their experiences.[8] They respected, understood and identified with the rural population, towards whom they had a generally protective, paternalistic attitude.

Lockhart's recommendation that, so far as possible, the organization of local governance already existing in the New Territories be maintained accorded with the aim of disrupting the daily life of the inhabitants as little as possible.[9] Consequently, District Officers turned to clan leaders and village elders for informal advice. This was formalized in 1926 into a system of Tsz Yi advisers.[10] The villages were allowed to continue with the mixture of written and oral customs, local rules, norms and expectations based upon the Confucianism which had been inculcated into the population. In the towns, an informal system of management by community and residential organization, led by local worthies including shopkeepers and other businessmen, was also allowed to continue.[11]

The attitude of the better District Officers contrasted with that of the senior civil service in urban Hong Kong where an arrogant, pompous and inward-looking frame of mind took hold during the decades before the Japanese invasion and occupation. They certainly had no interest in the New Territories, except perhaps for the recreational opportunities which it allowed. They made little attempt to win the support of urban Chinese inhabitants whom they regarded as mere sojourners in a British colony. In this they reflected the views of the expatriate population.

Each District Officer was an Assistant Land Officer. Land Registers were opened at the district offices where all documents and judgments affecting land were to be recorded by memoranda summarizing their contents. Forms of transfer, mortgage and lease were devised for use in the New Territories. Land Officers were given power to decide all questions and disputes concerning land summarily. They were enjoined to recognize and enforce any Chinese custom or customary right. They were also given a supervisory role over customary landholding institutions.

Authority of a more muscular variety backed the civil administration. Security was one of the priorities of the new rulers. The trouble in April 1899 was fresh in mind. Lockhart was well aware that the peace of the territory had occasionally been disrupted by village feuds, pirate attacks and raids by gangs from Shumchun. He also knew of the territory's reputed triad connections. In the early 1900s police stations were built at various, usually prominent, points around the territory under

8. Kenneth Barnett, Austin Coates, David Akers-Jones, Denis Bray, James Hayes, Brian Wilson, and Patrick Hase have all written about their experiences in the New Territories administration.
9. Tsang, *Governing Hong Kong*, p 33.
10. Baker, *Sheung Shui*, pp 13–14.
11. Hayes, *The Hong Kong Region*, xxii, pp 80–84.

the supervision of the long-serving, no-nonsense police chief, Francis May. Apart from at Taipo and Kowloon City, there were stations at Ping Shan and Au Tau, deep in the sphere of influence of the troublesome Tangs, and at Sha Tau Kok on the new border. A little later stations were added at Tai O at the western end of Lantau and at Sheung Shui, the domain of the Liu clan in the north of the territory. Following up on the defence theme recited in the Convention, a military camp was established at Kwantei near Fanling. At the end of the decade, military roads and blockhouses were built in the Kowloon Hills. In 1912 a cordon of military posts was erected along the frontier to protect against raiding bands.[12]

Political Representation

Although the practice of informal consultation of rural elders had been in place since 1899, a system of representation of ordinary villagers had to wait until the late 1940s when elected village representatives and rural committees were founded. The village representative was an intermediary between the District Office and the population, making suggestions, forwarding complaints, explaining plans. In theory the representative was elected but in practice he (the representative was always male) emerged by a sort of consensus within the village as to who was appropriate: this involved a mixture of a candidate's willingness to serve, seniority within the village, standing within the community, level of education and experience, and acceptability to the District Officer.[13]

Village representatives elected the members of the rural committees, including their chairmen and vice-chairmen. Committee members became spokesmen and intermediaries for the district. The chairmen and vice-chairmen became members of the Heung Yee Kuk (along with a number of special councillors) and, in turn, they elected the executive committee of the kuk.[14]

Numbers and Occupations of Population

There is no accurate count of the number of people dwelling in the newly ceded area in 1899, although there are a number of estimates. Lockhart put the figure at more than 100,000 but this included Shumchun which he expected, wrongly, would become part of the extended colony. Baker suggests the figure should be a little more than 84,000. The 1901 census, which ought to be more accurate than estimates, has 102,254. This includes the population of New Kowloon and those who lived on boats, so the number dwelling in the villages must have been considerably fewer. By the time of the 1911 census the population had fallen to 94,246, of whom 13,624

12. Sayer, *Years of Discretion*, pp 85–86, 103 and 113.
13. James Hayes, *Friends and Teachers: Hong Kong and Its People 1953–1987* (Hong Kong: Hong Kong University Press, 1996), pp 307–309 (*Friends and Teachers*).
14. Baker, *Sheung Shui*, pp 13–14 and 27; Hayes, *Friends and Teachers*, p 308.

were in New Kowloon and 9,855 were boat people. By 1921 it had fallen further, to 82,947.[15] This decline in the New Territories population seems to have continued a trend that had set in during the nineteenth century.

At the time of the British takeover the occupations of country folk were mainly farming and fishing. The farming was predominantly rice-growing, although sugar, sweet potatoes, peanuts, fruit, bean curd, soy, herbs and tea were also cultivated. Livestock were raised, mainly pigs and buffalo. There was some grass-growing and wood-cutting. The fishing was largely in coastal communities but there was a little inshore fishing too. Oyster beds and salt pans were to be found in the west.[16] In the hills to the east and in the centre were several long-established stone quarries. A few worked as artisans such as carpenters and builders. A growing number had found work away from their villages.

Emigration

Why the fall in the New Territories population in the early days of British rule? Emigration certainly played a role. Even before the territory became part of Hong Kong in 1898 but increasingly as the twentieth century progressed, the difficulty of making a living from agriculture led men to seek employment in the city or on ships or abroad, leaving the women to work the fields. Rice growing was hard toil with two crops a year to be planted, tended, gathered and threshed. Urban Hong Kong needed construction, dock and factory workers. Emigration to various parts of the world had long been a practice amongst rural folk from south-east China, including San On. Goldfields in California and Australia, railroads in Canada and the United States of America, and ships from the United Kingdom had drawn economic migrants. Among less likely destinations, South America, the Straits Settlements, Borneo, Jamaica and the Seychelles all provided work for coolies.[17] During the 1880s, San On had become a recruiting ground for shipping companies looking for merchant seamen willing to work at low wages.[18] Though the men expected to return to their villages and generally did so, the experience had given them an idea of the opportunities that lay beyond the countryside and which might tempt them into permanent departure.

The incorporation of southern San On into Hong Kong brought better communications and more contact with the west. It led also to improvements in education and greater knowledge of the outside world. Nevertheless, during the early decades of the twentieth century most New Territories villages remained remote from

15. Hayes, *The Great Difference* (book), Ch 4.
16. Hayes, *The Hong Kong Region*, pp 33–35.
17. Maurice Freedman, 'Emigration from the New Territories', Ch 12 in *The Study of Chinese Society*; Palmer, 'Surface-Subsoil' 48, fns 116 and 118').
18. Michael Palmer, 'Lineage and Urban Development in a New Territories Market Town', in Hugh Baker and Stephen Freuchtwang (eds), *A New State in Old Settings: Studies in the Social Anthropology of China in Memory of Maurice Freedman* (Oxford: JASO, 1991), p 76 ('Lineage and Urban Development').

metropolitan Hong Kong. Beyond New Kowloon, development was restrained and largely confined to the established market towns and the vicinity of new roads and railways.

Grants of New Land

Most of the land in the New Territories had not been disposed of by the block Crown leases. The policy of the administration in the first four decades of the twentieth century was to sell or let vacant land, usually by public auction, on standard terms and conditions. If the land was remote and small, it would be sold by direct arrangement with a purchaser (private treaty) rather than by auction. The standard conditions of these new grants were published by notice in the Government Gazette. They contained no restrictions upon use but did contain restrictions upon the height of any building which might be erected: no more than two storeys. In 1934 this was supplemented by a height limit of twenty-five feet, with each storey to be at least ten feet high and a maximum site coverage of 66 per cent of the lot plus any special conditions for the lot in question. Buildings had to be completed within twenty-four months.[19] After the Second World War, standard conditions fell out of use in favour of conditions tailored to the particular lot.[20]

Population Movement

Demand for new land was spurred by a reversal in the decline of the territory's population. The 1931 census showed the New Territories as having 98,157 people. There was an influx of refugees, mainly poor peasant farmers, fleeing communist disturbances of the 1920s and 1930s in north-east Guangdong. They were mainly vegetable growers who found a ready market in Kowloon and Hong Kong.[21] The 1920s were not prosperous, however. In Hong Kong, as elsewhere, the 1930s was a time of economic depression. There was an influx of refugees in 1938 after the Japanese took over Canton.[22]

Between the world wars the recruitment of New Territories men to work on ships was at its height. In his study of life in Sheung Shui, Baker recounts how, once Kowloon and Hong Kong became more accessible, an outflow began of men from the settlements of that district. The flow was at first a trickle, the majority finding work as crew of ocean-going ships calling at Hong Kong. By the 1960s the flow had become steady: the estimate of the number of villagers overseas was between

19. The principal Gazette Notices were GN 365 of 1906 and GN 364 of 1934. See Nissim, *Land Administration*, p 22.
20. The use of standard general conditions was discontinued in 1985 by GN 1409.
21. Hayes, *The Great Difference* (book), Ch 4.
22. Palmer, 'Lineage and Urban Development', pp 76–77; Jack M. Potter, *Capitalism and the Chinese Peasant: Social and Economic Change in a Hong Kong Village* (Berkeley and Los Angeles: University of California Press, 1968), p 8 (*Capitalism and The Chinese Peasant*).

one and two hundred. They sent back remittances to their families and intended to return on retirement.[23]

The 1940s was a decade of upheaval: regional conflict, world and civil war, Japanese invasion and occupation, neglect and destruction of buildings, forced repatriation of the population to their native places on the mainland, then return of many of those people to Hong Kong in and after 1945. Some farmers who had fled from the Japanese in the early 1940s became caught up in the turbulence of the mainland in the latter part of the decade and never returned. Others, skilled in handling livestock and growing vegetables rather than the traditional rice, took the opportunity to avoid the turmoil and immigrated to Hong Kong.[24] The dislocation of the war years stimulated change throughout Hong Kong, including the New Territories.[25]

The great influx to Hong Kong of refugees from the civil war led to shortage of housing and land. In the summer of 1950 alone an estimated 700,000 Chinese came to Hong Kong. Most of the expanded population went to the urban areas where squatter huts abounded but the New Territories, with its greater space, attracted a share of the newcomers: its population was estimated at 265,000 in 1955, more than two-and-a-half times the 1931 figure. By 1961 the number was 456,404.[26] Many of these new settlers squatted on government or private land, building makeshift dwellings there. Farmers from the mainland rented land from local owners and cultivated vegetables for consumption in the metropolis of Hong Kong–Kowloon.

During this post-war era intensive industrialization began, tempting rural inhabitants to take up factory work, which was more lucrative than farming. These inhabitants were largely women, especially younger ones. New Territories men had long preferred work in town, on ships or abroad to tending the land. Rice cultivation declined rapidly in the 1950s and had almost disappeared by the end of the next decade. Growing rice was less profitable than vegetables so vegetable growers could afford higher rents. Indigenous rice farmers gave up and some moved away. The land was left idle or rented to incomers. Dr Hugh Baker noted that in Wei Nei, one of the Sheung Shui hamlets that he studied, the previously predominant agricultural occupations of the natives had so fallen away that by the late 1960s only 12 of the population of 120 were engaged in farming.[27] It was estimated that at that time the number of the Liu clan from Sheung Shui working overseas was between 100 and 200. The rising population of the northern part of the colony led to a boom at the neighbouring market town of Shek Wu Hui and the founding of a new market

23. Baker, *Sheung Shui*, p 205.
24. Hayes, *The Great Difference* (book), Ch 6; Baker, *Sheung Shui*, p 207; Chan Kwok-shing, 'The Making of a Market Town in Rural Hong Kong, The Luen Wu Market', in Lee Pui-tak (ed), *Colonial Hong Kong and Modern China: Interaction and Reintegration* (Hong Kong: Hong Kong University Press, 2005), p 92 ('A Market Town').
25. Baker, *Sheung Shui*, p 206.
26. Almost 20% of the 1955 total, and more than 10% of the 1961 total, were boat people.
27. Baker, *Sheung Shui*, pp 22 and 205–207.

area at Luen Wu Hui, Fanling. These developments across the whole region may be described as an agricultural revolution.[28]

Records kept by District Officers in the middle of the last century show that men from many villages were working in metropolitan Hong Kong or abroad. For instance, in the 1950s the village of Pak Kong in Sai Kung in the western part of the territory had a population of 265 of whom only 220 were actually resident, the rest being either abroad or in Hong Kong or Kowloon; five or six were in the United Kingdom and more than ten at sea. At the larger settlement of Sha Kok Mei next to Sai Kung town, about one-fifth out of its 526 people were thought to be abroad or shortly going abroad; restaurants and laundries in London were a favourite destination; 48 were seamen. Further along the coast at Tai Mong Tsai, nine of the village's 39 men were working in town and five or six in the United Kingdom. At the large village of Tung Chung on the north coast of Lantau, 70 of the population of 991 was estimated to be working abroad.[29]

Coincidentally, British passports became available to New Territories inhabitants as residents of British territory, facilitating work overseas and permanent emigration. Loan funds were established to finance emigration. Chinese restaurants and laundries in Europe replaced ships as the main source of overseas work. The Man lineage of Santin to the east of Yuen Long became the operators of, and supplier of employees to, a flourishing network of restaurants in the United Kingdom.[30] They also had restaurants in Holland. Former padi farmers thereby became cooks and kitchen workers. One may wonder how this transformation was achieved. One restauranteur explained to Dr Baker that half-an-hour's training was all that was required. 'Tell them to use plenty of ginger, bean sprouts and dried citrus peel, give them a wok and a bottle of soy sauce and they know all there is to know about "Chinese cooking".'[31] This explains the Chinese cuisine to be found in Britain.

During three decades from 1950 there was a great expansion in the number of Chinese restaurants in Great Britain. They were nearly all staffed by people from the New Territories. They worked hard, with little time for entertainment or contact with the locals, but the income was good. They were able to send money home to fund the building of a spacious house for retirement.

Emigration to Europe became even easier when an enterprising New Territories businessman from the Man clan arranged seats at discounted prices, with generous baggage allowance, for indigenous people on charter flights and later with the major British airline. Destinations were not confined to Europe. South-east Asia, Borneo,

28. Palmer, 'Lineage and Urban Development', p 84.
29. John Strickland (ed), *Southern District Officer Reports* (Hong Kong: Hong Kong University Press, 2010), pp 68, 240–242, 259–262. The authors of the records are Austin Coates and James Hayes.
30. Palmer, 'Lineage and Urban Development', pp 72 and 104.
31. Hugh D. R. Baker, 'The Hong Kong Chinese in the United Kingdom', Ch 16 in Ronald Skeldon (ed), *Reluctant Exiles? Migration from Hong Kong and the New Overseas Chinese* (Hong Kong: Hong Kong University Press, 1994), p 295. Emigrant Mans were forbears of the protagonists in *Man Leung v Man Yuet Kwai* [2013] 2 HKLRD 1122.

Jamaica and the Seychelles all benefited from the New Territories people's contribution to the Chinese diaspora.[32]

In the course of research during the late 1960s into the occupancy of houses at the village of Sheung Tsuen, near Shek Kong in the Pat Heung district, Howard Nelson found a low average rate of occupancy and a number of abandoned houses. He attributed this in part to migration but also pointed out that it was rare for Chinese deliberately to leave their ancestral home for good. Instead they would embark on what was intended to be an extended sojourn abroad, in the hope of eventual return. Nelson suggested that the abandonment was due to the absence of a mechanism in customary law whereby a non-returning migrant's land could be transferred to kinsmen or fellow villagers, even after the migrant's death had been reported or become virtually certain, and to the shame attached to selling a house.[33]

More recently, Hong Kong people have taken advantage of special migrant schemes offered by high-immigration countries such as Canada and Australia and also by less prosperous nations in need of investment. Modern emigrants who held rural land would be more likely to sell than abandon it and the probability was that it would end up in the hands of a developer or speculator. Such owners might have no immediate use for the land, leaving it vacant whilst acquiring nearby lots so as to assemble a site more viable for building and whilst waiting for property prices to rise.

In the latter half of the twentieth century emigration from the rural areas was more than matched by the influx of people from elsewhere. The incomers were predominantly from China, notably eastern Guangdong, escaping famine or seeking a better life. Influxes were apt to come in surges. During twenty-five days in the Spring of 1962 an estimated 70,000 people crossed into the New Territories. Many were sent back. Those that were not and who were farmers, finding uncultivated land, turned it into vegetable plots and orchards or raised pigs and poultry to make a living. They put up temporary quarters, essentially huts and shacks. They did not know, and may not have cared, who the owner was but they did know that here was land that ought to be put to economic use. That indeed is one of the justifications for the legal sanctioning of the takeover of unused land by a long-term trespasser: it encourages efficient use of a scarce resource. In the rural setting it is more likely than with urban property that the claimant entered without any permission, in other words an instance of plain squatting.[34] Where the land taken over was Crown land, the administration would often bow to reality and grant the intruders licences to occupy at an annual fee. The newcomers also rented land from villagers. A common scenario with uncontested applications for declarations of title by

32. Hayes, *The Great Difference* (book), pp 142, 160.
33. H. G. H. Nelson, 'The Chinese Descent System and the Occupancy Level of Village Houses', 9 *Journal of the Hong Kong Branch of the Royal Asiatic Society* 113, pp 113, 120 and 123, fn 21 ('The Chinese Descent System').
34. Rural examples are: *Tsang Cho Kiu v Lam Tsat Fuk*, HCMP 1077/2013 (10 December 2013); *Ying Fai v Chan Bo Cheung*, HCA 891/2012 (28 January 2015); *Chan Michael v PR of Tam Siu Fung, dec'd*, HCMP 745/2015 (7 April 2017); *Wong Pui Ling v Leung Kit Fun Beatrice Benedict* [2017] 3 HKLRD 700.

long-term occupiers of land is that the claimants or their forbears had been tenants of the property and they or their family had simply stayed on after the landlord had died or otherwise ceased to collect rent.[35]

Famine, economic dislocation and social upheavals in China ensured that the flood of migrants continued throughout the 1960s with consequent pressure upon housing and land in Hong Kong. By 1970 the forbears of most of the residents of the New Territories were from elsewhere and most of the houses there were what the government called 'temporary structures', that is to say unauthorized and makeshift constructions.

Development

In 1899 the islands and rural areas had almost no infrastructure. There were no properly surfaced roads outside New Kowloon, only paths and tracks which mostly zigzagged over the narrow divisions between padi fields. Some of the wider paths had flagstones, but they were unsuitable for horses. The main means of access from Hong Kong was by boat, impracticable in bad weather. Land transport was powered by oxen or humans: carts, trucks and rickshaws. There was no electricity, gas or running water in the villages.

The new government set about building some metalled roads. Construction of a highway, of standard width with one lane in each direction, from New Kowloon to Taipo and thereafter, as Castle Peak Road, encircling the main body of the territory was soon started. The previous land route to Taipo had been a steep footpath through a mountain pass to Shatin. The new Taipo Road was completed by the end of 1901 and extended to Fanling by 1913. It began at the top of the wide tree-lined and largely undeveloped boulevard running from the south to the north of the Kowloon peninsula. The boulevard was initially named Robinson after one recent governor, then re-named after Sir Matthew Nathan, the governor who succeeded Blake. Nathan had been secretary of the Colonial Defence Committee advising Chamberlain, the Secretary of State. He was in office when the planning of the thoroughfare had begun and was an army engineer by background. He was however more interested in another project, the railway that was planned to connect Kowloon with Canton.

This railway had been foreshadowed in the 1898 Convention. The British section from Hung Hom to the new border was ready by 1910 although Nathan had already departed by then. The Chinese section on to Canton was not to be completed until 1924 and even then there was no link to the railway system of the rest of China. There was also a narrow-gauge branch line from Fanling to Sha Tau Kok with open carriages, alongside a new road running north-east from Fanling

35. Examples of overstaying tenants obtaining possessory title are: *Wong Wing Man v Wong Chung On*, DCMP 1009/2013 (4 April 2014); *Shue Huei Yue v Tan Chung Meng*, DCCJ 2294/2013 (1 August 2014); *Ip Ying Kung v Louie Hong Sue Gay*, DCCJ 4719/2015 (17 August 2016).

Station to Leung Yeuk Tau. This line lost custom after that road was extended to Sha Tau Kok and closed in 1928.[36]

The main line opened up the territory to recreation for city dwellers. A full-size golf course with clubhouse was created at Ping Kong, south of Sheung Shui, although the course was known by the name of the then nearest station, Fanling. Also in the vicinity of the line, a country club, a steeplechase racecourse and hunting and riding facilities were established. Villas for the wealthy and for the Governor were built. Pleasure beaches and later hotels opened just off the Castle Peak Road. A large military camp was set out at San Wai to the north-east of Fanling, next to the racecourse.

Telephone lines were quickly laid. Thirty miles of lines were achieved within the first eight months of the new administration, linking the main centres. However, the whole of the eastern portion of the territory remained unconnected to Kowloon by road or rail, as of course did the islands.

In 1914 the old market at Yuen Long was replaced by a new market funded by private initiative. The Hop Yick Company which built the new market was formed by villagers, mainly from the vicinity. In 1935 the market expanded to 48 shops. Soon after, the town acquired its first cinema. Despite this and despite being one of the larger centres, Yuen Long's population was only around 3,000.[37] Another of the larger towns, Tsuen Wan, was much closer to urban Kowloon. During the 1930s it housed several factories, making porcelain, bricks and beer, precursors of what was to follow.

Village men went to the city in search of employment. They continued to work on ships and a few ventured to Europe. Water shortages spurred the construction of a new reservoir in the foothills above Tsuen Wan to supply expanding Kowloon. During the mid-1930s another was constructed above the first and was named to commemorate the golden jubilee of King George V. For the most part, however, there was little development of the territory during the years up to 1941. There had been some delight at the republican revolution in China in 1911. The strikes of the mid-1920s that so disrupted Hong Kong's trade had no effect in country parts, except that workers returned to their villages for the duration. The agitation by owners concerning building land had subsided. Most villages remained remote with no paved roads, electricity, piped water or gas. The economy was subdued. The rural scene was settled and quiet. But that was about to change.

Japanese Occupation

Japanese troops had occupied large parts of China in the late 1930s and were poised on the border with Hong Kong for months before their invasion and rapid conquest

36. One of the branch line's locomotives can be viewed at the Hong Kong Railway Museum next to the old Taipo Market Station and the façade of one of the stations still stands alongside the Sha Tau Kok Road.
37. Potter, *Capitalism and the Chinese Peasant*, p 8; Akers-Jones, *Feeling the Stones*, p 38.

in December 1941. The military buffer which British commanders had requested forty-three years earlier for the defence of the colony provided by the Convention of Peking proved useless against a numerous, agile and well-armed infantry. The defensive line near the new reservoirs in the hills above Kowloon was quickly overwhelmed. The invaders progressed by the simple expedient of bicycling and marching down the railway line that the Convention had provided for.

The Japanese were interested in Hong Kong for its port and military facilities. They forced the depopulation of the built-up areas and began a reign of terror. They were little concerned with the rural parts, not having sufficient personnel to police them. They occasionally ventured into the hinterland in groups and with caution, for the countryside was the centre of resistance to the occupation, led by the East River Column which had its base in remote villages of the Sai Kung peninsula. The column was composed of Chinese irregular soldiers with communist sympathies. The Japanese massacred villagers at Luk Keng whom they suspected of aiding the resistance.

For civilians, the 44 months of Japanese rule was a time of privation. There was little food and not enough wood for cooking and heating. A villager, long-term head of Mau Tso Nam village at Fei Ngor Shan between Shatin and Sai Kung, born in 1923 and alive in 2018 recalled that people had to eat the bark of trees for nourishment. They could earn a pittance doing coolie work for the Japanese army, though the soldiers took a 'cut' of 50 per cent of the villagers' pay.[38] The worst threat however came not from Japanese troops but from gangs of Chinese thugs who would raid villages looking for booty. The remoter villages were terribly exposed. The inhabitants fled further into the hills, returning to their ransacked homes the next day after a cold night on the mountainside.

At Santin there were random killings of villagers of all ages by Japanese troops. A mass grave was dug behind an ancestral hall. Conditions were just as grim for the more prosperous villages of Ping Shan. There was little work; commerce was at a standstill. Landlords took land back from tenants and farmed it themselves or with hired help. Food was short there too. The wealthier villagers had salted fish, rice and vegetables; the poorer ones made do with rice gruel. Malnutrition was rife.[39] The deprivations and dislocation of the war years paved the way for change, which was to come rapidly after 1945.

Post-war Development

After the Japanese surrender, the British military were determined that there would be no repeat of the abject defeat of 1941. Men and resources were poured into Hong Kong. Construction of facilities for the army and air force in the late 1940s and

38. Interview with Mr Cheng Gau Hung, April 2018.
39. Potter, *Capitalism and the Chinese Peasant*, pp 38–39.

early 1950s provided a distinct economic fillip. New barracks, roads and ranges provided work for contractors and gave rural areas a complex of connections. The presence of tens of thousands of military personnel injected spending into the local economy. The communist takeover of mainland China and consequent influx of refugees sustained the threat. Airfields were constructed at Shatin and at Sek Kong where the main military camp was built. That camp was well connected by new or improved roads to Taipo, Kam Tin, Tsuen Wan, and Sheung Shui where shops, bars, restaurants, and other establishments catered for the needs of soldiers. A dozen other camps were opened, permanent or temporary. Many of the local population thus came into contact with Westerners for the first time.

The returning colonial government was enthused with the reforms of the age. This led to improvements in housing, health, welfare, education, and town planning. Given the scale of the difficulties facing Hong Kong, attention naturally focused on urban improvements. In the New Territories, help was given to farmers: establishment of the Agriculture, Forestry and Fisheries Department in 1946; formation of co-operatives for fisherfolk and vegetable-growers and of the Kadoorie Agricultural Aid Organisation. New schools were built.

Even these well-meaning initiatives were capable of subversion by country folk. The vegetable marketing organization charged a commission and did not guarantee prices. To avoid the commission, enterprising (and mainly female) cultivators set up their own small street markets, at least one of which (at Luen Wu Hui, Fanling) was so successful that it became a regular event and led local entrepreneurs to develop the area with shops. The market area at Shek Wu Hui was also rebuilt in the 1950s by local entrepreneurs following a fire. Many of the investors were businessmen from resident lineages.[40]

Tseung Kwan O, then known as Junk Bay, became the site of major resettlement of Nationalist troops and sympathizers who had fled across the border at the end of the Chinese civil war. They were placed far from the centre of Hong Kong, where they might cause the least trouble. They built a shanty town clinging to the hillside.

Repeated summer flooding during the last years of the 1950s set in motion drainage schemes in large parts of the north-west New Territories.[41] However, the threat from floods caused by intense summer rains continued until the end of the century when the principal rivers were turned into large concrete channels, with generous overflow areas, by the Drainage Services Department.

The rural electrification scheme which began in 1961 brought power to 450 villages within five years. A fourfold increase in the New Territories population was recorded between the censuses of 1931 and 1961. The figures, however, disguised a drop in population during the war years and rises in population during the late 1930s and throughout the post-war era. The increase, however, was modest by comparison with what was to come.

---

40. Chan, 'A Market Town', Ch 5.
41. Akers-Jones, *Feeling the Stones*, p 37.

The 1950s floods were followed by 1960s draught. The driest year on record was 1963.[42] In September 1962 the most destructive typhoon in living memory, Wanda, caused wide damage and loss of life: 130 died and 2,000 craft were destroyed. Wanda, which coincided with a high tide, passed over the territory then returned to wreak more havoc. There was a storm surge at Tolo Harbour. The radar station at Tate's Cairn was wrecked. There were more typhoons in 1964.

The drought, combined with heavy demand for water from the dying industry, led to water rationing. The need for new reservoirs was met by giant schemes at Shek Pik in the west of Lantau Island, Plover Cove near Taipo and High Island at Sai Kung which resulted in forced relocations of many villagers.[43] Even so, Hong Kong was to suffer a water shortage and rationing into the 1980s, largely because of the demand from industry.

The Kowloon Canton Railway, with just one train per hour, and the original Taipo Road built in the early 1900s remained the principal ways for New Territories people to reach Kowloon during the early 1960s. However, in 1967 the first of what were to become five sets of vehicular tunnels through the hills linking the main part of the New Territories with Kowloon was opened, bringing country closer to town. The Lion Rock Tunnel was conceived as a means of carrying water from the Plover Cove reservoir but plans were extended to provide a road link. Initially that was a single tube with one lane in each direction. This swiftly proved inadequate so in 1973 another tube began to be driven parallel to it and was completed in 1975, enabling each tube to carry two lanes of traffic in one direction.

Resumption and Compensation

These and other improvements brought into focus the process of compulsory purchase of land which was required for public purposes. The process, called 'resumption' on the pretence that the government had previously possessed all the land so was merely re-taking it, had caused difficulties for years. The 1898 Convention had promised no expropriations of land except for official purposes and at a fair price. The extension of Hong Kong law to the New Territories soon thereafter brought in the recent legislation which enabled the government to take land from owners. This power was initially used mainly in New Kowloon. Villagers there had their land seized and were paid only its agricultural value. The legislation dictated that compensation would be the value of the resumed land for the purposes for which it could currently be lawfully used. No allowance was to be made for enhancement in value as a result of the prospect of development—the so-called 'hope value'—which meant the compensation would be less than the market value since a purchaser in the open market would have reflected the hope value in his bid.

42. Only 901.1 mm of rain was recorded that year.

43. Akers-Jones, *Feeling the Stones*, p 40; Hayes, 'The Great Difference' (article), 145.

It was little use explaining to owners that the Crown leases which had been imposed upon them forbad any buildings without government permission. Their expectation of benefiting financially from absorption into the city had been dashed. It was the government which was going to get the value of any building on their property and that building would not necessarily be for official purposes as envisaged by the Convention. Naturally, they felt cheated: the new government had promised that their landed interests would be protected and that there would be no expropriations, yet here it was taking their cherished land and short-changing them so soon.

The low amount of resumption compensation was one of two running sores that poisoned relations between the New Territories Administration and the Heung Yee Kuk for decades. The other was the administration's desire to control rural development. This was largely done by use of the covenants in Crown leases. Permission to build was either denied or granted only in exchange for a fat premium. Administrators called this process conversion of the land to building status.

The balance of power between the wars was with the government. Land values and demand for building were low. China, now a republic but torn by internal strife and no stronger than it had been under the Ching, was in no position to help disgruntled land owners. Hong Kong planners did not yet need a great deal of land so the number of offended owners was relatively small. That started to change with the foundation of the Heung Yee Kuk in the mid-1920s. The big change however came after the Second World War for then town planning had become the watchword and the government needed much more land for reservoirs, roads, military installations and so on. Once the massive expansion of housing through new towns was being planned, the time had come to be more generous.

Administrators came up with a scheme to circumvent the meanness of statutory compensation. They would make extra payments to dispossessed owners on an ex gratia basis. They would offer them a cash amount for purchase of the land. As an alternative, they would offer them a share in the added value stemming from development but in an indirect way which would have a gambling element attractive to the Hong Kong psyche. That element would be even more attractive by being in the nature of a one-way bet in a booming property market. Those whose agricultural land was taken were to be allowed to exchange it for an amount of building land elsewhere. There would be plenty of that once the new town schemes got under way. They would be given a letter from the government promising that the land which had been taken could be exchanged for a certain amount of future building land. These Land Exchange Entitlements, or 'Letters B', could also be sold in the market which evolved for such documents. So the dispossessed landowner could obtain cash for his entitlement whenever he wished.[44] The proportion of development land which would be exchanged was two square feet for every five square feet

44. Letters B were offer letters issued where resumption proceedings had started. The rarer Letters A were used where resumption processes had not yet begun.

of agricultural land taken. This formula was calculated on the basis of an estimate that in every five square feet to be developed, three would be required for roads and other amenities. The two square feet for buildings proved far more valuable than five square feet of non-building land.

The government started issuing these letters which proved more popular than money with landowners as a means of compensation. Their market value escalated far quicker than that of any other investment. One reason for this was that the amount of building land created could not keep pace with the amount committed to by the certificates. The shortage of developable land resulted in surges in land prices and in the value of the certificates. Speculators and developers eagerly bought certificates from former landowners.

By 1976, realizing that with these certificates it had entered into commitments that were very expensive and would likely become even more so, the government started to offer as compensation for newly resumed land the equivalent of the current market value of certificates. This did not work, for owners realized that certificates would continue to increase in value so it was better to have them than the cash. So, after a review, the exchange formula was revised. Entitlements could in future be issued at the 5:2 ratio for up to only half the land taken, the rest would be compensated at a set amount of cash which would be regularly reviewed in the light of the market for such entitlements but which was well below the market value. But there was still insufficient land to meet the commitments and land values and compensation rates continued to go up.

If it was an attempt to buy off rural complaints, the Letters B system was not very successful and was hideously expensive. But it did give landowners a stake in the property game and allowed them a slice of the prosperity of late twentieth-century Hong Kong.

5

Preservation of Custom

Socially, southern San On naturally shared the traits of rural south China. The inhabitants had a strong sense of tradition and inheritance of Chinese civilization, with an emphasis upon Confucianism. This was reflected not least in the importance of family and lineage. People took pride in their genealogy, their institutions, and the history of their village. They practiced rites and followed their own rules and norms, both written and oral. There was reverence for ancestors and for cultural practices. This inculcated a sense of cohesion, stability, and continuity. It also encouraged a conservative outlook: men wore their hair in a pigtail and dressed in gowns and tunics. There was mistrust of novelty and coolness towards outsiders. It must also have encouraged a feeling of self-sufficiency.[1]

The new masters were well aware of the centrality of custom to the daily life of the Chinese peasant. Lockhart had counselled that as much of the existing set-up as possible should be preserved. Blake had promised no interference with good customs. Yet the ceded area was to be an integral part of Hong Kong which had a common law legal system in which the role of custom was distinctly limited. How was custom to be given legal force? The answer was by a mix of colonial principle and statute.

Chinese Custom and Customary Right

Whilst the process of ascertaining titles was under way, several attempts were made to underpin the land settlement by legislation. The Land Court (New Territories) Ordinance 1900 was the first to declare all land in the extension to be the property of the Crown, consequent upon the Order in Council and preliminary to the issuing of Crown leases. The ordinance also provided for District Officers, District Land Registries and registration of deeds. It recognized that land could be held in the name of an institution of family or clan lineage.[2]

1. Hayes, *The Hong Kong Region*, pp xix and 55; Sayer, *Years of Discretion*, p 110.
2. After a protest by a member of the Legislative Council at the way in which the Land Court Ordinance had been passed, it was replaced in essentially the same terms by the New Territories Land Court Ordinance, 1900. All together, there were three Land Court ordinances.

As the Land Court approached the conclusion of its work, a new piece of legislation, the New Territories Land Ordinance 1905, was passed. This applied to all land in the extension, although the Governor was given power to exempt land from its provisions. The ordinance established a special, simplified land regime in the territory. It provided for the registration of instruments affecting land there, using simple forms for the recording of sales, mortgages, and leases and gave the Land Officer (District Officers) power to decide all land disputes, except those involving the most valuable property, summarily.[3] Decision-making was to be informal, with no right of audience for legal practitioners. The judgment of the Land Officer was to be conclusive, subject to an appeal to a Supreme Court judge if the value of the subject matter was certified by the officer to exceed HK$2,000 or if the judge gave permission.

The 1905 ordinance gave the Land Officer power to recognize and enforce any Chinese custom or customary right in relation to land. So the father-and-mother official was able to decide land cases in accordance with the traditions of the people, not the imported common law of England. This jurisdiction was repeated (with some changes to the monetary limits) in subsequent legislation and lasted until 1961 when by amendment to the New Territories Ordinance the Land Officer's adjudicative powers were transferred to the courts. The Supreme Court always had jurisdiction over more valuable land and likewise had power to recognize and enforce any Chinese custom and customary right.

Despite its recognition of Chinese custom, the 1905 ordinance did interfere to some extent with customary rules. It required (in section 13) land held in the name of a clan, family or t'ong to have managers and provided for those managers to be registered, and it conferred upon the managers power to deal with the land as if they were sole owners, subject to the consent of the Land Officer. It also required trustees to be appointed for minors who held land. These provisions were repeated in the New Territories Regulation Ordinance, 1910.[4] They were carried forward into Part II of the New Territories Ordinance and have survived (with changes in section number) through to the present. In practice, most New Territories properties, notably those in New Kowloon, in the new towns and in villa-type developments, are exempted from Part II. Broadly, Part II applies to rural or village land but not to urban or suburban areas.

In consequence of the statutory power devolved upon District Officers and the courts to recognize and enforce Chinese custom and customary right affecting land, the rural New Territories are normally credited as the principal place in the HKSAR in which customary law is still applied. This is not incorrect, but misses certain subtleties in the position.

3. More precisely, all disputes except if the Crown was a party or if the capital or annual value of the land exceeded HK$5,000 or the annual value HK$500.
4. No 34 of 1910. The provisions are currently in s 15 of the New Territories Ordinance (Cap 97).

What was to be recognized and enforced was 'Chinese custom and customary right' affecting land, rather than Chinese law and custom or Chinese customary law. Accordingly, the custom which might be enforced need not have achieved the status of law. It could instead be a long-followed practice or a moral right recognized by convention or tradition. Nevertheless, before a practice can qualify as custom, it must be of sufficient antiquity and be generally accepted by those who practice it. It must be something more than a social convention.[5] So, for instance, the widespread habit in the villages of referring to a wife by the first personal name of her husband followed by a suffix ('ma' or 'leung' or 'shum' or 'po') is or was a convention rather than a custom (except in the loose sense).[6]

The term 'customary right' is ambiguous. It may simply refer to moral rights recognized by custom, in which case it adds nothing to 'custom', or it may refer to a custom which has hardened into a law. In the latter sense 'right' is used as synonymous with 'law', which is one of the established meanings of the imprecise word 'right'. This seems to have been the intention of the drafters of the legislation, so that District Officers acting as Land Officers could recognize and enforce customary law as well as mere custom.

Under the New Territories Ordinance custom and customary right was applicable only to land. This was generously defined to include rents and profits derived from land, as well as land covered by water such as the fish ponds found in the flatlands of the north-west, shares and every estate or interest in land and easements affecting land, but it did not extend to money or land exchange entitlements held by a customary body.[7] However, the statutory power to enforce custom and customary right in relation to land was in addition to Chinese law and custom which already had some limited application to the whole of Hong Kong in 1905.

Chinese Law and Custom

Customary law is one of the sources of law in Hong Kong. This was the case before Hong Kong became British, remained so throughout the years of British sovereignty (154 years on Hong Kong Island, 137 years in southern Kowloon and 99 years in the New Territories) and, by virtue of Articles 8 and 18 of the Basic Law, has remained so ever since. The preservation of customary law during the colonial period is owed to the principle applied in British colonies that, unless it is repugnant to fundamental tenets of English law, the law which existed at the founding of the colony (the so-called pre-cessional law) continues to apply, until replaced by any new law.[8] In

5. *Lui Yuk Ping v Chow To* [1962] 3 HKLR 515, 533 (Macfee J).
6. As in 'Fuk Ma', used in Santin according to evidence in *Man Leung v Man Yuet Kwai* [2013] 2 HKLRD 1122 (Godfrey Lam J).
7. *Tang Che Tai v Tang On Kwai* [2008] 3 HKC 521; *Lok Tin Choi v Lai Kwai Lin* [2015] 2 HKLRD 448, [2015] 3 HKC 283; *Kan Fat-tat v Kan Yin-tat* [1987] 4 HKLR 516.
8. *Ho Tsz Tsun v Ho Au Shi* (1915) 10 HKLR 69, [1911–1925] HKC 185; *Re Tse Lai Chiu, dec'd* [1969] HKLR 159, [1946–1972] HKC 160; *Tang Che Tai v Tang On Kwai* [2008] 3 HKC 521.

many colonies the pre-existing law was known as native law and custom. In the case of Hong Kong, the pre-existing law was called 'Chinese law and custom' or less frequently 'Chinese laws and usages' (the phrase favoured in probate matters). These labels are somewhat misleading in that they suggest that there were two types of pre-cessional law: the law of imperial China laid down by the central authorities and the customs or usages of the local population. The labels in fact employ two words to indicate a single concept (hendiadys). Consequently, the phrases 'Chinese law and custom' and 'Chinese laws and usages' are usually treated as singular, not plural.[9]

This is appropriate because although in nineteenth-century China there were imperial codes and regulations which were separate from local custom, those statutes were intertwined with custom. Their content usually reflected custom, assumed the existence of custom, and was interpreted in accordance with custom. Customs and usages which had prevailed for centuries were part of Ching law. Custom for its part governed daily life and filled the interstices of the statutory law. The Great Ching Code (Da Ch'ing Lu Li) was essentially a statute of punishments for transgressions of custom. For the most part the code did not explicitly enact rules, it stated punishments for failure to follow rules, those rules being implicit and customary. An example is article 78(3) implicitly forbidding adoption of a son from outside the clan which states that: 'If someone adopts a son of a different surname, thereby causing confusion in the clan, he will receive 60 strokes of the heavy bamboo'. In similar style article 87 decrees family cohesion by stipulating: 'During the lifetime of grandparents or parents the sons or grandsons are not allowed to set up separate establishments . . . nor divide the family property, under a penalty of one hundred blows.' It would be a misconception to regard statute as one thing and custom as quite another. Customary rules and practices were ancient and widespread throughout the Chinese Empire.[10]

The Ching code consisted of principal rules or Lu (sometimes called statutes) and subsidiary rules or Li (sub-statutes). The Lu were often of great antiquity, being passed from dynasty to dynasty and tended to state the proper principle, often based on Confucian ideals. The Li were more numerous and more recent. They usually embodied the actual practice and supplemented, qualified and even contradicted the principle; in other words, they reflected the popular custom. Accordingly and contrary to what might be expected, the sub-statutes were newer law and were therefore more important.[11] Confusion about Chinese traditional law has been sown in Western minds by the fact that the sub-statutes were so numerous that often they were not translated into English. Then there might appear to be a conflict between

9. Peter Wesley-Smith, 'Chinese Law and Custom as a Source of Law', Ch 12 in *The Sources of Hong Kong Law* (Hong Kong: Hong Kong University Press, 1994), p 205 ('Chinese Law and Custom').

10. Mills-Owens J in *Re Tse Lai Chiu, dec'd*, above, 175; Jamieson, *Chinese Family and Commercial Law*, p 4; Carol Tan, 'Chinese Wills under the Laws of Hong Kong' [1999] 29 HKLJ 93, 109.

11. Jamieson, *Chinese Family and Commercial Law*, p 9; *Liu Ying Lan v Liu Tung Yiu* [2003] 3 HKLRD 249, 266. In addition, there were edicts, circulars and judicial precedents.

the law and the custom. Occasionally there really was such a conflict (landholding and mortgages providing examples) and a Hong Kong court would be presented with a choice of which to apply, perhaps without knowing it.[12]

Another way of looking at the imperial system is to regard it as a combination of law and Confucianism. The latter was the favoured political philosophy of the Han dynasty which began in the second century BC. Dr Hugh Baker suggests that 'from the Han to the 20th century there was a kind of mix of Confucianism and Legalism in place'.[13] The Confucian aspects were customary.

This relationship between imperial law and custom explains the seemingly perplexing declarations by Hong Kong judges that the customary law applicable in the New Territories is the law of the Ching dynasty as modified by local custom.[14] The Ching law, though statutory, reflected custom so could itself be described as a kind of written national customary law. By and large it also accommodated local variations. There was, however, one important aspect of the law in Guangdong Province and other parts of China in which the imperial law did not accommodate local custom but was flatly contradicted by it. This was in respect of landholding. As explained in Chapter 6, the official ownership rules were circumvented and ignored by land owners and users. A pragmatic, parallel system grew up that was followed so widely and for so many generations that it became established and dignified with the description 'customary landholding' or 'customary title'. This shows the vigour of custom, although it also owed something to the weak position of the imperial magistrate in enforcing the statutory law. Inconsistency between the customary and the official rules, and the question of which should prevail, is generally not reflected in the judicial approach to Chinese law and custom. Fortunately, there is no need to do so because in the case of land in the New Territories what is (by statute) to be applied is Chinese custom and customary right rather than Chinese law.[15]

At the time of the British takeover of the New Territories, custom ruled there not only with regard to land. It was woven into the fabric of life. It reflected Confucian principles and everyday realities, so was more readily followed than a statute might be. Attempts to overcome customary practices by legislation were accordingly rare and might become frustrated by the population's adherence to those practices. An example is the reform of customary mortgages (*dian*) which foundered in the face of the arrangements to which the population was accustomed.[16]

Therefore in 1898 the pre-existing law in the New Territories was a combination of imperial statute and national and local custom. Yet following the takeover,

12. Henry McAleavey, 'Chinese Law in Hong Kong: The Choice of Sources' in J. N. D. Anderson (ed), *Changing Law in Developing Countries* (London: George Allen and Unwin Ltd, 1963), p 258.
13. Hugh D. R. Baker, 'Customary Law and the New Territories', Paper No 7, Hong Kong Culture & Society Programme Occasional Paper Series (Hong Kong: Centre of Asian Studies, The University of Hong Kong, 2009), p 3: based upon an oral presentation at the Centre of Asian Studies.
14. *Chu Tak Hing v Chu Chan Cheung Kiu* [1968] HKLR 542; *Wong Kam Ying v Man Chi Tai* [1967] HKLR 201, 211 (Huggins J); *Lai Hay On v Commissioner of Rating and Valuation* [2010] 3 HKLRD 286.
15. New Territories Ordinance (Cap 97) s 13; see further below.
16. McAleavy, 'Chinese Law in Hong Kong', p 261.

the laws of Hong Kong were almost immediately extended to the territory. Those laws primarily comprised local ordinances and English common law, the latter being applicable by virtue of a succession of Supreme Court Ordinances.[17] They would have over-ridden custom had their application not been subject to a qualification that the relevant English law must not be inapplicable to the circumstances of the colony or its inhabitants. It was under this rather opaque exception that judges were able to apply Chinese law and custom where they deemed it appropriate. One such circumstance was where a dispute concerned land in the New Territories. By this route therefore customary law continued to apply immediately after 1898. That application was reinforced in 1905 when the first of the statutes regulating the New Territories was enacted enabling District Officers as Land Officers to recognize and enforce any Chinese custom or customary right affecting land.[18]

It has been suggested that there is no difference between Chinese custom and customary right and Chinese customary law, but this is not so. The statutory power is wider in that it included but was not confined to custom or right falling short of law. It was therefore open to a District Officer to take into account customary practices in reaching judgments or exercising administrative discretion. The wide wording of the power meant that officers did not need to distinguish between customary law and mere custom. This is as well, for the border between the two is elusive. Both require a usage or habit that is longstanding and which is accepted, approved and followed by the population that practices it. A leading scholar of customary law has written: 'The binding force of custom ultimately rests on the fact that it is habitually obeyed by those subject to it: if not fortified by established usage, it is not law'.[19] However, law has connotations of order, regularity and certainty that go beyond habit and usage. So, before it can amount to law, the practice must be identifiable with reasonable certainty and be of sufficient antiquity, although this is undefined. The custom must also have been regularly enforced; this requires the existence of some enforcement body, individual or mechanism. It may also be that the evidence of the existence, content and length of the practice of the custom must be supported by documents before it can be called law.[20]

The requirements to be satisfied before an English court would recognize a custom as having the force of law do not apply to Chinese customary law. So the length of the practice need not date back to 'time immemorial'.[21] But for a practice to amount to a custom, it must have been followed for a very long time, for that is inherent in the notion of custom and even more in the notion of custom amounting

17. Supreme Court Ordinance, No 15 of 1844, No 2 of 1846 and No 12 of 1873: see *Chinese Law and Custom in Hong Kong*, report of committee chaired by George Strickland, Solicitor-General (Hong Kong: Government Printer, 1953), p 4 (Strickland Report).
18. Wesley-Smith, *Chinese Law and Custom*, p 209.
19. Antony Allott, *Essays in African Law, with Special Reference to the Law of Ghana* (London: Butterworths, 1960), p 89.
20. Wesley-Smith, *Chinese Law and Custom*, p 210.
21. *Tang Choy Hong v Tang Shing Mo* (1949) 33 HKLR 58, 65; *Tang Ho-foon v Leung Sek* [1953–1955] DCLR 152, 156. Time immemorial in English law is taken to be prior to be the start of the reign of King Richard I in 1189.

to law. Likewise the English requirement that a custom must be reasonable does not apply, although a weak version of this remains in the rule that Chinese custom must not be so extreme as to violate fundamental principles.

The requirement that the practice be identifiable with certainty is not necessarily inherent in the notion of custom but it is inherent in the idea of law. One of the components of the rule of law is that law should be certain. If a law, or in the present context an alleged custom, is drawn too widely or vaguely, there is a risk that it will affect people or property which it was never intended to do or will otherwise result in injustice. In one New Territories case, a claimed custom regarding the distribution of property was found to be too uncertain for the court to accept.[22]

The virtues of customary law are that it is flexible and local. In consequence it can adapt to changing circumstances, particularly social circumstances, in a particular district. Its vices are that it is imprecise and often unwritten, which means that there can be uncertainty as to its content, scope and application. There is a further vice, the danger that customs, being ancient, will be primitive and uncivilized. That is why to qualify as law a custom must not be contrary to fundamental principles.[23] So a custom which amounted to, or to condonation of, slavery or of torture would not be recognized. Originally this restriction was framed in terms of violation of tenets of English law or of common law. Nowadays it is probably better put as being contrary to the rule of law or of human rights.

Did the customs observed in 1898 in the area that became the New Territories have the quality of law about them? They had a strong moral element. They dealt with everyday problems: matters of the family, the village, the lineage, the farm, the market. They had been habitually followed and for a long time. But that is not enough. To constitute law, there must be means of enforcement. Dr James Hayes has said:

> Application of customary law rested upon public opinion. The consensus view was a powerful force. People were usually acquainted with one another and everyone was presumed to know the rules. Deviation from accepted practice was soon known and usually condemned. Social and economic sanctions of different degree were applied to offenders, including the ultimate deterrent of expulsion from the lineage or village, even execution.[24]

Disputes between lineage members were no doubt arbitrated by senior members. Disputes between families within a village or collection of villages were settled with the help of mediators—mutual friends, headmen and so on. Lineages administered their own rules. Some of those rules were written down, with punishments prescribed. Villages had their own defence force which, although principally

22. *Kan Fat-tat v Kan Yin-tat* [1987] 4 HKLR 516, 541.
23. Strickland Report, p 4. The traditional treatment of 'mui tsai' would probably have offended this principle.
24. James W. Hayes, 'Colonial Administration in British Hong Kong and Chinese Customary Law', lecture available online at https://archive.org.

concerned with fighting other villages and repulsing marauders, helped to keep order. Resort to the magistrate was a formidable step and almost unheard of.[25]

On Dr Hayes' account there was enforcement, if only social condemnation and ostracization for minor violations. But social pressure is not enough to make a custom a law. Who meted out the more serious punishments? According to Dr Hayes:

> They were administered by the elders and the local gentry, with public consent and official support, and carried much weight within what was virtually a closed society. Behind the elders stood the more powerful figure of the county magistrate, to whom serious offenders could be referred, or in some cases even conveyed bodily.[26]

So the local elite performed the task of police and judges. As a privileged class themselves subject to the customs they sought to impose, this is far from ideal. The magistrate's back-up, no matter how remote and infrequent, is important in the promotion of custom to law, indicating as it does official support for the system and involvement of an outside authority.

In considering the role of custom in everyday life during the late Ching period, one should beware of an inclination by Western admirers of the Chinese social set-up to overlook its flaws and talk up its virtues. There is a possibility that in economic matters at least there may have been one law for the peasants and another for the gentry, that is to say the senior members of the powerful clans enjoying close relations with the Assistant Magistrate. For instance, customary restrictions upon alienation of land seem to have been more loosely applied to wealthy landowners. One might protest that there is always one law for the rich and another for the poor regardless of the nature of the system, but law consisting of unwritten alleged custom is particularly prone to subversion by the realities of power and human relationships.

Scope of Application of Custom

Since Chinese law and custom is part of Hong Kong law, it might be expected that the subjects of its application are potentially limitless. Indeed, one judge observed that the judicial power in the New Territories Ordinance to apply custom and customary right in relation to land should be regarded as a duty: the court must apply it.[27] Despite this interpretation, the wording ('have power to recognize and enforce any Chinese custom or customary right') is plainly permissive and discretionary. Judges have generally been astute to confine custom to its proper sphere and not

25. Baker, 'Customary Law and The New Territories', p 10.
26. Hayes, 'Colonial Administration in British Hong Kong and Chinese Customary Law'.
27. Mills-Owens J in *Tang Kai-chung v Tang Chik-shang* [1970] HKLR 276, 310.

let it displace common law and statute where this is judged inappropriate or even where it is inconvenient.

That sphere was and is substantive rights in two areas in particular, the law of property and the law regarding personal relations. Thus issues of custom have featured particularly in cases concerning marriage, adoption, and succession (to personal as well as real property) by Chinese persons in Hong Kong, in addition to cases about land in the rural New Territories.[28] Statutory change has reduced the application of custom in family matters. Section 5 of the Wills Ordinance 1970 abolished section 3 of a previous Wills Ordinance whereby any will of a Chinese testator was to be taken to be lawfully made if made according to Chinese laws or usages.[29] The impact of this was limited because traditional Chinese people were content that customary inheritance rules should apply and rarely made wills directing how their property should be distributed.[30] To greater effect were the Marriage Reform Ordinance 1971 which abolished concubinage and Chinese Modern Marriages (those celebrated simply at an open ceremony in front of witnesses). In 1973, Chinese-style adoptions were made illegal by the Adoption Ordinance.

These changes in family law did not affect previously acquired status so those who had already married or been adopted according to custom remained married or adopted. Consequently, customary law continued to apply to some extent in those areas. Transitional provisions in the new ordinances ensured continuing application of the old law. In addition, the outcome of modern disputes about entitlement to property might turn upon questions concerning past customary marriages, adoptions and successions. Issues of customary law are therefore not confined to land in the rural New Territories. Every year, about five or six cases involving Chinese customary law are considered by the courts at various levels.[31]

Until 1961 customary law was not the preserve of the courts alone. District Officers also had power to apply and enforce custom and customary right in relation to land. This they did as special magistrates determining minor civil disputes. It seems likely that they had resort to customary rules more frequently than the courts do now. On one District Officer's account, the discretion was exercised by allowing the parties to choose whether they wished the magistrate to try their case according to custom or according to common law.[32] This was a dubious procedure, first because the discretion was that of the District Officer not the parties, and second because the statutory intention in giving the officer this power was not to exclude the general law (common law and statute) but to supplement it where appropriate

28. Technically, land which is not exempted from the application of Part II of the New Territories Ordinance (Cap 97). On the limitation to Chinese, see the Strickland Report and Daffyd M. E. Evans, 'Common law in a Chinese setting: The Kernel or The Nut?' (1971) 1 HKLJ 9, 26.
29. Tan, 'Chinese Wills under the Laws of Hong Kong"', pp 107, 119–121.
30. Baker, *Customary Law and The New Territories*, p 16.
31. Lutz-Christian Wolff, 'What is a Conflict of Laws?' [2016] 46 HKLJ 849, 864.
32. Coates, *Myself a Mandarin*, pp 123–129.

with customary rules. But it is likely that the six decades of informal adjudication by District Officers was the heyday of customary law in Hong Kong.

Once professional judges took sole jurisdiction, a sterner attitude prevailed. Shortly before that, the Chief Justice declared that Chinese law and custom prevails only if the corresponding English law is inapplicable in that it cannot be applied without injustice or oppression and if it is not shown to be excluded by legislation.[33] This however is going too far, for it ignores the positive power to apply Chinese customary right given by section 13 of the New Territories Ordinance. High Court and District judges have not allowed custom to intrude upon court procedure and practice, so matters of evidence and limitation of actions are not governed by customary law.[34] Nor, for the most part, have they allowed custom to displace statute. So where certain formalities are laid down by statute, the fact that those formalities are not required by custom does not absolve parties from following them. An illustration is the formalities necessary upon a sale and purchase of land. Statute dating back to 1677 in England and adopted in British colonies including Hong Kong requires, as a safeguard against false allegations of an informal transfer of land, that to be enforceable a contract for the sale or other disposal of land be in writing and signed by the party against whom enforcement is sought.[35] Yet the practice in customary sales of land was that the purchaser would not sign the agreement, only the middlemen and witnesses (and sometimes the vendor) would.[36] Nevertheless, the Hong Kong courts insisted upon observance of the statute so that if the purchaser refused to proceed and the vendor sought enforcement of an oral or unsigned paper sale agreement and the purchaser resisted, the courts would not force the agreement upon him even though custom recognized the agreement as valid.

The reason for this is that statutory provisions take precedence over custom, unless the provisions themselves permit the custom to be followed. This is of course a considerable curb upon the scope of customary rules. Where punishment for breach of a customary requirement is physical chastisement, application of that punishment may well involve a breach of the Hong Kong criminal law of assault or worse. The Ching Code is full of such punishments. They were supplemented by local practices. The customary punishment for adultery in parts of China, including what became the New Territories, was drowning. Dr Baker recalls an incident from 1961 in which a couple were saved from life-threatening village sanction only by the timely intervention of the Hong Kong Police.[37] Less dramatically and away from the criminal sphere, the law of land registration, being statute-based, applies

33. Hogan CJ in *Wong Yu Shi (No 1) v Wong King Kuen* [1957] 2 HKLR 420, 443.
34. *Leung Kuen Fai v Tang Kwong Yu T'ong* [2002] 2 HKLRD 705; cf *Tsang Wing Lung v Tsang Lun* [1993] 2 HKLR 23, [1992] 2 HKC 440 and *To Kan Chi v Pui Man Yau*, HCMP 562/1992 (26 November 1998).
35. Since 1984 by s 3 of the Conveyancing and Property Ordinance (Cap 219); before that by the Law Amendment and Reform (Consolidation) Ordinance (Cap 23).
36. Jamieson, *Chinese Family and Commercial Law*, p 96.
37. Baker, *Customary Law and The New Territories*, p 10.

to rural land even though custom (as opposed to imperial statute) did not provide for registration of documents affecting land.

More recently, the customary practice of restricting rights of inheritance of property to males has been abolished by statute. The legislative act was not however a measure explicitly contradicting the practice but rather the removal from the New Territories Ordinance of provisions which in effect prevented rural land from being the subject of a will. In consequence of the amendment, a landowner may therefore devise land to his wife and daughters or others, as well as his sons, on his demise. Long before that reform, the courts had held that customary law was not to be applied to questions of testamentary capacity or interpretation of a will.[38] In all these areas customary law has been unable to survive contact with the common law and statute. The one exception is in respect of partition of land and even that exception is dubious.

A less obvious but just as potent restraint upon the impact of custom is administrative. One view is that the very existence of a new, efficient, accessible, decisive, and better-staffed government meant that the population looked to the authorities more readily for help and led to custom becoming more defined and less flexible: ironically, the imposition of Western administration produced stricter adherence to custom than existed before.[39] But this may be exaggerated. The memoirs of one District Officer suggest that he at least much preferred applying customary law because of its very flexibility: the 'custom of the country' was the application of sensible and practical solutions rather than hard rules.[40]

Government policy and executive act have both reduced custom's sphere of influence. Once the new administrators had decided to issue Crown leases to owners of land and had determined that there could be only one such owner, the traditional division of title between imperial grantee and permitted long-term occupier of the land could not persist. The customary interests of the former were therefore abolished (or possibly postponed: see the chapter on Article 40) by the new government's decision not to grant them a lease of their land and not to register their imperial deeds. Conversely, in those few cases in which the new governors granted a long lease to the imperial grantee, the customary interests of occupiers were overridden by the administrative act of ignoring the latter's interests.

The block Crown leases that were issued in 1905 and 1907 cemented the administrative interference in the customary rights of landowners, extending the effect of that interference until June 1997. The length of those leases meant that the potentially perpetual customary interests of land holders were replaced by interests which expired after seventy-five years with a possible extension for another twenty-four

38. *Re Tse Lai Chu dec'd* [1969] HKLR 202.
39. Peter Wesley-Smith, 'Some Legal Problems Relating to Land in the New Territories' in Alan Birch (ed), *The New Territories and Its Future* (Hong Kong: Royal Asiatic Society, 1982), quoting Nelson.
40. Austin Coates, *Myself a Mandarin*, passim. One must bear in mind, however, that this book was written as much for entertainment effect as factual accuracy.

years less three days. The content of those leases further circumscribed customary rights by imposing restrictions upon the use of the land. The principal restriction was the condition against building upon the land without government permission. Apparently, Ching law did not impose such a restriction. Whether local custom also did not do so, is not so clear.[41] But if there were no customary restrictions, that changed on issue of the Crown leases.

After 1907 administrators in the New Territories made successive attempts to employ the leases' requirement of government permission to build as a means of extracting additional revenue from landowners by charging a premium for the giving of permission. If, as seems to have been the case, under imperial rule no such payment was required by the authorities, this too was administrative interference in customary rights. But if prior to 1899 other informal yet customary payments to the authorities or other parties had been expected of landowners, these in turn would have been abolished by the new land settlement.

Part of that settlement was legislation for the registration of deeds affecting land, that registration providing evidence of ownership of and encumbrances upon the land. Supposedly this replaced the legal requirement that deeds and ownership be recorded at the imperial magistracy so was only a modest change from the previous system. However, as explained in the next chapter, the previous system was more honoured in the breach than the observance. In practice, owners rarely registered changes in ownership because of the cost and difficulty of so doing and the magistrate lacked the resources to enforce the law against them. Since the new system of registration of deeds was run by a relatively efficient and accessible registry supported by a speedy method of resolving disputes (by the Land Officer), the opportunity for the evolution of informal methods of dealing in land was circumscribed, thereby constituting another administrative constraint upon custom.

Legislation also played a role in the land settlement. Successive ordinances provided for regulation of customary land matters. By and large their provisions built upon the customary establishment. Traditional communal institutions (t'so t'ong) were allowed to continue but rules were introduced requiring that the institutions have managers, that those managers be approved and registered by the District Office, that the managers be empowered to deal with the institution's land and that transactions in that land be pre-approved and recorded by the office. At that time no attempt was made to interfere with the internal workings of the institutions. Judges have, however, subsequently provided that interference by superimposing a creation of Western jurisprudence, the trust, upon t'so t'ong.[42] Thus we find a further source of incursion upon customary norms, the judicial, to lay alongside the societal, the legislative and the administrative.

The best-known example of administrative interference with customary rights is the Small House Policy. The details of this policy and its evolution are explored in

41. This is examined in the chapters on small houses and Article 40 of the Basic Law.
42. See Chapters 8 and 9.

later chapters but the general effect of the policy was to channel and control a pre-existing practice regarding the building of houses upon village land. That control has been so effective that the custom has been overwhelmed by the administrative rules contained in the policy. As a result, it has become nearly impossible to distinguish between the custom and the policy and there is general confusion of the one with the other. There must be serious doubt as to whether the custom now has any separate existence.

When introduced in 1972 the policy was in fact merely the latest attempt by the Hong Kong government to regulate the construction of domestic houses in rural areas. There had been previous attempts, notably in the 1920s and the 1950s, using a combination of governmental powers under the block leases, internal District Office rules and executive diktat. They were not as far-reaching as the 1972 attempt, nor were they as successful because, unlike the Small House Policy initially, they ran into opposition from the rural community. Nevertheless, those attempts themselves constituted administrative interference in the small house custom.

There is a further source of interference in customary rights which is difficult to define but may best be described as systemic or institutional. The interference stems from the absorption or conversion of part of the jurisdictional area originally governed by custom (namely imperial China) into a new jurisdiction (namely Hong Kong) with established processes of adjudication and law enforcement. These processes involve not only frameworks and practices alien to custom but also ways of thinking foreign to it.[43] So, for instance, the rules about admissibility of evidence in court may lead to relevant and accurate testimony concerning the content of custom not being heard. Likewise, the concept of judicial precedent, with its requirement that a current decision be consistent with previous decisions on similar facts, tends to harden rules which, left to custom, might be flexible and susceptible to inconsistency. Professor Dafydd Evans, a specialist in probate and succession, reflected on this in his inaugural lecture from the Chair of Law at the University of Hong Kong. 'So,' he said,

> the courts began to apply customary law as part of the law binding on the courts and the parties, binding in a way in which customary law had never been conceived to be. In so doing the judges changed the nature of customary law for all time: they made it susceptible . . . to the modus operandi of the common law.[44]

This phenomenon might also lead to perpetuation of inaccuracies about the custom. By admitting the evidence of experts on customary law, the courts have exposed themselves to a corps of specialists whose views tend to reflect those of each other so as to create a collective consensus as to what the custom is or was. Were the first judicial decision upon a particular aspect of custom to be based on incomplete information about or false interpretation of the custom, that decision,

43. Wesley-Smith, *Chinese Law and Custom*, p 223.
44. Evans, 'Common Law in a Chinese Setting', 27.

although inaccurate, might well influence the decisions of subsequent judges, or the views of later experts, on the same or similar aspects. Dr Peter Wesley-Smith has remarked upon the tendency for materials concerning custom to feed upon themselves, with one expert's view being quoted in a judgment and that judgment being cited by an expert in another case.[45]

A small but clear example of this phenomenon is provided by judicial decisions concerning a Chinese temple. In China most temples and associated structures were regarded as the collective property of the institution (usually a monastery or nunnery) by which they were operated. Land on which such religious organizations stood was registered in the name of the organization even though the organization had no separate existence from that of the individuals who ran it.[46] In litigation at the beginning of the twenty-first century about ownership of a large public temple near Tuen Mun, the undisputed expert evidence was to the effect that the land belonged to the whole clergy of the faith of the temple. Yet the trial judge misinterpreted or misunderstood this and in his judgment recorded that the temple lands belonged to 'all the people of that faith'. This inaccuracy was repeated by both the Court of Appeal and the Court of Final Appeal.[47]

Early District Officers in the New Territories, charged with honouring Chinese custom and customary right, were not lawyers so might have escaped these traps, but they were well-educated and saw the merit of consistency in decision making. Accordingly, they built up a list of points about custom that they had come across to inform each other and pass on to their successors. The list, known as the bible, sadly was lost in the Second World War so it is not possible to check its verisimilitude. There is a risk, however, that, well-meaning though it was, it contained infelicities. Certainly, the list assumed the wrong date as at which to ascertain the custom.[48] By assuming the relevant custom was that which existed at the time of the creation of the New Territories, the District Officers' endeavour perpetrated a misconception, namely that custom is never-changing, in effect frozen at about the date upon which Chinese imperial jurisdiction over the New Territories ceased.

An illustration of the dangers of institutional reliance upon experts is the evolution of understanding of the custom regarding alienation of lineage (t'so t'ong) land. In litigation during the 1960s concerning the sale of lineage land upon which part of the Lai Chi Kok Amusement Park stood, the courts enforced a contract by the t'so managers to sell the land to a company. This was despite the evidence of a village elder that by custom such land was inalienable. The Chief Justice recorded but did not act upon that evidence, perhaps because it did not come from an acknowledged

45. Wesley-Smith, *Chinese Law and Custom*, p 216.
46. Anthony R. Dicks, 'The Ownership of Buddhist Temples and the Civil Status of the Clergy in China' in Clara Bulfoni (ed), *Religious Traditions and Social Transformation in Contemporary Asia* (Rome: Biblioteca Ambrosiana, Bulzoni Editore, 2012), pp 25–26.
47. *To Kan Chi v Pui Man Yau*, HCMP 562/1992 (26 November 1998) para 61; [2000] 3 HKLRD 756, 762 (CFA).
48. 20 April 1899 instead of 1 July 1898 (the date of the Second Convention of Peking): Wesley-Smith, *Chinese Law and Custom*, p 222. Another list has been compiled by a post-war District Officer, Brian Wilson.

expert, although it is difficult to see who could have been more authoritative about local (as opposed to national Chinese) custom.[49] Yet in 1970 another judge accepted the assertion of an experienced District Officer (called as an expert) that t'so t'ong land was inalienable.[50] The District Officer's information however was out of date. Expert evidence from Chinese law scholars in more recent decisions has elucidated the position so that the present understanding is that the inalienability of customary land is an ideal rather than a practice and the land may be sold if it is not ancestral in nature (i.e. income from it is not devoted to ancestor worship) and if all current members—or perhaps the majority of members—agree and that, even if it is ancestral, the land may be sold if circumstances are compelling and all members agree. This is further explored in Chapter 7.

The institutional effect of the common law system is not confined to the consequences of procedural practice. Lawyers trained in that system share not just a way of thinking but a core of learning which they habitually employ to analyse legal problems. One of those core areas is the law of trusts. When faced with a problem concerning traditional Chinese institutions which bear superficial similarities to a Western trust, it is only natural for lawyers to reach for the familiar body of law concerning trusts. So, dealing with the case of a Chinese landowner who put his land into a traditional institution (a t'so) and then changed his mind and attempted to say that the land remained his, the judge looked for guidance not to customary law but to the law of trusts and found there the principle that someone who settles (founds) a trust may not revoke the trust once the settlement is complete.[51] Similarly a judge who saw a ready answer in the law of trusts to a problem concerning a Chinese customary institution (a t'so) was content to equate aspects of the institution with some, but not all, of those of a Western trust and thereby impose upon those institutions the rules of an alien legal culture. In order to reach that equation the judge had to ignore certain powerful objections (such as that that the founder of the t'so could not have intended a trust since it was unknown to the Chinese), overlook certain contrary indications in the New Territories Ordinance and misinterpret a Crown Lease. One of the contrary indications was the very provision of the ordinance empowering the court to apply Chinese custom and customary right. Yet the judge did not ignore this entirely: on the contrary, he interpreted it (dubiously) as requiring the court to apply custom but then inconsistently added the trust on top of the customary rules. The lure of a familiar body of law seems to have been compelling. Subsequently numerous other Hong Kong judges have been unable to resist the lure too, with the result that Chinese customary land institutions have become known as Chinese customary trusts of land, something of an achievement given that the trust did not exist in Ching China.[52]

49. *Lai Chi Kok Amusement Park Co Ltd (No 1) v Tsang Tin-sun* [1965] HKLR 413.
50. *Tang Kai-chung v Tang Chik-shang* [1970] HKLR 276.
51. *Chu Tak Hing v Chu Chan Cheung Kiu* [1968] HKLR 542.
52. This subject is treated at greater length in Ch 9.

Custom of What and Where?

The power of the courts (formerly also the District Officers) is to apply Chinese custom and customary right to land in the New Territories. In theory the custom to be applied is that of the Chinese empire but custom was far from a unitary body throughout that empire. It differed from place to place, indeed the essence of custom was that it was local. So the question arises, the custom of which place or institution was to be applied in Hong Kong?

The expression 'Chinese law and custom' suggests that the custom to be applied was that of the whole of China, the jurisdiction in which the New Territories was located before its absorption into Hong Kong. At that time and for long after, the culture of the territory was overwhelmingly Chinese. After creation of the New Territories, the population remained adjacent to China and for fifty years people passed freely between the jurisdictions. The approach adopted by Hong Kong judges, that the relevant customary law is that of the Ching dynasty as modified by local custom, suggests that national as well as local rules are pertinent.

Nevertheless, it has been suggested that the relevant custom for Hong Kong is that of Guangdong Province, the vast Cantonese-speaking southern region out of which Hong Kong was carved and from which the ancestors of most of its population originated.[53] This rather assumes that the area of a people's historical identity equates with the area of the origin of their customs. The assumption may be correct in respect of some customs but is unlikely to be correct in respect of all of them. We know that customary landholding evolved in an area wider than Guangdong, extending throughout southern China and even beyond. The most prolific historian of the New Territories in the English language, Dr Hayes, maintains that customary practices were more confined in geographical scope, varying from district to district, from sub-district (heung) to sub-district, and even from village to village.

In one case the custom contended for was that of the district (Ping Shan) or the clan that dominated it: at the time they may have been one and the same.[54] In another, it was that of a particular village.[55] Cases concerning the custom of a t'ong and a t'so have also arisen.[56] The position seems to be that, provided that land in the New Territories is the subject of the dispute, custom may be relied upon and the reach of that custom may be as broad or as narrow as occasion demands.

53. E. S. Haydon, 'The Choice of Chinese Customary Law in Hong Kong' (1962) 11 *International and Comparative Law Quarterly* 231, 247.
54. *Tang Choy Hung v Tang Shing Mo* (1949) 33 HKLR 58, 65.
55. *Chan Pui v Chan Yan Kit* (1950) 34 HKLR 297, 300–306 (notice to tenant to quit).
56. *Lai Chi Kok Amusement Park Co Ltd (No 1) v Tsang Tin-sun* [1965] HKLR 413, 423 (appointment of managers); *Tang Kai-chung v Tang Chik-sang* [1970] HKLR 276, 298 (partition).

Ascertainment of Custom

Although Chinese law and custom had become part of the law of Hong Kong and was familiar to the bulk of the population, it was an importation from another jurisdiction as far as the lawyers and judges of Hong Kong were concerned. At the turn, and throughout much, of the twentieth century the judiciary was staffed by (male) expatriate officers, mainly from the Colonial Legal Service and the Colonial Judicial Service. A few of them might have some knowledge of native law from their experience in other colonies but Chinese custom was not something with which they were familiar. How were they to be informed of its content? The answer was through legal precedent, treatises, studies, reports and argument in the normal way and also through expert evidence of the relevant practices.

Consequently, a small body of experts in Chinese law and custom grew up, mostly university professors and legal practitioners familiar through study and sometimes experience with the laws of China but also current and former government officers who had acquired practical local knowledge of the subject. Somewhat ironically, most of these experts were not Chinese. The limited number of experts is itself a concern. 'The problem is that there are so few if any experts, and probably none who cannot be contradicted by others of similar qualifications' observed Dr Wesley-Smith in 1982.[57] The number of qualified experts has hardly expanded since then.

A further weakness of reliance upon experts is that their expertise is in general Chinese law and custom, not in local custom. Factual evidence of the latter might be given by long-term residents of the district but Hong Kong judges have shown themselves wary of such testimony. There is reason for this since a villager may be partisan, being a relative of or sympathizer with one of the parties, or may be in a position of conflict of interest, may have limited knowledge of the subject matter, may be unable to distinguish law from mere custom and may be imprecise. Professional witnesses are not immune to similar vices. Academic experts easily fall into the temptation to lecture the court rather than to assist it. Non-lawyers tend to stray from their proper role of objectivity, their reports degenerating into argument and tendentiousness and trespassing upon the province of the judge, in effect becoming advocates of their client's cause.

Yet it is difficult to see who else would be able to give evidence of local custom but a longtime resident. Sometimes one feels that the judge rejects local evidence as a short cut to deciding or avoiding a difficult point. So, for instance, in the case of a fung shui tree which potentially raised an issue of choice of law (whether to apply common law or Chinese customary law) the evidence of local custom from villagers was rejected because, according to the trial judge, they were 'not experts on

57. Peter Wesley-Smith, 'Research Materials for Hong Kong Legal Studies', paper for Centre of Asian Studies, University of Hong Kong, September 1982.

customary law' and at the highest they could give evidence of traditional practices.[58] Whether these could be elevated to the status of custom or customary right was a question on which the indigenous male complaining that his family's sacred tree had been cut down had 'failed to file any admissible evidence'. But surely whether a practice is also a custom is not a matter of evidence but of judicial deduction from what the court has been told about the practice, the court's power to enforce custom being found in section 13 of the New Territories Ordinance. Similarly, in other judgments, submissions that a practice or provision is contrary to customary law have been summarily rejected on the grounds that there was 'no evidence' of the alleged custom, as if customary law could be proved only by experts, despite its being part of Hong Kong law.[59] One is left with the impression that common law judges are uncomfortable with customary law and treat it as an alien body which is better avoided unless there is a professed expert to guide them through it.

Since Chinese law and custom is part of Hong Kong law, it is possible to ascertain it in the normal fashion of consulting written authorities such as case reports and law treatises and hearing argument by legal representatives.[60] But it is difficult to do so because of the paucity of relevant prior decided cases and legal writing.[61] Customary law was the law of a previous jurisdiction, akin to foreign law, and its content is in effect a question of fact. The appeal court explained in the late 1960s that as Chinese law was part of the law of the land, the courts could indeed purport to find it in authoritative textbooks and cases but there was a long practice in Hong Kong, endorsed in a number of judicial decisions, of taking expert evidence on such law. This was a departure from normal practice but was a modification based on local circumstances. However, it should not be taken to supplant the court's right to inform itself by other means, the judges added.[62] More recently the Court of Final Appeal has explained that, although Chinese law and custom is applied as local rather than foreign law, the practice has been to receive and act on expert evidence of it. Though 'perhaps anomalous' it is 'pragmatic and well established'.[63] Questions of custom have been decided without experts and, since the existence of a custom is a matter of fact there is no reason that witnesses who have experience of the custom should not be heard, but judges tend to be reassured by the assistance of experts in what for most of them is an unfamiliar area.[64]

58. *Wong Sui Yeung v Chiu Kwong Wing* [2005] 3 HKLRD 495.
59. Eg, *Ng Shiu Hung v Sai Kung District Officer*, HCAL 2683/2000 (26 April 2001) (re suggestion that DO's statutory power to appoint replacement manager is contrary to customary law); *Brisilver Investment Ltd v Wong Fat Tso* [1999] 3 HKC 567 (re partition where applicant is not a t'so t'ong member); *Tang Kam Wah v Tang Ming Yat*, HCA 10141/1998 (26 November 2002) (no evidence of customary role of managers); *Kan Fat-tat v Kan Yin-tat* [1987] HKLR 516 (no evidence of custom re mode of distribution); *Re Man Sham Chung Wui*, HCMP 2417/2007 (21 January 2010) (no evidence that majority consent needed for sale).
60. *Lui Yuk Ping v Chow To* [1962] HKLR 515; see too *Wong Yu Shi (No 1) v Wong Ying Kuen* [1957] HKLR 420, 438.
61. *Ng Ying Ho v Tam Suen Yu* [1963] 4 HKLR 923, 925.
62. *Re Tse Lai Tsu, Dec'd* [1969] HKLR 159, 175–177, 194.
63. *Suen Toi Lee v Yau Yee Ping* (2001) 4 HKCFAR 474.
64. *Wong Kam Ying v Man Chi Tai* [1967] HKLR 201, where in the absence of expert evidence Huggins J relied

More than half a century has passed since the appeal court's explanation of the modification of practice. During that time numerous cases concerning points of customary law have been considered by Hong Kong courts and the evidence and conclusions recorded in written reasons for decision. Those points and cases, even the unreported ones, are readily ascertainable as a result of technological advances. Occasionally judges do rely on evidence of custom recounted in prior judgments.[65] Some of the principles of Chinese custom, for instance the preferential treatment of males, are now so well known that they may be said to have achieved sufficient notoriety for a judge to take judicial notice of them without requiring formal proof.[66] At the same time, the size of the judiciary, like the case law and the legal profession, has increased exponentially so that now the majority of judges speaks and reads Chinese, thus enabling the Chinese statute law to be read in the original. The scope for application of custom has decreased considerably over those years. New issues do arise but usually as a result of a novel external factor such as the need to resume land for infrastructural projects; because of their novelty, custom rarely has any contribution to make to their resolution. Does the need for this procedural modification still exist?

Relevant Date of Custom

Chinese customary law became, or more precisely continued to be, part of the law applicable to the New Territories on their creation in 1898. Does that mean that the customary law of that date (the date of reception into Hong Kong law as applied to the New Territories) is the law applicable today and was applicable throughout the period in between? The definition adopted by judges, that customary law is the law of the Ching dynasty as modified by local custom, would seem to suggest so. Adoption of a definition which referred to any later date would risk incorporating subsequent developments in the law of mainland China into Hong Kong law. Expert evidence given in numerous cases involving Chinese law and custom has assumed that what is applicable is the customs at the time of the cession, in other words the pre-British law.

Yet all custom evolved over time and it does not cease doing so at a certain point. It can change further: like the common law, it adapts to meet new circumstances.[67] The customs applicable in the New Territories were not frozen in 1898. As explained by one judge, the date of reception of the customary law is merely the starting point: one looks to that date to ascertain the applicability of the customary

upon written texts. In *Fan Kam Ching v Yau Shiu Hing* [1986] DCLR 14 the judge complained about the lack of expert evidence.

65. Eg, *Tang Tak Sum v Tang Kai Fong* [2015] 1 HKLRD 286 where the requirements for endowments in perpetuity set out by an expert in *Re Lau Wai Chau* [1998] 1 HKLRD 179 were referred to.
66. *Lai Suk Yi v Hau Tso Hee*, HCA 215/2014 (20 May 2018). See too *Tang Ho-foon v Leung Sek* [1953–1955] DCLR 152, 156.
67. *Yau Tin Sung v Yan Wan Loi* [1984] 2 HKLR 15, 22 (Liu J).

law and the basic rules as they then existed and thereafter one applies those rules subject to any developments that may have taken place since that date.[68] This is 'the living customary law'.

Are the relevant developments confined to those which have occurred in Hong Kong or can developments in Chinese custom elsewhere be taken into account? One judge has suggested that modifications only in Hong Kong are relevant and refused to take into account decisions outside the colony and new interpretations of the Ching code.[69] But this seems unduly narrow for the reality had been that the New Territories was part of a county within the Guangdong province of China. There was a close cultural, social and linguistic connection between the rural populations on either side of the border. For the first fifty years local residents moved freely across the border. Even thereafter peasant farmers crossed it daily. The imperial code which had applied before 1899 continued in China for more than thirty years and continued to be subject to judicial interpretation there. In the event, Hong Kong courts have quite willingly heard evidence of customs and decisions about custom taken on the mainland or in Chinese societies elsewhere.[70]

Whilst the idea of living customary law is attractive, the reality is that the habitat in which it dwells has become progressively smaller during the 120 years since its reception into the law of the New Territories. The opportunities for the practice and application of custom have narrowed, curtailed by incursions from statute, legal and administrative practice and modern attitudes.

One would expect any evolution to be slow and gradual anyway, since this is inherent in the nature of custom. One might also expect the evolution to depend upon the subject-matter of the custom. Where the custom concerns personal relations, for instance, it might adapt with the generations since what is involved is social change. Where the custom concerns land, the evolution might well be slower.

The picture becomes complicated because, although custom might change, the circumstances to which it might apply also change and are prone to do so faster than the custom. Outside influences intrude upon traditional life. The greatest outside influence upon rural life in recent years has been the demand for land to use for purposes undreamed of in the nineteenth century and the accompanying great increase in value of land. For instance, custom had no experience of dealing with the state's compulsory taking of land in exchange for compensation or with the division of those proceeds between those entitled to a share of it. Hence when lands owned by family institutions were resumed, there were no customary rules to apply to the division of the compensation between members. Those entitled were left to sort the dispute out by negotiated compromise.

68. Huggins J in *Wong Kam Ying v Man Chi Tai* [1967] HKLR 201 at 211.
69. *Wong Ying Kuen v Wong Yu Shi* [1946–1972] HKC 478 (Briggs J).
70. *Ho Tsz Tsun v Ho Au Shi* (1915) 10 HKLR 69, [1911–1925] HKC 185 (evidence from President of the High Court in Kwangtung); *Kan Fat-tat v Kan Yin-tat* [1987] 4 HKLR 516; *Tang Che Tai v Tang On Kwai* [2008] 3 HKC 521 (judgments of High Court in Nanking referred to).

Twentieth-Century Evolution?

Since Chinese custom and customary law have continued, albeit in stunted form, since 1898, in what ways might it have changed during that time? One suggestion is that the treatment of women has altered. Another is that certain customary practices in New Kowloon have departed from those in rural areas. A third is that the distribution of resumption compensation between members of customary bodies is acquiring a customary aspect.

These suggestions are reactions to the impact of social forces, which is the way that new practices develop. The education and emancipation of women during the twentieth century and the economic necessity in a modern economy for them to seek work outside the village led to their acquiring a greater role external to the home.

The separate administrative treatment from 1899 of the urbanizing areas immediately to the north of Boundary Street which led to the rapid development of New Kowloon was almost bound to have an impact on the practices of the population dwelling there, including those in the villages. It seems that the Chinese custom of not making a will was soon eroded and that urban Chinese took to the Western practice quite quickly. Not only that, they made provision for wives and daughters in those wills.[71]

Protection of Traditional Rights

Customary law in Hong Kong received a new lease of life upon inauguration of the Basic Law of the HKSAR in 1997. Article 8 of that law states that the laws previously in force in Hong Kong shall be maintained. This specifically includes customary law. Section 13 of the New Territories Ordinance, with its power of the courts to recognize Chinese custom and customary right in relation to land, was of course part of the law previously in force. More intriguingly, by Article 40 of the Basic Law the lawful traditional rights of indigenous inhabitants of the New Territories are to be protected by the HKSAR. No one knows quite what Article 40 means but it seems likely that there is an overlap between traditional rights and customary ones. Article 40 is discussed in Chapter 14. It would be surprising if traditional rights did not refer to, or at least include, customs which existed in imperial China in 1898. The position with regard to the holding, acquisition and transfer of land at that time is outlined in the next two chapters.

71. Stephen Selby, 'Everything You Wanted to Know About Chinese Customary Law (But Were Afraid to Ask)' (1991) 21 HKLJ 45 ('Chinese Customary Law').

6

Customary Landholding: Skin and Bones

Colonial administrators who set about registering the land and its owners in the new acquisition soon discovered that for many pieces of land there were two different claimants to ownership and that both claimants had a plausible case. This was because of the system of ownership which had grown up in parts of China, including Guangdong, during the late imperial era. The practice with regard to land ownership had evolved as a pragmatic answer to practical needs and without regard to official constraints or legal formalities.

There were two striking things about this customary practice. First, it permitted land to have two owners, one official and the other unofficial. Second, it was unauthorized in that it was not approved by the imperial authorities. Indeed, it was in direct defiance of Ching (Qing) law. Here, then, was another example of New Territories people's disdain for the rules.

Imperial Law

Practically all land in China was held in common tenure (or mintian) from the emperor. The imperial code decreed that all land belonged to the emperor who could grant it to his subjects. The grant was by deed which, because it was embossed with a red seal, was known as a red deed. The grantee had to pay tax, the tax being a combination of land and poll tax although it could be regarded as the equivalent of rental for the land. He was also required to register the deed; this required payment of fees.[1] Otherwise, common tenure was not unlike freehold in the common law system. The nature of the tenure and the amount of tax levied did not depend upon whether buildings were erected.[2]

Tax was charged on all cultivated land. Occupation of land without payment of tax was a criminal act. Only the grantee or his servant, agent, or short-term tenant was permitted to farm the land. Only one person could own the land: joint ownership was not allowed. Long-term lettings and assignments (sales) were also not allowed

1. Jamieson, *Chinese Family and Commercial Law*, Chapter V. Apart from payment of tax and registration, a third incident of ownership was provision of certain services involving labour but these had fallen into disuse.
2. *Winfat Enterprises (HK) Co Ltd v Attorney General* [1983] HKLR 211 (Kempster J).

without permission. Any purchaser or long-term tenant was required to acquire a fresh imperial grant, to register this and thereafter pay land tax. Registration meant the opening of a fresh heading for which a 3 per cent transfer fee and various incidentals were charged.[3]

Since much of southern China had been sparsely populated and was in effect a frontier area far from central control, much of the land had not been the subject of an imperial grant and remained the property of the state. The authorities encouraged the cultivation of unoccupied and ungranted land, so-called waste. Title to such land could be acquired by taking possession and cultivating it and then following a certain procedure, applying to the district magistrate for a grant. If no other claimant came forward, a deed would be granted. Tax on such land did not become payable for some years.[4] Although no purchase price would be charged, registration fees and eventually tax would have to be paid. This was a considerable disincentive so in many instances claimants did not apply and simply continued in occupation. If their occupation continued for a long time, the occupiers might come to be regarded as owners of the former waste ground and their landholding as customary.

This was the how the imperial authorities intended the system of common tenure to work. The practice which had evolved in southern China, and in other areas of the country remote from central control, was quite different.[5]

Customary Tenure

By contrast, the customary system permitted land to have more than one owner. That in itself was not unfamiliar to members of the Land Court, for the common law of England had long recognized several types of co-ownership. What was different in San On (Xin'an) and other counties of southern China was that the co-owners did not share the same rights over the land. One was the official owner, holding in common tenure and recognized by imperial authorities. This was the holder of the red deed proving that he was registered as the owner and was obliged to pay the land tax which served as a kind of government rent. The other owner had the right to actual use and occupation of the land. Frequently this owner was a lineage institution which let the land to one of its members for his family's use. This owner might instead be the tiller (or cultivator) himself or he might have let the surface rights to someone else. For ease of exposition, however, let us call this owner the user or occupier even if it was a lineage association or an individual who had let out his entitlement.

The user had no imperial deed, only (at most) a paper issued by the first owner acknowledging and recording their arrangements, called a white deed. Those

3. Hase, *Custom*, Ch 1, p 31.
4. Expert evidence of Anthony Dicks in *Winfat Enterprises (Hong Kong) Co Ltd v Attorney-General*, above; Jamieson, *Chinese Family and Commercial Law*, p 103.
5. Jamieson notes similar double ownership existed in Kiangsu (Jiangsu) in central China: ibid, pp 98 and 108.

arrangements were unofficial and informal, indeed they might not be written down at all for their agreement could be purely oral. The user paid no land tax, at least not directly, but instead paid money to the other owner to be allowed to use the land. This payment might be regarded as rent paid to the official owner for use of his land or it might be regarded as reimbursement to him of the land tax. It was not unusual for the registered owner to look upon the payment as rent and therefore think of the occupier as a tenant. At the same time the occupier might look upon the payment as tax and therefore think of himself as an unofficial successor owner of the land. The fact that the arrangement was perpetual and that the amount of payment did not increase over time is consistent with the latter interpretation. So is the fact that the rights were capable of being inherited, passing from father to son.

Moreover, the picture was complicated in that the precise arrangements might differ from locality to locality, as might the practical realities. There seems little doubt that occupiers of land in and around smaller villages in the central and northern sectors of the mainland New Territories were subordinate to the great clans and their lineage institutions based in larger villages nearby which claimed ownership of the district even when they had no imperial grant. By contrast, users of land on the periphery, in Sai Kung and the islands, had greater independence from the registered owners and might more justifiably regard themselves as true owners of the land.[6]

Nature of Joint Ownership

On initial encounter the customary arrangement between subsoil and surface owners for the use of land would suggest that in common law terms the two parties were landlord and tenant, and that therefore this was not co-ownership or concurrent ownership or divided ownership (a division between equals) but a letting of the land by lessor to lessee. In this relationship the lesser interest, that of the tenant, is carved out of the greater one belonging to the registered owner. But there are difficulties with this analysis. A lease is a grant of a period of exclusive possession for a term at a rent.[7] So, if the letting here was truly perpetual, there was no term, no end to the letting. The interests of the user were without limit of time: there was no expiry of the right to use. This violates the very nature of a common law lease which is a grant of possession that lasts for a term of years and so by definition ends at a certain date.[8] Further, the rent charged to users was immutable and much below the market level, neither of which is characteristic of a true lease. Nor could the grant by the registered owner be construed as for the lifetime of the user, in effect a life

6. Hayes, *The Hong Kong Region*, xix; Watson and Watson, *Village Life*, Ch 7.
7. *Street v Mountford* [1985] AC 809.
8. *Berrisford v Mexfield* [2011] UKSC 52, [2011] 3 WLR 1091.

interest. The rights of the user were understood to be heritable, passing to heirs on his demise.[9]

Professor Michael Palmer however suggests that there was a term, that the holding of the occupier was for five or ten years, this being implied or understood if not expressed. Watson says that around Santin the Man clan granted tenancies for terms of three to eight years.[10] On these accounts, the user's interest was a fixed-term tenancy but was perpetual in the sense that it would be renewed if the occupier so desired. In other words, the term was not perpetual but the letting was perpetually renewable. The land would revert to the registered owner only if the occupier failed to pay the rent or died without heirs.

This may be why civil servants who became familiar with the customary arrangements in the early twentieth century and subsequent writers habitually referred to the interest of the user as a 'perpetual tenancy'. The description reflects the idea that the user's rights are subsidiary or derivative, having been created out of those of the officially-recognized owner, yet last longer than those of a normal lessee or termor. The adoption of the phrase may owe something to 'Ulster custom' whereby agricultural land in the northern counties of Ireland was let to farmers for fixed terms but with automatic right to renewal. This would have been known to informed opinion throughout the British Empire because of late nineteenth-century political agitation in Ireland for land reform there.[11]

However, the suggestion that the arrangements amounted to a lease did not find favour with the Hong Kong officials who had responsibility for the investigation, award and registration of Crown leases after 1898. They thought that normally the occupier had more than a leasehold. Their analysis was that his interest was similar to the common law form of tenure known as copyhold and that the payment he made to the registered owner was akin to a rentcharge. This conclusion may however have been coloured by their attitude towards the 'taxlords', as they called the red deed holders who did not farm their own land. Once officers of the Land Court discovered that the imperial grantees of the great clans were in the habit of claiming more land than they were entitled to and letting it out to peasants, living off the rentals and evading payment of the land tax whilst their tenants were in positions of semi-servitude, they determined that these taxlords should be eliminated from the land settlement. The officers saw themselves as carrying out a needed social reform. Most taxlords were denied a grant by the court.

There was another, more pragmatic, reason that administrators found the perpetual or perpetually-renewable lease suggestion unattractive. This was that they wished to grant Crown leases to the occupiers and charge them rent as soon as possible and to record the land ownership on a new register. To have two owners would

9. Palmer, 'Surface-Subsoil', 29; Watson and Watson, *Village Life*, p 152.

10. Palmer, 'Surface-Subsoil', 26.

11. The Ulster custom would certainly have been known to the Governor of Hong Kong in 1899, Sir Henry Blake, who as a resident magistrate in his native western Ireland had had to punish land reform agitators.

be cumbersome. In which order would they appear on the record? Who would be liable to pay the Crown rent? Great Britain had itself been granted a term of only ninety-nine years by the Emperor of China. A perpetual lease would last longer than that, as would the imperial grant to the registered owner.

In certain cases the notion that the cultivators were merely lessees was tolerably accurate, but the relationship between the registered owner and the actual occupier was not the same in every instance. In some areas the position of the occupier was indeed precarious and was analogous to that of a fixed short-term tenant. This was especially true for land near villages close to the centres of power of the great clan lineages. These villages were effectively satellites subjugated to the will of those clans who held the imperial grants for land in the villages or who had asserted sovereignty over that land on the basis that it was within their sphere of influence.[12] In the majority of instances, however, 'lessee' hardly did justice to the status of the user. According to custom, he had the right to remain so long as he wished and honoured the arrangement and also the right to pass the land on to successors, either by inheritance or sale. Those rights were not absolute. If he failed to pay the rent or to cultivate or died without heirs, the land reverted to the registered owner, but such instances were exceptional. If in financial difficulties, or unwilling to farm, the occupier could sell the land. If he had no heirs, he could adopt a kinsman as his successor.[13]

It would certainly be inaccurate to describe the occupier's status as licensee of the red deed holder. The occupier had more than mere permission from the latter to use the land: he had exclusive possession. He could not be regarded as a squatter or adverse possessor either, for the registered owner had given consent to the occupation.

Initially, administrators thought that the occupier had a usufruct. This is a right in Roman law to use, and enjoy the fruits of, somebody else's land. The usufructuary could not change the character of the property and had to maintain it, to pay normal outgoings and to act as a responsible owner. In those respects the position of a cultivator in San On county was similar. The analogy breaks down, however, because the usufruct was usually a life interest whereas the interest of the San On occupier could be passed to successors.[14] For the same reason, comparison with the common law tenant for life is unsustainable.

Another suggestion, made by Gompertz the president of the Land Court, was that the arrangement was reminiscent of copyhold.[15] This was a form of tenure that had originated in feudal England whereby manors, tracts which had been assigned to tenants-in-chief (or lords of the manor), were divided and the divisions allotted

12. Hayes, *The Hong Kong Region*, p xix.
13. Palmer, 'Surface-Subsoil', pp 29, 83.
14. Dr Hase however seems to regard a usufruct as hereditable: Hase, *Custom*, Ch 2.
15. Palmer, 'Surface-Subsoil', 72, fn 184. Gompertz was initially a member of the court then later its president: see Ch 3.

to tenants and others for cultivation in exchange for rent. The terms on which they held their lot were a matter of the custom of the manor and were recorded on the manorial court roll with copies given to the tenants as evidence of their holding. Copyhold could pass from one tenant to another through surrender by one tenant followed by fresh grant and admission to the rolls of the manorial court of the successor tenant and, in the event of a tenant's death, the land devolved in accordance with custom.[16] There were certainly similarities between the landholding in southern San On and copyhold, the imperial grantee being like a tenant-in-chief, his lands being analogous to a manor and his grant to the surface owner being similar to that to a copyholder for cultivation purposes. The role of custom is also similar, as is the right to alienate. But in San On the land was not usually divided into portions, there was no customary court and the agreement was often oral. Also, the imperial Chinese government, unlike the British Crown, did not permit sale of the land to occupiers.

Nevertheless, after searching for a phrase to describe the interest which the occupier had, officers of the Land Court decided not upon copyhold but upon 'rent charge'. This was the term used for an arrangement popular in certain British cities, such as Manchester and Bristol, whereby the purchaser of property would pay, in addition the normal capital sum, a small annual amount to the vendor for the transfer of the property. The annual payment was sometimes referred to as a rent charge, sometimes as a ground (or chief, or quit) rent. It was in effect an instalment of the agreed total price for the land.[17]

The reference to 'rent' here might suggest a landlord-tenant relationship but the holder of a rent charge, unlike a landlord, retains no interest in the land. The word 'rent' is here used in its original sense of a payment; that sense is not confined to periodic payments by tenants in exchange for the right to use land for a term (technically 'rent service', habitually shortened to 'rent' or 'rental'). The rent payable by the occupier in customary tenure was fixed and was only a fraction of the market, or rack, rent that could have been commanded by a landlord from a tenant. Typically it was 3 to 5 per cent of the anticipated annual harvests of rice from the land; rack rents might be ten times that amount.[18] The modesty of the payment was similar to the level of a rent charge instalment.

In the customary system, the official owner was like the holder of a rent charge in that he had no right to use the land. However, the official owner, unlike the holder of a rent charge, did retain an interest in the land. The occupier's use of the land depended upon maintenance of that interest.

16. Charles Harpum, Stuart Bridge and Martin Dixon (eds), *Megarry & Wade: The Law of Real Property* (London: Sweet & Maxwell, 8th edn, 2012), Ch 2. Copyhold and its customs were abolished in England in 1925, copyhold titles becoming freehold.
17. Rent charges as methods of payment on sale of land were abolished in England in 1977.
18. Hase, *Custom*, Ch 2.

Accordingly, both rent charge and copyhold are the categories of landholding which most closely resemble Chinese customary tenure. However, analogies are ultimately futile, for customary tenure was flexible and had its own characteristics. What were those characteristics? How did the participants view their arrangements?

Divided Ownership: The Bones and the Skin

Professor Palmer has described the customary arrangement as 'divided ownership' of the land.[19] This seems more accurate than common or communal or co-ownership, for the customary system was not one of joint or concurrent use. In an attempt to convey the notion of divided ownership various phrases have been used in Chinese: 'one field, two lords', tax-paying fields and rent-paying fields, large rent and small rent, tax land and surface land. The most striking description, however, is colloquial, that of the one being the owner of the bones of the land (tei kwat, transliterated from Cantonese) and the other the owner of the skin of the land (tei pei). More prosaically, one is the subsoil owner and the other the topsoil or surface owner, the former being the holder of the imperial grant and registered as such at the magistracy and the latter being the occupier who enjoys use of the land by agreement with the former. The same categorization is suggested by writers who describe the subsoil owner as owner of the soil and the surface owner as owner of the face (mien) of the land.

The subsoil/topsoil (or soil/face) distinction is not literal but conceptual, shorthand for the division of ownership and the rights which each party had as a result of that division. The occupier's main right and interest was indeed to cultivate the topsoil and take the resulting produce but it would be inaccurate to conclude that this was the full extent of his rights. One writer has suggested that he was entitled to use the land generally, including the extraction of minerals, at least if they were near the surface, and to build upon the land.[20] There is some doubt about this, however. Another account has it that in traditional China if the subsoil and topsoil belonged to different proprietors, neither of them had the right to build a house or make a tomb on the land.[21] In one case the courts received evidence that there were no restrictions upon building upon the land and that any buildings belonged to whomever put them up.[22] The topsoil owner's freedom to do as he liked with the land no doubt depended upon the degree of control exercised by the subsoil owner. It was certainly the case that the subsoil owner's grant from the imperial authorities underpinned his grant to the occupier which could not exist without it: this is

19. Palmer, 'Surface-Subsoil', 6.
20. Hase, *Custom*, Ch 2.
21. Pierre Hoang, 'A Practical Treatise on Land Ownership', quoted by Allen Chun in *Unstructuring Chinese Society: The Fictions of Colonial Practice and the Changing Realities of 'Land' in the New Territories of Hong Kong* (Sydney: Harwood Academic Publishers, 2000), p 63 (*Unstructuring Chinese Society*).
22. *Winfat Enterprises (HK) Co Ltd v Attorney General*, above, at first instance and on appeal to the Privy Council [1985] AC 733, [1985] UKPC 8.

reflected in the notion of ownership of the subsoil. Equally, that reality is reflected in the idea of the official owner having the bones of the land, meaning its structure or essence. But the labels should not be taken to indicate that the registered owner had a concurrent right to use the land which was superior to that of the occupier or that the registered owner had rights over the layers beneath the surface which the occupier did not. The bones and skin distinction is, as Palmer has put it, a symbolic way of conceptualizing the long-term division of ownership.[23]

The essential content of the two interests was that, as between the owners, the subsoil owner had the right to receive payment from the topsoil owner who in turn had the exclusive right to use the land. The subsoil owner had the obligation (often not complied with) to pay the land tax to the authorities and the power to put the topsoil owner into possession. The topsoil owner had powers of disposition and alienation: he could let the land to a tenant, sell his rights to a successor or mortgage them to a lender, although these freedoms were in reality circumscribed by rules of his lineage or of the dominant local clan which forbade sales to outsiders. The subsoil owner could also sell or mortgage his rights, but could not put a purchaser or mortgagee into possession so long as the topsoil owner wished to continue to use the property.

It was registered owners' theoretical obligation to pay the land tax which led the Land Court to call them 'taxlords'. The reality however was that whilst they collected the rent, subsoil owners often disdained to pay the tax. Frequently they had little to do with what was nominally their land. The major subsoil owners collected the rent through paid agents who were always greedy and sometimes corrupt. These owners were for the most part absentee landlords, in effect rentiers enjoying proceeds from the land as an investment and the prestige that went with ownership of land. Sometimes they had no right to the land at all, and so no right to demand rent. Their 'rights' were based upon their influence with the authorities and their practical control of a certain area rather than upon imperial grant, and their demands were based upon extortion, coercion, deception and bluff.[24]

Nature of Payment

The money paid by the top-soiler to the sub-soiler may be regarded as rent or may be regarded as reimbursement (or pre-payment) of imperial tax. To some extent its nature depended on the power relationship between the parties and the physical proximity of the subsoil owner to the land. Subservient occupiers of land around satellite villages near to the seats of large, wealthy clans were treated as tenants holding on short leases at market rents. Occupiers further away from the dominion of the top-soil owner were more independent and regarded themselves as outright

23. Palmer, 'Surface-Subsoil', 10.
24. Palmer, 'Surface-Subsoil', 15–18, 61–66, 82 and 85; James H. Stewart Lockhart, 'Memorandum on Land' in HMSO, *Report on the New Territory at Hong Kong* (London: 1900); Watson and Watson, *Village Life*, Ch 7.

owners, looking upon their fixed low payments to far-away red deed holders as reflecting the amount of land tax and their position as less precarious than that of land users in the main body of the territory.

Divided ownership therefore meant different things to different top-soil owners and varied according to their particular circumstances. The nature of the payment was accordingly ambiguous. In customary times, there was no need to sort this out.

Origins of Divided Ownership

In imperial China the emperor made grants to favoured families, individuals or institutions. These were the red deed holders registered as owners at the imperial land registries kept by county magistrates. These holders were invariably wealthy people of influence or were organizations controlled by such people.

In the San On district the grantees were often lineage or clan-based institutions, t'ong or t'so, which held the land for the communal benefit of members of the clan or lineage. In the simplest arrangement, they would let the land to their members to farm, but the arrangement was usually more complicated than that. Particular members might become top soil owners then let out use of the land to others. The red-deed-holding institution might allow another t'so or t'ong to have the land in perpetuity in exchange for annual payments. But that did not mean that the second t'so t'ong would use the land itself: it would usually allow its members to farm the land, often on a rotating basis.

Where the imperial grantee had been an individual, his descendants might set up a lineage body which would acquire the tei pei rights and rent the land out to its members or others. But if that did not happen, owners who were members of prominent clans and were not interested (for reasons of status) in farming the land would be quite content to allow others to do so in exchange for payment, those others becoming the topsoil owners. The income received would have been an attraction to the subsoil owner, although, being fixed, its value would have declined over time. Another and perhaps greater attraction would have been the circumvention on restrictions on sale of land imposed by lineage custom.[25]

By the time of the survey at the turn of the twentieth century at least a quarter of New Territories land was nominally in the hands of clan, religious or business institutions. By then, these institutions had largely transferred control of their land to others in exchange for annual payments in cash or kind. Much of the rest of the land was registered in the names of men from branches of the great Cantonese-speaking lineages who had been the first to inhabit San On when it was re-populated following the coastal clearances of 1662–1669 and who claimed that their presence long pre-dated that. Two centuries later, members of these lineages regarded themselves as gentry and part of an elite. Their leaders were locally powerful and enjoyed good

25. See Ch 7.

connections with government officials. Their sons were well educated and prepared at study halls established by the clan to take the imperial examinations. Landholders from the lineages were identifiable by surname: Tang, Hau, Liu, Pang and Man. Each of them dominated certain parts of the territory, mainly fertile, flat and well-watered areas of the centre of the county (the northern New Territories) which their ancestors had settled.[26] But each also owned (or claimed to own) other, remoter, more rugged parts of the territory. There, the actual occupiers and claimants to topsoil rights, long-settled yet more recent incomers, tended to be Hakka.[27] The great clans exercised less influence over these hard-working, independent-spirited occupiers than over those near their native place. Anyway, they had no interest in farming marginal land. Often the occupiers had converted the land to cultivation at great effort and so had earned an interest in it. The lineages were content to share ownership with the topsoil claimants so long as they paid the rent.

Neither party to divided ownership had any motivation to regularize their arrangements by transferring official ownership into the name of the occupier. The subsoil owner did not wish to do so because it would have led to loss of influence and prestige as well as income. The topsoil owner did not wish to do so because it would have cost money and involved an arduous journey to the land registry at the county seat. The magistrate levied a transfer tax or charge of 3 per cent of the value plus various other fees for registering a new owner. So instead of having a red deed from the authorities, the occupier made do with a white deed from, or an oral agreement with, the holder of the red deed, who remained registered owner.[28]

The establishment and continuation of customary tenure was testament to the weakness of the imperial authorities. Magistrates were charged with enforcing the law but had many other duties too. There were very few magistrates: throughout China, each had to oversee, on average, more than a quarter of a million people. The further away from the capital Peking, the fewer the number of officials. Hong Kong was about as far away as it was possible to get.[29]

San On had four administrative divisions. What became the New Territories was situated in the largest division, called Guanfu, in the centre and south of the county. The county magistrate and the land register were at the main town, Namtou (Xin'an), in the west and itself one of the divisions. This was a considerable distance from Hong Kong in southern Guanfu. There were two other small divisions, one in the north-west (Fuyon), another to the east of Guanfu, called Dapeng. The Deputy Magistrate was at Dapeng. Fuyon and Guanfu each had an Assistant Magistrate. The Assistant Magistrate for Guanfu was stationed near the small market town of

26. Tang (Deng): Ping Shan, Yuen Long, Kam Tin and Taipo; Hau (Hu): Ho Sheung Heung and Kam Tsin; Liu (Liao): Sheung Shui and Kam Tsin; Pang (Peng): Fanling; Man (Wen): Santin and Tai Hang. Hugh D. R. Baker, 'The Five Great Clans of the New Territories' (1966) 6 *Journal of the Hong Kong Branch of the Royal Asiatic Society*, 25–47.
27. Palmer, 'Surface-Subsoil', 18–19.
28. Palmer, 'Surface-Subsoil', 25, 29.
29. Baker, 'Customary Law and the New Territories', p 5.

Shumchun (Shenzhen). The County Magistrate had a budget which purportedly supported 20 cavalrymen and 25 horses for keeping order, but there is no evidence of their actual existence. The money 'doubtless disappeared into one of the Magistrate's capacious sleeve pockets'.[30] He also had more than a dozen boats with which to watch the coast but this too seems to have been largely a phantom force.

The result of all this was that people in the villages of the county more or less governed themselves and the magistrate was content to allow this to happen. In the countryside local government was carried out by lineage organizations and other customary institutions under the auspices of clan leaders and village elders.

Crown Lessees

Faced with a choice between accepting the claim of a subsoil owner and that of a surface owner, the Land Court generally favoured the latter. This was especially the case where the rent received by the sub-soiler was lower than the proposed Crown rent. Early in the process of ascertainment and adjudication, red deeds were accepted as proof of ownership but as the court became wise to the division of ownership, topsoil owners were increasingly chosen as Crown lessee. Where cultivators accepted that they were mere termors of the person or entity registered at the imperial registry, the court allowed the claim of the latter.[31] This happened at Cheung Chau and Peng Chau, for instance, but not on Lantau.[32]

The refusal to recognize the claims of red deed holders naturally sparked resentment. This persisted for generations. Elders of the Tangs, one of the main clans who were deprived, at Ping Shan still complained about it in the 1960s. The Mans of Santin remained upset too.[33]

The holders of topsoil rights were naturally pleased to be promoted to registered ownership and to be released from subjugation to the subsoil owner. In the main body of the New Territories they became free of the dominant local lineage and the relatively higher rentals that red deed holders were able to charge. In the east and the islands, the largely independent Hakka occupiers were happy to be rid of absentee Punti landlords and their demanding agents.[34]

In the case of land owned by t'so t'ong, the practice was to grant the Crown lease to and to register the institution by name, followed by the names of the current managers. The managers were variously described as 'manager' or 'trustee' in the schedules to the leases.

30. Baker, *Customary Law and the New Territories*, p 7.
31. Palmer, 'Surface-Subsoil', 67–70; 72 fn 185.
32. Palmer, 'Surface-Subsoil', 73, fn 188.
33. Potter, *Capitalism and the Chinese Peasant*; Watson and Watson, *Village Life*, p 153.
34. Palmer, 'Surface-Subsoil', 58–61, 66, 85–86.

Other Traditional Land Rights

Custom recognized rights over land short of the outright possession characteristic of ownership or tenancy. A person or group might have a limited right to use land that belonged to another or which had no owner at all. Hillside ground around villages was often regarded as communal land from which villagers might cut wood and undergrowth, collect stone or build graves. Indeed, portions of hillsides were allocated to families. There they might graze livestock or even sell part to outsiders in search of a conspicuous and propitious grave site. The same held for temples and monasteries. This practice went on well into the twentieth century, to the aggravation of District Officers. Fruit-bearing bushes and trees might be divided between families.[35]

Customary law does not have the common law concept of fixtures under which objects attached to the land which are intended to be enjoyed with it, such as buildings, are part of the land. Hence a building might be under separate ownership from the land upon which it stood.[36] This idea, that rights over an object on the land could subsist separately from rights over the land, was brought out in an application that came before the High Court in 2005 concerning a tree.

The Case of the Fung Shui Tree

A three-storey house had been built by the owner of land at Ko Tong, a village in Sai Kung. One of the indigenous villagers complained that when building the house, construction workers had cut down his lychee tree. The villager said that, although the tree was not on his land, it was his family's fung shui tree and had been owned by them for more than a hundred years. He had, he claimed, inherited the tree from his ancestors pursuant to local and customary law. He sued the landowner, the supervisor of the works and the contractors. He also sued the village representative whom he accused of failing to protect his rights.

The villager's lawyers, evidently forgetting the law of fixtures, framed his pleaded case as a trespass or conversion of goods rather than as a violation of customary law. On this basis the claim had no hope of succeeding, for the land was not owned by the villager and the tree was not goods but part of the land. The village representative was under no duty to protect and enforce private property rights.

Although there was evidence from an elder regarding local practices, expert evidence of the relevant customary law was not obtained until just before the trial, six years after the start of proceedings, and was incomplete. This evidence would have transformed the claim but postponement of the trial would have been necessary so as to amend the pleadings and complete the expert's report. The judge refused to adjourn the trial because the complainant had had ample time to put his

35. Hayes, 'The Great Difference' (article), pp 143 and 146; Coates, *Myself a Mandarin*, Ch 10.
36. Expert evidence of Anthony Dicks SC in *Wong Sui Yeung v Chiu Kwong Wing* [2005] 3 HKLRD 495.

case in order and it would have been unjust to the defendants to delay the hearing further. Since the claim as framed was legally unsustainable, the judge granted an application by the defendants that the action could not be maintained.

So we were deprived of a modern judgment on this intriguing aspect of customary right. It seems that the indigene himself was not convinced that the tree would be recognized as his, for he repeatedly delayed the hearing, perhaps hoping for an offer from the defendants. He did however pursue an appeal. The Court of Appeal decided that the claim was vexatious and had been made to harass the defendants.

7

Customary Transfer of Land

In the customary system that existed at the end of the nineteenth century, land held by individuals might be sold or inherited or otherwise transferred to others by its owners. This applied to the rights of both the topsoil and the subsoil owner. However, rights held by t'so t'ong and similar institutions were in principle inalienable and were intended to be held by the institution in perpetuity.[1] There were in addition a number of constraints on the alienation of land held by individuals. These were essentially moral in nature, being based on convention and practice and containing a degree of flexibility.

The majority of private land was owned by individuals rather than institutions. It has been estimated that in 1905 at least a quarter of New Territories lots were held by kinship groups, t'so or t'ong.[2] Consistent with this, Professor Hugh Baker found in the 1960s that nearly 60 per cent of the cultivated land around Sheung Shui was held by individual households.[3] Prior to the absorption of their land into Hong Kong they had been topsoil owners controlling the land.

Sales

The role of the registered owner in a sale by the topsoil owner seems to have been limited to his being informed of the sale; there was no need for his consent to be sought or given.

Sales were carried out informally. Just as a sale by the red deed holder of topsoil rights was oral or by white paper, so an on-sale of those rights by the topsoil owner was transacted in the same manner. There were customary forms of white deed containing fairly standardized terms, the agreement being evidenced by witnesses and signed by the vendor but not by the purchaser. The deed would usually contain a recital that the land had been first offered to a kinsman who had declined it (this was often a fiction) and that middlemen or brokers had arranged the sale. The

1. See Ch 8 on Customary Institutions.
2. Hayes, 'The Great Difference' (article), 163, fn 33.
3. Baker, *Sheung Shui*, pp 170–173.

location of the land and agreed price would be stated and that it was an out-an-out sale (rather than something less such as a lease or mortgage).[4]

The middlemen usually were friends or neighbours of the seller. They could be as few as two or as many as ten in number. The involvement of middlemen was conventional not only because they acted as agents to match buyer with seller but also to serve as guarantors of good faith and against fraud. Their involvement ensured that the transaction was widely known. Their reward was a small commission or a feast paid for out of the proceeds of sale.

In the unusual case that the sale was to be registered, the head of the village would seal the deed preparatory to its registration. The purchaser would then take the deed to the district magistracy for registration, official sealing and transfer of the liability to pay land tax.[5] A slip showing liability to pay the tax was cut off the old deed and pasted onto the new one, a process known as 'passing the cut-off' (kwo-ko). This was necessary for the purchaser to obtain a valid title and if it were not done, the land would become liable to confiscation. But that was theoretical. The custom was not to register the transfer, for registration fees were 3 per cent of the price and yamen and other fees took the expense to 5 or 6 per cent. In consequence, where the new deed was registered, the price stated was often lower than the actual price: the vendor would execute two deeds, one giving the actual price and the other the lower figure. The former would be retained by the purchaser as a receipt of payment, the latter would be tendered for registration and stamping. The version received back from the magistrate had attached to it an official endorsement (or 'tail") and a red seal. This was the red deed. The endorsement set out the names of vendor and purchaser, the sub-district (the hundred or tything) in which the land was situate and the amount of land tax liability.

If a deed of transfer was not sealed, endorsed and stamped, it was known as a white deed. Such a deed gave no official title but in those parts of China in which the law was not enforced, this unofficial, unauthorized method of transfer had taken root and white deeds were readily accepted as evidence of ownership. Shanxi to the south-west of Peking was one such part. Guangdong in the far south was another, and of course this included Hong Kong and what became the New Territories. This unlawful method of transfer was so common that it had in effect superseded the lawful method. After 1898 the new administrators had to come to terms with it. They styled it customary title.

Restraints and Constraints

Land which had been bought by the disposer or created by him out of waste could be sold and bought freely but this was not so with inherited land in or near the village.

---

4. Jamieson, *Chinese Family and Commercial Law*, pp 96–99; Hayes, 'The Great Difference' (article), 143.
5. The registration process is summarized in *Beautiglory Investment Ltd v Tang Yet Tai Tong* [1993] 2 HKC 591 at 595.

Land which had been passed on by forbears was liable to be regarded as ancestral in nature and attracted customary restraints upon alienation. Although this land did not belong to the clan or family, they were regarded as being interested in its disposal. Dr Patrick Hase describes this as clan brethren having a collateral interest in the land.[6] This is a useful way of conceptualizing the wider family's involvement in any decision to alienate the land, so long as it is appreciated that the 'interest' is not a legal one. The concept of family property is not part of the law of Hong Kong.[7] Hence this 'interest' could not be enforced (except perhaps by complaint to clan elders) but was a moral right to be consulted and to express a view. The point is that land that had been inherited from ancestors was expected to remain within the family and as a result usually did so because the current owner would be reluctant to disappoint his relatives. Generally speaking, the greater the number of generations through which the land had been passed down, the greater the expectation of its being kept by the owner. The present holders of the land were regarded as custodians of the wealth earned by their ancestors for the benefit of their descendants.

The constraints were moral, not legal. They were based on local usage. Many clans had rules, written or understood, which prohibited or restricted sales by their members. Generally, these took the form that clan members could sell properties only to other members or that they first had to be offered to other members or to those who owned adjoining properties. There were no uniform rules: usages varied from clan to clan and from place to place, even within a relatively confined area. Accordingly, such rules did not constitute customary law: they were merely local practices. In his evidence for a divorce case in which the husband resisted having to sell property in his native village near Yuen Long in order to pay maintenance to his former wife, one eminent customary law expert said that he could not recall any instance in which a custom restricting an individual from disposing of land had been proved or recognized. In the same case the long-serving village representative testified that a land owner would be cast out by fellow clansmen if he ever sold land outside the clan over their objections, although he was unable to give an example of this when pressed.[8]

In his study of the occupancy of houses at Sheung Tsuen, Pat Heung, Howard Nelson found that the villagers thought it very shameful to sell a house—even more shameful than selling land. The strongest attachment was to inherited houses. Consequently sales were rare, often re-sales of bought, rather than sales of inherited, properties. Buyers usually had another house already and were expanding their holdings. Sales were more numerous in harsh economic times.[9]

---

6. Hase, *Custom*, Ch 5.
7. *Re Tse Lai Chiu, dec'd* [1969] HKLR 159, per Hogan CJ; *Kan Fat-tat v Kan Yin-tat* [1987] 4 HKLR 516, per Robert Tang Dep-J.
8. *Siu Kwok Kwan v Tsang Wan Hing*, DCCJ 4940/1992 (De Souza Dep-DJ, 14 June 1995).
9. Nelson, 'The Chinese Descent System and the Occupancy Level of Village Houses', 116–117.

The strength of expectation that ancestral land would be retained and shame of failing to do so meant that sales of rural land were unusual. In some villages for long periods they simply did not take place.[10] When sales did occur, the transaction might take the form of a mortgage so as to disguise the sale and in the hope that the seller would be able to redeem it at a future and better time. This was particularly the case with land held by the larger lineages near to their areas of settlement and influence.

The moral constraints upon sale of inherited land meant that when it did occur it might well be indicative of insurmountable difficulties: famine, disaster, death in the family. Consequently, sales tended to be in smaller villages with poorer land. Sales were in the first instance normally to a close kinsman so as to keep the land within the family. Where the subsoil owner of the land to whom rent was paid was a kinship estate, the moral imperative to keep the land within the members and the clan was all the stronger. Accordingly, the buyer was usually another member of the clan. Sales to outsiders were permitted only in extremis.[11]

Where the sale was carried out by deed or recorded in writing, there would usually be a preamble explaining the circumstances which dictated the transaction. The need to raise living expenses was a reason commonly given. Sometimes the deed would be signed by the vendor's sons so as to show their consent and prevent them from later disputing their father's sale of family land.

These at least were the moral rules for ordinary villagers. Powerful members of the elite in the large clans were, it seems, exempt from the rules, or perhaps it would be accurate to say that exceptional circumstances were more easily found where they wished to sell inherited land.[12]

Sales after 1899

The initial intention of British administrators had been that the customary system would continue with sales being recorded on a new land register which would serve as a register of title. This plan was soon abandoned and a survey carried out with the intention to issue leases to those found to be owners. It seems that in the meantime a few New Territories transactions were recorded on the established deeds register on Hong Kong island in much the same way that, in theory, had happened on the imperial register before the takeover. Once the new Crown leases had been granted and land registries for the New Territories had been set up, sales continued in the customary fashion and should have been recorded by the District Office. But often they were not because the sales were informal and the availability of registration was not appreciated. The process of registration involved a summary of the principal provisions of the deed of sale, such as the names of the parties and the properties,

10. Hase, *Custom*, 122.
11. Hase, *Custom*, Ch 5.
12. Hase, *Custom*, Ch 5.

being registered. This was the memorial of the deed. Memorials would also be recorded of other deeds or documents entered into concerning the land, such as mortgages. The process was simpler and speedier than that for registering deeds at the urban land registry.

New Territories inhabitants blithely continued with customary methods of alienating land, 'either because they did not know or because they did not care that the British administration now provided for other ways of dealing with land transfer'.[13] The customary, informal style of sale agreement continued to be used well into the twentieth century and, as in imperial times, might not be registered. This is shown by the facts in a case which was eventually to reach the Privy Council for decision in London. The son of the Crown grantee of a house had not been registered as owner in succession to his late father, yet in 1934 he sold the house. The sale was evidenced by a Chinese document headed (in translation) 'Conveyancing on Sale of Tiled House' which recited that the son had succeeded to the house and was now short of money, that none of his brothers was prepared to take it, and that the purchaser had been introduced by a middleman and agreed to purchase it. (The document did not say so, but the son was believed to be an opium addict and the purchaser was the village representative and a supplier of opium.) The document went on to say that the parties had inspected the house that day and, after negotiation involving the middlemen, the market price had been determined at $200, which had been paid in full. It declared that there was no prior mortgage or subsequent sale and that people such as uncles and nephews could not repudiate or resist the sale: 'Just like severed rattan, one stroke of the pen is forever and can never be recalled'. The sale was the will of the parties, the document concluded, there had been no compulsion or coercion: 'For fear that words of mouth bear no evidence, this instrument of absolute sale of the tiled house is made as proof'. The document was signed by the middleman, witnesses and its writer, but not by buyer or seller. The expert evidence was that this was a valid sale in customary law.[14]

The agreement was acted upon. Possession of the house was given to the purchaser who paid the full price (perhaps in the form of a set-off against debts for opium supplied). By the 1990s the purchaser's sons had been in possession for years. The trouble was that the son had never been registered with the District Office as successor to his father, nor had the purchaser registered the sale agreement on the land register. They both had followed the customary way even though the new system had been in place for almost thirty years at the time of the sale.

---

13. Godfrey J in *Beautiglory Investment Ltd v Tang Yet Tai Tong*, above.
14. *Wu Koon Tai v Wu Yau Loi* [1997] AC 179, PC; [1995] 2 HKC 732, [1996] 2 HKLR 477, CA.

Customary Mortgages

The raising of money by mortgage of the land was forbidden by imperial law. Here again, however, the population disdained the rules. By 1898 unauthorized mortgages had been used for generations and had long been part of the economic set-up in the countryside. They continued long after 1899.

Customary mortgage, or dian (pawning), was in form a conditional sale and was known as a mortgage-sale (dian mai). The landowner-mortgagor (the maker of the dian) would transfer possession of the mortgaged land to the purchaser (the holder of the dian) in exchange for payment of a proportion of the sale value of the land. Typically, the proportion was between 60 and 80 per cent of the value. The holder thereby acquired the right to use the land and keep all the income from it. No rent was charged to the mortgagee for occupation. The lump-sum payment was in effect a payment of rent in advance. No interest was charged by the mortgagee on the payment. The period of use and of the mortgage was not fixed. The mortgage could be redeemed many years, even generations, later on re-payment of the original price.

Accordingly, the mortgage loan was transformed into money in payment of the price for use of the land. Interest upon the money was replaced by enjoyment of the land and its produce. In these respects, and also the unlimited term of the mortgage and the perpetual right to repay, the arrangement resembled a so-called 'Welsh mortgage', a type of loan secured by transfer of land that used to be common in Wales and Ireland. The element of transfer of the property to mortgagee was also familiar. Mortgages by conveyance of the estate in the land were common in urban Hong Kong until 1984 when security for loans by charge over the land became available.[15]

The effect of this was similar to a sale of the surface rights but in appearance the dian involved a temporary transfer as it could be paid off at any time. Accordingly, it was the preferred method of alienation of land held by the larger lineages near to their principal villages where control of land was a sensitive political matter. Indeed, there was a presumption that an apparent sale of old family land was a mortgage-sale rather than an absolute sale. For the maker of the dian, there was hope of re-gaining possession of the land eventually. For the dian holder, the attraction was the gaining of use of the land (and its rent and profits) without the demeaning appearance of being the tiller of the soil.[16]

Mortgage to a fellow clan member was more acceptable than to a stranger because it meant that in the event of default and the mortgagee's taking permanent possession, the land would remain within the family. Mortgage to an outsider was discouraged because this brought the risk of the land passing out of clan control and might be a method of circumventing the moral ban upon alienation.

15. Under the Conveyancing and Property Ordinance 1984, now Cap 219.
16. Palmer, 'Surface-Subsoil', 100–101.

These mortgages ought to have been registered but rarely were, again because of the expense and inconvenience of opening a new heading on the imperial register. The habit continued into the twentieth century. Nelson mentions the case of a registered owner who sixty years earlier had handed possession of his land to a lender as payment for a debt. The lender and his descendants farmed the land for thirty years before the successor of the registered owner discovered his entitlement to the land and demanded possession. The dispute went to the District Officer who sagaciously decided in favour of the occupier on the grounds that no one would voluntarily hand land over to another without a good reason.

The difficulty of distinguishing this type of mortgage from an outright sale led to the passing of an imperial law to the effect that if the deed was meant to be a mortgage, a right of redemption should be expressly reserved and that if it was meant to be a sale only, the deed should state this and that there was no right of redemption. The law also provided that any right of redemption be exercised within thirty years from the date of the transfer. This statute seems to have had little effect: an instance of custom persevering in the face of imperial act. The customary practice received support in the interpretation of an old deed by a Hong Kong judge that an 'outright sale' and an 'outright purchase' did not lead to a transfer of ownership.[17]

There was another type of customary mortgage, the mortgage-pledge or tien tang. This type was meant to be temporary security for money lent. The property did not change hands: the mortgagee did not gain possession. As a result, there was no need for any registration of the transaction. There was a written record or memorandum of the terms of the loan and the title deeds were deposited with the mortgagee. In this it was reminiscent of an equitable mortgage in English law. There was an agreed time for repayment of the loan and redemption of the mortgage. Failing repayment, the mortgagee could foreclose and sell the land. However, not being registered as the owner and not being in possession, the mortgagee might run into difficulties in selling. If the proceeds of sale were insufficient to meet the debt, it was doubtful whether the mortgagee could sue for the balance.[18]

The old styles of customary mortgage continued to be used after the incorporation of the New Territories into Hong Kong. For instance, the background evidence concerning land at Ping Shan in a case that was tried in 1993 disclosed a mortgage-sale in 1903.[19]

Succession and Inheritance

In San On county succession to real property following the death of its owner was governed entirely by customary rules. The official system did not recognize inheritance of land: any would-be successor had to apply for a fresh imperial grant.

17. *Beautiglory Investment Ltd v Tang Yet Tai Tong*, above.
18. Jamieson, *Chinese Family and Commercial Law*, pp 101–102.
19. *Beautiglory Investment Ltd v Tang Yet Tai Tong*, above.

There was no room within the customary rules of succession for a will by the deceased to be considered. Nor did custom allow any procedure for the grant to a member of the family of administration of a deceased's estate.[20] Customary law required an equal division of the deceased's property and largely excluded its voluntary disposition by gift or will.[21] Anyway, by and large, Chinese peasants did not make wills. It was considered bad luck to contemplate death in this, or any other, way. Moreover, they conceptualized their farmland as belonging to the family. They were 'living together with property in common' in accordance with the traditional saying, so it was not for the father as landowner to dispose of it by will. Deceaseds' wishes were sometimes expressed in writing but these were in effect requests to the heirs to be of good behaviour which would not normally be ignored.

Family land

The traditional Chinese view was that property was, subject to certain limited exceptions, attributable to the family or household (ka or ga) rather than to the individual. The family comprised the common male descent group. This was a continuum which included deceased ancestors and unborn children as well as the living. The duty of members currently alive was to pass the property which they had received from their ancestors to their descendants. Accordingly, the death of the most senior member had no effect on ownership and no re-registration was required. The family survived and continued to hold the land. The only change was in the headship of the living family members.[22]

Male-only inheritance

The custom was that only males, more precisely sons, could inherit. Widows and daughters could not succeed to land. The reason for this was that females were from a different clan and village: if they were allowed to inherit the land, it would pass out of the control of the clan and lineage, thereby diminishing their wealth.[23] Were a daughter able to take the land, she would 'export' it to her husband's family when she married for her husband would invariably be from another village.

Consequently, the rule throughout China was that on a man's death all his real and personal property was to be equally divided among all his male children. This was so irrespective of whether the children were born of the first wife (tsai), of a replacement wife (tin fong) after the death of the first, of a secondary wife (tsip or

20. *Wu Koon Tai v Wu Yau Loi* [1995] 2 HKC 732, 748 (Liu J).
21. Expert evidence of Anthony Dicks QC in *Tsang Wing Lung v Tsang Lun*, HCA 7770/1997 (Sharwood Dep-J, 8 September 1992).
22. The concept of family property is not part of the law of Hong Kong: *Re Tse Lai Chiu, dec'd* [1969] HKLR 159; *Kan Fat-tat v Kan Yin-tat* [1987] 4 HKLR 516.
23. Selby, 'Chinese Customary Law', 55.

'concubine') or of a female servant in the household.[24] If the deceased had only one son, the son alone inherited the land. If there was more than one son, both or all the sons inherited the deceased's land jointly. A man could disinherit a son only in the rarest circumstances.[25]

Rights of females

Although female members of the household, or ka, did not participate in the division of the common property, they were entitled to support from that property so long as they remained within the household. Widows with sons were entitled to maintenance for life or until they left the family. This usually meant that they managed the family land and so had control of the income from it. A widow could prevent the son from taking a portion of the estate without her consent. A widow with no son who did not remarry was entitled to her late husband's share of the family property.

Daughters were entitled to support until they married, and when they were about to marry they would be given a dowry if the family's income could fund it. The provision of a good dowry was a matter of face for the daughter's family. At marriage a daughter had if possible to be endowed with a minimum of household equipment, clothing, jewellery and money to take to her new home. In well-to-do families, the daughter might even be given some land.[26] On marriage daughters lost the right to be supported by their parental family, so if they married prior to their father's death, they had no entitlement to anything from his estate. Family property passed to natural daughters only in the rare instance that there was no son in the household and no male relative of the correct generation eligible to be adopted as a son. This was the safety net provided by Article 88 of the Ching Code so as to prevent the land from being forfeit to the government.

Adoption

Continuation of the male family line was deemed so important that if a man had no male children, he was permitted to adopt a son formally. It was even possible for an heir to be adopted by his widow after the man had died. She, supervised by the family elders, would select an appropriate relative as successor. The widow was expected but could not be forced to adopt. There were no rules as to what would happen if no elders survived to supervise the adoption.

24. Jamieson, *Chinese Family and Commercial Law*, pp 24–25, 102; Ching Code, Li 1 to s 88; expert evidence of Professor Chang Wejen in *Yau Kwai v Yau Kar Siu* [2004] 4 HKC 141 at 148–149 and of Anthony Dicks in *Kan v Kan*, above. An illegitimate son born to a woman outside the household was to receive a half share, according to Professor Chang.
25. *Wu Koon Tai v Wu Yau Loi* [1995] 2 HKC 732, 749 (Liu J).
26. Maurice Freedman, 'Kinship and Religion in China', Ch 15 in *The Study of Chinese Society*. Presumably the land would be outside the village.

The widow might transfer part of the property to the heir but keep some to fund her maintenance. So long as there was one qualified agnatic male available to succeed, the line would continue, so if there were no nephews available, there would have to be a search within the clan to find the last man standing. Posthumous adoption was quite common. In his study of villagers at Santin, Watson found that 11 per cent of men of the Man clan died without natural heirs.[27]

The adoptee was supposed to be from the next generation of the man's agnatic kindred in a certain defined order (the closer related, the better) which, if followed, allowed the adopted son to succeed to the property. The Ching code laid down rules of succession to be followed, one set for an adoption when the man was still alive, another for an adoption by the widow after his death. The code did not stipulate any procedure or ceremony for adoption, however. An adoption would be valid if the adopting parents in the presence of the adoptee declared him to be adopted by them in front of their clansmen and held a simple ceremony. No documents were prescribed by the state. In the ceremony the adoptee had to worship the tablets of his new ancestors and serve tea to his new parents and senior members of the family in the presence of relatives.[28]

However, simple though the ceremony of formal adoption was, the rules were there to be bent if not broken as far as villagers were concerned. Informal adoption was common in the New Territories, especially where the adoptee was from outside the clan. Informal adoption required no ceremony. In one instance during the mid-twentieth century, a widow from one village was married for a second time to a man surnamed Tang from the neighbouring village. She brought her son, surnamed Chan, to the new village and at their wedding banquet her new husband declared that the son was his. The practice was to turn a blind eye to the imperial law which prohibited adoption from another surname. Such a son or 'courtesy child' (i-sze) was entitled to a share in the division of his adoptive father's property, the share not being fixed. But if he inherited property from his original village, he was taken to have returned to the original village and was not allowed to inherit from his adoptive family.[29]

Adoption was quite common, as shown by two twenty-first-century cases each of which involved two disputed adoptions. Since the process was informal there could be a disagreement as to whether a certain male had been adopted so as to inherit land. In that event, a judge has to consider all the evidence and decide whether there had been a valid adoption. One of the cases was a dispute over inheritance of land within a lineage of the Hau clan from Ho Sheung Heung. The earlier of two adoptions in that case was performed about eighty years before the time

27. James Watson, 'Agnates and Outsiders' in *Village Life*, pp 55–68.
28. Expert evidence of H. C. Mui in *Tang Cho Sang Wayne v Chim Siu Wah*, HCA A6666/1993 (13 June 1995).
29. Ching Code, Li 3 of s 78; expert evidence of H. C. Mui in *Tang Cho Sang Wayne v Chim Siu Wah*, above; expert evidence of Professor Baker in *Tsang Yuet Mui v Wan On*, HCMP 2314/2012 (23 September 2014), where registration of the only male heir had wrongly been rejected by the District Officer.

of the trial by the widow after the death of her husband, the adoptive father. The adoptee was surnamed Chau and thus not a blood relative, so the adoption was strictly illegal. The other adoption had taken place in 1965 and was of the son of a close relative. The occurrence of both adoptions was challenged. The later one was easier to prove: the adoptee himself, though a child at the time of adoption, was able to give evidence of the care and attention given to him by the adopter and of what he had been told by his mother and siblings, as well as of his role at and after the funeral of the adopter. There was oral evidence from witnesses of what the adopter had said and of what was common knowledge in the village. By contrast, all witnesses to the first adoption were deceased. In assessing whether it had taken place, the court considered hearsay from living witnesses of what they had heard from previous generations, contents of ancestral tablets, the conduct of the adoptee in venerating his adoptive ancestors on visits to ancestral tombs during Ching Ming and other festivals, the adoptee's role in arranging repair and renovation of graves of ancestors from his adoptive line and his conduct at funerals. The court found both adoptions to be proven. Similar assessment of the evidence of two disputed adoptions was carried out in the case of adoptions that had occurred at Sha Tau Kok.[30]

Informal adoptions ignored not only the proper process but also the rules of generational correctness. According to the Ching code, the adopted son was supposed to be from a generation below that of his adoptive father; the code prescribed the correct order. This was especially important in the case of post-mortem adoption. Yet country people allowed someone from the same generation as the father, a younger brother or cousin for instance, to be adopted.

Daughters could inherit only if there was a complete failure of natural or adopted male heirs. This was highly unlikely, not only because of the possibility of adoption of a son but also because an adoption could take place after the man's decease and the likelihood was that there would be a male successor within the clan. Yet it did happen to a family at Sheung Shui. The landowning father had died during the Japanese occupation, leaving a widow, two daughters and two brothers. He had not adopted a son, nor did his widow do so. Years later, after the widow died, one of the daughters (the plaintiff) endeavoured to be registered as successor but was rejected by the District Office because she was not male. The son of one of the brothers, who was the deceased's nearest and only male relative, no doubt with some confidence, claimed to succeed instead. Normally he would have done so but the courts ruled against him and in favour of the daughters. The reason was that he had already inherited land from his own father in 1960. This made him ineligible to succeed to his uncle, the deceased. He could not be loyal to two families at once. Once he had succeeded to the male line of his natural family, he could not cross over to be the heir of an adoptive line. That would deprive his natural family of their property. Although there was nothing express about this in Article 78 of the

30. *Yap Sui Kong v Yip Fong Tim*, HCA 1409/2013 (31 July 2017); appeal allowed in part, retrial ordered: CACV 191/2017 (26 Sepember 2018).

Ching code which dealt with succession to property, customary law did not allow the property of one line to be mixed with that of another, so he could not inherit from both his father and his uncle. Since there was no eligible male heir, the household had become extinct. That meant that the daughters succeeded to the property under Article 88(2) of the code.[31]

Division of property

In the normal case of the deceased leaving sons, they continued to hold the land jointly until a division of the land was carried out. Until that division (fan ka), all of them would have to join in any deed of transfer of the land. Adult sons might well have married and have had children by the time of their father's demise or by the time of the division. In that event, each of them headed a fong, or apartment, of his own. Pending the division, the land might be managed with consent by a senior member of the family or each fong might take a turn at managing it. Any extraordinary use of the land, such as a lease or mortgage, would have to be approved by all the fong. Consequently, none of the individual co-owners could sell or encumber the entire undivided property without the consent of all the others. It seems however to have been quite common for a son to mortgage or sell his joint interest in the property pending its division without the other sons' consent.[32]

Division between the sons or fong was a matter for discussion and agreement. Where the principal wife had not outlived the deceased, division would be postponed for a decent period for observance of rites. Before the division, a certain sum would be set aside for the marriage expenses of any unmarried daughter. Any division agreed during the lifetime of the widow required her consent. By statute, it could not be carried into effect until she had passed away. After that, a son could insist upon the carrying out of the division unless the land had been specifically dedicated to common purposes such as ancestor worship.

The division was per stirpes, that is to say equal between the fongs or sons and irrespective of the number of male children each son had. The eldest son usually received a larger share of the land because he had greater family duties but in general (and subject to local variations) the shares of the other sons would be the same. Although the property was to be divided between them, because of practicalities and family sensibilities, that might not happen for a long time, even for generations. Led by the widow and the eldest son, the family continued to live off the land together. Only once the widow had died would division actually take place. Then, it might prove difficult to gather the brothers together to reach agreement on the precise allocation between them, especially once it had become common for

31. *Liu Ying Lan v Liu Tung You* [2003] 3 HKLRD 249.

32. Evidence of Anthony Dicks QC in *Yau Kwai v Yau Kar Siu* [2004] 4 HKC 141 at 150. However, the judge in that case was not convinced that sons had an identifiable interest until division had taken place.

men to work abroad and in metropolitan Hong Kong.[33] The longer that division was postponed, the more difficult it must have been to disrupt existing arrangements. For instance, if one of the sons had remained living with the mother and cultivating the father's land whilst his brothers married and lived elsewhere, splitting the family land so as to deprive that son of use of some of it might seem inequitable. Physical division would also not be sensible if it resulted in plots that were uneconomic to farm. There was no pressure to register the land with the imperial magistrate as having new owners; quite the contrary, for that would involve heavy transfer fees. So the land might remain in the joint ownership of the deceased's sons as if it were family property.[34] The sons could make this more formal by putting all or most of the jointly-held land (perhaps together with other land that they owned) into a kinship body (t'so) dedicated to their father.

The reason that the eldest son took a larger portion was that he had the responsibility of providing for his mother and unmarried sisters. He also had to arrange ancestor worship. If the land was large enough to permit it, part might be set aside by the eldest son so that income from that part would fund ancestral rites.[35] That part would be regarded as common property and might be put under a t'so.[36] Similarly, part of the land, such as a floor for threshing rice, might be set aside for communal use.

Should one of the sons die after the father had done so but before division, that son's share passed to his own sons, then their sons, and so on down the male line. If he had no son, his share went to his brothers equally, in other words back into the pot as a kind of joint tenancy.

When one or more of the sons was a minor when the division was carried out, he would receive an equal share and a guardian would be appointed to look after his share. The guardian would be an adult member of the family, often the widow. The New Territories Ordinance formalized this practice by providing for appointment of a trustee for a minor.[37]

Joint ownership

During the period in which the land was in the possession of the sons jointly, their position was similar to that of co-parceners at common law. Although the normal inheritance rule in England prior to legislative intervention was that the eldest son took all (primogeniture), this did not apply where the deceased landowner's children were all female or where the land was copyhold.[38] Also, there were regional

33. Hase, *Custom*, Ch 2; Selby, 'Chinese Customary Law', 72.
34. Hase suggests (*Custom*, Ch 4) that if the land continued undivided over generations, it would start to be treated as if held on 'trust', by which is presumably meant family property similar to that of a t'so.
35. Selby, 'Chinese Customary Law', 73.
36. Hase, *Custom*, Ch 5.
37. Now s 18 of the New Territories Ordinance (Cap 97): see below.
38. For copyhold, see Ch 6.

customary exceptions where inheritance by sons jointly was allowed. In these cases, the inheriting children were co-parceners (or parceners). They held the land in undivided shares and between themselves resembled tenants-in-common. Each co-parcener had the right at common law to have the land partitioned and distributed. Upon partition, the co-parcenery would end and each family headed by one of the sons became a household in its own right holding a portion of the divided property.[39]

Succession under the New Territories Ordinance

After 1905, the customary method of male-only succession was regulated by the legislation that became the New Territories Ordinance and applied through a simplified system of registration. Unless a grant of probate or administration had been made by the High Court within three months of the death (such a short time that it rendered the possibility impracticable), the Land Officer was required to register the name of a person who was entitled to succeed in accordance with customary law.[40] Upon that registration the land vested in the successor. Since the laws of probate and administration of estates did not in practice apply to rural land, the applicant for registration as successor simply had to prove the death of the owner, his own identity and his relationship with the deceased and pay any fee required by the Land Office. The new registered owner became liable for any death duties and debts of the deceased.

This simple regulation no doubt seemed a harmless way of keeping track of inheritance. There was one thing wrong with it though: it was not in keeping with the usages and expectations of the population. Since they thought of land as belonging to the family, not to an individual, the concept of succession was foreign to them. The customary rules which the western mind characterized as succession were simply a natural part of life: sons took nominal charge of the land when their father died but the family continued to live and work on the land at least until the mother passed away. If there was some departure from the norm, that would be agreed between them and perhaps written down and witnessed, but that was all. They had no concept of registering a successor. As far as they were concerned, the imperial registry was better avoided. This attitude, being traditional, naturally continued long after civil servants and lawyers came from Hong Kong with their rules, forms, notices, and registers. The new land register, for all its efficiency, soon became out of date.

39. As part of the 1925 land law reforms in England and Wales, co-parcenery land became subject to a trust for the land to be sold and the proceeds divided between those entitled.

40. New Territories Ordinance (Cap 97) s 13 (power to apply customary law) and s 17 (registration of successors, abolished in 1994: see below). Section 17 registration was described in *Chan Shun Ho v Chak Hok Ping* (1925) 20 HKLR 1, 12, as merely an alternative to the normal application for probate and administration but this was so only for three months following the death.

The registration provided for in section 17 is registration of the name of the successor, not registration as the new owner on the New Territories land register. It consists of the Land Officer recording details of the application and, after determining in accordance with custom whether the applicant is the successor, of his notice approving it. Registration on the Land Register is registration of documents, not names or title, and comes later.[41]

Although the section 17 procedure was straightforward and convenient, it also made fraudulent or mistaken registrations easier for it hinged upon the Land Officer correctly ascertaining the identity of the person asking to be registered as successor and upon that person being the only one entitled to succeed to the property. In villages, deaths of landholders soon became known within the community. Villagers tended to be closely related and share the same surname. Impersonation or deceit was relatively easy. Also, errors sometimes occurred. The fraud or mistake might not be detected for a long time. Since the entitled successor would usually be in possession and the established arrangements for use of the land were prone to continue, he might not bother to register his entitlement for many years or at all.

Illustrative of this is a case concerning twenty-one lots near Yuen Long originally registered in the name of Lam Kam Tak. A succession for these lots to one Lam Shui Yan had been approved and registered in 1947. Apparently, the District Office had been told by the applicant for succession that Lam Kam Tak had died in 1939 and that the applicant was the deceased's nephew. In turn, Lam Shui Yan's nephews had been registered as his successors in the late 1990s. The plaintiff claimed to be the adopted son of Lam Kam Tak and so entitled to succeed to the lots. He said that his father had died in 1963 and that he had been in possession of the lots since then. He alleged that Lam Shui Yan had not been his father's nephew and that the registrations had been obtained by fraud. Lam Shui Yan's nephews, the defendants, were thought to be living in Holland and did not defend the claim. On the plaintiff's application for judgment by default, the judge made a declaration that the successions ought not to have been approved. She declined to make a finding of fraud without a trial.[42]

Another example of the dangers of section 17 occurred when a landowner died leaving a wife, a concubine, an oldest adopted son and one son by each of his wife and concubine. The adopted son alone was registered as successor despite the custom that all sons inherited equally. He, together with concubine and the deceased's brother, planned to sell the land. The widow complained to the District Officer who intervened and proposed to name all three sons as successors with the widow and the concubine as trustees for their respective sons who were still minors. Ultimately, the eldest son, the widow and the concubine agreed to divide the estate equally. The District Officer allowed that, but it was only because of the registration regime that the problem had arisen in the first place for the adopted

41. *Wing Tung Yick v Attorney General* [1997] 4 HKC 432.
42. *Lam Shing Shou v Lam Hon Man*, HCA 361/2001 (Chu J, 15 January 2002).

son probably assumed that once he was registered as the only successor, he alone owned the land.[43]

In another instance of misuse of section 17, two out of four brothers contrived to be registered as successors to their father in 1945, excluding the other two whom they did not mention to the District Office. One of the latter, who had been in China since the Japanese occupation, returned to his native village in 1982. He succeeded in his claim for a share of the income received from the land over the years.[44]

The informality with which changes in ownership could be effected, by simple registration of an individual claiming to be a successor, also laid the system open to corruption. Wherever administrative power is given, dark practices are possible. By and large the District Officers were men of probity. However, although they could speak Cantonese, they might not have been alert to devious devices nor able to guard against dishonest underlings. An official who was responsible for scrutinizing a claim to succeed was in a position to influence the outcome. He could invite reward for his efforts. He would also have been able to divert the land to a friend or an entity which he controlled. At least one former clerk at the Land Office in Taipo became extremely wealthy through personal land acquisitions there.

In the unlikely event that an application for representation of an estate of a New Territories landowner had been taken out and granted within the short deadline imposed by section 17 of the New Territories Ordinance, the probability (given the traditional Chinese dislike of wills) was that the deceased was intestate. In that event, section 11 of the Intestate Estates Ordinance (Cap 173) applies Chinese custom and customary right to the land, so the customary rules set out above would have applied anyway.

Trustees for Minors

A problem identified by the new authorities after 1899 when looking at inheritance of land was that of ownership by minors. In the harsh conditions of the countryside of that era, many men died young, leaving a widow and infant children. Richer, older men might take much younger secondary wives in the search for a male heir and again leave a young son, or they might adopt a baby from a brother or other close agnate and pass away soon after. As has been seen, it was possible for a young heir to be adopted by his widow or other family after the owner's death. The customary rules of succession dictated that the sons, not the spouse, inherited the land. Yet the sons, or some of them, were not old enough to manage the father's estate.

The custom in these circumstances was to appoint a guardian to care for the land until the heir was old enough to take over. This was built into statute with the enactment of what is now section 18 of the New Territories Ordinance which

43. Related by Chun in *Unstructuring Chinese Society*, pp 73–74, relying upon the account of Nelson.

44. *Tsang Wing Lung v Tsang Lun* [1992] 2 HKC 440.

empowers the Land Officer to appoint a 'fit and proper person' to be trustee of the land during the heir's minority and to remove that trustee and appoint another in his or her place. The appointment had to be registered in the appropriate Land Office. The record would normally state the name of the minor followed by 'with ABC as trustee'. Upon registration, the land which is the subject of the trust vests in the trustee 'for all the estate and interest of the minor therein' and the trustee is given power to deal with the land as if beneficial owner. The appointment of a trustee under section 18 lasts for as long as the successor is a minor. Upon his attaining the age of majority, the trusteeship ceases by operation of law.

The appointment of trustees for minors is an aspect of inheritance of individually-owned property, but the convention was and is to refer to the arrangement as a t'so with the trustee in the position of manager. However, although the Chinese character for this arrangement may be pronounced by a sound similar to that for the family endowment of land known as a t'so (dealt with in the next two chapters), it is a separate character with a separate meaning.

After the minor has achieved adulthood, a memorial is entered at the land registry removing the name of the trustee and re-vesting the property in the son, thereby ending the trust. Upon registration of the removal, the land divests from the trustees. The trustees, if still alive, sign on the memorial to signify their understanding of the termination. The son used to be registered as successor under section 17 of the New Territories Ordinance. Initially the Land Office simply deleted all reference to the trusteeship from the register. Then it was thought that an order vesting the land in the son was necessary. Finally, the previous practice was restored.[45]

Where a trustee appointed under section 18 is replaced, the section provides that the land shall vest in any new trustee (as well as any continuing one).

Female Inheritance

During the first fifty years or more of British rule, village wives had little reason to object to the traditional system. They understood the reasons for succession to be reserved to males. They themselves indirectly benefited from it in two ways. First, custom dictated that they be provided for by their sons, either by being allowed to remain in the marital home or by being accommodated at the expense of the sons. Their way of life would continue after the loss of their husband. Secondly, their sons, not someone nominated by their husband and not their daughters, would inherit the land and keep it within the family. So long as the traditional manner of life continued, they had no cause to complain.

But traditional ways began to unravel in the latter half of the twentieth century. Husbands, children, and wives themselves found work and living opportunities

45. *In the Matter of the Trustee Ordinance*, HCMP 2133/1987 (2 November 1987) and HCMP 2382/1987 (22 January 1988).

away from the village. Life became more secure and comfortable as health care was extended and piped water, gas and electricity reached the countryside. Universal education spread knowledge and fresh values to villages, as did radio and television. New and improved roads, railways and public transport brought a different pace and perspective to rural life. Urban life, in the guise of new towns, came closer to the countryside. So did essentially urban practices such as divorce. Rustic people born into this changed environment could see that the old ways were out of date. By the end of the 1980s the time was over-ripe for alteration of the rules of inheritance. Rural husbands were already making wills containing provision for widows and daughters. Even though tradition did not recognize such testaments, the modern family tended to do otherwise and District Officers did not resist.

The route was opened for wives to inherit land from their husbands by an amendment to the New Territories Ordinance in the summer of 1994. The change abolished section 17's simple alternative procedure for registration of successors. The change was fiercely resisted by older indigenous people, including some women. Lau Wong Fat, the chairman of the Heung Yee Kuk and its Legislative Council member, denounced the proposal. There were angry protests outside the Legislative Council. It was to no avail. The government did not negotiate this time. Practices by indigenous males regarding re-sale of village houses had already put them in bad odour with the general public. For the kuk, it was a rare defeat.

The change was initiated by a thoroughly cosmopolitan female legislator, Christine Loh. It was in truth a very modest amendment: in future, it would be possible for land in the rural areas to be left to females by will. The customary rules of succession could still be followed by those who wished to do so. The rancour soon died down. An attempt by Mr Lau to have the change declared a breach of human rights on the ground that it was a violation of the right of an ethnic minority to enjoy their culture failed completely. The legislative amendments did not prevent an indigenous inhabitant from making a will in favour of male descendants to the exclusion of female descendants if he wished to keep the custom. One of the judges complained that the statement of claim drafted on behalf of Mr Lau read like a political manifesto.[46]

It might also have been pointed out that in Hong Kong the indigenous were not an ethnic group, being Han Chinese like the great majority of the population, having no shared religion and no separate language. Although it is sometimes asserted that the indigenous are ethnically diverse, presumably on the basis that there are Punti and Hakka indigenes, this too is wide of the mark.

A quarter of a century later, the 1994 protests seem to have been a fuss about very little, almost a non-event. Husbands, brothers and sons do not see why their wives, sisters and daughters should have been excluded from the prosperity brought

46. *Lau Wong Fat v Attorney General* [1997] HKLRD 553 (Litton VP).

by the escalation of land values in recent decades.[47] There is even a case for saying that customary practices in respect of female inheritance have altered. The protests about the modest amendment did show that the rural lobby was still able to galvanize support to an extent and in a way that few interest groups could muster. But it also showed the limits of the power of that lobby when it was opposed by public opinion and a determined administration.

47. Hayes, *The Great Difference* (book), pp 149–150. The change was made in 1994 by the New Territories Land (Exemption) Ordinance (Cap 452).

8

Customary Institutions

In 1899 much of the land in the new territory was found to be occupied by members of lineages within clans and was claimed to be owned by the lineage. The clans were extended families having the same surname. The lineages consisted of part of the clan, so they shared the surname but did not include all the (male) members of the clan. The land was held by an association composed of members of the lineage and named after one of their common ancestors. Other areas were held in the name of a variety of customary organizations and dedicated to communal use. Where this was so, ownership of the land was awarded to the organization or association, granted to them in their names by the block Crown leases and placed on the new land register in those names.

The commonest of these traditional landholding organizations, the t'so and the family t'ong, were forms of lineage endowment by which estates of land were held in the common ownership of current male descendants of a particular deceased ancestor. The endowments were devoted to purposes connected with and confined to the lineage to which those descendants belonged and were enjoyed by those descendants during their lifetimes. The dedications of land had been made by ancestors for the furtherance of those purposes, usually many years earlier. Other customary organizations such as temples, monasteries, schools, commercial bodies and communal entities also held property in the New Territories. These were not lineage associations but had been founded by people with common interests for shared purposes. Such entities were instances of t'ong, although not of the family variety.

T'so T'ong

The two types of lineage association, the t'so and the family t'ong, are so frequently encountered and are so similar that they are habitually referred to in combination as t'so t'ong. They are endowments of land for the benefit of living, deceased and future members of a segment of a clan. Their primary activity is worship of ancestors. Both associations are rooted in Confucian ideals of veneration of ancestors, filial duty, preservation of family structure, and maintenance of hierarchy. They also reflect traditional ideas of patrilineal descent and the importance of males. They were encouraged, or at least tolerated, by imperial authorities. They existed throughout southern China, for instance in Fujian and Hunan as well as Guangdong, and spread abroad with emigrants from those parts. In Vietnam they were known as 'cult funds'.[1] They were forbidden in Malaysia because they offend the rule against perpetual settlements and were abolished in mainland China. Yet they live on in Hong Kong.

According to Nissim, there are about 4,000 t'so and 2,000 t'ong in the New Territories, controlling roughly 6,000 acres of land.[2] In 2018 in the North District alone there were 1,718 registered t'sos and 615 registered t'ongs.[3] The consensus is that between a quarter and a third of New Territories land was held by customary institutions.[4] But the proportion varied from place to place. It also varied over time. In his 1960s study of the Tangs at Ping Shan, Potter found that 93 per cent of their land was ancestral and owned by the clan, whilst in the same era Baker's estimate of the proportion of Liu land around Sheung Shui held for kinship-ritual was 52 per cent.[5]

In recent decades t'so t'ong holdings have been eroded by government resumption of their land for public purposes and by sale of their land, usually to developers. New t'so t'ong are discouraged by the administration and no new t'so t'ong will be registered, yet there is nothing to stop further land being transferred to existing ones. At the Fung Yuen valley a few miles north-east of Taipo, for instance, the amount of t'so t'ong land increased between 1905 and 1978, even while the holdings of individual members of the local clans decreased through sales to outsiders.[6]

At the turn of the twentieth century, the largest subsoil owners, holders of imperial grants, were often t'ong or t'so lineage estates.[7] Since Crown leases were usually awarded to actual occupiers (surface owners), ownership by t'so t'ong recorded in the block leases would not fully reflect the extent of their holdings. The largest subsoil owner on Lantau Island was the Li Kau Yuen T'ong. On Lamma Island it was the Iu Yi Yin T'ong. The rights of both were not recognized, the Land Court favouring cultivators. By contrast, on Cheung Chau the subsoil owner, the Wong Wai Chuk T'ong, was exceptionally granted a Crown lease—the effect of which had to be reversed by legislation ninety years later.[8]

The Home Affairs Department maintains a register of t'so t'ong, their managers and their constitutions at New Territories District Offices. T'so t'ong land is entitled (on application) to exemption from the requirement to pay government rent at 3

1. Palmer, 'Surface-Subsoil', 97, citing Rawski; H. McAleavy, 'Chinese Law in Hong Kong: The Choice of Sources'.
2. Nissim, *Land Administration and Practice in Hong Kong*, Ch 16, p 140. Selby however put the amount as 6,000 hectares: 'Chinese Customary Law'.
3. Information from the District Office, North, October 2018.
4. Hase, *Custom*, Ch 4; Hayes, 'The Great Difference' (article), 158.
5. Potter, *Capitalism and the Chinese Peasant*.
6. Judith Strauch, 'Community and Kinship in Southeastern China: The View from the Multilineage Villages of Hong Kong', (1983) 43 *Journal of Asian Studies* 21.
7. Palmer, 'Surface-Subsoil', 97.
8. Block Crown Lease (Cheung Chau) Ordinance (Cap 488), 8 September 1995.

per cent of rateable value. The justification for this is difficult to discern. T'so T'ong are not charitable in nature but private organizations founded for the benefit of groups of individuals who invest in property to fund institutional operations. Some have very large rental incomes indeed. This may be another instance of indulgence of indigenous interests by the authorities. Land held by these institutions was originally largely used for agriculture but there is no customary restriction upon usage and today the land is often put to more profitable purposes, such as open storage. More prosperous t'so t'ong invest in commercial property.

T'so t'ong have no exact equivalent in the common law, although they contain elements which are familiar to common lawyers. Since they have no existence separate from that of their members, they are not corporations but a form of unincorporated association similar to a club, with a fluctuating body of members.[9] Their theoretically endless continuation means that they are dispositions of property in perpetuity, a type of land settlement which elsewhere (including Hong Kong) as a matter of policy was made illegal, first by the courts and later by legislation, because it ties up the property for ever and prevents its alienation, thus inhibiting its commercial exploitation.

Each member (living male descendant) receives a direct interest in the land which resembles a life estate. The merging of a deceased member's interest into those of the remaining members resembles the right of survivorship characteristic of the common law joint tenancy. Unity of possession, unity of interest and unity of title are also present as with joint tenancy, but not unity of time. The interest of each member vests at birth and ends at death, occasions which will occur at different times for each member. The holding of the member's interest in equal undivided shares is a characteristic of the other major form of co-ownership at common law, the tenancy-in-common.

Attempts to understand or describe t'sos and t'ongs have led to inaccurate labels being applied to them. Historians, sociologists, anthropologists, journalists and civil servants may perhaps be forgiven for use of loose terminology here but lawyers have no excuse. T'sos have often been called corporate, no doubt reflecting the idea that they are long-established bodies which persist beyond the lifetimes of those that compose them and so seem to be a distinct entity. But in law they are not incorporated bodies and have no existence separate from their members for the time being. They are at best quasi-corporate. They have been described as charitable, but they are not because they are private, not public, in nature. Although they may support worthy objects, enjoyment of the benefit of those objects is confined to a segment of a section of the population, certain male members of a lineage within a clan, and does not extend to the general public.[10] Given that their predominant purpose is worship of ancestors, they appear to have a religious connotation but the worshipping is private, not public, and so they are not trusts for the advancement of

9. *Ip Cheung Kwok v Ip Siu Bun* [1988] HKC 437.
10. *Ip Cheung Kwok v Ip Siu Bun*, above; *Yeap Cheah Neo v Ong Chong Neo* (1875) LR 6 PC 381.

religion, a form of charitable trust. Nor are they religious in the sense of worship of a deity. They are nevertheless habitually called trusts but, as will be recounted in the next chapter, they could not have been established or intended by their founders as trusts for the simple reason that neither Chinese custom nor imperial law had such a word or concept. If an English word is required to describe t'so t'ong, a number are available of which endowment and foundation are probably the most serviceable.

T'so

The character for t'so (祖) means the male descendants of the deceased person whose name precedes that character. It also signifies 'ancestor' or 'lineage'. The Cantonese sound for the character is sometimes rendered in English as 'jou', the Mandarin as 'zu'.

A t'so is an organization named after a common male forbear of its members that holds land for communal purposes of a part of a clan, that part (or segment, as anthropologists say) being males directly descended from the forbear, including its founders: in other words, a lineage. Most, but not all, t'sos are of long standing, having been established in the seventeenth or eighteenth centuries or even earlier. Accordingly, the land held by t'sos passes down the generations and is often referred to as ancestral land. Since the t'so is not an entity separate from its members, it consists of its members. Consequently, the members own the t'so land. The members are the currently-living direct male descendants of the nominated ancestor. Their interest is for life: it begins automatically at birth and ends automatically on death. The land, or income from it, is enjoyed by each member until he dies. He cannot pass his interest to others by assignment or will since it is not transferable or heritable. On a member's demise, the interest merges back into the property of the surviving members. The t'so continues despite changes in membership: in principle it is perpetual.[11]

A t'so is usually created after the death of the land-owning forbear by his (male) heirs. In so doing they may be obeying instructions given by the forbear himself during his lifetime.[12] The creators need not be of the generation immediately following that of the landowner: grandsons or even remoter direct kin may found the t'so. One motivation for placing land into a t'so was to avoid the family argument that may accompany division of the property between heirs. A t'so is always named after the common ancestor rather than the founder, with the character for t'so appended. Occasionally a living male person may form a t'so for land which he has acquired.

11. The classic, much cited, definition of a t'so is by Mills-Owens J in *Tang Kai-chung v Tang Chik-shang* [1970] HKLR 276 at 279–280. The definition is expressly general and summary in nature so is not completely accurate.
12. *Li Tang Shi v Li Wai Kwong* [1969] HKLR 367.

Baker, however, thought that the formation of a t'so was always on a posthumous basis by descendants.[13]

The t'so is intended to benefit the clan or lineage by providing money for ancestral worship, maintenance of shrines and graves, and care and education of members of the family, with any surplus income being distributed amongst living members.

The majority of t'so have only modest landholdings and nearly all their income is spent on ancestral matters. Well managed t'sos of larger lineages, however, generate substantial investment income which can provide generous, regular financial support to their members.

The custom is said to be to preserve the t'so land intact and to pass it on to succeeding generations. However, this is more a historical aspiration than a hard rule as it seems quite readily to give way when the immediate financial advantage of the members dictates otherwise.

T'ong

T'ongs (or tohng) have been described judicially as 'essentially in the nature of unincorporated associations composed of individuals and with continuous succession through patrilineal descent from their founding members'.[14] In these respects a t'ong is indistinguishable from a t'so. However, the description t'ong (meaning hall) covers a variety of associations, not necessarily lineage or clan-based, not necessarily owning land and not necessarily operating in the New Territories.

Business t'ongs

New Territories residents formed associations for investment of money to provide themselves with benefits. Accordingly, t'ongs can be business partnerships or co-operatives formed between clansmen or between friends and associates. If formed by clansmen, they are sometimes called wui. If made between friends or associates, they are sometimes called heung.[15]

Members of the wui or heung can be t'so t'ong or individuals. They contribute land or money to buy land to be held by the institution, thereby pooling resources for investment under the custodianship of a manager. Therefore, members can be individual owners of separate pieces of wui land or joint owners of wui land. Members have considerable power in supervising the manager. Such commercial t'ongs have been known to have written internal rules, similar to articles of association. Shares

13. Baker, *Sheung Shui*, p 100.
14. *Secretary for Justice v To Kan Chi* (2000) 3 HKCFAR 481, [2000] 3 HKLRD 756. The mandarin is 'tang'.
15. *Tang Man Kit v Hip Hing Timber Co Ltd* [2003] 4 HKC 278; *Man Ping Nam v Man Mei Kwai*, HCA 9852/1998 (21 May 2002).

(or shek) in the wui are allocated and may be tradeable within the membership or outside it depending upon its constitution.[16]

A t'ong might be formed to rent or buy premises from which to operate a business and thereafter to account for profits.[17] Similarly, a t'ong can be formed in order to raise capital for a project. T'ongs can also be set up to purchase land with contributions from subscribers and build houses for them to live in, the subscribers holding shares or using parts of the land proportionate to their contributions.[18]

Religious t'ongs

A common type of t'ong is the religious foundation: temples, monasteries, nunneries. They were known by a variety of names.[19] In imperial China, land was frequently registered in the name of monasteries and temples and treated as the property of the institution. The same happened to large public temples in the New Territories both before and after 1898.[20] In the case of larger monasteries, their land is held in the name of the monastery.[21] The land is owned by all members of the clergy or sangha of the faith in question. In the case of smaller monasteries in which monks reside as if in a family, ownership lies with the resident clergy. Heads of Buddhist monasteries and Taoist temples were forbidden to sell or charge the institution's land although in some instances this did not prevent the abbot or senior monk from regarding the land as his, perhaps because of his power to nominate a successor. Income from donations, subscriptions, fees and so forth is put towards expenses.

There are, however, different types of temple. Rich laymen, typically members of the same local clan, might own a temple privately. Similarly, wealthy families of different surnames but from the same village might each place land into common ownership of a t'ong so as to endow a temple dedicated to a deity or revered figure such as the Buddha or Tin Hau. Small village temples usually belong to the indigenous inhabitants of that village, through a t'ong of which they are all members.[22] These foundations are not charitable trusts for religious purposes. It is doubtful whether charitable trusts existed in Chinese customary law.[23] Registration of a temple under the Chinese Temples Ordinance does not affect its being in private ownership.[24] Agricultural land owned by temples was normally let to farmers on long or perpetually renewable leases.

---

16. *Man Ping Nam v Man Mei Kwai*, ibid; *Tang Yau Yi Tong v Tang Mou Shau Tso* [1996] 2 HKC 471; *Wah Yan Mo Fan Heung v Hip Hing Timber Co Ltd* [1999] 1 HKC 373.
17. Hase, *Custom*, p 103.
18. As in *Chan Wai Hung, manager of Hop Yi Tong v Chan Oi Fong*, HCA 764/2016 (27 August 2018).
19. Buddhist nunnery: She; Buddhist monastery: Tsi. Other nunneries: Yuen, Un and Siu Chuk.
20. Dicks, 'The Ownership of Buddhist Temples and the Civil Status of the Clergy in China'.
21. Selby, 'Chinese Customary Law', 66.
22. Dicks, above. *Secretary for Justice v To Kan Chi* (2000) 3 HKCFAR 481, [2000] 3 HKLRD 756: there it is mistakenly stated that public monasteries are owned by all the people, rather than all the clergy, of that faith.
23. *To Kan Chi v Pui Man Yau*, CACV 32/1999 (3 February 2000).
24. Cap 153; *To Kan Chi v Pui Man Yau*, ibid.

One of Hong Kong's oldest temples, the Tsing Wan Kun at the Tsing Shan Monastery near Tuen Mun, was the subject of a dispute about ownership at the beginning of the century. The temple had been granted the land on which it stood and some surrounding lots by block Crown lease in 1905. The current abbot claimed ownership on the basis that a predecessor priest of the temple had purchased some of the land. The To clan from nearby villages, which had appointed the abbot, also claimed ownership. The Secretary for Justice joined the contest, asserting that as the monastery was registered under the Chinese Temples Ordinance, it was a charitable trust of the religious sort for the benefit of the public. The temple's assets were found by the courts to be in the private ownership of the Tos and not to be a charitable trust. Registration under the ordinance, which is concerned with control not status, did not turn the monastery into a charity.[25]

Social and educational t'ongs

People from the same native place may establish social fraternities as t'ongs. Similarly, a group of like-minded scholars might set up scholastic societies. Associations founded to finance educational prizes may also take the form of a t'ong.

Community t'ongs

An entire village could be owned by a tong in which all registered resident householders are members and are expected to perform various duties.[26] T'ongs of a municipal sort were formed for purposes of common defence of villages, purchasing weapons, recruiting volunteer fighters (braves) and building walls and gates. A less belligerent community use was the provision of facilities, such as meeting halls and schools, within a village. These areas would be colloquially referred to as belonging to Ah Kung, the founder of the village. The latter might not hold land, its activities being funded by fees and subscriptions with all heads of household as members and the village head as manager.[27] The community might also endow a hospital, with land for its site or funding put into a t'ong by donors.[28]

A t'ong could in addition be used to receive donations intended for some specific scheme or worthy purpose, such as the provision of graves or the meeting of the costs of emigration to the 'gold mountains' of California and Australia. Contributions would be used to buy land as an investment with a steady income.

25. *Secretary for Justice v To Kan Chi*, above; the Chinese Temples Ordinance (Cap 153).
26. *Tang Poon Lap v Tang Kam Kai*, CACV 99/2004 (1 September 2005).
27. Selby, 'Chinese Customary Law', 59; Hase, *Custom*, p 103.
28. This occurred at Kowloon City, Cheung Chau and Yuen Long.

How many types?

It was this variety no doubt which led the Hong Kong legislature to use the Cantonese collective term 't'ong' in its law concerning land in the New Territories. There was no term in English that adequately covered the variety of t'ongs that exist, although perhaps 'foundations' comes closest. By contrast, t'sos were referred to as families or clans.[29] This nomenclature is not exactly accurate for members of a t'so rarely comprise all members of a clan or even a family. They do, however, come from one clan and have a common surname. All types of t'ong are the subject of the regulatory provisions in Part II of the New Territories Ordinance, provided that they hold land in the territory.

The range of purposes served by t'ongs has led one historian to categorize them as comprising different types of trust. So, it is said, there are family, commercial, communal, charitable and ancestral trusts.[30] However, this is misleading because the majority of t'ongs were founded to serve more than one purpose. Indeed, commercial and communal t'ongs were a minority and truly charitable ones were unusual. Similarly, a suggestion by Hayes that there are four types of t'ong is inaccurate.[31] In truth, the variety is as wide as the worthy causes that could be thought of in the agricultural society in which t'ongs arose.

Purposes of t'ongs

Most New Territories family t'ongs have been created by a land owner during his lifetime to ensure that land is held by his descendants for the collective benefit of its (all male) members. The founder's intention is usually to keep the land intact so that all his descendants benefit, thereby avoiding arguments about division of the land and ensuring that funds are available for t'ong purposes. As with t'so, the purposes of family t'ongs include ancestral worship (rituals and graves), maintenance of the family temple or ancestral hall (*tsz t'ong*) and education of members, but extend also to support for the welfare, health, social activities and businesses of members. Thus a t'ong has greater responsibilities than a t'so. Even so, it is not a charity. Where investments by managers of a t'ong have been astute, the material benefits distributed to members can be valuable despite the tendency of members to increase in number over time.

A t'ong, unlike a t'so, usually builds a hall to house ancestral tablets, hold rituals and conduct meetings. A hall is not, however, essential, nor is a lineage restricted to one hall. Many t'ongs, especially in smaller villages, confine themselves to a hall and an occasional feast. Only a small amount of land is needed to pay for such activities.

---

29. New Territories Ordinance (Cap 97) s 15.
30. Hase, *Custom*, p 99.
31. *Tang Yau Yi Tong v Tang Mou Shau Tso* [1995] 2 HKC 245; Lockhart in *Report on the New Territory for the Year 1900*, Hong Kong Sessional Papers No 28/1901, suggested there were four major categories of t'ong.

A t'ong does not necessarily use the formal name of the ancestor or family: for example, it may use a lucky or auspicious name or an alias. This assists in avoiding charges of self-glorification. An example is the Liu Man Shek T'ong, the possessor of one of the most impressive (and much renovated for the delectation of visitors) ancestral halls in Hong Kong, to be found in the centre of old Sheung Shui. The name of the t'ong's focal ancestor is Liu Chung Kit.

A t'ong does not need to use 'Tong' in its name. T'ongs which are not of the family type commonly do not. Even family t'ongs do not. For example, yuen (literally a garden) is the style used for family t'ong in the Taipo district.[32]

Common Features of T'so and T'ong

The shared attributes of t'so and family t'ong have led to the distinction between them becoming blurred and to their being referred to collectively and colloquially as t'so t'ong. In both: the land is held by all members for the common benefit of the lineage; members are direct agnatic descendants of a common male ancestor; members have only a life interest with no rights of succession; the land is supposedly inalienable and indivisible, so is to be preserved intact for the benefit of ancestors, living members and future generations; the institution is perpetual and, once established, the founders may not revoke their decision. Their land is sometimes referred to collectively as ancestral or lineage estates.

The institutions derive income from rent and, occasionally, sale of their property as well as other investments. Originally, the land was almost entirely put to agricultural use. It would be let to a farmer who might well be a member of the t'so t'ong. A common practice was for each *fong* (branch of the family, or household) among the clan to take turns to use the land and to pay communal expenses from the income derived. In recent times the land has been let for higher-yielding commercial or industrial purposes. Nevertheless, t'so t'ong are not intended to be profit-making enterprises. Income would be spent or distributed. Risky investments would be avoided, for these would jeopardize the patrimony.[33]

Both types of lineage group were important to social stability during the Ching period. Central government was then weak and remote so customary institutions instead provided local authority. Lineage leaders made decisions, enforced custom and settled disputes. This partially explains why so many t'so t'ong, owning so much land, were to be found in San On. Inevitably, incorporation into Hong Kong weakened the prestige and influence of the institutions and their leaders. Order thereafter rested more upon the District Office, the police and the courts.[34] Economic opportunities expanded, social attitudes changed, the numbers and composition of the New Territories population expanded. A long decline in the significance of

32. *Chu Tak Hing v Chu Chan Cheung Kiu* [1968] HKLR 542.
33. Palmer, 'Surface-Subsoil', 78–80.
34. Freedman, 'Shifts of Power in the Hong Kong New Territories', Ch 11 in *The Study of Chinese Society*.

these customary bodies began, yet they played a part in rural life throughout the twentieth century.

A less endearing feature common to t'sos and family t'ongs is that they are apt to be riven by dissent and argument. This is understandable given that their membership is composed of men of indigenous background with their inclination to disputation and given that the membership lacks the moderating influence of women. The potential for disputation is increased by the institutions being predominantly concerned nowadays with two things which are said to drive men mad, land and money. Members are more concerned with furthering their individual financial interests than with maintaining the cohesion of the extended family. The amount of litigation concerning t'so t'ong land, and the issues raised there, suggests this. That the members are related does not seem to make a difference, for the ancestral bond is now weak.

The conduct of the internal affairs of a t'so t'ong is in theory a matter for the membership. Customs and practices will have evolved over decades and centuries and in accordance with the size and wealth of the institution. Larger organizations might have more defined rules, which might be written down (for instance in family annals), on such matters as the collection and investment of income and the keeping of accounts, the election and dismissal of managers and the alienation of land.[35] Occasionally the institution might have become a registered company with articles of association.[36]

Ancestor worship

The over-arching purpose of t'sos and family t'ongs was what has come to be known as ancestor worship. This is the commemoration and veneration of past generations, in particular the male forbear at the apex of the lineage. In the case of a t'ong, he is the founder who first placed land into the t'ong. In the case of a t'so, he is the ancestor who first accumulated land which was later put into the t'so by his descendants.

The cult of the ancestor has been described as the 'spiritual representation of the kinship tie', a ritual vehicle of communication between living and dead members of the lineage and a symbol of its unity.[37] This involves procession to, and devotion and offerings such as fruit and flowers at, the graves or urns of past generations at festivals such as Ching Ming, cleaning and tending to those graves, a communal feast afterwards, the placing of the name of the ancestor on tablets at a shrine in the village temple (the tablets were formerly wooden but now are paper), the performance of rites and worship at a shrine with paper tablets inside the home.

The expenses of these activities and the upkeep of the temple are provided by the land and other assets of the t'so t'ong. Regular income may be augmented by

35. Hase, *Custom*, p 78.
36. Selby, 'Chinese Customary Law', 55 and 63–64.
37. Baker, *Sheung Shui*, p 61.

donations from lineage members. Poorer bodies have to limit those members who may attend the feast and the range of foods provided there.[38]

Formation of T'so T'ong

Founding an endowment

Most t'so t'ong were endowed before the time that the New Territories came into existence. A segment of kin would set aside land as a t'so for veneration of their ancestor, to ensure that his name did not fade away or his grave decay. The traditional method of formation was to draw up an agreement between fongs to establish the endowment and to report to the county magistrate pursuant to an imperial decree which permitted this, with a request that the land should be held by the institution. The land would then be entered at the imperial registry in the name of the institution. In the New Territories this was replaced by grant and registration: those t'so t'ong which were in possession at the time of the survey were granted the land by Crown lease, followed by registration at the land registry as owner and registration of managers with the District Office; those created after 1905 were founded by registration of the t'so t'ong by heirs or owners following demonstration to the Land Officer of intent to set up the foundation and appointment, approval, and registration of managers.[39]

Where a t'ong was established by the man after whom it was to be named rather than his heirs, the dedication of the land to the t'ong had to be carried out during his lifetime (inter vivos) rather than by will which would take effect after death. This is because customary law did not recognize wills.[40] Likewise, a t'so could not be set up under the wills of descendants. So where a father who owned land in 1939 wrote a 'division of property' between the fongs (families) of his four sons, directing that one son was to collect rent and use the proceeds for ancestor worship, that was not an effective foundation of a t'so t'ong.[41] His heirs however might have executed his wishes by placing all the land into a t'so named after him with rules that followed his directions.

Revoking the endowment

Once the founder had done all in his power that was necessary to put the t'so t'ong in place, he could not revoke the endowment. This emerged from the saga of Mr

38. Baker, *Sheung Shui*, p 115.
39. Evidence of Professor Cheng and Anthony Dicks SC in *Tang Tak Sum v Tang Kai Fong* [2015] 1 HKLRD 286.
40. *Lau Leng Chau v Lau Yuk Kai* (2000) 3 HKCFAR 98; in *Tang Tak Sum v Tang Kai Fong*, ibid, evidence that it was acceptable in custom if arrangements for the foundation and the appointment of managers had been made during the founder's lifetime to take effect following his death came too late to be admitted.
41. *Tang Tak Sum v Tang Kai Fong*, ibid.

Chu Tak Hing.[42] During his lifetime Mr Chu, late of Taipo, liked land and women. As a young man he began work as a lowly clerk at the lands section of the Taipo District Office. He ended his career there in 1941 as chief clerk. In between, he somehow amassed a considerable estate despite his modest salary. He would not purchase land under his own name but under three others: Chu Tak Yam Tong, Chu Nam Yuen and Chu Wai Chi. The purchase deeds conveyed the land to one of those names with a friend or relative as the *sze lei* (manager or trustee) and the land was registered as such. After retirement he purchased further property which was conveyed to Chu Tak Yam Tong.

Mr Chu's personal life was typical of that of a rich Chinese man in former times. Originally and no doubt before he acquired impressive land holdings, he had a wife and a son by her but they both died. Later he had a tin fong (replacement wife) who bore him a son. Then he acquired a secondary wife or concubine. She too bore him a son. In 1949, after acquisition of most of the property, he formed a relationship with a second concubine. She became his favourite and they had three sons. He bought her a home and supported her living but it seems this was not enough. Around 1960 he had a change of heart about the settlements he had made earlier. He claimed that all the land was his own and that in fact the three names to whom the land had been conveyed were each his alias. This claim was not popular with the rest of his family, including his eldest surviving son (born of the first concubine) and the widow of his older son (born to the tin fong) whom earlier had been helping him to manage his property.

Mr Chu tried to persuade the District Officer to allow him to sell some of the property. He made a statutory declaration that the names were his aliases. The District Officer refused. Mr Chu pressed his eldest son to write to the District Office asking to be removed as a manager and declaring that the land was his father's alone. The son at first resisted but later signed such a letter as an act of filial duty. The District Officer was unmoved. Mr Chu persisted in trying to regain control of the land until he died in 1964. His executors took up the struggle, arguing that the land belonged either to Mr Chu personally or to t'ongs of which he was the sole beneficiary and so was part of his estate to be distributed in accordance with his will under which the second concubine and her children would benefit. The children of his earlier wives said that the land had been put into family t'ongs for the benefit of his male descendants in accordance with Chinese law and custom.

The judge, Mr Justice Scholes, had no difficulty in deciding that Mr Chu had intended to form traditional t'ongs to hold the land. He had put that intention into effect by having the properties conveyed to the relevant t'ongs with managers, by having the conveyances and the managers registered at the District Office, Taipo and by lodging a list of members with that office. The three names that Mr Chu had used were not his aliases, the judge found, nor were they his private t'ongs. Mr

42. *Chu Tak Hing v Chu Chan Cheung Kiu*, above.

Chu had used the procedure under what became section 15 of the New Territories Ordinance to set up t'ongs to benefit his male descendants. The evidence showed that before his change of mind Mr Chu had kept books listing the properties and the beneficiaries and declaring the importance of land and lineage.

The claim that the t'ongs were private was effectively sunk by the evidence from one of Mr Chu's former colleagues, a Mr Cheung, clerk in charge of the Land Office in Taipo. Mr Cheung was adamant that land registered in the name of a t'ong belongs to the t'ong. Mr Cheung had never heard of a private t'ong; no such thing would be registered. So long as the t'ong was mentioned in the title deeds and managers were mentioned afterwards (presumably in the registration), it would be considered an organization. There was no need to use 't'ong' in the name, Mr Cheung explained, many t'ongs set up around Taipo before the war had used '*yuen*' instead.

But could Mr Chu dis-establish the t'ongs and retake the land? He evidently had wished to do so and the land had after all been his. Mr Cheung said no: a man who settles property in a t'ong name, appoints managers for it and supplies lists of its members cannot afterwards claim that the land is his. But it is unclear whether Mr Cheung was relating the customary position or simply the attitude of the registry. Rather than invoke custom, the judge relied upon the law of trusts, apparently unconcerned at the incongruity of applying modern English law to an ancient Chinese institution. There he found authority that a settlement is binding upon the settlor of a trust once he has done everything necessary to transfer the property into the trust and render the settlement binding upon him.[43] Mr Chu had undoubtedly done so.

There was no evidence before Scholes J as to the customary attitude towards attempts by the founders of a t'so t'ong to undo their work. The three t'ongs established by Mr Chu had been running for upwards of twenty years before he changed his mind. Presumably during that time rental income had accrued and been used to support his male offspring and three living wives. It seems doubtful that any system of law would permit that arrangement to be unwound. However, it would not be surprising to find that where the founder had also been the sole owner of the settled land, was still alive, was in pressing need and all his male lineage descendants agreed, custom would allow the t'so t'ong to be wound back. The customary law had a similarly nuanced attitude towards sales of both family and individually-owned land.

Motives of Founders

What would have impelled landowners to place their land into a t'so or a t'ong? When the founder was also the sole owner, the main motive must have been to avoid the consequences of the application of the customary law of succession to

43. *Milroy v Lord* [1861–73] AER 783; *Re Rose* [1952] 1 All ER 1217.

property. This required that the land be divided between the owner's sons after his death. If the owner wished his land to remain intact, he would convert it into t'ong land during his lifetime. In consequence, the land could be enjoyed communally by his sons and, through them, their wives and mothers and the founder's unmarried daughters too. This promoted family cohesion, avoiding the arguments that might erupt over the division of the land. It also made economic sense in that a larger piece of land could be cultivated more efficiently than several smaller plots. Even if an initial division of the land would have resulted in viable farming, continued sub-division, for generation after generation, would eventually make farming uneconomic. So turning the land to communal use increased the chances that future generations would continue to farm and live on the land. It also increased the likelihood that there would be funds available for veneration of the founder's name after death and for the upkeep of his grave, thus ensuring him a kind of immortality.

In the case of a t'so, the founders were usually male descendants of later generations. They wished to mark the achievements of their forbear and show their gratitude to him in an act of filial piety. That is why they would have used his name in the title of the t'so. But they also would have wanted to avoid any dissent and economic detriment arising from division of the land.[44]

Membership

Birthright

In customary practice, membership of t'so t'ong of the lineage variety is confined to males in the direct line of male descent from the focal ancestor.[45] The land devolves upon a new-born member automatically. In principle therefore members cannot be expelled. Birth of males is traditionally marked in annual ceremonies: at new year, the Hakka sacrifice a pig, the Punti raise a red lantern (dim dang) in front of the main altar of their temple to introduce the new member to his ancestors. His name is noted by the clan's secretary or recorder. Upon registration as manager, a new manager provides a list of members to the District Office which endeavours to check its accuracy. Adoption is the one exception to qualification by birth for membership of lineage institutions. An adopted son could be a member.[46]

Membership is a lifetime privilege which ends automatically upon death. Following decease of a member his name would be deleted from the record by the secretary.[47]

44. Selby, 'Chinese Customary Law', 58.
45. *Tang Yau Yi Tong v Tang Mou Shau Tso* [1996] 2 HKC 471.
46. *Tsang Ka Fai v Tsang Wan Kiu*, HCA 1769/2006 (22 January 2014).
47. *Leung Kuen Fai v Tang Kwong Yu T'ong* [2002] 2 HKLRD 705, 722 F-H.

Proof of entitlement

In the case of community and other non-familial t'ongs membership is not confined to those of a single lineage or even a single surname. When, following receipt of a large amount of resumption compensation, managers of a t'ong at a village near Tuen Mun ceased (on the instructions of members) to make money distributions to long-settled villagers who did not have the surname (To) of the great majority of its members, a resident surnamed Tang successfully sued for payment. In deciding that the claimant was a member of the t'ong, the judge took into account past lists of members submitted to the District Office by new managers and the testimony of senior members of the t'ong. He considered the contributions of the claimant to village activities in money, labour and kind over many years and past practice with regard to ceremonies, distributions and attendance at feasts. He found that lanterns had been raised in the village temple at lunar new year for the births of those of three different surnames, including Tang, and that pork, fruit and sugar payments and invitations to clay-pot feasts (pun choi) had been similarly made. So, despite the contentions of the managers that the t'ong had been founded by the To clan who had provided the property which funded its activities, the claimant was found to be a member.[48] A similar examination of the evidence was carried out in cases where the identity of a claimant to membership was in issue.[49]

Different t'so t'ong can have the same membership whilst maintaining separate identities. Their identity derives from the land, so if the land of one institution differs from that of another, they are distinct entities despite their membership being the same. They will prepare separate accounts and may have different managers.

A man may be a member of a number of different t'sos or t'ongs, so long as he is in the male line of descent from the focal ancestor of each of them. Dr Hugh Baker gave the example of his next-door neighbour at Sheung Shui who was of the eighteenth generation of a lineage and a member of seven different t'so t'ong, each focused upon an ancestor of various prior generations.

Women's entitlements

The purpose of t'sos and family t'ongs is to provide for members of the family, past, present and future, including women. A wife has the same interest as her husband. A widow can receive her deceased husband's share as maintenance.[50] Unmarried daughters also have some rights of support.[51] A married daughter who takes care of an elderly parent is given preferential treatment by the t'so.

48. *Tang Siu For v Tao Chi Shing*, HCA 2336/2004 (29 January 2007).
49. *Tang Poon Lap v Tang Kam Kai*, CACV 99/2004 (1 September 2005); *Hau Poon Sek v Hau Chi Kin*, HCA 2168/2004 (20 February 2009); *Tang Chi Chung (a Minor) by Tang Chai On v Tang Sun Yip*, CACV 48/2015 (28 August 2015).
50. *Tang Choy Hong v Tang Shing Mo* (1949) 33 HKLR 58.
51. Evidence of Professor Chan Weijen in *Mak Lai Chuen v Lau Kar Yau* [2009] 3 HKC 217, 222.

There was one type of t'so in which a widow had a special position, that formed after the death of, and named after, her husband without a son to hold the husband's property. Pending the adoption of an heir, the widow controlled the property. The extent to which a widow might spend the income from the t'so is a matter of disagreement between experts. She has a right to maintenance from and to manage the land. Certainly she is entitled to take sufficient to maintain her established livelihood. Whether she may go further and buy luxuries, live lavishly and even sell the property is unclear. One view is that she must not, for that would dissipate the patrimony to be passed to the sons; all she may do is to manage the estate and maintain herself from it, no more, pending adoption of an heir. Another view is that she is in effect the owner with complete control of the property and income until she dies or adopts a son and therefore may do with it what she likes until then.[52]

After appointing an heir, the widow might transfer part of the property to the heir whilst keeping some to fund her maintenance. Alternatively, she could make the whole property over to the heir who would then have to provide for her maintenance.

Although women may not be members, it seems that in certain institutions at least they may be managers, if only temporary ones. Moreover, practice may be changing. Females born or married into the institution may benefit to the extent decided by the membership, so although not admitted as members, wives and widows may receive a share of annual and special payments to members in certain t'so t'ong.

Who benefits?

Despite one of the aims of customary family institutions being the relief of poverty, it is not necessarily the poorer members who benefit more than the richer from the income generated by the land of t'so t'ong. On the contrary, elders and managers, who almost inevitably are drawn from the wealthier members, are in a position to exploit for gain the influence which their status gives them.

Members have a proprietary interest in their t'so t'ong's land. In customary law they were joint owners. Under the law of trusts, they are beneficiaries with equitable interests. Their interest is sufficient to allow them to sue individually.[53]

As generations go by, the links between members inevitably weaken as they grow more distant. Each male descendant has his own fong (room or apartment) of the extended family. Within each fong may be smaller families (ka) and then households (wu).[54] Antagonism between branches and families can often arise, especially disputes about money and benefits.

52. These contrasting views were given by the experts in *Tang Choy Hong v Tang Shing Mo*, above. Gibson CJ found it unnecessary to decide the point.
53. *Man Ping Nam v Man Mei Kwai*, HCA 9852/1998 (1 February 2002).
54. Hakka did not use the terms ka and wu but they did use ting, meaning male individual.

Managers

Neither t'ong nor t'so being legal entities, they are what lawyers refer to as unincorporated associations. Consequently, they must act through authorized individuals. By custom t'ong and t'so had managers or sze lei, appointed by the members, to represent them. The nomenclature is interchangeable and indiscriminate: manager, sze lei and trustee are synonymous.[55]

Section 15 of the New Territories Ordinance formalized this practice by requiring that a manager be appointed. Despite the section's use of the singular, usually there was more than one manager. It has been suggested that a t'ong can act only through managers registered under section 15, but insofar as this implies that an unregistered manager is not a valid manager it is incorrect. An unregistered manager may be engaged by the membership to run the affairs of their organization and to represent them. Accordingly, he may be appointed to represent them in litigation. What he lacks is the right to dispose of and deal in the organization's property as if he were the sole owner, for this power is given by the statute to registered managers only.[56]

Managers are appointed by the members, not by the government, but the appointment must be notified and proved to, and approved by, the District Office (Home Affairs Department) which then registers the manager pursuant to section 15. The appointment is a matter of the body's internal practice so it is not open to outsiders to challenge the appointment.[57]

The office of manager is often filled by more worldly members. Managers are not paid a salary but members often allow them 'shoe money' and opportunities for profit frequently arise in larger institutions. Purchasers of t'so t'ong land apparently are expected to pay managers a signing fee or 'tea money' or to contribute to a 'family fund'. Poorer and less-informed villagers may be unaware of the manipulation that goes on even though they hold shares in the land.[58]

The appointment of the manager can be by the majority of members rather than unanimously and is often by consensus among clan elders. The one legal requirement is that the process of appointment must be fair.[59] A manager is usually a senior male member of the t'so t'ong but there have been instances of a deceased manager's widow succeeding him. For example, the widow of the founder who died without issue is commonly recognized as the temporary manager pending the naming of an heir, as illustrated by a case from Sai Kung. The facts in a case concerning a t'so in

55. Liu JA in *Tang Yau Yi Tong v Tang Mou Shau Tso* [1996] 2 HKC 471; *Li Tang Shi v Li Wai Kwong* [1969] HKLR 367.
56. *Ip Cheung Kwok v Ip Siu Bun* [1988] HKC 347; *Shenzhen Luohu Runan Industrial Ltd Co v Un Yau Kung Tso*, HCMP 2320/2000 (17 December 2001).
57. *Tang Man Kit v Hip Hing Timber Co Ltd* [2003] 4 HKC 278.
58. H. G. H. Nelson, Review of *Capitalism and the Chinese Peasant*, (1968) VII *Journal of the Hong Kong Branch of the Royal Asiatic Society*.
59. *To Kin Wah v Tuen Mun District Officer (No 2)* [2003] 4 HKC 213.

Kam Tin reveal that its manager from 1950 to 1978 had been a Madam Chung. The defendant t'so in another case was represented by a female manager.[60]

A manager as an agent if not a trustee owes fiduciary duties to the members. Accordingly in his management of the t'so t'ong a manager must use the due diligence and reasonable care which the ordinary prudent man of business would exercise, he must act honestly and reasonably and he must pay equitable compensation for breach of duty.[61] He must tender accounts and documents, such as tenancy agreements and receipts. He must not make a profit from the office he holds.

Managers must act jointly and unanimously: it has been so held on the basis that a manager is a trustee.[62] Anyway, customary law requires unanimity, or at least absence of disagreement, since each manager represents a different branch of the clan. Unanimity requires that all managers consent, not that all sign the document creating the transaction.[63]

Traditionally a manager would be appointed for life or until retirement, although more recently some t'so t'ong have stipulated a term of office. A manager's appointment terminates when he dies. There is no need for the appointment to be 'cancelled' following the death.[64]

Upon the death of one manager the surviving manager(s) does not become the sole manager and has no authority to act alone; a replacement must be appointed, or a decision not to replace the deceased made, at a properly convened meeting of the family.[65] Perhaps such a decision can be inferred from failure to appoint a replacement for a deceased manager over many years. A vacancy might be left open if the member who is next in line for appointment is thought unsuited to the role.[66] The demise of a manager, and disagreement about his replacement, can paralyse a t'so t'ong.

Managers are responsible for the day-to-day administration of the t'so t'ongs land and affairs. Larger institutions sometimes appoint management committees, the more junior members of which act as assistants to help the managers with routine tasks such as rent collection and book-keeping.[67]

---

60. Respectively: *Li Tang Shi v Li Wai Kwong* [1969] HKLR 367; *Pang Lai Yung v Wong Hoi Lam*, HCMP 1742/2004 (9 January 2008); *Brisilver Investment Ltd v Wong Fat Tso*, HCMP 2038/1997 (18 July 2000).
61. *Man Fong Hang v Man Ping Nam*, HCA 7935/1998 (11 December 2003); [2005] 1 HKC 535 (CA); undisturbed on further appeal (2006) 9 HKCFAR 674.
62. *Tang Kam Wah v Tang Ming Yat*, HCA 10141/1998 (26 November 2002).
63. *So Kee Transportation Co Ltd v Secretary for Environment, Land and Works*, CACV 363/2005 (12 October 2006).
64. *Chan Choy Fong v Secretary for Home Affairs* [1998] HKLR 431, [1997] 4 HKC 122.
65. *Mak Lai Chuen v Lau Kar Yau* [2009] 3 HKC 217.
66. Selby, 'Chinese Customary Law', p 60.
67. Ng Wing Kit, 'Statutory and Judicial Control over Managers (Sze Lei) of Tso Tong' (2015), unpublished research thesis, Faculty of Law, University of Hong Kong.

Division and Sale of T'so T'ong Land

Although the land is in principle inalienable and must be preserved, it may be sold if all current members consent and, where not held for ancestor worship, if only a majority consent.[68] Sale of communal ancestral property took place in traditional China in cases of necessity if unanimous consent of members was obtained. By the beginning of the twentieth century the prohibition on the sale of ancestral property had only moral force in China.

Furthermore, local custom might allow the sale if the heads of all fong acted together in the alienation or if a general meeting of the lineage or clan decided upon it or if the alienation was carried out and subsequently ratified by them as a whole.[69] However, the head of only one of several fong cannot validly sell ancestral land. The heads of all fong must agree or the land must have been divided and distributed to the individual fong before a sale by one can be effective.[70]

Despite their statutory power to dispose of t'so t'ong property as if they were its sole owners, in customary practice managers may not dispose of the lineage's property against the wishes of the members.[71] Yet in the Lai Chi Kok case, the manager apparently did just that without condemnation by the court.

Division of ancestral land is not contrary to Chinese law and custom.[72] Division is often a prelude to sale of parts of the land. Although it has been suggested judicially that the Partition Ordinance, which empowers the court to divide jointly-owned land (or the proceeds of its sale) between its co-owners, does not apply to t'so land, the ordinance is general law containing no exception for customary land. The suggestion, based upon sentiments outdated even when it was made, was not necessary to the decision since the ordinance had not then been brought into force. So the suggestion is not binding and it may be possible to achieve a division by an application and order under the Partition Ordinance under which the court has discretion whether to allow partition. One of the factors to be considered by the court is the attitude of the membership, so if the moral imperative to retain the land intact motivates sufficient numbers of them or if one fong opposes the proposed division, custom may prevail. Where the t'so t'ong is merely a shareholder in the land and not its sole owner, the customary restraint upon partition does not apply to the other owners.[73]

Consent to division or sale from the Home Affairs Department (District Office) is also required by virtue of section 15 of the New Territories Ordinance. Since

68. *Man Ping Nam v Man Tim Lup* [2011] 1 HKLRD 427.
69. Judgment of the Supreme Court of Nanking in 1928 cited by Anthony Dicks SC in evidence in *Kan v Kan*, above.
70. *Tang Woung Shiu v Tang Kun Yeung* [2003] 1 HKC 195.
71. Ibid.
72. *Beautiglory Investment Ltd v Tang Yet Tai Tong* [1993] 2 HKC 591.
73. *Tang Kai-chung v Tang Chik-shang* [1970] HKLR 276 (decided shortly before the Partition Ordinance became law); *Brisilver Investment Ltd v Wong Fat Tso* [1999] 3 HKC 567; *Beautiglory Investment Ltd v Tang Yet Tai Tong*, ibid.

many clan members live abroad and may be untraceable, the department's practice is to require consent of a certain percentage of members, varying between 50 and 80 per cent according to the district involved, before it will proceed to consider an application for consent. In reality it seems that the land can be alienated if the rewards are attractive enough to the members and they can make out a plausible reason for needing the proceeds of sale.

Resumption Compensation

The need for buildings to accommodate the expansion of Hong Kong's population and economy in the second half of the last century meant that institutional as well as private land had to be taken by the government for the construction of new towns and a variety of public projects. Although members might complain that t'so t'ong land was inalienable, they were given no choice for the government's statutory powers overrode customary principles. Sale was compulsory, whatever promises might have been made at the time of the Second Convention of Peking.

The compensation was on the whole generous, however. The government paid owners more than the market price for agricultural land, which is what most of it was. The offer included a discretionary ex gratia element, meant as a sweetener to keep rustic mouths closed.

When it came to sale of ancestral estates, however, there was a complication. The land belonged to the members jointly, as individuals. How were the proceeds to be divided between them? There was no customary answer because this question had not arisen in the past. The New Territories Ordinance was silent on the point. Its direction that managers were to have powers as if they were sole owners was sufficient to enable them to receive the compensation on behalf of the members but did not empower them to divide and distribute the proceeds.

In theory, all members should agree upon a solution, to be negotiated between them and brokered by the elders. Once discussion starts, however, questions arise. Not all families and households are equal in size. Those whose fong have modest numbers will want an equal division between fong. Those from the more populous fong prefer an equal division between individual members. Which is it to be? The inequalities that can arise after many generations are illustrated by one dispute over division of compensation. Originally there had been six sons, each heading a *fong*. However, one *fong* had become extinct. Of the others, one had just five members, three had between five and twenty-two members and the remainder had 151 members. Naturally, members of the last were arguing for equal distribution between all members.[74]

74. *Tang Che Tai v Tang On Kwai* [2008] 3 HKC 521.

Distribution of Proceeds

Compensation in principle should be handled in the same manner as other income such as rental. But there is no uniformity between different t'sos and t'ongs as to how income and assets should be dealt with and anyway the compensation is a large lump sum, not a relatively modest periodic payment like rent.[75] Even after some of the money has been set aside to meet regular future expenses, there will be a healthy surplus and surpluses were traditionally distributed to members in cash or kind. Distribution of income is a matter for the lineage group, not the District Officer.[76] Once the expenses of ancestor worship have been met, income is spent on other purposes of the t'so t'ong. These include payments to members ('pork money' and 'relief of poverty money' or pai-ji) and can be considerable in lineages of richer clans. Most t'so t'ongs' landholdings are small, however, and their income is entirely taken up with ancestral expenditure. Payouts to members occur only if land is sold or resumed.

There is no customary requirement that surpluses be distributed. Members can decide on the use of surplus income generated from t'so property because customary law did not forbid this and if unanimous consent is given by members, there will be no one to object.[77] But in making their decision and any distribution consequent upon their decision, they must conform with the requirements of Chinese law and custom since a t'so t'ong is a customary institution. This requires unanimity 'in some form'.[78] The membership was usually agreed that the bonanza should be shared between them rather than saved or invested. What they could not agree upon was the basis upon which everyone's share should be calculated.

There is plenty of scope for dissension about distribution of the lump sum from resumption. Since sale was not contemplated by the founders or subsequent members, there will rarely be any pre-agreed rule about division of the proceeds. In recent decades most litigation concerning t'so t'ong has arisen directly or indirectly from internal disputes as to whether such surpluses are to be distributed equally to each member (per capita) or to each family or fong comprising the membership (per stirpes). Another possibility would be distribution according to household. Customary law has no answer because in traditional China sales of ancestral land were not supposed to take place and government compensation upon forfeiture of land was unknown. The only occasions upon which land was compulsory taken back was when the landholder committed treason or rebellion. So unless the disputants can reach a compromise, the money remains in a bank account or with the government.

75. Selby, 'Chinese Customary Law', p 68.
76. *Tang Choy Hong v Tang Shing Mo* (1949) 33 HKLR 58, 62.
77. *Tang Che Tai v Tang On Kwai*, above.
78. *Secretary for Justice v To Kan Chi* (2000) 3 HKCFAR 481, 493.

Per Capita or Per Stirpes?

The arguments in favour of distribution per stirpes are that this is the custom for inheritance and was the initial method used by the founders of the t'so t'ong, shares in the land being divided equally between sons irrespective of the size of their respective families. A distribution per capita is said to be arbitrary since the number of shares varies according to the time of distribution and to be unfair on younger sons who at that time are likely to have fewer descendants than older sons. The arguments for per capita distribution are that the purpose of removing land from the family and putting it under a t'so t'ong was to prevent per stirpes division and allow all the male descendants to benefit, that inheritance rules are irrelevant to distributions of income, that money distributions are usually to each member not each fong and that treating each member as an equal is less divisive, more 'democratic' and more in tune with the times. There is also the reality that since each member has to agree to a distribution, in exchange for his consent he can reasonably expect to be treated in the same way as every other member.

Judicial reflections upon the mode of distribution, beyond saying that it is a matter for the membership, are strictly irrelevant but as far as they go, they show a preference for per stirpes distribution. In his lengthy judgment in the struggle between factions of the Tangs of Ping Shan about partition of their t'so's land during the late 1960s, Mills-Owens J was told by the witnesses that the traditional method of division was per stirpes. Having recorded that the decision to sell t'so land and share the proceeds amongst members was controlled by the clan in family meeting, he reflected that distribution on a per capita basis was an innovation, the product of a bargaining process at the meeting during deliberations over whether to agree to the sale rather than of custom.

But why should the fact that distribution per capita was agreed at a meeting and was the result of negotiation preclude that mode from being an emerging custom? The judge seemed to assume that custom is ancient, immutable, and fossilized rather than alive and adaptable. The essence of custom is its flexibility and ability to respond to changing circumstances. The opportunity for the lineage to adopt the per capita mode itself arose from a custom which had emerged in China during the late Ching and been followed in the New Territories, namely the rule that the decision to sell clan land must be unanimous.

Mills-Owens J stopped short of expressing an opinion about which method of distribution was in line with custom. An evaluation of relevant considerations and what might have been the customary attitude was however given in the dispute between the Kan brothers of Tsung Pak Long village. There, in a similarly long and wide-ranging judgment, Deputy Judge Tang said:

> *Per stirpes* division in China, as I understand it, provides for equal division amongst the sons of the relevant direct ascendant. Given a desire to achieve equality amongst the sons, I believe that to be the only fair method of distribution. A division *per*

> *capita* such that each male descendant living at the time of the distribution, regardless of generation, should have an equal share, would not be fair to the younger sons, who are likely to have less [*sic*] descendants on death of the relevant ascendant which is the earliest time at which one could insist upon division.

The judge added that per capita division seemed to him arbitrary. It was unsatisfactory because the number of shares may vary according to the time of distribution. He concluded that per stirpes division of family property was both reasonable and right. He then considered whether the same mode of distribution should apply to t'so properties and concluded that it should.

Deputy Judge Tang pointed out that t'so land was commonly cultivated by rotation between the stirps. Although distributions of ceremonial pork were made on an equal basis between those at the ceremony, he thought that was done as an inducement to attend the ceremony. Although education allowances were paid to male descendants individually, that was only to be expected from the purpose and nature of the benefit which would be paid to all who qualify, he said. Similarly payments for the relief of poverty would depend upon individual circumstances. So 'if I am free to say what the mode of distribution ought to be, I think I am strongly inclined in favour of *per stirpes* distribution'.[79] But later the judge concluded he was not free to say that after all.

The deputy judge did not deal with the fact that annual cash distributions (sometimes euphemistically referred to as 'pork') are often on a per capita basis. Perhaps he would have said that the tradition was, or should have been, to pay per stirpes but that the only way to obtain the support of all the stirps would have been to pay out per capita. But that this and all other applications of a per capita basis can be explained does not alter the fact that it is used. All practices have their reasons.

There was undoubtedly no custom regarding division of resumption proceeds in imperial China, for resumption did not happen there and distributions were not supposed to take place at all. There could hardly have been one in the New Territories until the late twentieth century since resumption did not become commonplace before then, so the custom would have lacked the necessary antiquity. Any such local custom would anyway require clear evidence, which would be hard to gather. The customary position was that such a dispute should be the subject of conciliation. The participants were admonished to seek harmony and not be impious.

Disputes within the institution that are not governed by its rules are normally settled by negotiation with the elders (those of the senior generations, not necessarily the oldest members) acting as mediators.[80] Usually the compromise employs a mixture of the two methods. There is however a distinct bias in favour of distribution per capita in modern settlements between members. This is not surprising

79. *Kan Fat-tat v Kan Yin-tat* [1987] 4 HKLR 516, 542–543.
80. Selby, 'Chinese Customary Law', p 63.

given that the whole membership must consent to a distribution. It may have been an innovation fifty years ago, but two generations have passed since Mills-Owens J's judgment and many more sales and resumptions and distributions have taken place. The ability of custom to adapt to new circumstances is one of its attributes. Distributions on a predominantly per capita basis have become the norm. Can it be said that they are now customary?

The origins of the adoption of per capita in negotiation and bargaining, far from being reprehensible, are rooted in custom. Asked what the attitude of the imperial magistrate would have been to a squabble about division of the compensation, Anthony Dicks, one of the experts in the Kan case, replied that the magistrate would not have expressed a view but would have sent them away to their villages for conciliation in the traditional Chinese way. That makes sense but the sums at stake nowadays usually mean that litigation is a viable option.

Perpetuities

Since t'so and t'ong land is intended by its founders to pass from generation to generation for ever, the land held by these institutions offends the rule against perpetuities. This is a rule of common law, and later statute, which forbids the tying-up of land by perpetual settlement of it for countless generations. The rule, which is also called the rule against remoteness of vesting, is based on policy. If land may not be sold, this prejudices trade and commerce. It also causes distress and frustration to families whose estates are fettered by such settlements, as numerous lineages with t'sos and t'ongs have found. But as they are customary institutions and custom is recognized in relation to land, the rule does not apply to them provided the land is in the New Territories.[81]

However, once the land has been converted into money, that exemption from the rule ceases, for it applies only to land. The proceeds of sale or resumption would therefore appear to fall foul of the rule and thus be liable to be returned to the settlor (for whom the money is said to be held on resulting trust) rather than held by the t'so t'ong. This would be inconvenient and contrary to expectations, to say the least, and has led the Court of Appeal to find a circuitous and rather doubtful way of nevertheless applying customary law to the proceeds. The solution of one judge was to interpret the word 'land' (defined in section 2 of the New Territories Ordinance) to include proceeds from land: he pointed out that rent and profits from land are expressly within the definition and did not see why other money derived from the land should not also be included. In support of this, it might be added that the statutory definition is not stated to be exhaustive so would be capable of expansion if the context dictated this. The majority of the court, however, was not

81. *Tang Kai-chung v Tang Chik-shang*, above, at 295; *Kan Fat-tat v Kan Yin-tat*, above; *Leung Kuen Fai v Tang Kwong Yu T'ong* [2002] 2 HKLRD 705.

willing to stretch the definition. Instead they reasoned that it would be unjust to apply the rule to the proceeds since it would lead to the dissolution of the customary institution and undermine clan cohesion. They pointed out that both common law and customary law are part of the laws previously in force in Hong Kong which were extended by the Basic Law; and that prior to 1997 application of the common law (of which the rule was part) was expressly subject to a proviso that it would not apply if local circumstances meant that to do so would cause injustice; this was such a circumstance.[82]

The majority reasoning is open to question: first, because the law latterly which contained the proviso, the Application of English Laws Ordinance of 1966, was one of the ordinances which was expressly not continued after 1997; and second, because it assumes that the institution holds no other land or the means of acquiring any and so would have to be dissolved once the rule applied. The route taken by the judge in the minority has an attractive simplicity but is legally questionable. Yet another solution, and one apparently favoured by the Court of Final Appeal, is to say that the subject matter is not money but the institution holding it and, since t'so t'ong are customary institutions, customary law applies to all their assets.

Equally, the court might have said that customary law has precedence in t'so t'ong matters and that these institutions had been holding bank accounts containing money as part of their resources for generations without objection so the practice was now part of custom. They had also been holding without objection Land Exchange Entitlements, which are choses in action not land, granted by the government in consideration for property which had been resumed.

Another legal justification for the holding by t'so t'ong of assets other than land would be through Article 40 of the Basic Law. This protects the lawful traditional rights and interests of the indigenous population. T'so t'ong must have held cash ever since this form of payment of rent became available and certainly long enough for this to be called a tradition.

Dissolution

Over time, t'so t'ongs tend to become unmanageable. The number of members increases with the generations yet the body's income cannot keep pace. So the distributions diminish and the lineage ties loosen. Inevitably, members begin to question whether their institution is worth preserving and their minds turn towards liquidating it and sharing out its property. Minor t'sos are often dissolved within a few generations.

Despite the determination of their founders that lineage bodies should be perpetual, in life nothing lasts forever, so it must be possible to terminate them. One might expect customary law to say nothing on the topic since dissolution would

82. *Tang Che Tai v Tang On Kwai*, above; *Lok Tin Choi v Lai Kwai Lin* [2015] 2 HKLRD 448, [2015] 3 HKC 283.

be contrary to the nature and purpose of their foundation. Nevertheless, according to evidence accepted by the Court of Final Appeal, ancestral t'so t'ong may be divided between the founders' male descendants if they unanimously agree to do so. Agreement can be by the heads of each fong on behalf of their members, at least if there is no indication of dissent from a member. On such a division, the t'so t'ong is dissolved.[83] Yet it could be a misnomer to call this dissolution, for the institution might have other assets, including a hall or temple, and new property could be put into the t'so so as to continue its function.

If t'so t'ong are regarded as purely landholding bodies, the alienation of all their land would demand that they cease to exist. But t'so t'ong undoubtedly have purposes beyond the owning of land: ancestor worship, welfare of members, and so on. Land ownership is a means of earning income to sustain those purposes. Yet land is not their only source of income. The difference lies in precisely what is being considered. If it is a t'so t'ong within section 15 of the New Territories Ordinance, land is essential, for the section applies to clans, families and t'ongs that hold land from the government. If it is a t'so t'ong that falls outside the section, however, land is not essential. The institution can pursue its objectives using other assets.

Since customary law does not contemplate dissolution, we may look to the common law for assistance as to when dissolution occurs. T'so t'ong are unincorporated associations, that is to say groups of people joined together for a common lawful purpose. Unincorporated associations can be dissolved if the purpose for which the association was founded (their substratum) has ceased to exist. Mere inactivity of the association is not sufficient: it may be dormant but not dead. A really prolonged period of inactivity might be enough but one has to look to the wider circumstances as well, asking why the association has not been functioning and whether it might spring into action again. The circumstances might indicate that the association has ceased even after a short period of inactivity. The question is whether, put together, the facts carry sufficient evidence that the society is at an end.[84]

Applying that approach to a t'so t'ong, one would look first at whether and when it had stopped carrying out its functions. In the case of ancestral t'so t'ong this would mean its members ceasing to maintain its hall or temple and to perform rituals such as grave sweeping and holding feasts. One would ask whether there are any current members: if the male line had died out, that would be a strong indicator, although there could be female family members still living or the possibility of adoption of heirs to revive the line, in which case, if they received support from the t'so t'ong, a function would remain. Perhaps most importantly, one would investigate whether the institution continued to hold land. If all the land, including that devoted to ancestral matters, had been alienated, there would be no rental income to finance operations. However, there might be other assets and income.

83. *Re Estate of Lau Wai Chau* (2000) 3 HKCFAR 98, [2000] 1 HKC 681.
84. *GKN Bolts & Nuts Sports and Social Club* [1982] 1 WLR 774, 779 (Megarry VC).

In addition to being unincorporated associations, t'so t'ong have been held to amount to trusts, or rather their land has been said to be held on trust by managers for their members. If correct, this presumably means that the trust must also be terminated if the t'so t'ong is to be dissolved.

Future of Lineage Endowments

Although land held by t'ong and t'so passes from generation to generation perpetually, such land is gradually being sold off to developers and resumed by the government for public purposes. Little income is generated from agriculture and more lucrative uses are now controlled by planning restrictions. This and loosening family ties tempt the members to agree that the land be sold.

Most New Territories folk agree that these ancestral estates are anachronistic and troublesome. As long ago as 1968, younger and better educated villagers at Ping Shan told Potter that they would rather divide up the ancestral property and have done with lineage affairs because internal disputes were so common. The feeling was that the institutions were old-fashioned, out-of-date, and unimportant.[85] Leadership positions in lineage bodies had long ceased to carry power and influence, that aspect having passed to village representatives, rural committee chairmen and members of the Heung Yee Kuk, soon to be joined by members of District Boards. Twenty years later, the working group set up by the New Territories Administration received similar sentiments. Almost all the current generation of members and managers, regardless of age, expressed the view that Chinese custom in t'so t'ong matters should be brought up to date.[86]

Yet the group's report concluded that t'so t'ong were alive and healthy and important for village unity. Customary practices were found to be still widespread. The overwhelming majority of New Territories people interviewed by the group disagreed that customary land management practices were outmoded and served them badly. They thought them better suited to their situation than Western practices. They did not regard the New Territories Ordinance as redundant.[87] Similarly, Potter noted that common landholdings were about the only thing that held ancestral groups together. Since, due to mutual suspicion and distrust, it was difficult to persuade members to sell the land, the institutions continued. Worshipping ceremonies, though simpler than before, were still observed. The institutions were adaptable and had survived for centuries.[88]

The working group recommended only a few changes to the system, almost none of which have been implemented. Instead, the government and the courts

85. Potter, *Capitalism and the Chinese Peasant*, pp 167–168.
86. Report of the Working Group on the New Territories Ordinance (Cap 97) (April 1988), para 3.54 (Working Group Report).
87. Working Group Report, chapter II, paras 7–10; Annex 3, para 3.58.
88. Potter, *Capitalism and the Chinese Peasant*, pp 169–171.

between them have managed to make the existing provisions work either by ignoring them, by interpreting them creatively or by supplementing them with administrative rules.

The modern attitude is to adapt these old institutions to work for the current members. Where outright sale or resumption is not available, the land will be let for lucrative but decidedly non-traditional uses or be put into a joint venture with a developer so as to exploit ding house rights. The latter is shown by an episode in which managers sold and assigned t'so land in 1997, purportedly for $3.88m, to developers for division into house plots and transfer into names of indigenous males for small house applications. The managers falsely told the District Office that the $3.88m was to be used for repair of t'so property, ancestor worship and education of members' children. In fact, only a deposit of HK$200,000 was paid; the true consideration was that the t'so was to receive five houses once built. But the property market fell and processing of applications for building licences was delayed so the land remained vacant and producing no income for seventeen years until the court declared the assignments void. A sympathetic judge allowed the t'so to back out of the deal even though the steps which had been taken to implement it could hardly be described as minimal.[89]

T'so and t'ong are inadequate forms of landholding for undertaking development. Dissent between members, adhesion to patrilineal and other traditional values, and vacancies in the office of manager almost guarantee that projects will be delayed. A landholder who wishes to dedicate his land to the benefit of future generations is nowadays likely to use a private company and give shares to his children and grandchildren.

89. *Tang Teng Hong Tso v Cheung Tin Wah* [2014] 4 HKC 515.

9

Regulation of Customary Institutions

Self-government

We have seen that the initial inclination of Hong Kong administrators was to leave customary matters as much as possible to the native population and govern with a light touch. Yet when it came to t'so t'ong, there was potential for trouble, because of their large membership and the extent and value of the land which they possessed. Owners who consisted of a large body of individuals provided an obstacle to the collection of Crown rent. They were not corporations, with directors and a personality separate from their members, which could be pursued in the name of the corporation. Each member could hardly be expected to pay the fraction of the rent attributable to his interest in the land. Nor could the covenants in the Crown lease, such as the restriction on building without government consent, be enforced against each of the members individually. That would be unwieldy and impracticable. One could not be expected to deal directly with dozens, perhaps hundreds, of difficult and disputatious country people.

Most customary institutions did however have supervisors or managers (sze lei) who looked after their affairs. They tended to be older and better educated than the body of members. The solution was to make these individuals rather than the membership as a whole liable for paying the rent and observing the terms of the lease. Why stop there? Should the t'so t'ong wish to let out its land, it would be sensible for the managers to be given power to sign the lease. Likewise, if it wished to sell the land or accept government compensation for acquiring the land, how much more convenient it would be to deal through the managers only. So giving the managers powers over the institution's property was the answer. If the institution had no manager, it would be required to appoint one. This would be expedient for all concerned.

At the same time, giving these managers full power over the property carried risks. The managers might be dishonest and defraud the members. For instance they might let the property to their friends or associates at a low rent, perhaps in return for some personal benefit. The managers might be domineering personalities who would force their views upon the members, perhaps ignoring the objections of a minority to sign an agreement to sell some of the ancestral land. So there had to be safeguards. Consequently, some fairly rudimentary regulation of t'so t'ong was introduced as part of the settlement and refined by legislation in the early twentieth century.

Similarly, the courts initially adopted a non-interventionist attitude towards these customary bodies. In the late 1940s the Chief Justice, responding to the administration's horror at the thought of taking responsibility beyond the limits of statute, declined to interfere in the internal affairs of a t'ong. Shades of this attitude could be found even into the 1990s. Yet the courts increasingly found themselves drawn in to disputes concerning kinship land, largely as a result of the enormous inflation of land values in the latter half of the twentieth century. Judges found readily to hand an English law institution, the trust, which exhibited superficial similarities to the design of t'so t'ong. At first tentatively, then with increasing confidence, judges applied the law of trusts to these customary emanations so that in the first decades of the twenty-first century judicial directives were even made concerning their governance.

This chapter describes and traces the development of statutory, administrative and judicial rules concerning t'so t'ong. It begins with the statutory controls the wording of which, somewhat ironically, is almost unchanged since they were introduced in 1905.

Section 15 of the New Territories Ordinance

Section 15 is badly organized and unnecessarily convoluted. Its twofold purpose is, however, easy enough to discern from its contents: first, to facilitate transactions regarding the land by managers as representatives of t'so t'ong; and second, to protect members from malpractice by managers.[1] The section provides for a supervisory role by the Home Affairs Department, through its District Offices, regarding the appointment of managers and their dealings in the property of t'so t'ong. This role has been described as that of a quasi-trustee but a better description would be quasi-regulator. Recognition of an organization as coming within section 15 by the DO cannot be challenged.[2]

A reading of section 15 gives the impression that the District Officer has four distinct roles with respect to t'so t'ong. First, he approves the appointment of and registers their managers. Second, he can cancel the appointment of a manager. Third, his consent is required to the disposal of or dealings in t'so t'ong land. Fourth, he witnesses the execution of land instruments. In addition, he supervises the appointment of trustees for minors (males aged under 18 years who own rural land) and consents to dealings by those trustees in the land of a minor. These last two responsibilities arise under section 18 and are not really concerned with land held

1. *Lai Chi Kok Amusement Park Co Ltd (No 2) v Tsang Tin-sun* [1966] HKLR 124, 130 (Briggs J). The contents of the section originated in the New Territories Land Ordinance 1905.
2. Selby, 'Chinese Customary Law', 68. *Tang Man Kit v Hip Hing Timber Co Ltd*, CACV 137/2002 (13 May 2005).

by t'so t'ong, although it is customary to refer to the arrangement whereby a trustee looks after land for a minor as a t'so.

The impression given by section 15 is deceptive for one of the four District Office roles is defunct and two have been greatly curtailed. At the same time, those functions which remain have become the subject of panoply of internal administrative rules that challenge the suggestion that internal operation is entirely a matter for the members.

Approval of Appointment and Registration of Managers

The first responsibility of the DO mentioned in section 15, the approval of the appointment and registration of t'so t'ong managers, remains in full force. Under custom it was usual to have a manager, in fact more than one. The opening sentence of the section makes this compulsory.

Section 15 talks of 'a manager' in the singular. In smaller t'so t'ong there may well be only one manager. There is often little or no competition to fill the position. There may be a convention that the elder son succeeds his father to the post. Larger t'so t'ong habitually have several managers, typically with one representing each division of the family, or fong.

The DO satisfies himself that the appointment of a manager is in accord with the internal rules of the institution and that members are content before approving it. Notices are displayed in the village and objections invited. Administrative practice has developed a complex of forms, lists, interviews, notices, and approvals, all set out in a manual for the guidance of staff, as a condition of and prelude to consent. DOs have teams of liaison officers to assist with t'so t'ong matters.

The officer's task is to approve the appointment, not the candidate. Whether a manager's appointment is by election or selection or otherwise is also not a matter for the DO to decide. His only legal concern is that the overall process be fair.[3] So, for instance, if the notice convening a meeting at which the manager was chosen was misleading or if signatures signifying members' consent to the appointment are suspect, those would be grounds upon which not to approve the appointment. He and the liaison staff are not in a position to adjudicate on disputed facts, such as an allegation that the established method of selection has not been followed. Nor are they concerned as to the suitability, integrity or propriety of the appointee.

Can members change the process of appointment, moving, say, to election by majority from some other method, such as nomination by elders, previously used? If the previous method is time-honoured, it seems doubtful that it can be changed unless all members consent, or at least unless no member protests. It might be objected that any alteration in a long-established method would be a breach of custom and therefore contrary to section 13 of the New Territories Ordinance. But

3. *To Kin Wah v Tuen Mun District Officer (No 2)* [2003] 4 HKC 213.

that would be to confuse the custom of the t'so t'ong (being its internal rules) with Chinese custom and customary right. The latter consists of the practices and laws which governed the conduct of the general and local population at the time of the creation of the New Territories with some room for evolution since then. Only if customary law recognized that the internal rules were immutable would members be legally bound to follow previous practice. This seems unlikely since the method of choosing a manager is only a question of procedure within a private institution. Custom, even local custom, seems not to have been concerned with internal governance of customary institutions.

If the members disagree as to the accepted method of selection of a manager, all the DO can do is to try to discover the basis upon which the disputants allege that a particular method has been adopted. If the rules are recorded in writing, it should be possible to ascertain who is correct. If they are a matter of previous practice, minutes of meetings and recollections of older members may be of assistance. Otherwise, the liaison officers may try to broker a settlement of the dispute or suggest that a meeting be held in order to decide on a way of proceeding. Often, however, the sides are entrenched and no way forward is possible. Without a manager, or without a full complement of managers, the t'so t'ong becomes unable to operate.

Another way in which a stalemate is reached is where the rules for choosing a manager are clear but they have been rendered unworkable because their content has been ill thought out. This occurred in a t'so at Kam Tin which had two requirements for being its manager. First, the candidate must be the most senior clansman and, second, he must be confirmed by majority vote of the members. The senior was easily identified but he did not succeed in obtaining majority support.

Even though an election or selection has taken place, there may be objections to the appointee made to the DO. This presents a difficulty, especially if the objectors do not want their identities to be revealed or are not willing to co-operate in an investigation. The office has to consider whether the objections have any basis and any relevance, which requires enquiries and analysis.

Only a small minority of managerial appointments cause difficulty, however. A more frequent source of complication lies with the list of current members that a new manager is expected to present to the DO. One might have thought that membership was really an internal matter yet the DO takes upon itself verification of the membership, comparing the proffered list with previous lists and calling for explanation of differences between the two, even referring to recent membership lists of associated t'so t'ong for assistance. Where a t'ong is based on the community rather than a section of a clan or lineage, its membership can be very wide, consisting of all the indigenous or even the whole population of a village or group of villages (heung), and is accordingly difficult to check.

If satisfied regarding the appointment of a manager, the DO will register the manager's name. Registration is on the t'so t'ong register, a computerized database kept by the t'so t'ong section of the office. Registration is a time-consuming business for a manager and the office. New managers often do not bother to go through the process. What effect does failure to register have? Does it mean that transactions carried out by the manager are ineffective?

In a case in which a sale agreement had been entered into by managers whose appointment had been reported to but not yet approved or registered by the DO, nor had the sale been consented to by or executed before the District Officer, Litton JA said the agreement was at best conditional: the requirement of consent was not trivial and could not be disregarded. Yet in a later case a majority of the Court of Appeal manifested a more lenient approach, suggesting that consent was a mere administrative requirement.[4]

However, consent to a transaction is one thing, approval and registration of managers quite another. Without the latter, managers lack the appearance of authority and the statutory power of disposal and dealing. In customary law, decisions concerning transactions are for the membership as a whole, not just the managers. Yet one must ask what action of an unregistered manager is being called into question, by whom and for what purpose. The Court of Final Appeal has distinguished between title and capacity to sue.[5] Registration of managers goes to title but unregistered managers may sue, eg for rent due. Capacity to sue is a matter of internal administration of the t'so t'ong and outsiders may not challenge this.

Failure to prove the appointment of a new manager or the first ever manager within three months of that appointment may, according to section 15, lead to the government re-entering the land thereby forfeiting it from the t'so t'ong. This is notional, for the penalty is quite disproportionate to the omission. Many changes in management have gone unreported for years and the organization has continued to function. It is only if the manager is required to take some step in relation to persons outside the t'so t'ong that registration comes into focus. Asked about the penalty, one District Officer exclaimed: 'Ten thousand people would rally if I exercised the power!' It is doubtful that there has ever been such a re-entry even though omission to inform the office of a new manager must be common. The penalty is probably a heavy-handed way of emphasizing the importance of reporting that there is a new manager so that he can be approved and registered. Yet reporting, approval and registration are procedural or regulatory matters failure to observe which should not result in such extreme consequences. Indeed, registration and penalties for non-registration ought not to be dealt with in primary legislation but by regulations made in a schedule to the ordinance. This modern practice was not fashionable at the time that the New Territories Ordinance was drafted. The power has remained, unrespected and unused, awaiting amendment that never comes. It stands in express contradiction of the assertion that the government does not interfere in t'so t'ong internal matters, as does the next power.

4. *Light Ocean Investments Ltd v Enway Development Ltd* [1994] 3 HKC 31; *Man Ping Nam v Man Mei Kwai*, CACV 193/2002 (11 December 2002).
5. *Hip Hing Timber Co Ltd v Tang Man Kit* (2004) 7 HKCFAR 212.

Cancellation of Manager's Appointment

The DO may cancel the appointment of the manager(s) for good cause, and appoint and register a new manager.[6] Examples of good cause would be maladministration, misappropriation of funds, and forgery of signatures on documents leading to doubts as to the manager's representativeness.[7] So too would physical or mental incapacity to perform the tasks of management. This power is extreme given that this part of section 15 provides for administrative interference in domestic affairs, contrary to the supposed approach of leaving them to the members. Perhaps because of this, and because cancellation of a manager's appointment involves sensitive considerations, the power is sparingly used.[8] District Officers are however occasionally asked by disgruntled members to remove managers. The requests are usually the result of internal disagreements and the complainants are seldom able to point to anything which might qualify as a good reason for cancelling the appointment.

One instance of purported cancellation occurred during the 1960s in the case of Li Tang Shi, an elderly woman managing a t'so at Nam Pin Wai, Sai Kung, and the widow of Li Wah Fuk. He had died sixty years earlier, leaving land but no children. It was an unusual type of t'so in that it had been set up soon after the death of her husband, not by his male heirs but by members of the Li clan, apparently to protect the young widow pending the adoption of a male successor. She and two men from the clan had been made managers but the two had died and she became sole manager. She lived off the income from the land, as a widow was entitled to do. The first defendant Li Wai Kwong, being the nearest male relative of Li Wah Fuk from the appropriate rank, was heir apparent but, after some vacillation, the widow refused to adopt him, an unprecedented refusal which caused consternation to clan elders. She disappeared from the village. The first defendant sought help from the DO. Eventually the first defendant was appointed as an additional manager, apparently by the then District Officer, David Akers-Jones, who was anxious to resolve the impasse but was plainly interfering in the affairs of the t'so without any lawful power. The first defendant later demanded that the widow's appointment be cancelled, alleging that she had not been performing her customary duties regarding grave ceremonies and the re-interment of ancestors, had not prepared accounts, was too old and feeble and had left the village. These charges were eventually denied by letter when the widow re-appeared and (probably with the help of her brother who was a justice of the peace) engaged lawyers but the DO said that this was not good enough and her response should deal with the specific criticisms. Another District Officer held a peremptory hearing at a meeting attended by the widow's eminent barrister, Mr (later Sir) Oswald Cheung, who had been led to believe that

6. New Territories Ordinance (Cap 97) s 15.
7. *Ng Shiu Hung v Sai Kung District Officer*, HCAL 2683/2000 (26 April 2001).
8. During interviews in the autumn of 2018 the District Officers for both Yuen Long and the North District in 2018 said they had never exercised the power of cancellation.

the meeting was to be a preliminary discussion. The officer thought there had been too many delays and, despite Mr Cheung's objections and the absence of Madam Li, said he would decide the matter immediately and declared the widow's appointment cancelled.

Perhaps we see in these actions an echo of the then recently abolished power of District Officers to decide small local disputes informally and apply custom as a kind of father of the people. Certainly Mr Akers-Jones who was to give expert evidence before the judge (astonishingly, since he was also a participant in the facts of the case and an employee of one of the defendants) thought that the widow was defying custom in not adopting the first defendant. He asserted that if the widow failed to adopt, the clan elders could do so, but the village head, who gave evidence, denied this and Mr Henry Hu, a renowned teacher of customary law from Wah Yan College, told the court that no one could dictate who or when a widow could adopt.

The decision to cancel Madam Li's appointment was challenged in court. The government was the second defendant. Mr Justice Briggs held that the procedure used had not conformed with elementary fairness. Although section 15 laid down no procedure to be followed where the officer was considering exercising his power of cancellation, it was a serious step which affected the widow's dignity and income so the rules of natural justice should have been followed: it was not for the widow to disprove the charges, the complainants should have given evidence and been examined and the widow should have been allowed an opportunity to be heard. The appointment of the first defendant as an additional manager was also found invalid by the judge who pointed out that under section 15 the making of an appointment was by the t'so, not the District Officer who had 'taken a chance' (as the judge delicately put it) in an effort to resolve matters. If the officer had first removed the widow properly, he could have appointed the first defendant in her place.[9]

Since section 15 does not stipulate the procedure by which managers may be removed by the authorities, it is not obligatory to conduct a trial as happened, though ham-fistedly, in the case of Madam Li. Instead, and probably more appropriately, an inquiry could have taken place with the complaints against her being investigated and assessed before (if any of them proved substantiated) putting them to her and her advisers. What is clear from the judicial review is that if the DO decides to conduct a formal hearing, he must use proper procedure and act fairly.

According to the expert Mr Hu, under custom a widow could not be removed from management of her husband's t'so on grounds of age or feebleness. Presumably this is because of her right to maintenance from the land and her relationship with the deceased. But the judge observed that this did not impinge upon the power of the DO to remove her if he considers that good cause has been shown. Statute was more powerful than custom.

9. *Li Tang Shi v Li Wai Kwong* [1969] HKLR 367; confirmed on appeal [1969] HKLR 629. See Daffyd M. E. Evans, 'The Widow Who Would Not Adopt' (1971) 1 HKLJ 84.

A more recent removal of managers by a DO was also challenged, this time unsuccessfully, in a case from Nga Tsin Wai in Sai Kung. Following complaints from t'so members, investigation led to doubts about the representativeness of recently approved managers. This was partly because one of the longer serving managers artlessly admitted to the liaison officer that the managers knew that some of the documents supporting the application for registration of new managers had been signed on behalf of members who could not be contacted—he regarded it as traditional practice. Perhaps this also illustrates a traditional attitude towards bureaucratic impositions.[10]

The judge rejected a suggestion that the power to cancel a manager's appointment for good cause was contrary to Chinese customary law by which a manager is appointed for life. There was no evidence of custom before the court. Anyway, the power was contained in an express statutory provision. Again, custom gave way to statute.

Witnessing of Land Instruments

The District Office's defunct role is the witnessing and execution of land instruments. The relevant sentence in the section is: 'Every instrument relating to land held by a clan, family or *t'ong*, which is signed by the registered manager thereof in the presence of the Land Officer in the presence of the Land Officer and is attested by him, shall be as effectual for all purposes as if it had been executed and signed by all members of the said clan, family or *t'ong*.' The witnessing of instruments was a service provided by the office for the convenience of country people who might find that engaging the services of solicitors was formidable and expensive. Although the sentence might seem to imply that any instrument executed by a manager other than in the presence of the Land Officer will not be effective and that the only other way of carrying out a valid execution is to have all the members of the t'so t'ong sign, this is not its intent or effect. As explained in the Lai Chi Kok Amusement Park case, section 15 merely provides a means of valid execution by managers alternative to that before a solicitor or made informally.[11] Earlier in the section a properly appointed, approved and registered manager is given 'full power to dispose of or in any way deal with' the land of the t'so t'ong 'as if he were the sole owner thereof, subject to the consent of the Secretary for Home Affairs'. This means that such a manager may validly execute instruments to carry out a transaction provided that he obtains consent to it from the District Land Office. This requirement of consent is separate from the Land Officer's power of attestation. The one is concerned with validity of a transaction, the other with validity of an instrument carrying through

10. *Ng Shiu Hung v Sai Kung District Officer*, above.
11. Blair-Kerr J in *Lai Chi Kok Amusement Park Co Ltd (No 1) v Tsang Tin-sun* [1965] HKLR 413 at 417.

a transaction. But of course if the documents have been executed in front of the District Officer, he must have consented to the transaction which they implement.

The DO's 'counter service' for witnessing instruments became less and less used as the twentieth century progressed and indigenous people grew more knowledgeable and their land more valuable. Although the service was still being referred to in government documents in 1986, it seems that it was a victim of the transfer of responsibility for land matters from the District Office (part of the Home Affairs Department) to the new, specialist District Land Office (a division of the Lands Department) in 1982. In a way this was symptomatic of the change of focus from concern about the welfare of rural people, which characterized the DO before urbanization of the New Territories, to concern about proper administrative practice which dominates the modern civil service.

Since use of the attestation service was never mandatory under section 15 and was not the only means of effecting valid execution of documents, its loss is of no great moment. The continuing reference in the section to execution before the Land Officer is a hangover from an earlier era. Its elimination would be one of a number of desirable reforms to statutory regulation of t'so t'ongs.

Consent to Transactions

The DO role which has diminished but not disappeared is the giving of consent to land transactions by t'so t'ong managers. This role rests upon the phrase 'subject to the consent of the District Officer' which immediately follows and qualifies the power given to registered managers to deal in their t'so or t'ong's land as if they alone owned it.

On the modest foundations of this phrase the Home Affairs Department has erected an elaborate superstructure of formality set out in the same manual as the procedure for approving managerial appointments. Divisions, sales, assignments, mortgages, tenancies and lease modifications require an application by the manager on behalf of the t'so t'ong (using a form, of course), the opening of a file, an interview with the applicant who must bring along proof of identity and of the lineage's ownership of the land (such as a chap chiu extract from the rent roll or receipts for government rent), a list of members and proof of their consent to the transaction. The last can be a letter signed by members or minutes of a meeting containing the names of those attending at which the proposed transaction was discussed and decided upon. The form must state why the proposal is beneficial to the members. The office checks with the Land Registry all the property registered as belonging to the t'so t'ong to see whether it includes the property affected by the transaction and whether the property is free from encumbrances. It will then post notices concerning the proposal and the members' list on the boards of the appropriate village and DO. Copies will be sent to the relevant village representative for indigenous inhabitants and rural committee. If there are no objections within one month, the

T'so T'ong Registry prepares a consent letter for the District Officer's approval. The signed letter is given to the applicant or his legal representative in person and a copy is passed to the District Land Office to arrange for its entry on the Land Register.

This lengthy procedure incorporates the administration's understanding of the requirements of custom. The first customary rule, that the members be unanimous in agreeing to the transaction is manifest in the provision of a list of members, proof of their consent and absence of any objection after publicity has been given. The second rule, that the dealing be necessary, is reflected in the requirement that a reason be given for it on the form and the potential for investigation of the reason by a liaison officer. But the procedural manual does not specify that the reason show that the sale be necessary as custom required, only that it be to the advantage of the t'so t'ong.

When there is an objection to the transaction, progress with it inevitably becomes delayed while investigations take place. A senior liaison officer will ascertain the nature and seriousness of the objection and report to the DO who may uphold the objection and therefore refuse consent or reject the objection and endorse the application. The DO may attempt mediation between the objector and the managers. Most objections concern money—the price or the amount of rent and the distribution of proceeds between members.

An objector does not have to provide a reason, or perhaps the reason that the land is ancestral and so should not be alienated is implicit. Nor does the objector have to act consistently. A challenge by the purchaser to the DO's refusal of consent to a sale of ancestral wui land where there was only one dissentient was rejected by the Court of Appeal. This was despite the objector having earlier attended a meeting of members at which he indicated support for the proposed sale. It seems he later changed his mind after discussing the proposal with his son who thought the price offered was unreasonable. The written objection was lodged after the formal sale and purchase agreement had been signed by the managers. The court reluctantly refused to order that the managers perform the agreement because DO consent had not been given.[12]

An irony of the elaborate procedures before consent will be given to a dealing is that, as far as the law is concerned, no formality for the giving of consent is required. It is simply a question of whether the District Office has indicated somehow its lack of opposition to the proposed dealing. This emerged when the manager of a t'so gave notice to quit to a tenant who argued that termination of his tenancy was a dealing in land within section 15 which had not been approved by the office. There was evidence that the DO had written to the manager encouraging termination of the tenancy so that government plans for use of the land could be implemented. Consent could therefore be inferred.[13]

12. *Million Way Ltd v To Shing Wo* [2011] 2 HKLRD 1017.
13. *Liu Chun Kui v Liu Wing Fat*, HCA 1115/1995 (2 December 1997).

Manager's Power of Dealing

Upon approval of appointment and registration, a manager has, in the words of section 15, 'full power to dispose of or in any way deal with the said land as if he were the sole owner thereof'. This is for convenience of effectuating transactions concerning the land, otherwise all members of the t'so t'ong would have to sign any instrument affecting the land and the government would have to pursue all of them for any unpaid rent or breach of other covenant in the government lease. Contrary to what is sometimes asserted, the words do not make the managers sole owners or give them legal title to the land; rather, the managers are given powers of dealing and disposal *as if* they were sole owners. In other words, the managers are to be treated as owners for purposes only of disposal of and dealing in the land so that the other party to the transaction may rely upon the managers having authority. But it is only as though they were the owners, they are not in fact so. Ownership stems from the government grant, not section 15. The grant is to the t'so t'ong, so its members are the owners.

This fiction of ownership by managers is as much for the convenience of the administration as it is for the convenience of members of t'so t'ong. Levying and collection of Crown rent was the dynamic of the 1905 land settlement, of which section 15 was part and which the section itself facilitates. Enforcement of government controls, such as those in the Buildings Ordinance and the Town Planning Ordinance, is similarly made easier since the authorities can look to the managers to comply with their orders.[14] The acceptance of resumption compensation is another function facilitated by the fiction: the authorities have only to pay the managers, not each member individually.

Looking at the fiction from the point of view of members of a t'so or t'ong, the ability of managers to carry out lettings and sales of the land is obviously expedient. It might well be impossible in larger institutions to locate all their members to sign a lease or assignment. But the empowerment of managers to act for all the members in such serious matters carries risk. The internal rules of most t'so t'ong, if not the custom in the New Territories as a whole, is that any important decisions such as these require consent of the membership, often unanimous consent. That is no safeguard though if the managers are clothed with ostensible authority to represent the membership in land dealings, as they are by section 15. The managers might arrange a letting or sale without reference to the membership. The acts of the manager cannot be overridden by the members.[15] This is where the requirement of Land Office consent was designed to come into play. The administration would check to ascertain whether the proposed transaction had been approved by the membership or was in accordance with the rules of the institution or custom of the country. The requirement was to protect members against a dishonest manager.

14. *AG v Lam Mei Chai* [1997] 1 HKC 22.
15. *Light Ocean Investments Ltd v Enway Development Ltd*, above.

It has been suggested by one judge of appeal that protection of members is not a purpose of section 15 and that its only purpose is facilitation of conveyancing.[16] This was despite the existence of previous appellate dicta in the Lai Chi Kok Amusement Park case that part of the mischief at which the section had been aimed was malpractice by managers.[17] The judge prayed in aid as part of the context of section 15's enactment Blake's 1898 proclamation that the customs of the people of the New Territories would not be interfered with. But the phrase Blake actually used was 'good customs': the absence of oversight of t'so t'ong managers in imperial times can hardly be described as a good custom. At the time he made the proclamation Blake would barely have been aware of the malpractices of t'so t'ong managers. During the succeeding six years before the legislation was put in place the administration had an opportunity to acquaint itself with the realities of the New Territories and discover what caused difficulty. One such was dissent within t'so t'ong and one cause of that dissent was the conduct of their managers. As part of the context, the judge also referred to the undeveloped nature of the New Territories at the time that section 15 was enacted. Surely more relevant, but not mentioned, was the great amount of land and therefore wealth held by t'so t'ong in 1905 which was to be put under the statutory power of managers. Even if the past conduct of managers had been exemplary, section 15 placed temptation in their way and precautions against exploitation of their position would have been desirable. The analysis of the other judges who considered the purpose of section 15 in the same case is more convincing. They concluded that the section was part of a statutory scheme regulating the management of traditional land, one purpose of which was to protect members against the depredations of managers.[18]

In fact indigenous people did not trust t'so t'ong managers, even though they might be from the same lineage. For that reason they favoured the appointment of better educated clan members (ideally those who had passed the imperial examinations) as managers since they were felt to be less likely to defraud the members. If such a candidate was not available, members preferred the appointment of wealthier men since, aside from the attraction of their business acumen, such men would have less need to supplement their resources from lineage income and were more likely to have property to which the members could look for compensation should the manager abscond with the rents.

Even before section 15 gave them greater powers, managers used their position to extract advantages from the income of clan lands under their charge. In the days when tenants paid rent in rice, managers would skim off a part for themselves, a practice made easier by the small tolerances that were allowed in the accounts for wastage. A more sophisticated scheme was to take the cash received in rental and

16. Le Pichon JA in *Man Ping Nam v Man Tim Lup* [2011] 1 HKLRD 427.
17. *Lai Chi Kok Amusement Park Co Ltd (No 2) v Tsang Tin-sun* [1966] HKLR 124 at 130 (Briggs J).
18. Peter Cheung JA in *Man Ping Nam v Man Tim Lup*, above, and Andrew Cheung J (as he was) at first instance: HCA 9835/1998 (1 February 2002).

make short-term loans at interest, returning the taken funds before the time for presentation of the annual accounts to the membership but retaining the interest. Another ruse was to use the rental as capital in the manager's private business. If the manager was an elder, he might simply spend the lineage income on himself, feeling entitled to do so, and immune from criticism, by reason of his status. Then there was the 'tea money' and the signing fees which managers expected from those who benefited from performance of the manager's functions or use of his influence such as new or renewing tenants of clan land and those interested in using or buying that land. The rent or price might be an under-value and the tenant or buyer might be a relative, or introduced by a relative, of the manager, or might be a company in which he had an interest.

Interviewees complained to a government working group about such attitudes and practices in the mid-1980s. Jack Potter found them rife at Ping Shan in the early 1960s. It would be naïve to think that they do not go back a lot further. Only the amounts and the opportunities involved have increased with the years.[19]

Given that background, there seems little doubt that one of the purposes of section 15 was indeed to protect the membership of t'so t'ong from predatory managers. Another judge in the same appeal thought so, agreeing with the view expressed in the Lai Chi Kok Amusement Park case years earlier. In the light of this, it is astonishing that the administration has ceased supervising the grant of leases of t'so t'ong land—the more so that it has done so with the permission of the judiciary.

Division and Sale of Land

The District Office still supervises the sale of t'so t'ong land. A sale is certainly a 'disposal' within section 15. In a way it is a surprise that the DO is ever called upon to do this, for fundamentally lineage land should not be sold. The intention of the founders was that the land should be held for ever so as to fund ancestor worship, provide benefits for its members and bind the lineage together. The principle of non-alienability was enshrined in imperial statute.

Another fundamental was that ancestral land was indivisible: it must continue to be held as one estate so as to promote lineage cohesion and stability. Consequently, where different factions or fong hold differing views as to how their land is to be dealt with, the solution of partitioning the land between them so that each can handle part of the land in a different fashion would in theory not be available. A desire to divide the land often precedes a decision to sell it.

Despite the principle, in practice ancestral land is frequently sold. The practice started long before the temptations created by the escalation in value of New Territories land in the final quarter of the last century. Kinship land was allowed to be sold in nineteenth-century imperial China, provided that two conditions were

19. Working Group Report, para 3.51; Potter, *Capitalism and the Chinese Peasant*, pp 103–104.

satisfied: first, that the members unanimously agreed to the sale; and second, that the sale was necessary. These may seem formidable obstacles to a sale, yet both have been eroded over time.

In Ping Shan, Potter found little deference to the idea of preserving Tang clan land for the benefit of the lineage. By 1961 ancestral land was already being sold to private buyers. 'Men talk about land deals incessantly, especially those who own land or have shares in large ancestral estates,' he observed. Some of those doing the talking were themselves engaged in land brokerage. The old rule that ancestral land should be offered for sale to members of the lineage before it could be sold to outsiders was disregarded, because the prices anticipated were beyond the means of villagers.[20] At the same time members of the clan were bickering about division and sale of their land and the allocation of the proceeds between them. One dispute was as to whether hundreds of lots owned by a single t'so which had grown in size to 233 members (from one hundred, forty years previously) should be divided up between its nine fongs (or t'ongs) so that those which wished to liquidate their interests could do so. The fongs with the two smallest number of male descendants were those applying to do so. This became a landmark decision concerning the law applicable to t'sos.[21] The judge refused to allow partition, reasoning that to do so would abrogate custom and lead to the disintegration of the t'so with adverse consequences for the social structure of the clan. He was persuaded of these arguments by the expert on custom called by the defendants, the former District Officer David Akers-Jones, who evidently was unaware of the tolerance of the sale of kinship land during Ching times and the pragmatic attitude towards such sales within clans. It may be that Mr Akers-Jones relied upon what he had been told by older members of the lineage who presented an idealized version of the custom rather than what actually was done. Given the widespread and enthusiastic sale of t'so t'ong land in subsequent decades the judgment reads today as old-fashioned and more than a little ironic.

Sale of lineage land may no longer be forbidden or even exceptional but it is such a large step that custom requires that it should be approved by members. Approval is usually obtained at a meeting. The need for unanimity has been diluted. Instead of it being obligatory, whether it is required has become a question of evidence as to the custom of the t'so t'ong.[22] The meaning of unanimity has also been changed: a member's approval may be inferred from knowledge of the proposed sale and failure to object to it. Consent of all the heads of fong (ka, or apartment), rather than all the members, may be enough.

Is consent of the head the equivalent of obtaining the consent of all the members of that fong? The answer seems to be that it can be, but only if the head undoubtedly has authority to act on behalf of all his members by their express giving of that authority (eg by letter) or if by the clear practice of the t'so t'ong the consent of the

20. Potter, ibid, p 101.
21. *Tang Kai-chung v Tang Chik-shang* [1970] HKLR 276.
22. *Man Ping Nam v Man Mei Kwai* [2011] 1 HKLRD 427; Selby, 'Chinese Customary Law', p 63.

head is deemed to be sufficient. Normally one would not expect a head to disregard a member's disagreement though equally one would not expect a member to contradict the wishes of the head of his fong or the majority of its members. If, despite the head's consent, there is evidence of dissent from a member, the head's consent would not be acceptable as an indication of unanimity.[23]

There is often disagreement concerning a sale. Objections are less to do with the principle that the land should never be sold (although that is a reason that may be given, if only to conceal the real reasons for opposition) than with suspicion of the motives of those who promote the sale and the not unfounded fear that other members may secretly benefit more from the sale than the objector. Such attitudes led to the Lai Chi Kok Amusement Park dispute and they were common in Ping Shan in the 1960s, acting as a brake on the disposal of clan land.[24]

Since the assumption was that the interests of future generations should be protected, sale was supposedly a last resort. For instance, the need to raise money for much-needed repairs to the village temple or to the tombs of ancestors would be sufficient reason to break with tradition. But the necessity asserted has become increasingly tenuous and may even be false. The District Office requires a reason for the sale to be given as a pre-condition to consenting to it but does not direct its staff that the reason must amount to necessity. Instead, the office requires that the sale must be for the benefit of the t'so t'ong, a less stringent requirement, and the reason may well be false. In at least two instances, managers told the office that the sale was needed to finance temple repairs whereas the truth was that they planned to sell it to a developer in exchange for ownership of houses to be built on part of the site.

Before an application for consent to sell will be considered by the DO a certain percentage of support from the membership is required by the administration. The percentage varies from district to district. In Yuen Long, which has the highest number of t'so t'ong, 50 per cent is required. In the North District, which has the second highest number, it is 80 per cent. This is because some members may be untraceable and it is therefore not practicable to insist that every member be consulted.[25]

Leases

In two decisions heard separately but delivered on the same day in December 2002 two judges of the Court of Appeal expressed the view that DO consent was not needed for a lease as opposed to a sale.[26] In the first, *Tang Man Kit*, Vice-President

23. *Re Estate of Lau Wai Chau* (2000) 3 HKCFAR 98, [2000] 1 HKC 681; *Tang Che Tai v Tang On Kwai* [2008] 3 HKC 521; *Kan Fat-tat v Kan Yin-tat* [1987] 4 HKLR 516, 535.
24. Potter, *Capitalism and the Chinese Peasant*, p 101.
25. Selby, 'Chinese Customary Law', 68, 114–115.
26. *Tang Man Kit v Hip Hing Timber Co Ltd*, CACV 137/2002 (13 May 2005); *Man Ping Nam v Man Mei Kwai*, CACV 193/2002 (11 December 2002).

Rogers' reasoning (with which Madam Justice of Appeal Le Pichon agreed) was that the letting of land is an act of management rather than a disposal or dealing.[27] A similar conclusion was reached, though by a more circuitous route, by Le Pichon JA in her reflections in the second case, *Man Ping Nam v Man Mei Kwan*.[28] Both Rogers VP and Le Pichon JA relied heavily upon rather selective accounts of the historical background to the New Territories Ordinance to conclude that the intention had been to have minimal interference in customary land matters and thus to require consent for disposition by sale but not by lease or other instrument. As has been seen, Le Pichon JA even doubted that protection of members from malpractices by managers was one of the purposes of section 15.

This interpretation of section 15 is undoubtedly pragmatic and no doubt came as a relief to both administrators and managers. The requirement of consent to a letting was not well known and, even where known, was roundly ignored by managers. Previously, lettings were informal affairs in which the tenant was a member of the lineage and the rent was modest. Commercial tenancies made with companies had become far more frequent and valuable following the increase in cross-border trade and a court decision which allowed old schedule land to be used for purposes other than agriculture, both in the 1980s.

However, the distinction between management and dealing seems spurious. No doubt leasing out is an act of management, but then so is a sale, which would be one of the manager's final acts of management of the land sold. Being an act of management does not prevent it also being a dealing or even a disposition. It is striking that neither judge referred to any authority in which disposal or dealing had been defined or construed.[29] It is difficult to reconcile their conclusion with the usual understanding of what a disposal is.

Land is disposed of when it is conveyed away by the owner to another. That other does not have to be a buyer: he could be a lessee or a mortgagee. The disposal consists of the assignment of the owner's interest to the other party in completion of the transaction. The difference between a sale, a leasing (or letting) and a mortgage lies in the length of alienation. Assignment following sale is for the duration of the rest of the government lease. Conveyance following an agreement to lease (or tenancy agreement) is for a shorter period, although it might be only one day shorter. Assignment by mortgage was, until 1984, also permanent in theory though temporary in practice since the mortgagee retained a right to redeem the mortgage by paying off the loan; since 1984 an assignment has not been used and the mortgage takes the form of a charge over the land. All are alienations of the land, disposing of an interest in it. In both sale and letting, the interests disposed of are

27. *Tang Man Kit v Hip Hing Timber Co Ltd* [2003] 4 HKC 278.
28. *Man Ping Nam v Man Mei Kwai*, CACV 193/2002 (11 December 2002) HKCAH. This part of her judgment is irrelevant to the outcome (obiter dicta) since the judge expressly declined to reach a definite conclusion on the point and the outcome was decided by all three judges on another point.
29. Eg, *Bromley LBC v Greater London Council* [1983] 1 AC 768 and *Prescott v Birmingham Corporation* [1955] Ch 219.

leasehold. In the case of a conveyance on sale the interest is the balance of the term of the government lease. In the case of a lease, the interest is a lesser term carved out of the government lease by under-lease. In both cases the assignment is a disposal, irrespective of the length of the interest granted. So the conclusion that the requirement of consent in section 15 does not apply to a letting is at odds with the usual understanding of land lawyers that a lease, if by deed, is a disposal of land for a limited period. Even if not by deed (as is common with short tenancies, generally those for three years or fewer) the tenancy agreement is a dealing with the land. The drafter of section 15, who would surely have been familiar with conveyancing usage, may well have added a reference to dealings in order to catch tenancy agreements as well as leases by deed. On the face of it, he went even further, for 'in any way deal with' is designed to cover all sorts of land transactions: licences, rights of way, rights to water, informal mortgages, terminations of tenancy and so on. One item which the phrase does not cover (although for a time the misconception took hold that it did) is resumption of the land by the government. That occurs under a statutory power and is a unilateral, compulsory taking of the land.

The reasoning concerning disposals and dealings of the other judges in *Man Ping Nam* who dealt with the point is more persuasive. Both the trial judge, Deputy Judge Andrew Cheung, and Peter Cheung JA concluded that a letting was a dealing. They regarded section 15 as part of the regulation of traditional landholding imposed by the British administration and as drawn in deliberately wide terms, covering a number of aspects of t'so t'ong. The clarification of a clear chain of title (by monitoring of sales) was only one such aspect. They regarded the purposes of the consent requirement in section 15 as obvious from its content: to restrict the power of the manager and to protect members of the t'ong. As Cheung JA pointed out, under Chinese customary law a manager could not alienate clan land without the consent of all the members but section 15 instead (for ease of conveyancing) gave the manager alone full power of disposal and dealing. The consent requirement was to ensure that there was no abuse of that new power since the Land Officer had to ascertain from members whether they had any objection to the disposal or dealing. In that way, the requirement was actually supporting the customary practice. Any regulatory mechanism imposed in 1905, Cheung JA explained, would have had some impact upon existing customs. One needs to fit customary law into the regulatory framework, not the other way around.

The judicial reflections upon whether consent to lettings is needed in the two cases are not binding. In both, the issue was not vital to the decision since the appeal was decided on another ground. Only two of the appeal judges in *Man Ping Nam* actually expressed a view on the issue and they disagreed about it. Moreover, the decision in *Tang Man Kit* was subsequently declared a nullity by the Court of Final Appeal because it had been heard by two judges only when three should have done so. The *Tang Man Kit* appeal was later re-heard by a panel of three which included Cheung JA who had said that consent was required in *Man Ping Nam*. Whilst maintaining his view that consent was necessary, he felt that, as a matter of precedent, he had to follow what he described as the majority view in *Man Ping Nam* that consent was not necessary. Yet, to complicate matters further, he was mistaken in thinking that there had been a majority view. In *Man Ping Nam* only he and Le Pichon JA had expressed an opinion on the issue: the third judge, Stone J, had declined to do so and decided the appeal solely on a different point. So the upshot is that there was only one valid relevant appeal and in it the judges were evenly split on the issue.

Despite this, DOs have been conducting themselves for years now on the assumption that the observations of Rogers VP and Le Pichon JA about lettings are correct. The question is unlikely ever to go to a higher level and if it did, there would be tremendous pressure on the Court of Final Appeal to make the law conform with the practice of landlords not seeking consent and DOs not giving it. The judicial resort to a strained interpretation of 'dispose of or in any way deal with' is really another illustration of how outmoded section 15 is and of the need for its amendment. That will not happen, however, for t'so t'ong land is a sensitive issue and reform concerning it would undoubtedly have political ramifications going well beyond the meaning of a few words in the section. So the judges will have to continue to display creativity in their reasoning so as to bring the law into line with reality.

Less controversial is the Court of Appeal's view that absence of official consent would at most render a lease voidable and that whether it would be avoided would depend upon the circumstances.[30] The question here is what 'subject to the consent of' the District Land Officer means. Do those words make consent a pre-condition to the effectiveness of the disposal or dealing? Or are they merely normative, indicating that consent ought to be obtained? Grammatically, they seem to qualify the 'full power' of the registered manager to dispose of or deal in the land as if he were its sole owner. In other words, without that consent, the manager's power is doubtful and anyone dealing with the manager ought for his own protection to resort to the members (or, if the t'so t'ong rules permit, the elders or heads of fong) as being those who, aside from the section, have power to deal. Needless to say, such an interpretation would be undesirable result from a practical point of view.

Control of Trustees

By finding, or more often supposing, that t'so t'ong are trusts judges have imported a ready-made set of rules for controlling managers. These rules may not have been required in that the customary law already laid down similar rules but the law of trusts, unlike customary law, at least has the virtue of being well understood by those who have to deal with the legal aspects of customary institutions, namely judges and

30. *Man Ping Nam v Man Mei Kwai*, CACV 193/2002 (11 December 2002); *Tang Man Kit v Hip Hing Timber Co Ltd* [2003] 4 HKC 278; cf Yuen J [2001] 4 HKC 11.

practitioners trained in the common law. The ready acceptance of the notion that these institutions are trusts must owe something to the comfort of familiarity. The roots of the notion are now wide but they are not deep. There has never been a sustained analysis or defence of the supposition. We will turn to consider the supposition later in this chapter.

What does the imposition of trust requirements mean for managers and members of t'so t'ong? The first and most basic matter is that a manager as a trustee owes fiduciary duties to the members. Accordingly, in management of the t'so t'ong he must use the due diligence and reasonable care which the ordinary prudent man of business would exercise, he must act honestly and reasonably and he must pay equitable compensation for breach of duty.[31] He must tender accounts and documents, such as tenancy agreements and receipts. He must not make a profit from the office.

Certain of these requirements sit oddly with the nature of a customary institution. T'sos and kinship t'ongs are not commercial enterprises run by businessmen. They have investments and income and their land is sometimes astonishingly valuable, but they are not operated for profit. Their managers are rarely professional people. Management can be onerous, that is why appointees of the wealthier lineages are allowed to have assistants. If so, the members may be quite content to allow the managers to earn an income (in the form of 'shoe money') for their efforts. But most t'so t'ong have modest holdings and limited income and most managers are volunteers; there is no competition for their position. The preparation of annual accounts with supporting documents is a customary practice that needs no imposition by the courts. Proposed tenancy agreements are routinely put before elders for scrutiny and endorsement, again as a matter of custom.

Another requirement said to be based on the law of trusts is that managers must act jointly and unanimously, so each must sign a lease to make it valid and binding.[32] Yet in *So Kee Transportation Co Ltd v Secretary for Environment, Land and Works* the Court of Appeal, reversing a decision of the Lands Tribunal, explained that it was not necessary for managers actually to sign the lease provided that they all consented to the making of the lease.[33] But again, the imposition is unnecessary for customary law requires unanimity, or at least absence of disagreement, since each manager represents a different branch of the clan.

In undertaking litigation on behalf of his institution a manager might expect that the costs would come from its common funds since (in the words of section 15) he is appointed and approved to represent it. The interposition of a trust, however,

31. *Man Fong Hang v Man Ping Nam*, HCA 7935/1998 (11 December 2003); [2005] 1 HKC 535 (CA); undisturbed on further appeal (2006) 9 HKCFAR 674.
32. *Tang Kam Wah v Tang Ming Yat*, HCA 10141/1998 (26 November 2002).
33. *So Kee Transportation Co Ltd v Secretary for Environment, Land and Works*, CACV 363/2005 (12 October 2006).

means that this expectation will be guaranteed only if he successfully makes a prior, separate, and costly application to the court for permission to use the funds.[34]

Are T'so T'ong Trusts?

The above account of judicial control of t'so t'ong assumes that the pronouncement that these customary bodies are trusts is correct. There is no doubt that this has taken root at lower levels of the courts where it has been held repeatedly that managers of t'so t'ong are trustees and the members beneficiaries. The repetition has become self-reinforcing, to the extent that one judge even declared that it was 'trite law' that t'sos were trusts.[35] The Court of Appeal has decided a number of cases on the supposition that t'so t'ong are trusts. Yet in none of those appeals has the supposition been squarely in issue. The supposition is somewhat curious since a trust is an English law concept which had no equivalent in Chinese law, whether statutory or customary, at the time of the British takeover in 1899 and the Crown grants of 1905 and 1907.

A trust divides ownership between legal and equitable. Legal ownership is formal and based on the common law. Equitable ownership is the underlying real or beneficial ownership recognized originally by the courts of equity in England. The trustee is the legal owner who holds the interest in the land. But the trustee holds it on trust for the beneficial owner who, although having no interest in the land, is entitled to its benefit. Chinese law does not recognize this division: the members of t'so t'ong are customary owners of the land. The managers are not the owners, except to the extent that they are also members. Their management function is administrative.

What is the basis for saying that t'so t'ong, even those founded long before English law came to Hong Kong, are trusts? There were very few reported cases concerning customary institutions until after the Second World War. Early judgments seem to have taken the trust analogy as obvious: the founders had settled the land onto a customary institution for the benefit of their descendants and the descendants as members of the institution had entrusted their managers with looking after the land for their benefit. The first attempt at an explanation appears to be the judgment in the dispute between warring factions of the Tang clan in 1969, *Tang Kai-chung v Tang Chik-shang*[36] (hereafter *Tang*) in which the institution of the t'so was first analysed. The analysis was performed with the benefit of expert evidence as to Chinese law and custom. One of the experts was David Akers-Jones, who at the time of the trial was in charge of government land policy and during the 1960s had been the DO for Yuen Long. Some members of the t'so wanted its land to be partitioned, others did not. The judge, Mr Justice Mills-Owens, decided that the

34. For a 'Beddoe Order' under Order 85 rule 2 of the Rules of the High Court (Cap 4A).
35. Chu J in *Tang Kam Wah v Tang Ming Yat*, HCA 10141/1998 (26 November 2002), para 68.
36. [1970] HKLR 276.

law of partition did not apply because t'so land was intended to be held perpetually and not to be alienated. He held that a t'so is a trust and the managers are trustees who are subject to the provisions of the Trustee Ordinance. However, this holding was hardly vital to his decision.

It is somewhat perplexing that Mills-Owens J thought the t'so to be a trust because early in the judgment he set out his understanding of what a t'so was and his understanding was inconsistent with its being anything to do with English law. 'Speaking generally,' he said,

> a tso may be shortly described as an ancient Chinese institution of ancestral land-holding whereby land derived from a common ancestor is enjoyed by his male descendants for the time being for their lifetimes and so from generation to generation indefinitely.

The descendant automatically becomes entitled at birth to the interest in the land for life, the judge explained, and on death that interest merges with the interests of the surviving members of the t'so, automatically enlarging their interests.[37] The interest of the male descendant described by the judge is an interest in the land, not in the t'so; there is no mention of the interest being merely beneficial. Indeed, in defining a t'so the judge does not mention the managers, the putative trustees and legal owners of the land, at all. In itself this is not surprising because in giving his definition the judge was confining himself to customary law and Chinese customary law has no conception equivalent to a trust.

In concluding that the t'so was a trust, the judge relied on the terms of the schedule to the block Crown lease of 1905 under which the land had been granted (or perhaps more accurately, re-granted) to the t'so by the new administration in the name of King Edward VII for the standard term of seventy-five years with right of renewal for a further twenty-four years less three days. The schedule was in common form with columns for the number of the lot, its size, its use, its address, the term, the name of the owner (i.e. grantee) in Chinese and in English, the Crown rent and so on. The entries under the columns were written in manuscript. Where the grantee of a particular lot was a customary institution, the practice was to place against the lot number the name of the t'so or t'ong and follow this with the names of the managers, all in Chinese. In the next column was what the judge called a translation, although it is more likely to have been a transliteration (a representation in alphabet form of the sound in Cantonese), of the Chinese names into English. In the case of t'sos and t'ongs there would be a transliteration of the name of the t'so or t'ong followed by the name of each manager. In the schedule in question, as no doubt in many others, this name was followed by '(trustee)'. On the basis of this parenthetical word, the judge concluded that the grant had been made to the managers as trustees in law.[38] In other words, the trust had been imposed by the government grant.

37. *Tang* at pp 279–280. Mills-Owens J was speaking generally and was attempting a short description.
38. *Tang* at p 304.

There are difficulties with this conclusion. First, it overlooks what is manifest from the contents of the schedule, that the name of the grantees in English followed by '(trustee)' is merely a translation of the Chinese entry in the immediately adjacent column and was not intended to add to what was shown by the Chinese characters. Only if the Chinese entry contained the equivalent of 'trustee' could that word have effect to impose a trust. The Chinese entry is not reproduced in the judgment but it seems highly unlikely that any indication of trusteeship would have been given there since the word for and concept of a trust was unknown in Chinese. The description favoured for the managers of a t'so was the Cantonese sze lei. This means nominee, manager, supervisor or administrator. In the nineteenth century there were no Chinese characters for a trustee.[39] The concept of a manager is different from that of a trustee. This is so in English and is apparent also in Chinese traditional usage from the custom that sze lei would not act without the approval of the members of the t'so.

The presence of parentheses around 'trustee' suggests that the description is incidental and may not have been used in the Chinese but is added to the English version to explain why there are both collective and individual names (those of the t'so and of the three managers) in the entry of owners. It is as if the clerk who filled in the columns by hand was concerned to indicate that each of the three individuals was not an owner as such but was a representative of the t'so. In other words, the clerk's choice of 'trustee' was not made in order to reflect a status or impose a trust but to emphasize that the grant was made to the t'so itself and to explain why three names follow the name of the t'so in the owner column. The description 'trustee' merely reflects the writer's interpretation of sze lei. Substance is given to this possibility by the fact that in the block lease schedules 'manager' and 'trustee' seem to have been used randomly. As was observed in a case decided a year before *Tang*, nothing turned on the word 'manager' or 'trustee' for they had been used indiscriminately on the Land Register. In a later case another judge stated that manager, trustee and sze lei were synonyms.[40] Dr Patrick Hase has observed that trustee tended to be used where the land was held for a minor or widow under section 18 of the New Territories Ordinance and manager was usually used for t'so t'ong.[41] If so, this would support the possibility that the parenthetical 'trustee' in *Tang* was indicative rather than definitive, or that it was simply a mistake.

In any event, the block lease schedules contain no words of grant: the schedules merely record details pursuant to the grant which is in the printed body of the lease. That body declared its purpose to be to grant a lease 'to the several persons, clans,

39. Evidence of Professor Chang Weijen in *Yau Kwai v Yau Kar Siu* [2004] 4 HKC 141 at 149. The modern Chinese term (信託), 'shun tolk' in Cantonese, is a twentieth-century commercial innovation. However, Jamieson mentions 'trusts' in China, presumably a loose term.

40. Respectively, Briggs J in *Li Tang Shi v Li Wai Kwong* [1969] HKLR 367 and Liu JA in *Tang Yau Yi Tong v Tang Mou Shau Tso* [1996] 2 HKC 471.

41. Hase, *Custom*, Ch 4.

families, and "t'ongs" whose names are set out in the Schedule hereunder written'.[42] The operative words in the *Tang* lease stated that the Crown granted to each lessee the piece of ground set out in the schedule opposite to the name of the lessee.[43] There was no mention there of any status or capacity except that of lessee. There was no indication that the grant is in any way qualified by the words in the schedule. The grantee named in the schedule was the t'so which, having no personality separate from its members, meant its members.

Since the grant was expressly to the t'so (the living male descendants of the ancestor after whom it is named) rather than to the individual managers, the intention cannot have been to constitute the managers as trustees. Trustees are by definition legal owners of the land which they hold on trust so, had the three names been truly trustees, the owner column in the schedule should have begun with them rather than the t'so, perhaps adding that they were holding on behalf of the t'so or its members. But this treatment would have been in defiance of the words quoted above from the start of the lease by which it is apparent that grantees could include clans, families and t'ongs.

A grant to the institution rather than to the managers as trustees would have been consistent with the nature of t'so and with the contemporaneous legislative treatment of them set out in Chapter 3. The provisions of what became section 15 of the New Territories Ordinance are inconsistent with a manager being a trustee. First, the section refers to the land being held in the name of a clan, family, or t'ong, not as being held by the managers as trustees for them. Second, the section deals with the appointment of a manager, not a manager and trustee; indeed it does not mention trust or trustee at all, in marked contrast to section 18 of the same Ordinance. Section 15 was interfering with the customary law by requiring the appointment of a manager and bestowing upon him powers of sole ownership. If the government's intention also had been to add to custom by imposing trustee duties upon the manager, one would have expected that to be in the legislation as well. Instead, the section refers to the members of the family or t'ong appointing a manager 'to represent it', in other words to act as their agent. If the manager had been intended to be a trustee, he would not have been a mere representative but the legal owner of the land. Since elsewhere in the ordinance (in the contemporaneous provision dealing with land held by minors, now section 18) and as part of the same settlement there is a reference to trustees, the absence of the use of that word in section 15 is unlikely to have been an oversight.[44] The section institutionalized and adapted the existing practice in t'so and t'ong of appointing a sze lei, or rather a number of sze lei, a manager or representative but not a trustee.

42. *Tang*, p 289. The wording reflects that used in contemporaneous legislation, now s 15 of the New Territories Ordinance (Cap 97).
43. *Tang*, p 290.
44. Section 18 of Cap 97. This argument was considered but rejected by Chu J in *Tang Kam Wah v Tang Ming Yat*, HCA 10141/1998 (26 November 2002), para 61, for reasons which are not convincing.

The third point about section 15 is that the express effect of the registration of the manager is that he is to have full power to dispose of and deal with the land as if he were the sole owner thereof. If managers were trustees, they would not need this power because they would already have them. It is axiomatic that trustees of land are legal owners of the land. It would make no sense for the legislature to bestow upon managers the power of disposal of the land *as if* they were sole owners unless the legislators, and the drafters of the legislation in the government, were of the view that the managers were not already the sole legal owners of the land and therefore not trustees.[45] The main difficulties which section 15 was designed to overcome, those of dealing with the t'so t'ong and of conveying its land, would not have been encountered if the managers were also trustees. Nor would the need for protection from dishonest managers have arisen, for the duties imposed in equity upon trustees would have provided protection to the members as beneficiaries.

The judicial interpretation of the schedule to the block lease in *Tang* was literal: 'trustee' meant trustee in law. However, in subsequent decades a contextual, rather than textual, approach has found favour so that the courts now look at the words used in their setting. This includes the factual and legal background as well as the practical objects which the words were intended to achieve.[46] The change raises the possibility that a different interpretation might now be put upon the government lease were the question of whether the grant was to managers as trustees to be squarely considered.

The possibility of such a consideration has been raised by a recent application in the High Court for leave to adduce expert evidence on the trust question. The case concerns a t'so holding land at Hong Lok Yuen near Taipo whose land was used as a playing field by a junior school there without payment of rent to the t'so. If the t'so is indeed a trust, the limitation period would not have expired which would deny to the occupiers a defence of adverse possession. This is because the relevant period in the case of a trust is not the usual twelve years since the taking of exclusive possession by the occupier but six years from the attaining of the age of majority of the youngest beneficiary. Since in the case of ancestral institutions new male descendants are continually being born, expiry of the limitation period is constantly being pushed back. In effect the t'so t'ong has immunity from the law of limitation which applies to other landowners.

The injustice of this, and the undermining effect it has upon the efficient use of land, is an indication that the trust concept ill fits land held under customary norms. Another indication is that the rule that forbids perpetual settlements of land, which operates in the public interest, has also been declared not to apply to t'so t'ong.[47] Further indications lie in the other exceptions to the general law of trusts that have to be made for 'customary trusts'. Unlike normal trusts, they cannot be

45. Most managers are members of the t'so or t'ong and therefore a joint owner but they are not the sole owners.
46. *Jumbo King Ltd v Faithful Properties Ltd* [1999] 3 HKLRD 757 at 773 (CFA).
47. *Tang*, pp 294–295.

created by will.[48] Their land does not need to be conveyed to the managers (the putative trustees) in order to constitute the trust. Instead, the settler transfers the land into the name of a body and appoints managers for that body. The requirement of signed writing for creation of a trust of land also does not apply. Most t'so t'ong were formed long before the imposition of this requirement when the New Territories became subject to Hong Kong law. Likewise, the rule that a declaration of trust must be in writing is not applicable. Nor is the trust, not being created in writing, registrable.[49] In the case of a trust of land, one would expect to find an express declaration of trust, in writing (often a will), signed by the founder, settling the land upon trustees in that capacity. None of this is expected in the case of t'so t'ong. These compromises of the law of trusts as applied to customary settlements must surely raise the question whether they really are trusts in the first place.

One eminent authority on Chinese customary law was firmly of the view that calling t'so t'ong customary trusts was a misconception. The late Anthony Dicks lamented that in one publication traditional institutions co-owning land were 'lumped together under an English legal category, trust, which not only has no Chinese equivalent but also into which none of them fits'. Whilst acknowledging that the label may have met the practical needs of colonial administrators, he deprecated its being 'foisted on the reader as if it represented some form of truth'.[50]

48. *Re Estate of Lau Wai Chau* (2000) 3 HKCFAR 98, [2000] 1 HKC 681.

49. Conveyancing and Property Ordinance (Cap 219) ss 4 and 6, re-enacting the Statute of Frauds 1677; Land Registration Ordinance (Cap 128) s 2.

50. Anthony Dicks QC, Review of *Custom, Land and Livelihood in Rural South China* in (2014) 54 *Journal of the Royal Asiatic Society Hong Kong Branch* 231–234. Similar sentiments were expressed by Professor Dicks in conversation with the author in 2012. See also Malcolm Merry, 'Are T'sos Really Trusts?' (2012) 42 HKLJ 669.

10

Small Houses

The New Territories of 1898 was typical of the rural China of that era. In China '[p]ractically the whole of the rural population lives in villages, being drawn together by a sense of mutual security' observed one authority on Chinese traditions and law.[1] The fending off of predatory bands by living in compact proximity to others of the same kin was one of the principal purposes of the village combination. San On contained hundreds of such compact villages, some with walls or ramparts or moats.

At the heart of every village surveyed at the turn of the twentieth century was a cluster of houses. They can be seen on the maps of the demarcation district that accompanied each block Crown lease, neat rectangles, usually arrayed in rows or terraces with the village temple at the centre. Often the village was in a valley beside a stream, numerous irregular small plots straggling along its banks and up the surrounding hillsides, a grove of trees behind the houses. The plots were the fields tended by the villagers for a living. The trees were the fung shui wood, sited to protect the inhabitants from evil influences.

A District Officer and former Land Bailiff, S. H. Peplow, writing at the end of the 1920s, remarked upon the sameness of the villages and the houses. Peplow went on to describe the houses.

> The average size of village house is 40 feet long and 12 feet wide, one storey . . . A wooden partition divides the long room into two, one being used as a sleeping compartment. The doors are of wood held together by a cheap lock and the floor is merely the earth beaten flat. If the occupants own any pigs or poultry, there may be a small shed at the back of the building for them, but more often than not they are kept at the back of the house.[2]

A similar description was found in an old District Office file uncovered in 1950:

> The houses are all of one room structures with the rear portion partitioned into a small dark sleeping chamber. A cockloft usually forms the upper ceiling of the sleeping chamber. Entrance to the sleeping chamber is always on your right as you go in, and the furniture in the main living room is simple and of varied items.

1. Jamieson, *Chinese Commercial and Family Law*, p 73. Jamieson had been British Consul in Shanghai.
2. Peplow, *Hong Kong About and Around*, quoted in Strickland (ed), *Southern District Officer Reports*, p 10.

> The family shrine (red papers with Chinese characters written on) occupies the centre of the partitioning wall, a few benches or stools would serve as seats for all occasions.[3]

The houses really were small. Most were no more than 436 square feet in size: 'yat fan dei' in the Cantonese phrase, one hundredth of an acre. The foundations were usually made of stone, the walls of brick and earth. The ground floor was a single room, for sitting, cooking, and eating. The rear portion might be screened off as a bedroom for the husband and wife. The floor consisted of packed mud. Above, and beneath a wooden pitched roof topped with tiles, might be a cockloft, for sleeping or storage. The interior was sparse and dark, with few if any windows. Outside the front there was often a small yard marked off by a low wall: this was a kitchen and latrine during the day and a compound for the family's chickens and pigs at night.[4]

A few of these old houses can still be seen, usually in a line at the old centre of the village. Some have been restored in show-villages near to new towns such as Yuen Long and Sheung Shui. Occasionally an unaltered one can be found, tumble-down and uncared for, now used for storage or nothing at all.

Such houses were common until well after the end of the Second World War. Writing in the late 1960s of his experiences and investigations earlier in that decade during 18 months researching in Sheung Shui, Dr Hugh Baker described the houses of the hamlets there. The houses were arrayed in terraces, all facing the same direction:

> one behind the other, a gap of only about six feet separating one row of houses from the next. The normal length of a terrace is six houses. The narrow alleys between the terraces are often paved with granite blocks, but in some cases with concrete. The houses are small, generally about 30 feet by 12 feet, and consist of one large room half covered by a cockloft, with a kitchen-cum-washhouse forming an entrance hall.[5]

A few houses in prosperous villages of 1898 were larger, some with two storeys. No doubt many villagers would have liked something greater than 436 square feet. Those who could afford more space would acquire two houses rather than build a larger one.[6] Wealthier inhabitants certainly built bigger and better houses as the twentieth century progressed. But for the most part small houses were all that the nineteenth-century rural subsistence economy could afford. Even if they could have been afforded, bigger buildings would have extended the village beyond the compactness that security dictated—robbery and piracy still plagued the south

3. Quoted in Hayes, *Friends and Teachers*, p 19.
4. Hayes, *The Hong Kong Region*, p 42; Hase, *Custom*, pp 13–14. Hase puts the internal area of a typical house at 340 sf.
5. Baker, *Sheung Shui*, pp 20–21.
6. Nelson, 'The Chinese Descent System', 113–123; Hase, *Custom*, p 14.

China coast and raids from rival villages were not unknown. Isolated farm houses were seldom, if ever, found.[7] New, larger houses would also have impinged upon the farmland upon which the villagers' livelihood depended. Where the village was walled or moated, room for expansion was physically restricted.

This then is what was originally meant by a traditional village-style or village-type house. They were also sometimes called small village houses, on account of their size. We know approximately how many of them there were at the turn of the twentieth century because of the great survey. No fewer than 35,957 building lots were recorded in the old schedules to the 477 block Crown leases. These accommodated a rural population estimated in 1898 to total about 84,000. Since a portion of that population would have been boat people, and another portion would have lived in the market towns, the average number of people occupying each house would have been between two and three only. However, the survey numbers for houses may not be reliable as indicative of dwellings. Howard Nelson, who conducted research in 1967 and 1968 at Sheung Tsuen, a village near Sek Kong in the Pat Heung district, found some houses there which were separated by an alley from their kitchens, yet each house and kitchen had been recorded by the surveyors as two buildings.[8]

Nelson observed that one household (meaning a group of kin sharing a common budget and a single stove) could be spread over several houses, often adjacent and sometimes with an interconnecting door. He also found that there were more habitable old structures in the village than recorded in the survey plans—structures which might have been used as cowsheds or pigsties or been in ruins at the time of the surveyors' visit. Equally, he suggests that the total number of houses recorded in the block leases may include a good many that were not fit for human habitation. Therefore, the numbers cannot be relied upon as precise. Even so, they do suggest that in the early twentieth century the villages were not over-crowded and that the demand to build more accommodation in the countryside would not have been great.

Ever since the forced evacuation of the coast in the seventeenth century, the southern part of Guangdong had been short of people. The toughness of the life contributed to this under-population. The climate was harsh, the terrain difficult. Contaminated wells, poor personal hygiene and bad food storage meant that diseases such as dysentery and malaria were common. The diet was poor. Danger lurked in the fields: snakes and wild boar, even the occasional tiger. Work hazards abounded. A cut might result in septicaemia. Deaths in childbirth and childhood were common. Adults rarely survived beyond the age of fifty years.

During the middle of the nineteenth-century southern China, including San On, mysteriously suffered a fall in population. This can have been only partially the

---

7. Jamieson, *Chinese Commercial and Family Law*, pp 73 and 74.
8. Nelson, 'The Chinese Descent System'.

result of emigration in search of job opportunities. It seems likely that the cause was some disease or other, although famine may have played a part.[9]

Small House Custom

Accordingly, when an extra household had to be accommodated there must often have been a vacant or ruined building that could be adapted or an unused house or lot within the village that could be occupied or built upon. The practice in at least the more prosperous parts was said to be that when a male member of the village married, if suitable land and sufficient money was available, his father as head of the family would build one of these small houses for his son's family.[10] Indigenous males were called 'ding' (meaning male) and such houses were known as ding (or ting) houses, ding ngok. The house would be on land which the father owned (that is to say, held on customary terms) within the village. His bride would be from another village: not from one immediately neighbouring the groom's village, for usually the relationship between adjacent villages was bad, their inhabitants being rivals if not enemies. As is usual with human beings, from football teams to nations, the closer and more alike they were, the more they disliked each other.

There is disagreement as to whether marriage was the occasion for the construction of a ding house. The Hong Kong government, which presumably investigated this and drew information from its civil servants across the territory, says that the custom was exercised on marriage. The Hung Yee Kuk, whose members might also be thought to be in a position to know, maintains that the construction of houses was not restricted to marriage. However, the kuk and its members are hardly impartial in this, having an interest in drawing the custom as widely as possible. Perhaps the practice differed from district to district or even from village to village. One can confidently assert that a young ding was unlikely to have need of a house of his own until he became married, so it would be natural that most houses were built on that occasion.

It is also unclear whether the house was to be built by the father or the son. Howard Nelson found that '[f]athers were under a clear obligation to provide each of their sons with a house when he marries'.[11] That was at Sheung Tsuen; one cannot rule out the possibility that the obligation was different in other villages or outside the relatively prosperous Pat Heung. The obligation is anyway not inconsistent with a son building a house if he had land. The reality may be that the father was more likely to be the one with land to spare or who could afford to buy land and build upon it. Nelson observed that when their son married, parents generally vacated and renovated their own house for the son to occupy and moved to a more modest

9. Hayes, *The Hong Kong Region*, pp 43, 106–110.
10. Joseph Lam Ding Kwok, Chief Land Executive, New Territories Administration, *The New Territories Small House Policy* (unpublished paper, February 1980). No source is given.
11. Nelson, 'The Chinese Descent System', p 116.

one. The background facts of a case from Tsung Pak Long near Sheung Shui showed that the family had been living in one village house, passed down from father to eldest son, for multiple generations with no suggestion of a father building a new house for the son.[12]

Formulation of the custom has proved elusive. The Heung Yee Kuk naturally puts it in wide and simple terms: their indigenous members have a 'birthright' to build a house. This leaves much to be debated. The summary by Denis Bray, the District Commissioner with carriage of the Small House Policy in the 1970s, is almost as succinct: sons of local inhabitants could build themselves a village house on their land in accordance with the orderly layout of the village.[13] This introduces one qualification yet leaves out others. The authors of Civic Exchange's first paper on the policy say that indigenes had the right to convert agricultural land into building land without any prior permission of the Ching government.[14] This may be correct but does not address what the custom was, i.e. what was done in practice. The custom is discussed further in the context of Article 40 of the Basic Law in Chapter 14.

There is a distinct possibility that the building of a house for sons was not a territory-wide phenomenon but differed from district to district or from clan to clan. The practice may have been confined to more prosperous villages whose inhabitants had the resources to construct new homes. In this sphere, as in others, the practice of the districts dominated by the prominent clans inhabiting the flat and fertile north and north-east of the territory may have been taken by administrators, academics, and observers as general. Villages in these districts have been the subjects of intense scrutiny by anthropologists and therefore their customs have received publicity and analysis. Yet they are by no means representative of all villages. Their size, wealth, antiquity, and location set them apart. The five clans that dominated these districts constituted less than a third of the indigenous population.

It is difficult to believe that in the late nineteenth century smaller communities in more rugged surroundings in the eastern section of the New Territories and on the islands followed the same custom. They did not have the money, the space, or the demand to build houses. Most families were poor. Invariably village houses were located in tight clusters for reasons of security and fung shui. Land outside the cluster was often unsuitable for building. Populations were steady or falling. During an interview in April 2018 the retired headman of a small 300-year-old, dual-clan Hakka village at Fei Ngor Shan (Kowloon Peak) stated that his clan had no tradition of the father giving a house to his son on marriage.[15]

---

12. *Kan Fattat v Kan Yintat* [1987] 4 HKLR 516.
13. Denis Bray, *Hong Kong Metamorphosis* (Hong Kong: Hong Kong University Press, 2001), p 163.
14. Lisa Hopkinson and Mandy Lao Man Lei, *Rethinking the Small House Policy* (Hong Kong: Civic Exchange, 2003).
15. Interview with Cheng Gau Hung (born 1923) of Mau Cho Nam, 8 April 2018. The village population had been 100–200 in the 1930s and about 100 post-war; currently it is about 150.

Dr James Hayes, the historian who was a District Officer at Sai Kung, at Tsuen Wan, and on the islands with more than three decades of experience, is sceptical about the alleged custom. He observes that in the 180 or so villages of those areas during the 1950s there were few new houses, suggesting that any such custom, if it had existed, had fallen away during the first half of the twentieth century. 'I consider the "custom" to be the ideal rather than the attainable . . . It could not be attained everywhere, and at all times, nor was it during the first fifty years of British rule.'[16]

By contrast, and consistent with the possibility that the practice varied from place to place, at Fung Yuen near Taipo, there was a spate of building outside the village confines in the 1860s and 1870s, then a pause for some 30 years, followed by more building. The last houses in the old Fung Yuen village of Mak Uk were put up in the 1940s and by the 1950s some houses there were in ruins.[17] But the Fung Yuen villages were in a fertile, secluded valley, close to water (Tolo Harbour) and a town, and inhabited by six relatively recent immigrant clans, so it was more prosperous than remote, small, single-lineage villages that typified Sai Kung and Lantau.

Building on the Custom

If there was a practice in his village of supplying a son with a new house or marriage or otherwise, in order to exercise it the villager needed both land and money. In the early decades of the twentieth century, economic conditions rarely permitted such expenditure. Indigenous males were driven or enticed to work in urban Kowloon and Hong Kong or abroad. The population of the villages did not grow. In fact after 1899 the population of the New Territories as a whole initially declined in number, a continuation of a trend that seemingly had begun in the middle of the century. If there was a vacant or derelict house in the village, it might be more economical and convenient to take over or rebuild on that lot rather than to build on other land. Most agricultural lots were small and irregular in shape and many were on sloping ground, so they were not conducive to construction. Besides, to build on agricultural land meant sacrifice of crops and income. In most villages, there would have been neither the wealth nor the demand for construction of numerous new houses.

However, the block Crown leases of the early twentieth century had envisaged that there might be such a demand. As regards 'old schedule' lots, that is land which had been occupied at the time of the survey and therefore the majority of the land within and around villages, the Crown leases introduced an element that originated in the common law of contract and of land rather than in Chinese custom. The leases contained a provision that government permission (licence) would be required for construction of buildings on any agricultural ground to which the lease applied. This enabled administrators to control construction of buildings on old schedule

16. E-mail communication from Dr Hayes to the author, 23 July 2012.
17. Strauch, 'Community and Kinship in Southeastern China', 36.

farmland and even to charge money for that permission. Exercise of the power was delegated by the Governor to District Officers.[18] In the event, it was soon decided not to charge a premium. The reasons for not doing so were political. The Peking Convention provided that there should be no expropriation of land and taking away the right to build might be construed as an expropriation. Both the Attorney General (the government legal adviser) and the Registrar General (the government land officer) doubted whether the new administration was entitled to extract any benefit from old schedule lots, presumably on the basis of the Convention's provisions. Villagers had not had to pay the Ching authorities for permission to build on their own land and protested loudly at any suggestion that they now do so. Not charging a premium would placate them. The new government had also promised not to interfere with landed interests and customs. Its approach was consistent with and indirectly acknowledged the old custom.

It would, however, be an exaggeration to say that the custom was continued under the new regime. The restriction on building in the block leases and the need for prior permission to build from the Hong Kong authorities were innovations which interfered with the customary position. Moreover, although the grant of building permission did not require a premium, it did result in an increase in the Crown rent charged on the developed lot.

There was also an economic reason for not charging a premium. The government wished to encourage development within the New Territories. Most of the native population there was poor by the standards of the rest of Hong Kong. Allowing them to build on their land would increase economic activity and confidence. No doubt for much the same reason in 1909 on the recommendation of the Hong Kong government the Secretary of State for the Colonies gave permission for the making by private treaty, rather than by sale at auction, of new grants (i.e. of land not covered by block Crown lease) of up to 1000 square feet for building small houses in rural areas. New land had in fact been sold since the turn of the century but always at auction and generally in the expanded Kowloon or in the vicinity of the new roads and railways. The making of direct grants for houses to residents of remoter parts would enable their villages to grow. Sale by private treaty did not extend to New Kowloon or easily accessible land on the coast, along the railway lines and near to new roads or anywhere likely to be the subject of development and the applicant had to be a bona fide villager wanting a house for his own occupation.

It seems that both the power to make private grants and the power to permit building on old agricultural land by giving the owner a building licence were sparingly used. The reason was not that District Officers discouraged building. Their attitude tended to the indulgent so as to foster good relations with natives. It was simply that there was little demand. Villages were not expanding or prospering. Indigenous men saw fresh and better opportunities in urban employment or work

18. GN 191/1906 (9 March 1906).

outside Hong Kong. They began to abandon the land. The rural population continued to fall.

During their early years as part of the colony, the attention of rural land owners was focused not on the construction of houses but on the level of ground rent that the new authorities charged them. In 1903, even before the issue of the block leases, eighteen elders of Shataukok protested against increases in Crown rent. Administrators summarily dismissed the complaint, saying that there had been no promise that the rent would not change or that it would not exceed the amounts payable to the imperial authorities. Internal government memoranda observed that the petitioners were quite well off and could afford to pay. In 1905 residents of Tung Chung on Lantau island also protested about increases in Crown rent. This too was rejected. However, the discontent was so widespread that the Governor, Sir Matthew Nathan, decided that it would be politic to promise that rents would not be further increased. On 11 July 1906 a proclamation was issued that Crown rent would not be raised during the term of the lease.

In an attempt to encourage purchase of land, in 1905 the reserve (or upset) price for sales by auction was set at the low level of HK$1 for every hundred square feet. Then in 1909 concessionary rates were set for sales of house sites within village areas by private treaty. The conditions upon which these concessions were made were the first appearance of a concern about the re-sale or letting of village houses to incomers, a concern which ran throughout the twentieth century. So as to prevent speculation and exploitation, it was stipulated that the privileges should be confined to real villagers who would actually live in the houses with their families.

The villages remained exclusionary places. Outsiders were not welcome and did not wish to live there. Anyway, the District Office would not give permission to non-natives to build there. There was no shortage of housing, so no demand to do so. Accordingly, the great majority of village house sites were sold by private treaty at a low price.

Free Building Licences

The restrictive condition against building without government consent is a means of regulating the use of land, a form of planning control, but it can also be used as a tool for raising revenue. The policy in urban Hong Kong was to obtain income from the betterment of land by charging a fee or premium for relaxation of restrictions upon development coupled with an increased annual Crown rent. The same practice was initially followed with regard to newly granted land in the New Territories. The Tung Chung villagers had complained about this as well as the increases in Crown rent. They had petitioned the Colonial Secretary in London about it. Their complaints had been rejected but the influential Cecil Clementi, who as a member of the Land Court had acquired knowledge of customary land practices, wrote to the Colonial Secretary stating that villagers believed that they were entitled to build on their own padi and that he considered that they had been nothing to stop them from doing so. The secretary responded by allowing District Officers to grant building licences to villagers free of charge.

Rural land management then entered a quiet period until the early 1920s. Years later, reflecting upon the evolution of land policy, a District Commissioner for the New Territories described it as the period of optimism 'when farmers were abandoning their land and it looked as if we could do what we liked'.[19] The optimism must have given administrators confidence to re-visit the question of charging for permission to build on, and for permission to lease out houses on, agricultural land. In 1923 the government determined to extend the practice of levying a premium for these permissions to land appearing in the schedules to block Crown leases. The government also confirmed that only 'native cottages' could be built on agricultural lots. District Officers were instructed accordingly. The rural reaction was sharp. Villagers argued that the new approach was inconsistent with the contents of the 1898 Convention and with assurances given in 1899. At Taipo a committee was organized to petition the Land Officer, the Governor and an official of the Chinese government. Their protests were initially rejected by the Hong Kong government. These grievances led to the formation the following year of the Coalition for Agriculture, Industry and Commerce in the Leased Territory, the forerunner of the Heung Yee Kuk.

The government offered a compromise on the premium issue: villagers who built for their own use would not have to pay a premium, only an increased rent. If they built and rented the house out, half premium would be charged plus additional rent. Non-villagers would have to pay both full premium and increased rent. This did not satisfy village representatives who petitioned the Governor Sir Reginald Stubbs. They argued that the new rules amounted to expropriation of their interests contrary to the terms of the Convention. At about the same time, government compulsory acquisition of land in rapidly-developing New Kowloon was causing disquiet. In April 1925 representatives of 671 villages petitioned the Secretary of State for the Colonies, Leo Amery, in London, enclosing a legal opinion to the effect that resumption was inconsistent with the terms of the Convention. The government postponed implementation of the new rules. There was then another petition, this to Sir Cecil Clementi the new governor who, as a Sinophile and a former officer of the Land Court, might be expected to be more sympathetic to rural interests. This may be why eventually Sir Cecil promised that no premium would be charged.[20]

Thus was established a pattern that was to be repeated several times in the course of the next ninety years. Concern about construction on agricultural land

---

19. Kenneth M. A. Barnett to Colonial Secretary, 20 September 1956, '"Conversion" of Agricultural Land to Building Status', HKRS 163, 1/2805.
20. S. H. Goo, 'The Small House Policy and Tso Tong Land', Ch 15 in Fu Hualing and John Gillespie (eds), *Resolving Land Disputes in East Asia: Exploring the Limits of Law* (Cambridge: Cambridge University Press, 2014).

and about rural houses being owned or rented by people who were not true villagers would lead to an attempt by the government to control the building of those houses. This would be resented by indigenous landowners who would organize resistance and protests, including petitions to Hong Kong authorities and later if necessary to sovereign authorities, arguing that the changes were in violation of the terms of the Convention and of Sir Henry Blake's promises or, later, the Basic Law. The local authorities would offer a concession which would be rejected. There would then be negotiation and a compromise would be struck. The compromise usually resulted in rural representatives obtaining much of what they had asked for. Legislators and the general public would not be consulted, or even informed, until later. The compromise would be put into effect by executive action only.

The discontent was quieted by the 1926 compromise but there was also another factor at play. In the mid-1920s the colony's economy entered a prolonged recession, curbing property values and transactions. Nobody wanted land in the New Territories. The recession was triggered by a general strike in 1925 and a boycott of Hong Kong goods, called after nationalist protestors in Shanghai and Canton had been shot by British troops. The downturn worsened in the 1930s as the worldwide slump affected all sectors of the Hong Kong economy, including shipping which had provided so many jobs for rural men. Incentives to build were offered but had little effect. Economic woes were exacerbated by the outbreak of war between China and Japan in 1937. Then in December 1941 war came to Hong Kong with the Japanese invasion and occupation. There would be no rural construction, only destruction, for the next four years.

A New Spirit

The return of British administration in September 1945 heralded a different era. During the war, a dedicated planning unit of exiled Hong Kong people had come up with ideas and worked out policies which included development of the New Territories. A '1946 outlook' pervaded the post-war administration. The economy sprang back to life. The restored Governor, Sir Mark Young, contemplated the introduction of elections. The sense of turning a fresh page was enhanced by the destruction of pre-war records and the recruitment of a cohort of younger senior civil servants.[21]

Town planning was very much part of the new spirit. Planning had become fashionable in Britain in the 1930s. In Hong Kong a Town Planning Ordinance had been enacted just before the war but had not been brought into effect and was anyway confined in application to the urban areas. Therefore in the New Territories the only means by which planning could be put into practice was through the terms of Crown leases and government conditions of grant.

21. Frank Welsh, *A History of Hong Kong* (London: Harper Collins, 1997), pp 433–434.

Whether it was from a sense of a new beginning or simply that memory of pre-war practices had faded cannot be said but from 1945 the government ceased to sell land for small houses by private treaty. Sales were nearly all by public auction, in accordance with general government policy. However, the majority were sold at concessionary rates, presumably reflecting the fact that those most likely to purchase them were indigenous villagers. Demand for land was stimulated by the post-war influx of refugees and immigrants, including the wealthy from China. In 1948 there were instances of rich mainlanders, including manufacturers from Shanghai, acquiring old schedule agricultural lots in order to build impressive country houses. Reacting to this in January 1949 the District Commissioner John Barrow initiated a prolonged debate about what he termed (echoing the words of the block Crown lease) conversion of land in the New Territories to building status, in other words the circumstances in which the restrictions upon construction on old schedule lots would be lifted. Although he could find no copy of Clementi's 1926 decree that there should be no premium for building on such lots, he discerned that the pre-war practice had been to charge conversion premium only on lots other than old schedule ones. He felt that 'the intention originally must have been that we should not charge a countryman premium for building a simple peasant house on his land', rather than for a luxurious villa.[22] Accordingly, a premium was to be extracted from land owners who wished to build unless they conformed to this description and they proposed to construct a modest house and live there with their families. Barrow composed some notes on land use for the guidance of District Officers reflecting this.

Of course, the new rules led to protests from the Heung Yee Kuk which petitioned Barrow the following November. The kuk wanted all private land to be exempt from premium. The Registrar General, Anuerin Jones, thought what he called a genuine New Territories resident should be allowed to build a house for himself and his family on his native ground. Barrow's successor, Mr K. Keen, was certain that the administration was entitled to charge but the question was whether it should do so. It was decided that the free building licence would remain for genuine villagers wishing to build a family home in the traditional style but that in other circumstances a premium would be required. Meanwhile a land boom was well under way as more and more people came to Hong Kong.

No doubt a desire to participate fully in this boom caused the Heung Yee Kuk not to let the matter lie. In 1956 it returned to the attack on the conversion policy. The usual pattern of demand, proposal, rejection, counter-proposal, discussion, and compromise, or something very like it, recurred. A petition from the chairman of the kuk to the then Governor, Sir Alexander Grantham, deployed familiar arguments based on the terms of the Peking Convention and promises made at the time of the British takeover to argue that extraction of any premium was an assault on the right of inhabitants to develop, use, and transfer village land.

22. Barnett, '"Conversion" of Agricultural Land in the New Territories to Building Status', Attachment 1, 15 January 1949, HKRS 163, 1/2805.

In advising the Colonial Secretary on the response, Kenneth Barnett, the Director of the New Territories Administration, wrote a lengthy review of the history of the land conversion policy. Listing the principles underlying the policy, Barnett gave primacy to the need for control of development and therefore the desirability of maintaining a requirement of permission to build. Other principles were the need to raise finance for services for developing areas, the need to encourage development where suitable and the need to tax the betterment of the land arising from allowing building. But he also identified the need to 'honour our undertakings towards the country people' so he distinguished farming areas and villages from developed and developing areas and concluded that a premium should not be necessary for granting permission to build on block lease land.[23] This was actuated more by the pragmatic consideration that auctions of village land rarely exceeded the upset price because only villagers were interested in buying than by acceptance of the kuk's arguments. Barnett recommended that the reply to the kuk should avoid mention of the Convention and other irrelevancies. Aneurin Jones was also confident that it would be legal to require permission before a house was built but he pointed out that the block Crown leases did not mention any payment being required. He was wary of saying that the Convention and the promises had no bearing on the matter. He was unable to come to a definite conclusion as to whether payment would be legally justifiable.

Time has proved Barnett correct to say that arguments based on what had been agreed and said in 1898 and 1899 were irrelevant. They were political rather than legal statements. The Convention was a treaty between nations, not justiciable in domestic courts.[24] The governor's proclamations were assurances of intent, analogous to a statement of policy or a political manifesto, and likewise had no legal status. As far as law and administrators were concerned, the important document was the Crown lease. The kuk's arguments were moral and political only.

Barnett was no enemy of rural interests. He was one of the most talented men to hold the various-titled positions which constituted head of administration in the New Territories. He had joined the Hong Kong civil service in 1934 and quickly shown his gift for languages and his love of Chinese culture. As an army officer and later prisoner of war he had displayed courage in daunting circumstances.[25] A scholar of Chinese, he was one of the founders of the Hong Kong Branch of the Royal Asiatic Society. During his time in the New Territories he had established good connections with rural leaders.[26]

23. Barnett, '"Conversion" of Agricultural Land in the New Territories to Building Status', Attachment 56, 3 July 1956, HKRS 163, 1/2805.
24. *Winfat Enterprises (HK) Co Ltd v Attorney General* [1988] 1 HKLR 5 (PC); [1984] HKLR 32 (CA).
25. Barnett had complained, in French, to a Swiss inspector of the prison camp of lack of food (Japanese soldiers were stealing prisoners' food parcels with the connivance of the commandant), which earned him solitary confinement and beatings; in 1946 his testimony helped to convict the commandant of war crimes.
26. Later Barnett founded the Census and Statistics Department and organized the 1961 census, the first full census in Hong Kong for thirty years, widely admired for its organization. After retirement he worked for the United Nations on census matters in Africa and Asia.

Trouble at the Kuk

One difference between the 1925 dispute (and another lesser eruption about premium and increased rent in the 1930s) and protests in the mid-1950s was the political context: in between times, the Japanese had first overrun and then been forced out of Hong Kong, China had been through the turmoil of international and civil war and the Communists had taken charge of the mainland. Towards the end of Barnett's tenure in the New Territories the Heung Yee Kuk was torn apart by an internal dispute. In 1957 there was a power struggle between a nationalistic traditionalist faction from long-established lineages intent on pushing rural land claims to the ultimate and a more moderate progressive group, centred on the existing leadership, which felt that the kuk should not provoke the Hong Kong authorities and should exploit the New Territories' good fortune in being part of an expanding British colony and aim to profit from the demand for their land. Representatives of the latter faction tended to come from parts adjacent to industrial or urban areas.

Elections of chairman and committee members took place in August 1959. Leaders of the former faction ('an unscrupulous bunch' according to Denis Bray, who was soon to become the Deputy District Commissioner) staged a coup by rigging the vote. They arranged for electors to be presented with an enormous list of candidates—hundreds of village representatives qualified to serve on the committee—and then gave perplexed electors a list of those for whom they should vote. The consequence of course was that the traditionalist faction's candidates were elected.

Government recognition of the kuk was withdrawn shortly before the tainted elections took place. Barnett himself attributed the trouble to the premature death of one of the kuk's leaders, presumably because this opened up possibilities for election of new leaders. In any event, the government considered it pragmatic to dissolve the existing kuk and reform it, placing it on a statutory basis. Barnett engaged in secret talks with the progressive faction. The Bill setting up the new organization was introduced to the Legislative Council by the Colonial Secretary (who spoke 'a lot of hot air', according to Bray) and was passed quickly. The land upon which the kuk's office in Taipo stood was resumed. The office was seized in an early morning raid, then the land was conveyed to the new statutory organization. The kuk's new leaders were considerably friendlier towards the authorities than their predecessors.[27]

A Sensitive Matter

It has been suggested that during the middle decades of the twentieth century there was a 'tacit agreement' between the government and indigenous villagers that the latter would be allowed to erect houses for their own use on their own land held

27. Bray, *Hong Kong Metamorphosis*, pp 97–101; Chun, *The Fictions of Colonial Practice and the Changing Realities of 'Land' in the New Territories*, p 143; Akers-Jones, *Feeling the Stones*, pp 29–30. The statute was the Heung Yee Kuk Ordinance (Cap 1097) passed in 1959.

under block lease.[28] This seems to be putting the matter too high. District Officers were no doubt sympathetic to the request of a villager who needed a home and could afford to build one on his own land. They may well have been sensitive to the desire of a father to supply a house to his son upon marriage. But 'agreement' suggests surrender by the government of its control over village development and a decision that it would not exercise the condition against building without Crown licence, neither of which happened.

At an internal meeting in February 1957 the principal officials of the government concluded that there was no legal obstacle to imposing a premium but that old schedule lots should continue to enjoy free conversion for the erection of genuine village houses. So, far from there being a tacit agreement, the truer position was that the government decided unilaterally not to exercise its rights because it wished to avoid trouble—it steered a pragmatic course, for the power to impose a premium was a sensitive political matter. Landholders within the rural community fiercely contested the making of payment which they saw as an affront to their traditional rights and a breach of promise and were prepared to complain loud and long about any attempt to make them pay.

So, when formally approving the policy concerning the grant of permission to build in the New Territories in 1957, the Executive Council decided that no premium would be required for a village-type house for occupation by a bona fide villager. But this was expressly subject to there being no planning or fung shui objections. The qualification concerning planning shows that the 1957 policy was not a simple continuation of the traditional small house right, still less acceptance of the arguments of rural landowners.

A Revised Policy

The 1957 policy imposed no restriction upon the size of village houses: this seems to have been recognition of existing practice and may explain the presence during the mid-twentieth century in villages of domestic houses greater than the traditional 436 square feet including the occasional house of four storeys. However, the policy did demand that the applicant be a bona fide villager, that the house be of a traditional type so as to be in keeping with the village (the term 'small house' had yet to enter official vocabulary) and that there be no objections to its siting. Any objections were invariably based on considerations of fung shui or of planning. The former objection would come from fellow villagers for whom protection of the good fortune of the village was of great importance; the latter came from the administration. Planning considerations assumed importance when general development policies for whole areas and particular layout plans for certain villages became more

28. Memorandum for the Executive Council, XCR (67), 28 February 1967, referred to by the Director of Audit, *Report on the Accounts of the Hong Kong Government for the Year ended 31st March 1987.*

common. By the late 1950s plans had been devised for Tsuen Wan, Shek Wu Hui (Sheung Shui), Sham Tseng and Tai Wai (Shatin).

There were, however, two difficulties with the application of the administrative approach towards the grant of free building permission. Who was a genuine, or bona fide, villager? And what was a village-type house? A bona fide villager certainly did not mean an urban outsider who desired to erect a spacious country home on some farmland that he had acquired. At the other extreme, it certainly included a man who had always lived in the village and who could trace his ancestry back through men to one who had lived there since the nineteenth century or before. But what about those living in the village whose families had settled there during the twentieth century? And what about those living outside the New Territories who had been born in the village and regarded it as their place of origin? Then there was the complication of new villages. Villages were founded after 1898, sometimes as offshoots of well-established settlements. Were long-term residents of these new villages bona fide villagers, even if their villages had no long history? Moreover, insistence upon the applicant being a genuine villager seemed a waste of effort. The block Crown lease contained no restriction upon alienation, so a bona fide villager could sell the house on to someone else quickly.

There were differing views about what constituted a village-type house. Must it be small? Must it have only one storey? Must it have been built from traditional materials? Must it have only one large room, possibly with cockloft over? Must the kitchen be situated at the front? How many windows were permitted and what size could they be? The traditional style of house was not attractive for modern living.

In 1959 Barnett's successor as District Commissioner for the New Territories, Ronald Holmes, resolved to cut through these difficulties. Holmes, a brave and wiry Yorkshireman fluent in Cantonese who had been a young government cadet before the Second World War and an intelligence officer during it, was an astute, decisive, and long-serving senior civil servant with a reputation as a trouble-shooter. Perhaps he sensed that the momentary weakness of the Heung Yee Kuk was an opportune time to take the initiative. The New Territories administration had become overwhelmed with work, in part because of its modest size and in part because of the influx of people into its sphere during the previous decade. Holmes thought that the administration of land could be made easier by dropping the requirements that the owner applicant be a bona fide villager and that the house be in traditional style, though he could see that a building free-for-all had to be avoided. In March 1959 he proposed to the Colonial Secretariat, the command centre of the Hong Kong Government, new rules for the conversion of land to building. The proposal did away with the notions of a bona fide villager and of a village-type house. Instead it employed the idea of a small house and a restriction of one such house to each family.

Holmes suggested that, provided there were no planning or fung shui objections, any owner of an old schedule lot should, as before, be given a free licence to build a house, but the house should be a small one. He defined small as a single-storey dwelling up to a maximum of 15 feet in height and occupying no more than 700 square feet of ground. This requirement was larger than the traditional type of house but it was what District Officers thought a contemporary poor man might afford and thus was likely to help those with genuine housing need. The officers called such houses bungalows. The requirement also happened to be the same as the restrictions imposed upon residential buildings on newly granted land in the 1930s. These small houses would be free of building controls: fortuitously, legislation to extend those controls to the New Territories was being drafted so an exemption could be written in for such houses. The height restriction would allow for the usual cockloft above the living room and for a traditional peaked roof, but not for two or more storeys. Holmes thought this would encourage farmers to replace wooden sheds with permanent and more hygienic buildings. Permission for a house of larger dimensions would attract a premium and require engagement of an architect.[29] A new Crown rent would be charged on the small house.

Although, somewhat disingenuously, Holmes presented these as merely slight modifications to the existing rules, the Colonial Secretariat had reservations about them. The secretariat feared that the proposals would not prevent urban dwellers from setting up weekend bungalows on old lots or prevent the establishment of a considerable number of houses in what once had been cultivated areas.[30] Nevertheless, the new rules were approved in June 1959, although with a stern warning that the issue of building licences for old lots should be closely controlled and confined to one per family.

The new rules were a distinct departure from previous policy. They in effect extended free building licences to those who were not bona fide villagers but who happened to own old schedule lots. They also limited what villagers might build. Holmes was well aware that this would not be welcome to the indigenous population. At the time, the change of policy was not revealed. It was regarded as too sensitive: 'political dynamite' according to Holmes. It might have been feared that announcing the new policy would rekindle faction-fighting within the Heung Yee Kuk. The anticipated explosion would not be about the giving of free licences to non-villagers but about the restrictions in size to 700 square feet and 15 feet in height with only one-storey, the imposition of payment for anything larger and the restriction to family use.

The new conversion rules were initially confined to old lots. The reason for this was presumably that prior to 1898 owners of land in private ownership had not been required to ask or pay for permission to build on that land. But this rather ignored that much new land had been granted by the Crown over subsequent decades and that an influx of people in recent years had stimulated demand

29. District Commissioner, New Territories (Holmes) to Colonial Secretary, confidential memorandum, 20 March 1959.
30. Colonial Secretariat (I. M. Lightbody) to DCNT (Holmes), confidential memorandum, 29 April 1959.

for residential buildings. A year later the Executive Council quietly approved the extension of the rules to new grants made before the Second World War, that is to say grants made in and between 1901 and 1941. This too was not publicized, for fear that it would set off demand for similar concessions regarding post-war grants which the administration discerned were often taken for speculation. The extension was a little surprising, for the argument that building restrictions broke promises made at the turn of the century and were tantamount to confiscation of traditional rights could hardly be made in respect of land first granted after 1900. In the event the extension was little used. Land which had been the subject of pre-war New Grants was generally on higher, more marginal ground, unsuitable for rice and for buildings.[31]

In remoter parts of the New Territories new buildings must have been rare. But the post-war city was spreading out as population pressures grew and transport improved. Rural landowners were keen to take advantage of this. Restrictions under the Crown lease were the only means of control upon buildings. The Buildings Ordinance, which had been overhauled in 1955, did not apply beyond the old urban area. New Kowloon was the only part of the New Territories to which building controls applied.

The extension of the Buildings Ordinance and its associated regulations to the whole New Territories was, however, about to pass through the Legislative Council. Among other things, these would require plans of new buildings to be drawn up by professionals and approved by the Building Authority, for the authority to give permission before work could start and for a permit to be granted before a house could be occupied. But the administration did not want villagers to incur such trouble and expense. To accommodate the new approach an exception was incorporated for a dwelling house with a roofed-over area of 700 square feet or fewer which was not more than 15 feet in height.[32] These houses were to become known within the administration as New Territories Exempted Houses. The ordinance and the exception applied to all buildings and all people throughout the whole New Territories. There was no privilege specific to the indigenous. As such, the ordinance and the revised policy marked a further departure from the old custom which had become subsumed by executive acts and by statute.

31. Barnett, 'Land Conversion in the New Territories', XCR 217/60, discussion paper for the Executive Council (1960).
32. Buildings Ordinance (Application to the New Territories) Ordinance (Cap 322), effective 1 January 1961. This was the first of (eventually) two ordinances of that name. Regulation 2 of the Buildings Ordinance (Application to the New Territories) Regulations provided that various provisions of the ordinance should not apply to the erection, alteration or demolition of certain buildings in the New Territories.

Rural Response

The new restrictions on size and the charging of a premium for a larger building were finally disclosed in June 1960 through a circular to village representatives from Holmes' substitute as District Commissioner, Arthur Walton. As feared, they received a fiery reception from the indigenous population. At Sheung Shui the Rural Committee and its legal advisers discussed the new policy and the impending extension of building controls to the New Territories with village representatives. They resolved to request an amendment to the policy and, if that should be rejected, to request the Heung Yee Kuk to start a self-government movement in the New Territories.[33] The District Officers must have been feeling the heat, for they raised the question of revising the restrictions at a meeting with Walton that September.

In November a group of kuk representatives toured the mainland New Territories to test opinion on land policy. They visited rural committees at Shatin, northern Sai Kung, Taipo, and Fanling, with the press in attendance to ensure that publicity would be given for the views expressed. The feeling was that landowners should be allowed to build without any restrictions unless the village had a planned layout. The size restrictions were denounced as unsuitable. Every villager should be allowed to build a house. Building licences should be free. No architect's plan should be required. Owners should be allowed use of land outside the village layout without payment. No premium should be charged for converting agricultural land to building land. Bitterness was voiced about the slowness, or complete lack, of response of the administration to house applications. At Fanling, however, there was more concern about the poor telephone system than about small houses.[34]

The kuk pressed for the 15-foot height limitation to be raised and the 700 square-foot size limitation to be dropped. They had some momentum for this since many existing houses exceeded the new limits. The maximum height for houses constructed on new grant land had been 25 feet with two storeys since the 1930s. They found a sympathetic ear in the District Officers. After one meeting with the officers and another with kuk representatives, Walton beat a retreat. He recommended to the Colonial Secretariat substitution of a limit of 25 feet and two storeys, provided that no reinforced concrete was used in the construction: a safety concern prompted by the Director of Buildings. However, Walton resisted the kuk's demand that a roofed-over area in excess of 700 square feet be allowed. The recommendation was approved. The poor man's bungalow had lasted but fifteen months.

Small houses were therefore getting larger and as they did, the traditional house was left behind. Also the practice of the government negotiating a private settlement of land difficulties with the kuk was further established. 'For some reason,' commented Ronald Holmes to the government's Political Adviser about the right to build on agricultural land, 'the leaders of New Territories opinion have shown, and

33. *Wah Kiu Man Po*, 26 July 1960; there is no mention of seeking approval for this from the PRC.
34. *Kung Sheung Yat Po*, 10 November 1960.

are likely to continue to show, less delicacy and forbearance than ordinary people in this kind of matter.'[35] Perhaps the reason was that rural people had discovered that being forceful with the administration brought results.

The government's fear that village houses would be built for occupation by non-villagers proved well founded. At the Ping Shan village of Hang Mei in 1962, eight new houses were constructed, five of them specifically for rental to outsiders. The building and letting of houses was a prime topic of conversation among the local population. Jack Potter observed:

> They often discuss such matters as the proper design and height of a house; how to build a house to get the maximum income from minimum construction costs; the amount of rental to be derived from each square foot of house space; new government regulations on the building of village houses; and how to get around the government building inspector.[36]

Since its constituents were so keenly interested in exploiting their housing, it is no surprise that the kuk continued to press for concessions. In representations to the authorities during the early 1960s, it argued that the size limitations on new houses were too severe and resulted in unsatisfactory living conditions. It said that the ban on the use of reinforced concrete was unreasonable. The pressure eventually worked. At a dinner given by the kuk in his honour in November 1964 the Governor, Sir David Trench, announced that two-storey houses of reinforced concrete with up to 1,000 square feet of covered area would be allowed by District Officers within village areas or their natural extensions, although with the caveat that standardized plans and a registered building contractor would have to be used. The caveat proved unpopular. In 1965 only seventy-five applications were made for premium-free licences to build. The kuk complained that it was difficult to engage architects who were willing to work on buildings in country areas.

So the pressure for more changes continued. In 1967 it was rewarded when the Executive Council removed the requirement for use of plans and engagement of a registered contractor. This was though subject to a proviso that the house was genuinely needed by the villager himself or his sons when they married. If no suitable land was available within the established village, the site could be within natural extensions of the village. The statutory exemption for small houses was accordingly amended with effect on 1 July 1967.[37] At the same time the permitted maximum dimensions were converted into metric measurements: 65.03 square metres instead of 700 square feet and 7.62 metres instead of 25 feet. Everybody continued to use the old figures.

Therefore 'small houses' continued to move away from the traditional design. Wood had long given way to concrete. Pitched roofs had been replaced by flat ones.

35. Confidential memorandum, 16 January 1961.
36. Potter, *Capitalism and the Chinese Peasant*, p 99.
37. Regulation 3, as amended, of the Buildings Ordinance (Application to the New Territories) Regulations.

Two storeys became more common. The new height limit, measured to the level of the main roof, or to the apex of a pitched roof, was widely adopted. The restriction to 15 feet if reinforced concrete were to be used was widely flouted. Later an extra half-floor at roof level was tolerated.[38]

Being allowed to build taller houses and do so without plans did not satisfy the kuk. New houses had to be within the confines of the villages or their natural extensions, a restriction which reflected traditional practice and gave the DO ability to plan village extensions. But the restriction reduced the amount of land available for building and held back the expansion of accommodation for villagers. An indigene who wanted a house had to find his own land in or around the village and such land was scarce. Even where land was available for sale, he had to compete with others who would usually out-bid him. So the kuk wanted villagers to be able to build outside the village and not to have to pay a premium for doing so. Administrators resisted this: they could see that it would encourage sale to outsiders. The kuk also wanted villagers to be allowed to build one house for each son free of premium regardless of the age of the son—in other words, to do away with the marriage requirement. Again administrators pushed back: they anticipated that the house would be let out until the son was old enough to live there or to sell it at a profit. This reflected the long-standing disagreement as to whether the custom was linked to the son's marriage; the kuk said that it was not, the government that it was. Officials thought that if they gave way on this, there would be disorderly development of houses which would be let to people who were not indigenous.

Village houses were becoming known and popular outside rural circles. Between 1905, the time of the block leases, and the start of the Small House Policy in 1972, 27,431 new grants were made for building purposes. This was aside from free building licences made to both indigenous and non-indigenous landowners. Certain desirable places such as Lamma Island near to Hong Kong Island and the Sai Kung peninsula proximate to Kai Tak airport, suffered an influx of new, largely expatriate, residents. Officials were sympathetic to rural complaints. For a time in the late 1960s sales of building plots at Lamma and Sai Kung were suspended. The government was prepared to restrict participation in auctions of village building land.

Government policy dictated that building land be sold by public auction. This created a problem for those whom administrators regarded as 'genuine villagers', by which they seem to have meant families of modest means who had settled in a village for generations and were unable to compete with the bids of outsiders. One solution attempted was to hold 'restricted' auctions in the village and at dawn. Another was to have a 'closed' auction in which only villagers were allowed to bid. But closed village auctions merely led to those who wished to bid colluding to

38. Dr Patrick Hase, quoted in Hopkinson and Lau, *Rethinking the Small House Policy*, 3.1.

divide up the lots which were for sale by agreeing amongst themselves that only one of them would bid for a particular lot.

Squatters

Simultaneously, the New Territories Administration had an additional housing problem, one faced by Hong Kong in general. This was the post-war influx of immigrants from mainland China. Millions of newcomers flooded into the colony and hundreds of thousands of them settled in the rural areas. They found there land to work and to live upon, sometimes as tenants, occasionally as owners but generally as squatters.

Pressure for more homes in the New Territories really began with that influx. The vacant land in the countryside was largely government land, although some of it belonged to private owners who had chosen or been forced by circumstances to abandon it or who had simply disappeared. This set the scene for numerous claims of title by adverse possession in later decades (see Chapter 15). The squatters put up huts, shacks and sheds on the empty land. In course of time many of these temporary dwellings became accepted by the authorities who granted the squatters licences to occupy (Crown land permits). By the beginning of the 1970s there were almost as many of these as there were traditional village houses, but almost as many again remained unapproved.[39] Accordingly, authorized village-type houses had become a minority among the dwellings in rural areas.

On government land the immigrants set up humble abodes of wood, brick, wire, stone, asbestos, and metal, small houses of a different sort from the traditional village-type construction. They were generally about 400 square feet in area and 12 feet in height, often with small dependencies such as pig sties and chicken sheds. These flimsy structures formed extensions of existing settlements or even new villages on their own. Politely termed 'cottage areas', they were in effect rural shanties or slums, and they constituted a health hazard, a safety concern, and an administrative headache.

The small staff of the various District Offices struggled to keep track of this problem. They could not prevent or control it, so they attempted to regularize it. Occupiers of Crown land were given permits to occupy the land or short-term tenancies. Where the land occupied was private, the owner (Crown lessee) was given a licence for the erection of the structures for a small annual fee which was usually paid by the occupier. If the squatting involved a change of use, the owner would be granted a temporary waiver of the restriction on use.

39. In 1972 a then-secret discussion paper for the Executive Council, XCR (72) 219, estimated that there were 43,000 traditional village houses, 36,000 lawful temporary houses, and 35,000 unlawful houses.

Rural Housing Crisis

By the late 1960s, the squatter problem, coupled with the recurrent complaints of the indigenous that their building rights had been denied, their land was being confiscated and that new village land was being sold beyond their means, led to perceptions of a rural housing crisis and a sense that something radical had to be done about it.

11

The Small House Policy

The lack of village land for houses was a problem that festered for years whilst representatives of government and the Heung Yee Kuk met. Discontent with this and other aspects of official practice in the New Territories, such as the sale of land at public auction and the compulsory acquisition ('resumption') of villagers' land, led the kuk in 1971 to form a special committee to fight for changes. Discontent reached a peak with a protest meeting, said to be attended by more than one thousand people, at Yuen Long in 1972. The meeting produced a list of demands to be made to the government.[1] Plans were announced to mobilize ten thousand people to march on Government House.

This no doubt startled the authorities. However, there were other pressures to act as well. The complaints of the indigenous population were only part of a wider issue of inadequate housing in the New Territories. Many of the structures in which people lived, not just the indigenous and not just in the villages, were makeshift and unhealthy.

The complaints of the indigenous lobby that they could not find or build houses in their villages and the needs of the numerous incomers pointed towards an overhaul of rural housing policy. At the same time, the requirement of space to accommodate the expanding urban population pointed to development of the New Territories and therefore the placation of those whose land would be needed for new towns. As a first step, the District Commissioner for the New Territories, Denis Bray, resorted to the tactic of his predecessors: he negotiated with the Heung Yee Kuk.

Having ascertained what the kuk wanted and what they might settle for, Bray with the assistance of his acting deputy, a former District Officer, Patrick Williamson, formulated proposals, packaged as a new policy resulting from a major review, to put before the Executive Council. He drew up a confidential discussion paper for submission via the Colonial Secretary to the council.[2] Exco considered and approved the proposals on Tuesday, 14 November 1972.

1. Bray, *Hong Kong Metamorphosis*, p 163.
2. XCR (72) 219; Bray, ibid, p 166.

The 'new policy with regard to small houses in the rural areas of the New Territories', or Small House Policy, was introduced by the Hong Kong government in December 1972. The policy is now synonymous with the housing privileges enjoyed by indigenous men and is usually regarded as the source of those privileges. However, neither of these presumptions is strictly accurate.

During the last decades of the twentieth century and the first decades of twenty-first century, the policy came to assume totemic qualities. To critics and opponents of the advantages enjoyed by native villagers, the policy was regarded as the embodiment of unwarranted aboriginal benefits, discriminatory and wasteful. To supporters and defenders of those benefits, the policy was regarded as the prime example of traditional entitlement. Each of these views places too much weight upon the policy and ignores its background and content. The background has been recounted in the previous chapter. The content was different from the way in which it was presented.

Presentation of the Policy

Although today the term 'Small House Policy' has become synonymous with indigenous building rights and privileges, that aspect was only part of the policy as originally envisaged, or at least as originally put forward. Equally, if not more, important was the position of the non-indigenous population, relatively recent settlers who lived in squatter huts and tin shacks (in official parlance, 'domestic structures built of temporary materials'), often clustered in so-called cottage areas, on government and private land. Following influxes during the previous quarter-century, these immigrants and their offspring were the majority of the rural population by 1972.

The plight of non-indigenes featured large in the discussion paper presented to ExCo in late 1972.[3] The paper pointed out that 58 per cent of the buildings in the rural New Territories were either unlawful houses or lawful temporary houses and that, according to the 1971 census, 40 per cent of squatters were in the New Territories despite their containing just 10 per cent of Hong Kong's population. The current land policy, the document asserted, perpetuated temporary structures, for their nature kept down the cost of taking back the land if it should be needed for public purposes.

On this, the paper was somewhat parsimonious with the truth. The lower cost of resumption was not the only consideration. A franker assessment would have acknowledged that the government had simply been overwhelmed by the inflow of immigrants during the previous two decades. The expansion of the public rental housing programme that was vital to the elimination of squatter areas was not yet under way. Most of the immigrants had settled in urban areas where matters were more pressing. In the relatively spacious New Territories, it had been easier and

3. XCR (72) 219.

pragmatic to allow things to continue, at least until the new towns which were then on the horizon had been built.

Even so, the paper was now proposing a change of course. As a first step towards the achievement of better building standards, permitted structures which had been on Crown land for more than ten years would be granted leases permitting the construction of village-type houses. Where the structure was on private land (and therefore subject to a Crown lease which restricted building) and irrespective of its age, licence to build would be given in place of the existing modification of the lease which temporarily allowed the structure. This power would be freely exercised in rural development areas. In each case, it was thought that the prospect of permanence would encourage householders to improve their living conditions by erecting proper buildings with up-to-date sanitation. The drawback with this proposal was that the householder would have to pay to the government the market price (a full premium) for purchase of the land. He would also have to pay the costs of construction. Most families occupying these humble structures would not be able to afford this and even for those who could, it would mean an enormous, if temporary, increase in housing costs that was unlikely to be attractive. The authors of the new policy must surely have realized this, which raises the suspicion that this aspect of their proposals was window-dressing and perhaps designed to deflect attention from the main purpose of the reform.

That purpose came next in the proposals. The District Commissioner wished to resolve 'a major anomaly in the system of disposal of land within village areas', the practice of holding closed village auctions. In order to achieve the market price, sales of government land had long been by open auction. To ensure that sales of building land within and around villages were to genuine villagers, this practice had been amended by restricting those who were entitled to bid for such land to those who had demonstrated need for housing to DO staff. This was achieved by not advertising the auction outside the village, holding the auction behind closed doors within the village and at an inconvenient time, and withdrawing the property from sale if non-villagers were bidding. In practice, the paper explained, there was rarely more than one bid. It proposed therefore that the auction be replaced by a direct sale to the villager, a private treaty grant.

ExCo members were told that each lot sold would not exceed 1,000 square feet in size with the area to be built-over 700 square feet and the buildings not to exceed two storeys or 25 feet. In other words, the existing maximum dimensions for exempted houses were to be maintained. The land was to be within the village environs. Each indigenous male over the age of 18 years (except those who already had new housing as a result of land clearances for government projects) could have one house built during his lifetime provided that he was not already adequately housed in accordance with village tradition. The grant was no longer to be tied to the son's marriage, a concession to the kuk. The paper suggested, with some exaggeration, that it was a minor concession and a compromise since the kuk had wanted no age restrictions.

The proposal to abandon restricted village auctions sounds reasonable enough, although to describe the holding of an auction as an anomaly that by implication required removal seems strange. Sale of government land by auction was the norm. The anomaly, if there was one, was that bidders were confined to villagers. This could have been removed by holding an auction open to all. But that would not have served the purpose of the District Commissioner, who wanted to carry out his agreement with the kuk to provide house sites exclusively for its constituents. This could be achieved by direct sale of building land to them but it would not have been expedient to state this baldly, so instead it was presented as the removal of an anomaly.

Ironically, what was proposed was in effect the creation of another anomaly, one which received no emphasis in the paper. The grants to indigenes ('genuine' or 'native' villagers), unlike those to other long-term residents of rural parts and to buyers elsewhere in Hong Kong, would not be at market price. The price would instead be two-thirds of the market level. Why such a proportion? It was the 'upset price' at village auctions, the minimum amount at which the government would be willing to sell. The reasoning was that since there was usually only one bidder at closed village auctions, the sale was normally at this price. No consideration seems to have been given to offering private treaty grants at market prices even though this was envisaged for sales to non-indigenous residents. Nor was it explained that there was normally only one bidder because villagers colluded in advance of the auction to allocate the lots to each other—in other words, they engaged in bid rigging.

The discussion paper makes no mention of another feature of the provision of building land for aboriginal males which distinguished it from land already occupied by licensees and squatters. Such provision would require that land in the vicinity of the villages be resumed by the government, purchased from its existing owners with public money. The land would then have to be made suitable for construction, and infrastructure, such as access roads, might well be needed too. This would involve government expenditure.

Nor was any mention made of the long-running agitation of members of the kuk for more building land and the deal struck shortly before the ExCo meeting with the kuk's leaders. The closest that the paper comes to acknowledging the underlying reality is that early on it says that small houses are of importance in rural areas and that regulation of their construction has been the subject of prolonged discussion between the kuk and the District Commissioner and that it states in its conclusion that abolition of closed village auctions in favour of private treaty grants would be 'reasonable and politically desirable'.

The overall impression given by the paper is of a subtly deceptive presentation of a sensitive change of position materially favouring one section of the rural population, dressed up as a major reform aimed at improving health and safety and preserving village identity. ExCo was duly persuaded and approved the policy. The principal author of the policy, Denis Bray, attended the ExCo meeting. So did his predecessor, David Akers-Jones.

Executive Council members were really the only people who needed to be persuaded since implementation required little more than a change in internal administrative rules. However, Mr Bray felt the need to convince the Legislative Council and the public at large. He used the opportunity, or rather excuse, that a small part of the new policy necessitated a minor relaxation of rules made under the Buildings Ordinance so as to allow the use (already widespread) of reinforced concrete in construction of buildings 25 feet in height, to make a speech in the Legislative Council. The relaxation might have been achieved without any speech or debate but Bray wanted publicity for his new policy. He spoke to LegCo on 29 November 1972, two days before the policy was to come into operation. An announcement was made to the press the same day, highlighting the changes and quoting Bray at length. The account given to LegCo and to the press was subtly different from that in the ExCo discussion paper.

To LegCo, Mr Bray explained that the changes had come about because of a review requested by the Heung Yee Kuk which had begun the previous year and which had led to an agreement with the kuk, which he thanked for its co-operation. He had arranged for the kuk's leaders to be present in the public gallery. By contrast with the ExCo paper, he gave prominence to aspects of the new approach which favoured indigenous applicants. Small house applications would be processed more quickly in future, he said: within six weeks of receipt, because they would be handled by District Officers, plans would not be needed, and private grants would be used. More sophisticated health standards would be required. There would be no more permits for temporary structures. Anyone would be able to build a small house in rural parts, he asserted, and owners of existing temporary structures and long-term permit holders would be allowed to redevelop their structures into small houses. Whilst Bray stated that areas for new houses would be better defined with uniform criteria, he did not mention the resumption of land to supply sites for indigenes only, nor that they alone would receive a discount on price. He concluded by saying that these were interim measures which would complement a future comprehensive development plan for the rural New Territories.

The price discount was however mentioned in the contemporary six-page announcement to press and public by the Government Information Services. But the direct sale of government land at two-thirds value was presented there as merely the third of four principal features of the new policy, worthy of just one sub-paragraph. No justification for the discount was given. The public could have been forgiven for thinking that the new policy was a much needed reform designed to alleviate poor housing conditions for everyone living in country areas. Humble abodes would be improved, over-crowding alleviated, disease, and dilapidation eliminated: all this at little cost to the public revenue.

On the same day as his speech, Bray communicated the details of the new policy by letter to the Heung Yee Kuk. Naturally, the letter dwelt upon the concessions to be given to indigenous inhabitants. Generally speaking, Bray told the kuk, during a villager's lifetime he would be entitled to one concessionary grant of land to build a small house. The letter omitted to mention the proviso contained in the ExCo paper that the applicant not be adequately housed in accordance with village tradition. Bray must have known that the kuk recognized no such restriction upon its constituents' alleged right to build.

So, as far as the government was concerned, the averred purpose of the new policy was to improve the rural housing stock. This was to be achieved by supplying more land for village housing on a systemized basis, requiring better building standards, and allowing non-indigenous residents to construct their own houses. There was no suggestion at that stage that preservation of the character of villages was an objective.

Another, less virtuous but more realistic, motive for the policy is hinted at by Dr James Hayes who at the time was serving in the New Territories Administration. He wrote that the policy was intended as recognition that villagers' land in many places had been, and would continue to be, affected by development and planning controls.[4] This is rather opaque but seems to be suggesting that the privileged provision of discounted development land made under the policy was compensation for loss of land elsewhere and for the refusal of the administration to allow new houses in villages that were earmarked for incorporation into a development plan. This is rather hard to understand since to qualify for a grant the applicant had to be indigenous to the village in which the land was situated: it could not be sold by the government to a displaced or disappointed indigene of another village. Perhaps Dr Hayes' point is more general. As a district officer he had experience of the resiting of villages to make way for public works projects and the inability of the administration to provide land upon which the removed villagers might continue their farming. Instead, they had to settle for compensation and a flat in a multi-storey development in one of the expanding towns. Their disappointment and disruption must have been observed with trepidation by villagers in other districts. By 1972 town planning in the New Territories still largely consisted of extensions to existing built-up areas such as Tsuen Wan and Taipo but it would have been apparent that development of entire new towns would be necessary in the near future to cope with housing needs and that the land for these towns would be in currently rural areas. The provision of subsidized government land for village housing was a way of signalling that the administration had the interests of villagers in mind and of subduing any trouble that future village removals might engender. In other words, the policy aimed to win rural co-operation for the development of the New Territories.

4. Hayes, *The Great Difference* (book), p 109.

Content of the Policy

So far as it concerned indigenous inhabitants, the policy was formulated to allow an adult indigenous man (ding) to apply for permission to erect for himself during his lifetime a small house on a suitable site within his own village or its environs. The object was said to be to regularize traditional practices whereby male villagers would build a family home on land that they owned. However, as was seen in the previous chapter, regularization had been in place throughout most of the previous seventy years during which customary rights had been incorporated with adaptations into land policy.

The policy is a set of internal administrative rules the main features of which were and are that land was to be made available for sale to indigenous inhabitants in or in the vicinity of villages exclusively for 700 square foot, three-storey houses. The land would be vacant government land or private land which the government would resume. Similarly, other long-term residents with homes on government land were to be allowed to buy that land to build a replacement house. The sales were to be by private treaty rather than auction. Where the inhabitant was indigenous, the price was to be below market level. The Buildings Ordinance would continue not to apply to such houses, so an architect need not be engaged.

Indigenous Inhabitants

Who were the 'indigenous inhabitants' who were to benefit from this largesse? According to the government, an indigenous inhabitant was a male person who was at least 18 years old and who had descended through the male line from a resident in 1898 of a recognized village. He did not have to have been born in that village, nor did he need to be resident within it. Females, no matter how long they had inhabited the village and even those who could trace their descent to a male resident of 1898, could not be indigenous. Nor could the many thousands of males who lived in recognized and other villages but were not descended from a male resident of 1898, irrespective of the fact that several generations of their forbears had inhabited a village. This meant that villages which had been founded after 1898 (there were a few, such as Lo Wu which owed its beginnings to the Kowloon-Canton Railway completed in 1910) could have no indigenous inhabitants. Neither could a village, such all those in New Kowloon, which was unlucky enough not to be recognized.

A recognized village is one on a list kept by the Director of Lands. A number of New Territories villages are not on the list, even though they existed in 1898. The list has been revised from time to time as villages have been added. Originally, in 1973 591 were listed. Ten years later there were 636. By 2019, there were 642. Somewhat confusingly, the list includes a number of villages founded since 1898. Although these villages cannot have indigenous inhabitants, the Small House Policy does allow applications to be made to build exempted houses in them. A successful applicant will be charged a full premium, in contrast with indigenous applicants. Licences to build at post-1898 villages are granted only to adult males descended through the male line from a resident in the village at the time that the village was founded. This restriction is mystifying given that by its nature the village had never been the subject of the nineteenth-century small house custom.

The definition of indigenous adopted in Hong Kong therefore owed nothing to race or creed or language or any of the other distinguishing features of aboriginal people in other places. It hinged instead upon the Chinese tradition of patrilineal descent. The definition seems to have been the creation of administrators. 'Indigenous inhabitant' is not two ideas but one. The 'inhabitant' does not refer to a current resident but to a historical one: an inhabitant of a village at the time that San On was part of imperial China.

The restrictions upon who could be regarded as an indigenous inhabitant had rational connections to custom and the past, but they also served the useful purpose of limiting the impact of the new policy. In 1972 no-one seems to have questioned the exclusion of females or of native males who could not demonstrate descent through a male line back to a certain village at a certain year. Presumably this was because the New Territories was regarded as a law unto itself and it was assumed that all the government was doing was crafting a rural housing policy which was consistent with custom.

Provision of Sites

The sites to be provided to those who wished to exercise their customs were to come from either existing government land or resumed private land. The pledge to provide sufficient building land and to do so on a systematic basis was an innovation which belies suggestions that the policy was merely a consolidation of previous practices. It also belies the suggestion that the policy was a continuation of the small house custom, for under the custom the indigene selected and owned the land upon which to build whereas under the policy new land for exempted houses was initially owned and selected by the government and released in accordance with the orderly layout of the village.

The boom in construction of small houses after 1972 meant that village boundaries could not accommodate the demand for building sites. Before implementation of the policy, construction was allowed by District Officers within the pattern of the village. Afterwards, construction was permitted within the village environs, defined as 300 feet of the outermost existing construction that existed in 1972. Later, for a time there were 'village expansion areas', space into which the new buildings were allowed to grow. Hence the policy heralded better planning of the development of villages. These areas were placed into abeyance in 1999 following the extension of planning laws to rural parts.

Land Exchange

For a variety of reasons the villager's land might be unsuitable for a 700 square foot house. Many plots identified in the great survey were tiny; others were awkwardly shaped; still others were situated on sloping ground. An indigene might hold several of these, scattered around and not close to the village. In such instances, the administration was willing to exchange that land for other, more suitable land by a procedure known as land exchange. Where the villager's land is insufficient on its own for a house, land officers may provide adjacent land, if available, by surrender and re-grant. The owner surrenders his existing land to the government which then re-grants it to the owner together with the extra land as one new lot so as to comprise an adequate house site.

Private Treaty Grant

In permitting house land to be sold by private treaty, the Small House Policy was departing from immediate past practice. During the years from 1945 to 1972 grants of land without auction, though possible, had been rare. They were employed for special purposes such as for the provision of a non-profit-making hospital. The premia charged for these grants varied but was normally a certain percentage of the market value. Departure from the norm of sale by auction was so unusual that in 1959 the Executive Council had ordered that nearly all grants by private treaty be referred to it.

So in this respect the policy was not a continuation of the previous practice but a reversion to an old one. The policy paper for ExCo in 1972 presented the use of private treaty as a revival of an old practice but it did not explain that private sales had been used in the early days of the New Territories because no one except native villagers had been interested in building houses in the remoter villages and that by the 1930s such grants had become rare. Nor did it say that in the post-war era private grants had come to be regarded as an exception to the general rule of sale by auction so as to obtain the best price for new land.

What Could Be Built

Instead of using the terminology of 'village type' houses, the policy continued the stipulation of maximum dimensions based upon the pre-existing practice with regard to the size of what was allowed within the exemption from Building Authority controls. In his autobiography Denis Bray claims credit for the idea of substituting dimensions for style, but in fact the idea was that of one of his predecessors, Ronald Holmes, as explained in the last chapter.[5] In 1959 Holmes had

5. Bray, *Hong Kong Metamorphosis*, pp 164–166.

suggested that the size of houses which villagers should be allowed to build should be restricted to 700 square feet and one storey and 15 feet in height. That had been adopted, although the subsequently the permitted height had soon been lifted to two storeys and 25 feet.

Bray's recollection is also faulty in respect of the inception of the exemption from the application of the Buildings Ordinance which saved villagers from having to employ architects and comply with other building regulations. He credits the 1972 policy with this but actually the exemption dates from 1961 (Holmes again being responsible) when the ordinance had been extended to the whole New Territories subject to the exemption.

In the 1980s, the maximum height allowed grew to 27 feet, being three storeys each of nine feet. The maximum permitted roofed area remained at 700 square feet. These dimensions are still in effect and are to be found in the schedule to the present legislation.[6] So the exemption currently requires the building to be of no more than three stories and 27 ft (8.3 m) in height, with a roofed-over area not exceeding 700 sf (65.03 sm) and a balcony or canopy not exceeding four feet (1.22 m). The thickness of the walls must be at least 6.89 in (175 mm) if of reinforced concrete or 13.39 in (340 mm) if of brick. There are also restrictions upon the height of any rooftop structures such as stairhood, water tank and parapet and requirements regarding kitchen, bathroom, toilet, septic tank, and drains. The exemption was introduced in 1961 so the maximum size of small houses had been laid down for more than a decade before the policy was initiated. Consequently a 'small house' is an example of what is officially known as a New Territories Exempted House (NTEH). A house of greater dimensions would not be a NTEH, so the Buildings Ordinance and regulations would apply to its construction. Once a NTEH has been built, any changes to it are subject to the ordinance and regulations. Any rural house within the dimensions, whether built for or occupied by indigenes or not, was an NTEH. The thinking continued to be that to enable small houses to be erected quickly and inexpensively, it should not be necessary for plans to be drawn up by architects and submitted to the Building Authority for approval, or for permission to be given by the Authority before construction could begin or before the house might be occupied.

Accordingly, the innovation which was introduced by the 1972 policy was not the restriction upon size but the provision of subsidized land to a certain class, namely ding, or indigenous adult males. This class was defined by reference to their gender and patrimony, so they did not have to be genuine villagers at all. They could have been born or be settled in Sydney or Soho and never have visited their family's ancestral home.

The provision of subsidized land was not entirely new for, as explained in the previous chapter, prior to 1972 village land sold by auction restricted to indigenous men was usually at below market price as a result of the bidders colluding to offer

6. The second Buildings Ordinance (Application to the New Territories) Ordinance (Cap 121).

the lowest amount acceptable to the government. What was novel was that the supply of building land around villages was increased and organized.

Free Building Licence

As before 1972, indeed almost since the creation of the New Territories, and in accordance with what was accepted by the administration to have been the custom, if a villager already owned suitable land, he could be given permission to build a small house thereon without a premium, a free building licence. The grant of the licence might however be upon certain conditions and in certain circumstances might even be refused. The continuation of this practice proved to be another valuable gift to indigenous males for, as will be explained in the next chapter, it was open to exploitation by them, acting in league with developers.

Benefits Granted

The Small House Policy bestowed or continued significant benefits upon the indigenous. It enabled them to acquire building land where previously they had none or where what they had was unsuitable for building. It subsidized the cost of that land. It enabled them to buy in priority to other potential purchasers. In the case of lots acquired by purchase from the Crown between 1901 and 1972, it allowed permission to be given to build without charge. It also allowed those who had old schedule land to build on it, despite the covenant in block Crown leases against building without government consent, and to do so without charge too. They had of course to pay the cost of erecting the house and might have to pay an increased Crown rent.

Building Covenant

The policy continued the existing requirement that the ding construct a house reasonably swiftly. The government grant of a new small house lot, or of licence to build upon an old one, would stipulate that a house must be constructed within a specified period. At the time of the introduction of the policy the period was 24 months, though it is now 36 months.

Non-alienation

Since the grant or licence was to be personal to the villager, for the purposes of family housing and at a reduced or nil premium, one would have expected them to contain a restriction upon sale or assignment of the land. The administration was well aware of the risk that rural houses would be constructed for resale rather than as living accommodation for the ding and his family. Yet, despite the custom that the small house be for the indigene's own use and despite the declared aim that the policy was to improve housing for rural people, the early grants and licences issued under the policy contained no clause forbidding alienation of the property.

This was changed in 1976, after an initial spate of resales of newly built village houses. The grantee was forbidden to transfer the land to someone who was not indigenous. This was an absolute prohibition, lasting for the length of the lease in the case of grants of government land and for five years from the date of the certificate of compliance (below) in other cases. Needless to say, the ban was unpopular with indigenous folk and the kuk was soon pushing for its abolition or relaxation.

As usual, the government gave way. In 1979 it agreed to waive the condition if the full premium was paid to the government by the owner. There was an exception in the case of a grant of government land within a village expansion area: there the restriction would not be waived for the first three years. Neither measure proved a practical obstacle to the resale of new houses.

Building Boom

Once the new policy was in place there was an immediate surge in the construction of new exempted houses. Denis Bray attributes this to a 'terrific pent-up demand for legitimate development' and describes how the thousandth building licence for a small house was issued within nine months. It would have been more accurate to say that there was a terrific demand for speculative gain. Development there certainly was, but it was not development to meet the housing needs, or improve the housing conditions, of indigenous families, which had been the declared aim. Only a minority of the houses were to be occupied by such families. Bray hardly realized, even thirty years later, what his policy had let loose. In his autobiography he claimed that he had warned the kuk that if the policy was abused 'we should scrap the whole thing' yet says he knew that it would not be long before houses would appear which looked nothing like the traditional village house and some would be sold to 'rich city slickers'. In fact it was the great majority of houses which were resold, and quickly, a risk which should have been apparent from so many of them having been erected under free building licence which, unlike new grants, contained no restriction upon alienation. Bray adds that if some New Territories residents made money out of the policy, he did not begrudge them that. He does not mention that far more money was made by developers, agents, businessmen and lawyers.[7] Nor is his claim that the new houses were created without a cent of public expenditure sustainable. There were infrastructural and administrative costs, not to mention the amount of premium and government rent foregone.

Once the policy was in place, there followed a quarter of a century of construction of village houses with only the loosest restrictions. Ding houses on land

7. Bray, *Hong Kong Metamorphosis*, pp 164–166.

supplied by the government were intended for occupation by villagers, yet the majority of them were immediately resold to others. A disproportionate number were built in more convenient and scenic locations, attractive to those seeking a country home or rural retreat.

Despite the pre-1972 complaint that insufficient building land was available to indigenous men, before long the majority of small house applications were for free building licences on land already owned by ding, rather than for grants of government land on which to build. This was because of schemes devised and refined by developers to take advantage of the rights of indigenous males to build on their own land, for their mutual benefit. These schemes are dealt with in the next chapter.

The explosion in the number of exempted houses, mostly 'Spanish style villas' with white walls and red trim, changed the appearance of the countryside. Three-storey houses seemed suddenly to be everywhere. It became apparent that the exemption of these houses from building controls may not have been a sound idea. More control over their construction was desirable.

1987 Reform: Certificates of Exemption

Consequently, on 16 October 1987 legislation became effective to replace the original ordinance extending building controls to the New Territories. Somewhat misleadingly, the new ordinance bore the same name as the old one.

The replacement legislation still exempted ding houses from the main controls but it brought in greater regulation of them. The permitted dimensions were hardly altered. However, the builder of such a house had first to obtain from the District Lands Office (DLO) certificates verifying that the house was to be exempt from the requirements of the Buildings Ordinance and regulations.[8] The grantee needed such certificates in respect of the building works, site formation works and drainage works before construction work could begin. The certificates were and are issued under sections 5 and 6 of the 1987 legislation by the DLO on behalf of the Director of Lands.[9] The effect of the certificates was that the relevant building provisions do not apply to the works or the building named in the certificates. However, a certificate may be made subject to conditions. Conditions relating to health and safety are often imposed. In *Rita Enterprise Co Ltd v District Lands Officer, Taipo*[10] a condition that planning permission for village-type development be obtained (the proposed house being on green belt) was upheld.

These certificates of exemption were soon pronounced by the courts to be documents of title.[11] This meant that, as far as conveyancing lawyers were concerned, there were two title regimes for village-type houses. One was for houses the

8. Buildings Ordinance (Application to the New Territories) Ordinance (Cap 121) s 4.
9. Ibid, ss 4–11.
10. [1996] 4 HKC 410. The power to impose conditions is in s 9 of Cap 121.
11. *Lui Kwok Wai v Chan Yiu Hing* [1995] 1 HKC 197; *Lo Chun Tak v Chan Foon Tai* [1991] 2 HKC 650.

construction of which had begun before 16 October 1987: a vendor of such a house did not need to show any certificate of exemption since the old law still applied to it. The other was for houses the construction of which had begun on or after 16 October 1987, the vendor of which had to provide such certificates (or an occupation permit showing that the Buildings Ordinance had been complied with).[12]

Certificate of Compliance and Letter of No Objection

After construction of the exempted house had been completed, the new law also required a certificate or letter stating that the covenants or conditions in the government grant had been complied with, and before the house could be occupied the DLO had to issue a letter stating that it had no objection to the house being occupied. The first served as proof that the building covenant and other conditions had been observed and therefore that there was no risk of government action for failure to comply with the Conditions. The builder and engineer engaged by the villager would submit a construction completion report and, if satisfied, the DLO would issue the certificate.

The other document which is needed before the house can be used is a letter from the DLO stating that it has no objection to the house being occupied. This is similar to an occupation permit.

So certificates of compliance and occupation permits, documents familiar to conveyancing lawyers in built-up Hong Kong, were now in effect required for village houses. Moreover, land administrators could impose conditions upon the issue of these documents thereby tightening control of development still further. All this was a far cry from the simple and inexpensive countryman's home that had been the vision of those who first promoted the exemption in the late 1950s. It seemed that the distinction between town and country was being eroded.

Village Zoning

The comprehensive planning that Bray envisaged did not arrive until the 1990s. Now most listed villages outside the country parks are the subject of planning. Those that are within or next to a new town have a village layout plan. Originally the plan was the work of the District Office but it has become part of the preparation of outline zoning plans. These layout plans usually provide for superior infrastructure to those for other villages.

In more rural parts, the Planning Department draws up plans which recognize a 'V zone', that is to say an area in which village-type houses may be built without planning permission. Designation of the zone takes in a number of factors: the terrain, slopes, demand for small houses, and so forth. However, exempted houses

12. *Wong On v Lam Shi Enterprises Ltd*, HCMP 2549/1995 (20 December 1995).

may be built outside the V zone too, in development permission areas, with permission from the Town Planning Board and approval of the DLO. The Board readily allows small houses to be constructed on agricultural land.[13] Indeed, most such applications are approved. The green belt around villages is far from inviolable.

The belated application of planning controls accounts for rural sprawl, the irregular arrangement of village-type houses that disfigures many villages. Typically, a ragged string of individual houses of varying age and design rubs shoulders with cramped developments of a few identical houses. These are usually on the periphery of the original village. The core of the settlement retains its older houses inhabited largely by those few 'genuine villagers' who remain in residence, enjoying their nominal government rent and exemption from rates. More and more land on the outer reaches of the village has been levelled, reclaimed from water or converted from waste, ready for more houses.

13. Lai, Ho, and Leung, *Change in Use of Land* (Hong Kong: Hong Kong University Press, 3rd edn), p 236.

12

Exploitation of Ding Rights

Use and Misuse

The supposed custom of indigenes building a small house in their village, as incorporated into, amended, and expanded by the Small House Policy, is one of the most criticized aspects of the Hong Kong housing and land regime. The criticism takes several forms. Some critics concentrate on the policy's profligate use of land; some upon its cost to the public finances; others upon its gender inequality; still others upon its deleterious environmental consequences. However, the main focus of the criticism is its unfairness to the community at large. The policy is claimed to bestow an unearned, outdated and unwarranted privilege upon a small section of the population. This unfairness is said to be exacerbated by the misuse or 'abuse' of the privilege. This chapter investigates what is meant by the privilege being abused and how this so-called abuse is carried out.

Underlying the charge of abuse is the assumption that the purpose of the policy was to provide better and more living space for the rural population. This assumption gains traction from the government's justification of the policy when it was introduced in the early 1970s. There was then claimed to be a rural housing crisis. Natives had been priced out of the housing market by outsiders who out-bid them at auctions of village building lots. The character and composition of villages was said to be under threat. The Heung Yee Kuk naturally emphasized these matters since it assisted their lobbying for the provision of land exclusively for their constituents. Arguments presented by administrators to legislators and the public for the introduction of the policy concentrated upon the need for and improvement of housing. Yet that aspect was down-played in their conversations with the kuk whose members regarded the building and sale of houses upon their land as their right.

Given that the public purpose of the policy was the provision of domestic accommodation for indigenous and other villagers, any practice which results in new houses not being lived in by them but being sold to and occupied by others can be described as a misuse of the policy. However, if the purpose of the policy was instead or in addition to appease the rural community by rewarding them for their co-operation in tolerating the new town development programme and by compensating them for the loss of land and culture which that programme entailed, there is no 'abuse' if the villagers benefit from the policy, whether that benefit consists of accommodation or of money. Likewise, if a purpose of the policy was to give native villagers a share of the prosperity being enjoyed by property owners in urban Hong Kong or to bestow a benefit comparable with the subsidies given to tenants of low-cost public rental housing and home purchase scheme flats, any material benefit resulting to them is defensible.

Consequently, the judgmental ideas 'abuse' and 'misuse' will be avoided here in favour of the more neutral idea 'exploitation'. This is so even while recognizing that a large proportion, probably a majority, of Hong Kong people believe that the Small House Policy should be abolished and that indigenous rights should not be allowed to be sold.

Anatomy of Exploitation

How does the exploitation take place? The common impression is that a villager is given a piece of land by the government on the basis that he is to build a house on it and live with his family in the house but instead, once the house has been built, he sells it to someone from outside the village, thereby turning the house into money.[1] In the early days of the policy this was one way in which villagers monetized their rights. Before December 1972 there was no subsidized government land on offer, so an indigene had to be relatively wealthy if he was to build a small house: he needed to have inherited or bought at market value a piece of land suitable for building, to pay a premium to the government, and to meet the costs of construction. But sales of one house by an individual ding acting alone soon became the exception rather than the rule.

The new policy changed the dynamic. For those indigenes who already had land, it guaranteed the giving of permission to build without payment of a premium. However, the pre-existing practice of District Officers already allowed them that, so the permission was merely confirmed by the policy. For those who did not have land, the new policy made more building plots available by instituting village expansion areas and reserving them for ding. The land was not available free of charge; a premium still had to be paid to the government. The premium was concessionary, not the full value, yet it was still a sizeable amount, generally about two-thirds of the market price. Construction costs also had to be paid, as did other expenses such as administrative fees. So participation was easier but many ding still could not afford to join in unassisted.

The terms upon which the government agreed to sell the land (Conditions of Grant) stipulated that the house must be built within a certain time, typically 36 months, and, from 1976, that the villager (grantee) could not sell, let, charge, part

1. Examples are in *Lau Kwai Kiu v Bian Xiantian* [2012] 4 HKC 313 and *Lou Siu Ping v Lam Tsz Man* [2012] 4 HKC 394.

with possession or otherwise alienate the land, other than to another indigene. Originally it was an absolute ban on resale to outsiders. This reflected the government's understanding that the house was for use as the grantee's residence but of course was at variance with the wishes of most grantees and with the attitude of village representatives and the kuk. However, after pressure from the kuk the no-alienation clause was relaxed to permit resale after five years from completion of construction to the satisfaction of administrators and the giving of a certificate of compliance with the terms of the Conditions of Grant issued (initially by the DO, later the District Lands Office or DLO). In the case of a house built on land owned by the indigene, the non-alienation period stipulated in the licence or exchange was three years. Greater flexibility was introduced in 1979 by allowing resale before completion of construction if the grantee paid to the government the difference between the reduced premium that he had been charged and the full market value of the land as at the time of application to the administration for permission to sell.

Consequently, the no-alienation clause impeded the quick re-sale of the house. It meant that anybody who agreed to buy the house and land from the grantee before the house had been built or during the non-alienation period thereafter would be taking a considerable risk. The agreement could not be registered, for then the authorities would discover the forbidden agreement. They might discover it by other means in which case under the terms of the grant the land would be at risk of government re-entry, i.e. the grant could be forfeited.

This was a risk, but it was not a great one and, from the point of view of both the villager as a keen seller and the buyer anxious to have a spacious country residence, one worth taking. It soon transpired that land administrators took a fairly relaxed view. The terms of grant envisaged that the house might be resold eventually. Speedy unauthorized resale at least meant that the house would be built, for the buyer's instalment payments of the price could be put towards construction and other costs.

So it was that during the later 1970s sales of village houses prior to completion of their construction became frequent. By the mid-1980s this was common knowledge. A thriving small industry arose around them in the New Territories, employing builders, estate agents and other intermediaries. So widespread and accepted was the pre-sale of new village houses that when eventually the courts were obliged to consider the legality of the practice, approval was given. Such sales were not contrary to public policy, the Court of Appeal pronounced, for the proceeds benefited the public revenue through the premium received; the sales helped indigenous males if they did not have the finances to build the house; also the sales helped to solve the housing problem because they meant that others besides the indigenous might live in pleasant village houses. The court described the transaction as merely 'jumping the gun': since resale would be allowed at the end of the period during which alienation was forbidden or upon payment of the balance of premium anyway, the sale was simply anticipating that event. Overall, the judges thought, more good than harm resulted, so such sales were not void as contrary to public policy.[2]

The judgment may be thought astonishing in its toleration and even to amount to encouragement of a breach of government grant. 'Jumping the gun' seems euphemistic, for the sale was undoubtedly a breach when it was agreed, even if it might not have been one if carried out later. The judgment may also be a little naïve. The judges evidently assumed that since he was the registered owner of the land, the grantee ding had paid for the land himself and had no hidden backers, but (as we shall see) this was rarely the case. The reasons for decision were delivered in late 1997, towards the end of a sustained period of inflation in property prices during which village houses had proved popular objects of speculation and profit. Shortly afterwards a crash in prices, brought on by the Asian Financial Crisis, exposed many problems with ding houses. More recent decisions of the courts have been notably less accommodating towards practices concerning such houses, as will be demonstrated in the next section.

The Small House Policy incorporated the pre-existing practice described earlier by which an aboriginal male who already had land might build a small house upon it. This may seem an inconsequential matter since building land had become so scarce and expensive as to be beyond the means of the average indigene, but that would be to underestimate Cantonese business ingenuity. The policy, and the custom before it, gave its beneficiaries something besides access to subsidized building land and something which others could not obtain, namely a right to build a house without paying a premium to the government. A wealthy urban man might be able to buy land in or near a village but he would not be able to build on it because of the covenant against doing so contained in the government grant. Unless he also happened to be indigenous, he would not have been able to obtain permission to build there, even on payment of a large premium. But if somehow the indigenous right to build could be married to the ownership of the land, it would be a different story.

The Reality

Most new village houses are not built or paid for by indigenous males. They are and have long been built and paid for by investors and developers, entrepreneurs whose business is based on exploitation of the administration's readiness, pursuant to the Small House Policy, to grant building licences to ding who have suitable land and to do so without any premium.

Typically, these entrepreneurs buy land in the vicinity of a listed village: within the V-zone or the green belt nearby. If the latter, they will have to apply for rezoning of the land for residential purposes but that is a straightforward, though time-consuming, process. The land is usually vacant or only lightly used and suitable

2. *Li Pui Wan v Wong Mei Yin* [1998] 1 HKLRD 84.

for building. Formerly it may have been used for agriculture or horticulture. These entrepreneurs may be villagers or acting in league with villagers and agents with local connections, either as investors themselves or as advisers.[3] They put together a building scheme, perhaps in joint venture with a developer. The developer is invariably small, a company specializing in construction of village houses either by itself or through sub-contracts with builders, and may itself have local connections. (Large developers prefer to build massive estates of flats and houses or medium sized estates of luxury villas.) The venture is organized through a partnership or a jointly owned company formed specifically to carry out the project. One participant may contribute the land, the other the various development costs.[4] One or both of the participants may lend money to the joint venture to finance the project, or the venture may borrow money from a finance company. The scheme might be the subject of a contract (sometimes called a co-operation agreement) or of a letter of intent: the latter is employed in order to deflect allegations that the venture will be in breach of the no-alienation provision in the contemplated government grant.

The land is then divided into plots or portions, each sufficient for a small house with maybe a garden. The division is carried out by a declaration by deed, called a deed-poll because there is only one party to it.[5] The entrepreneur and its agents will in the meantime have recruited males indigenous to the village or sub-district (heung) to which the house site appertains and willing to sell their right to build a house. Depending upon the number of houses planned, this can be quite a lengthy process because the original population of many villages has moved away. The recruits must not only be able to trace their male ancestry to a listed village in 1898 but also must not yet have exercised their right to build a house and must be willing to sign documents that they may not understand and to attend at the DLO. The indigene must be able to prove that he is descended from an 1898 male inhabitant through a genealogy or on the certification of the village representative or member of the local rural committee. It is not unknown for the representative or member to require consideration for his co-operation. The search for suitable males often extends to the city and overseas, whence many New Territories people have moved. It does not matter that the indigene was not born in the village, nor (provided that he says he is intending to return) that he does not live in the village. But he must be descended through the male line. The lure for him is a handsome reward for lending his name to the project: commonly HK$150,000 to HK$300,000 in the 1990s. Property price inflation since 2003 has increased the amount further after a fall at the turn of the century. Payments of half a million dollars or more

3. The scheme had been devised by the village head in *Yip Wai Hong v Yip Kai Tong* [2015] 4 HKC 435.
4. An example of such an arrangement is revealed by the background facts in *Yip Wai Hong v Yip Kai Tong*, ibid.
5. Since there is only one party, the edge of the top of the document is smooth (polled), in contrast with the serrated edge (indenture) traditionally used where there are two or more parties and each will have a copy, the edges of which fit together.

have become common. This payment may be described as a loan. Occasionally the reward is instead a flat in one of the houses within the scheme.

The accumulation of a collection of villagers qualified to receive house grants is so difficult and lengthy that there are businesses operated by intermediaries who specialize in it. The joint venturers may make an arrangement with such a business to buy the dings' rights from it.[6]

At this point there is a developer with land but no right to build on it and there are dings with a right to build but no land. The difficulty is solved by assignment (transfer) of a house plot to each ding by the real or true owner, the entrepreneur or developer who bought it. The ding thereby becomes the legal and registered owner of the plot. To give the appearance that this is a regular sale, a price will be named in the assignment papers but it will not actually be paid by the ding; the only money changing hands will be in the opposite direction, payment to the ding of a portion of the fee payable to him for use of his right, although this will not appear on the assignment. These initial amounts have various descriptions: 'sincerity money', 'fung shui money', 'welfare payment'.

In exchange, as part of the scheme and as security that it will be carried out, the indigene signs various documents. Foremost of these is Power of Attorney giving the entrepreneur or one of its directors authority to act on behalf of the ding in all matters to do with the land and house, including the making of applications to the DLO. There is usually a will, by which in the event of death, the ding leaves the property to the agent or developer and names the latter as executor of his estate. There may be a declaration of trust, by which the he states that he holds the property on trust for them. However, a declaration of trust is strictly not necessary since the law will deduce, by dint of the fact that the ding did not pay for the land, that he holds it on trust for whoever did pay for it. There may be a letter of intent, stating that he intends to re-transfer the land to the developer. There will also be a mortgage deed if the entrepreneur or developer wishes to use the land as security for a loan to finance the building. Lastly, a reassignment of the property executed by the ding will ensure that the legal ownership is returned to the true owner at that owner's wish.

Thus prepared, the entrepreneur can apply to the DLO as representative of the indigene for a licence to build a house on the land. The man will have to attend at the DLO to sign various papers, including a declaration that he is the owner of the land and, if resident abroad, that he intends to return to live in the village. Another instalment of the monetary reward will usually be payable to him after this.

If satisfied, the DLO then issues the licence to build the house. This is without charge (a free building licence) but an administrative fee is payable. The issuing of the licence will take time. Invariably, conditions are attached to the licence. The

6. Packages of dings with rights had been purchased by the developers in *Best Star Holdings Ltd v Lam Chun Hung*, HCA 409/2008 (22 February 2012) and in *Tiu Sum Fat v Shun Sing Development Ltd* [2010] 1 HKLRD 553, [2010] 1 HKC 258.

entrepreneurs and their agents can then start to look for purchasers for the completed house or units within it.

It may be years before construction is concluded and the house is finished and ready for occupation. Only then does the ding receive the final instalment of payment for his rights. He may never have seen the house, let alone the ultimate purchaser. Meanwhile that purchaser will have been paying instalments of the price and may have been given possession of the house. After the DLO has certified that the terms of the grant have been complied with, the purchaser will have to wait for the period of the ban on assignment to expire or (as the case may be) for an application to be made to lift the restriction on alienation and the top-up premium to be paid. The transfer of title is made in the ding's name under the power of attorney. To add to the complications, the purchaser may be a speculator who in turn has sold the house to an end-user.[7]

One Man's Experience

The indigenous male involved in such machinations is invariably unaware of the complexities of the scheme in which he is participating. As far as he is concerned, he has a traditional right but that right is useless to him unless he needs a house in his ancestral village and has the funds to buy land there and build on it. He is delighted to find that someone is willing to buy that right from him, turning it into cash.

Prime candidates for selling their rights are male descendants of 1898 villagers who have been born or have settled abroad. They may not even know of their rights. They certainly would not be told by the middlemen who seek them out that the sale involves deception and possible illegality. One such man, let us call him William, is a university graduate born in the United Kingdom of Hong Kong parents. He is unable to read or write Chinese. He now has no contact with his village forbears or relatives. William described what happened to him.[8] 'There was a friend of a friend in my circle of British-born Chinese friends. We all have similar backgrounds. Our parents are from Hong Kong but they immigrated to the UK in the 1960s or 70s to work.'

The friend of a friend was an acquaintance of someone who worked for a Hong Kong property developer. 'I didn't know the developer but the friend of a friend I've known for many years. He just came out and asked me, during a social event, if I had rights to land in Hong Kong. I didn't know much about the process. Thinking

7. Examples of such schemes can be seen in the facts described by the Court of Final Appeal in *HKSAR v Lau Kam Ying* (2013) CACC 422/2010 (28 March 2013), by the Court of Appeal CACV 43/2010 (26 March 2013) and the trial judge in the same case *Kan Wai Chung v Hau Wun Fai* [2016] 1 HKLRD 632, [2016] 1 HKC 278 and by the trial judges in *Best Sheen Development Ltd v Official Receiver* [2001] 1 HKLRD 866, [2001] 3 HKC 79, and *Lau Ting Tai v Chung Chun Kwong* [2010] 3 HKC 352.
8. William is not of course his real name.

about it now, he probably got a kick back because it was very "salesy" how he talked about it and answered my questions.'

The small house policy was not mentioned, nor was the process properly explained, says William. 'To be truthful I had no idea what it was about or how it worked, only that I could sign some paperwork and get a few thousand pounds . . . it seemed odd to me that someone would pay me for something I don't own and is intangible, and all I needed to do was sign some paperwork.'

What did he understand to be his role? 'I didn't see it as a role or even realize I was a pawn within a bigger organization. I was told, just sign paperwork and get some money', he explained. Nothing was mentioned about what the process actually entailed, the proprieties of it and what he was doing from a legal point of view. William was aware that the location of his familial village would make a difference to the amount he would be paid. He was told that there would be three payments and it would take three years from the first payment to the last.

In the event, the first payment was in 2010 or 2011 at a meeting at a coffee shop within a railway station in a large northern English city where a representative gave him papers to sign and half the agreed price. The middlemen realized that William could not understand written Chinese. An interpreter was present and four others, including William's brother. 'It was quite surreal' he says, 'they pulled out a wad of paper. The interpreter didn't translate word for word. Thinking back, he was vague and general in what he was saying. At the time I wasn't aware of the ramifications and was coming from a place of wanting to get easy money.' He was paid in cash. The meeting took about 30 minutes. William was not given a copy of the papers.

The second payment was in Hong Kong three years later when he went to the Land Registry at a town in the New Territories to sign documents before receiving a further 25 per cent. Present at that meeting was the village chief and a representative of the property company. He was told to simply sign the papers and he would receive the second payment. The officers of the District Office did not explain matters to him. This time he was given a cheque.

The third instalment, the final 25 per cent, was again to be in Hong Kong upon signing more papers which William subsequently learned were to be about legal transfer to the developers of the house that had been built. But the third signing and payment did not take place. The process stopped after news reports concerning participants going to jail for taking part in these schemes (see the section on Illegality later in this chapter). Samuel then found out how controversial the whole process is and felt that he'd been deceived. He now wishes that he had known the bigger picture and been able to build his own house.

Afterwards William compared experiences with other British born Chinese friends and, as he put it, 'uncovered a world of corruption'. Their individual experiences differ only slightly. One of them wished actually to build a house, so did not sell his rights. But approval of his application requires the support of the village chief who has been refusing to give it for more than 15 years. The friend suspects that the chief co-operates with the developers and receives payments for approving their deals.

Dangers

The whole process is complex and ingenious. It is also fraught with danger. This is especially the case for the ultimate purchaser or end-user. The developer may give that purchaser a guarantee that the house will be built but that is only as good as the financial viability of the developer. The parties dare not register the sale and purchase agreement and the other documents, since they have been made in breach of the Conditions of Grant, so there is a risk of the end-purchaser's interest being defeated by a later transaction which is registered first.[9] In one instance, during construction of the house the ding somehow managed to mortgage the land as security for a personal loan from a finance company despite the title deeds being kept by the developer's solicitor.[10] In another, the ding granted an informal mortgage over the property by deposit of the deeds with the developer.[11] There is always the chance of the indigene using his registered ownership as a basis for making a gift or a lease or entering into a second sale with a rival developer.[12] Similarly the holder of the Power of Attorney may use it to mortgage, let or sell the land for his own benefit.[13] The developer or entrepreneur may fail to make some payment to the government or fail to obtain the certificate of compliance or letter stating that there is no objection to the house being occupied, so that the title is defective.[14] The developer may become insolvent and go into liquidation before construction is completed. If the ding becomes bankrupt, the land will fall into the hands of the Official Receiver since it is registered in the man's name as legal owner.

Should the indigene become upset with the developer or think that his reward is insufficient, he may try to withdraw from the arrangement, perhaps attempting to enlist the support of the DLO. Similarly if one of the joint venturers becomes disenchanted, it may try to sabotage the scheme.

On top of all this, the scheme could be tainted by illegality, in which case the courts will not enforce it but neither will they order the return of money to parties who knew of the wrongdoing. The clearest example of such illegality is the deception practiced on the government by an indigene who declares that he is the sole owner of the land (he is the legal owner only; the true or beneficial owner is the person who supplied the land to him). If the land to be built upon includes common

9. By operation of s 3(1) and (2) of the Land Registration Ordinance (Cap 128).
10. *Lou Siu Ping v Lam Tsz Man* [2012] 4 HKC 394; the purchaser's solicitor was found negligent for not explaining the risks to her.
11. *Lau Kam Sing v Cheung Cho Development Ltd*, HCMP 361/2014 (22 October 2014).
12. As occurred in *Wah Hing Strategy Co Ltd v Tang Wai Hung*, HCA 16690/1999 (16 May 2014) and *Kan Wai Chung v Hau Wan Fai* [2016] 1 HKC 278.
13. As happened in *Lawin (HK) Ltd v Ng Yau Fong Yvonne*, HCA 640/2011 (16 February 2012).
14. Illustrated by the background facts in *Cheung Chi Kui v Li Siu Kwong*, HCMP 2990/2014 (18 May 2015).

property of a clan (t'ong and t'so land), a deception will almost certainly have been carried out by its managers in order to obtain permission from the District Office to sell it.[15] Illegality is further considered in the next section.

Then there is the commercial or investment risk. The various steps between the end-purchaser's agreement to buy of the property and delivery of the completed house to a purchaser may take so long that the market falls calamitously in the meantime. This happened in a number of cases in which, as a result of the collapse of land values in 1997 making sales unprofitable, schemes became frustrated, postponed or abandoned.

Illegality

The schemes for exploitation of the policy did not go unnoticed by the administration. Although the courts had given the green light to pre-sales of ding houses, that did not bind the government to grant building licences or provide subsidized land where the villager was in league with a developer. The administration tried to discourage the practice by changing the contents of the application form which the indigene was required to fill in when seeking a licence or small house grant.

In the 1970s and 1980s the form was relatively simple. The applicant had to warrant that he was a male indigenous villager and give his personal details, including his father's name and those of his male children. The abuse feared in those days was that the applicant was not really indigenous. A separate sheet at the end of the form was a statement confirming that the applicant's ancestors through the male line could be shown from village records as having resided in or about the village since before 1898, to be signed by the village representative or a member of the rural committee. The form also required the land upon which the house was to be built to be identified by demarcation district and lot number, and that land be registered in the name of the applicant.

In calling only for the land to be registered in the name of the applicant, the form did not address the manipulation described above whereby land that really belonged to the developer would be transferred into the name of the villager and the transfer registered, thereby making him the registered owner. The requirement of registration showed an administrator's understandable reliance upon the official record of ownership but ignored the fact that the land register was not a register of title. The status of registered owner meant merely that conveyancing documents showed that the land had been transferred into that owner's name, not that he was the true owner. By virtue of the documents, the villager was the owner at common law, the legal owner. But behind him stood the developer, the party who had paid for the land, and in the parallel system of law called equity, the land belonged to

15. As in *Super Keep Investment Ltd v Wong Kwok Wa*, CACV 195/2010 (15 April 2011) and *Tang Teng Hong Tso v Cheung Tin Wah* [2014] 4 HKC 515.

the developer. By virtue of the developer's having financed the acquisition of the land and of the villager not having paid for the transfer into his name, in the eyes of equity the villager held the land upon trust for the benefit of the developer. The latter was accordingly the equitable, or beneficial, owner. The trust arose or resulted from the financial reality. Where the villager had signed a declaration that he held the land on trust for the developer, there was no need for the resulting trust for the trust became express.

The administration, and the form, began to catch up with the realities in the 1990s. The guidance notes to the 1991 version of the form advised the applicant for a building licence that he should acquire 'sole ownership' of the land upon which he wished to put the small house. But there was no elaboration of what was meant by sole ownership so the phrase could be interpreted as meaning sole legal or registered ownership. In 1993 a statutory declaration was introduced. Such a declaration is a solemn, sworn statement under the Oaths and Declarations Ordinance.[16] The knowing making of a false or incomplete declaration is a criminal offence. The revised form said that the applicant 'may lodge a statutory declaration stating whether the lot under application is registered in his name' and the notes explained that the Director of Buildings and Lands might require such a declaration. But the scope of the declaration was confined to registered ownership so would not cover the beneficial ownership of a developer and the notes permitted the declaration to be made in front of the applicant's own solicitor (in reality engaged by the developer) rather than an independent commissioner for oaths, thus allowing the declaration to become just one of a sheath of papers that the applicant had to sign in order to obtain his money from the developer. The declaration was simply: 'I am the sole owner of [lot and demarcation district numbers] on which I wish to erect a small house.'[17]

In 1997 the declaration was expanded to add: 'I have never made and have no intention at present to make any private arrangements for my rights under the Small House Policy to be sold to other individual / a developer.' By using actual conduct, namely sale of rights, rather than the ambiguous notion of ownership, the new form was coming closer to the mark. The villager was still required to declare that he was registered owner, or (since 2001) 'sole legal and registered owner' of the land. The weakness of the new formula was that it referred to intention: the applicant could make the declaration then later say that he had changed his intention after making it. In 2001 the reference to intention was dropped but the wording expanded in other directions: 'I have never entered into any arrangement or agreement with any person(s) to transfer, alienate, dispose or otherwise deal with my rights in and over the Lot, including but not limited to the right to develop the Lot pursuant to any grant or approval to be issued by the Government.' This was not well received by

16. Cap 11.
17. App LXII to the 1993 form.

indigenous people. They thought it took away their right to build. To complicate matters, certain District Offices continued to use the old form.

There the declaration rested until July 2006 when it was quietly dropped. A deal had been done with the Heung Yee Kuk again. They had objected that the declaration criminalized a villager's behaviour. In fact, it criminalized a false statement in an application for grant of a valuable privilege. Nevertheless, the administration gave way and undertook to remove the declaration about ownership of the land from the application process. Instead, a warning was given that the grantee should not enter into any arrangement or agreement with any person to transfer, alienate, dispose or otherwise deal with rights in or over the subject lot, including the right to develop, because a term to that effect would be incorporated into the relevant licence or conditions of grant. Government representatives argued, or rather took comfort, that a term in the licence or grant would be as good as a statutory declaration, but they were deceiving themselves. A declaration as part of the application would discourage deception and would be punishable against the declarant alone by criminal sanctions and at an early stage in the process, perhaps before any licence to build had been given. A term in the licence or grant would take effect later and the breach might be discovered later still, which might be well after the house had been completed and sold. The sanction would affect not only the villager but also the developer and any later purchaser, for the effect would be to ruin the title to the house and land. A breach would entitle the government to re-enter the land, i.e. to cancel the grant and take back the land. This is an extreme sanction which is rarely used because it is usually disproportionate to the breach. So the likelihood was that the villager would get away with the breach.

Nevertheless, the statutory declaration had been in place for nine years. During that time, villagers and developers appear to have carried on regardless, entering into joint venture agreements and selling their right to build by masquerading as the real owners of the lot on which the house was to be built. There is no reason to believe that they ceased to do so after the term had been included in the grant.

Private Treaty Grant

Where the developer or entrepreneur has no or insufficient land to supply to the ding for the scheme, a grant of government land in the vicinity of the village is required. The application for a private grant of such land may be handled on the man's behalf by the entrepreneur or developer (perhaps acting in joint venture) using power of attorney. Apart from the Power, the indigene signs a Declaration of Trust and a Will. The ding must live in the village or state that he intends to return to it: this requirement is opposed by many indigenes but has been held not to be unconstitutional.[18] If the DLO is satisfied, a new grant is made with a restriction

18. *Koon Ping Leung v Director of Lands* [2012] 2 HKC 329.

upon alienation and a covenant to build within 36 months. The developer obtains the necessary certificates, builds the house and obtains the necessary consents. After that, or before, the house is sold to an end-purchaser who is given possession once the house is ready. The transfer follows payment of the balance of premium (or expiry of the no-alienation period). The risk for the end user is similar to that which attends purchase of a house built on private land: the documents between him and the entrepreneur cannot be registered; the developer may not pay the balance of premium; the developer/entrepreneur may not obtain all the documents and may go into liquidation. The risk is increased if there are no middlemen and the indigene is selling on his own initiative to the end-purchaser.

Sullied Reputation

So many people are usually involved in these schemes to exploit aboriginal small house rights that it is almost inevitable that sharp and dubious practices arise. These have become notorious and have sullied the reputation of the indigenous community.

13

Lawfulness of the Policy

The Small House Policy was devised in an era before a measure of democracy was introduced into Hong Kong's political system and before the advance of human rights into the then colony's legal system. Government in the New Territories was a matter for the District Commissioner and the various District Officers operating a kind of enlightened patriarchy that occasionally sought endorsement of their proposals from the Governor and the Executive Council and periodically troubled to explain their policies to the unelected Legislative Council. There were no District Councils or town boards in 1972. The only influential group there of any consequence was the Heung Yee Kuk, supposedly representing (in the words of its ordinance) 'the people of the New Territories'.

Accordingly, the policy was at first viewed as a peculiarly rural matter, almost a private arrangement between the District Commissioner and the kuk. The policy was instituted as a result of pressure from the kuk. Changes to the policy in its early years were refinements made in response to complaints by the kuk. No one thought to question the kuk's influence or to challenge the assumptions that lay behind the policy. It took several years for the impression that this was a measure for amelioration of the shortage and standard of rural housing to wear off. The curious conditions that the government imposed upon the availability of new land for village houses—that the applicant be an adult male and be descended through the male line since 1898—seemed to be no more than the perpetuation of historical curiosities. The reservation of new building land for houses in which such males and their families might live in their hereditary communities appeared justifiable. Besides, Hong Kong had greater matters on its mind as 1997 drew closer.

This benign view began to erode once word went around that the customary right was being used more as a commercial opportunity than as a means of providing family housing. The exploitation of the policy's privileges, related in the previous chapter, received more and more publicity as the property market soared during the late 1980s. By then, the future of Hong Kong as a Special Administrative Region of the People's Republic of China had been settled by the Sino-British Joint Declaration. There was little about indigenous rights in the declaration but that did not matter. The kuk's leaders had already set about protecting indigenous interests under the forthcoming regime.

To provide reassurance to Hong Kong people, a constitution for the SAR was drafted by a widely drawn committee. With a view to protecting basic rights after the handover, in the early 1990s the legislature enacted a Bill of Rights.[1] Both contained provisions outlawing discrimination. Legislation against discrimination on grounds of gender was also put in place.[2] However, the Small House Policy had been specifically excluded from its reach. There was no such reservation in the Bill of Rights Ordinance. The Basic Law contained nothing expressly about the policy but it did preserve indigenous traditional rights.

The question therefore arises as to whether the policy has been rendered to any degree unlawful as a result of these developments. In particular, there is a possibility that aspects of it are contrary to the Basic Law and therefore unconstitutional.

The Right to Equality

So far as concerns the right to build on subsidized land, the policy as formulated favours only indigenous males descended through the male line from an inhabitant in 1898 of a listed village. As such it discriminates between five sets of adult people, setting up four pairs of contrasts. First, it differentiates between male and female indigenous villagers (meaning descendants of inhabitants in 1898 of listed villages). Second, it differentiates between male indigenous villagers and non-indigenous villagers (post-1898 inhabitants of listed villages), both male and female. The latter may have the right to build, or rather re-build, if they happen to occupy a licensed or tolerated house, but unlike the indigenous they must pay a full price for the land. Third, it differentiates between male indigenous villagers of listed villages and inhabitants, both male and female and indigenous or otherwise, of villages that are not listed. Again, the latter may build if they are licensees but must pay full premium. Fourth, it differentiates between male indigenous villagers and the rest of the inhabitants of Hong Kong, who generally have no right to build even if they happen to own land.

The human rights principle applicable to all of these contrasts is that of equality before the law. Both the Basic Law and the Bill of Rights insist that all persons shall be equal before the law and are entitled to equal protection from the law without any discrimination.[3] The law shall prohibit any discrimination and guarantee to all equal and effective protection against discrimination on various grounds, including sex, social origin, birth and other status.[4] This can be called the right not to be

1. Hong Kong Bill of Rights Ordinance (Cap 383).
2. Sex Discrimination Ordinance (Cap 480).
3. Basic Law, Art 25; Bill of Rights, Art 22.
4. International Covenant on Civil and Political Rights (ICCPR), Art 26. The ICCPR is incorporated into the Basic Law by Basic Law Art 39. *Director of Immigration v QT* (2018) 21 HKCFAR 324, [2018] 4 HKC 403.

discriminated against. It reflects the concept that generally the law should accord identical treatment to comparable circumstances.

However, not all discrimination is unlawful. Differences in treatment between people can sometimes be justified. Consequently, it is open to a government or public authority accused of discrimination to convince a court that the discrimination is acceptable by satisfying the 'proportionality test'. This demands demonstration that the discrimination pursues a legitimate aim, that there is a rational connection between that aim and the difference in treatment, that the difference is proportionate, that is to say no more than necessary to accomplish the aim, and that a reasonable balance has been struck between societal benefits and the restriction. This provides flexibility, as does the principle that a court will give a 'margin of appreciation' to the legislature or the administration which has imposed the discrimination. Some leeway is allowed, being the scope for imposition of a discriminatory law or practice. Hence the court will not interfere unless the arrangement is manifestly without reasonable foundation. The degree of appreciation allowed depends upon the context. Where the discrimination is based upon certain core matters, those which go to respect for and dignity of the individual such as birth, gender or race, the courts apply severe scrutiny and the discrimination will rarely be acceptable. Greater flexibility is permitted in respect of discrimination concerning matters which are not regarded as core, particularly socio-economic rights such as those involving education and wealth. These types of right more readily involve questions of public interest and policy and so are usually for the legislative or administrative arms of government. So here the courts ask whether the restriction is manifestly without reasonable foundation, rather than whether it is no more than is necessary to accomplish the aim.[5]

The Small House Policy can be seen to strike at core values. The distinctions drawn in the contrasts above are based on birth (or descent) and social origin.[6] Consequently the policy violates the right to equality unless it can be shown to pursue a legitimate aim, that there is a rational connection between that aim and the discrimination and the discrimination is no more than that needed to accomplish the aim. What then are the aims of the policy?

As initially presented to the Executive and Legislative Councils the policy was intended to tackle rural housing need with the additional object of improving building standards. More house sites were needed for indigenous families in their villages. Badly built squatter and licensed houses needed to be replaced too. The houses should be built quickly and cheaply. Later, the administration gave an additional aim of the policy: preservation of village cohesion and identity. This aim was expressed in the 1990s, more than twenty years after the policy had been put into effect.

5. *R (Carson) v Work and Pensions Secretary* [2006] 1 AC 173.
6. *Tse Kwan Sang v Pat Heung Rural Committee* [1999] 3 HKLRD 267, 286 H-I.

There was a further aim, unspoken but deducible from the circumstances in which the policy came into being: placating rural interests. This was a political aim, so could not be spelt out and was certainly not legitimate in human rights terms. The Heung Yee Kuk had been pressing for years for more favourable treatment with regard to village houses. It enjoyed generally good relations with the district administration which was understandably keen to head off trouble and was under largely loose supervision by its masters in central Hong Kong. The reasons for the past, and continuing, indulgent attitude of the administration have already been explored.[7] No doubt that attitude made sense from the point of view of peace, order, and good government. By 1972 there was a new reason to maintain that attitude. Following the troubles of 1967, the Hong Kong government had embarked upon an enlightened phase under Sir Robert Black with the encouragement of a Labour government in London. Part of that phase was the improvement of housing and the elimination of the shanty towns that disfigured urban hillsides. The Small House Policy could be seen as an extension of that housing phase to the rural parts but as well, or perhaps instead, it was a means of paving the way for the new towns which Black's successor, Sir Murray Maclehose, determined had to be built if decent domestic accommodation was to be achieved for the colony's millions. Those towns could be built only in the New Territories and they would entail the compulsory acquisition of a great deal of land, much of it held by aboriginal owners. One way in which to keep those owners well-disposed was to compensate them generously for their land. Another was to allow them to build new houses, for themselves and their male offspring, in and around their native places.

Improvement in the rural housing stock however was a much more respectable aim. There is no doubt that the policy had some success in this respect. After the policy came into effect, applications for discounted land and permission to build on existing land greatly increased. Modern three-storey houses, with kitchens, bathrooms, running water and hygienic facilities, sprang up throughout the countryside. In his memoirs the District Commissioner in 1972, Denis Bray, congratulated himself on this.[8] The trouble was that the houses were rarely occupied by indigenous families. Most of them had been built to be re-sold. Consequently, if the aim is refined to be to improve living conditions for village natives, the policy cannot be counted a success.

There are further difficulties about the aim of improving rural housing as current justification for the policy. They are that the aim has been achieved and has anyway long been overtaken by events. More than forty years after inception of the policy, rural poverty had become unusual. Such as it was, poverty appeared in the remaining cottage areas of squatter and licensed occupiers, not in 2,100 square feet village houses. Widespread and good-quality public rental and home ownership scheme flats, many in the New Territories, had replaced villages as a source of

7. See Ch 3.
8. Bray, *Hong Kong Metamorphosis*, p 166.

economical housing. Building controls, applicable except to small houses in rural parts, ensured maintenance of health and safety standards. So too since 1991 did planning controls, and they applied to villages also. Even in the villages, the District Office's power to impose conditions upon land grants ensured that similar standards applied to new homes there. Bray envisaged that the policy would be temporary, pending more permanent arrangements. Those arrangements have now been in place for almost three decades.

Moreover, it is difficult to see a rational connection between the improvement of village houses and the differentiation between indigenous and non-indigenous inhabitants. Both types of villager occupied village housing. The express aim was to improve the houses occupied by both. The goal did not require better treatment (subsidized land and free building licences) to be given to one over the other.

Finally, the aim of improving the quality of houses can be said to be disproportionate to the discrimination involved: the policy and its discriminatory aspects are not 'no more than is necessary' to achieve the aim. There were and are alternative ways of achieving it without discriminating between residents. Principally these are the extension of building and planning legislation to small houses and the provision of subsidized public housing. The policy achieved improvements in the housing stock but did so at a high cost to public finances (in sale premium foregone and infrastructural costs incurred) and by bestowing excessive benefits upon one section of the population based upon their birth, descent and social origin. At the same time it used building land in a wasteful way at a time of pressing social need for more land for housing. The waste is compounded by the subversion of the policy from its original aims by practices previously described directed towards speculation and profit and involving dubious conduct.

Preservation of Indigenous Identity

Another justification sometimes given for the Small House Policy is that it promotes the cohesiveness of the indigenous community, providing them with housing in and around their traditional villages and in a manner consistent with the rural environment. This argument is undermined by the fact that the houses are largely occupied by people from outside the village. The buildings are certainly not high-rise so in that sense are in keeping with a village but they are much larger than the original small house of 436 square foot, with peaked roof containing one multi-purpose room with cockloft over. Few of them are surrounded by fields or adjacent to farms. By and large they are monotonous, rectangular suburban-style constructions.

Protection of indigenous culture is a legitimate objective that may permit departure from human rights norms. But the departure is acceptable only if denial of the same right to the non-indigenous is reasonable and necessary to preserve indigenous identity.[9] If the villages were the homogenous places of 120 years ago, with virtually all the inhabitants descended from one or two clans, there would be sense in giving preferential housing treatment to indigenous families. That is no longer the case: as recounted in earlier chapters, the rapid social change of the second half of the last century and the early years of this one have transformed life and landholding in even the smallest and remotest settlements. The population of most villages is no longer composed of aboriginal people only, as acknowledged by the Court of Final Appeal in a case about village elections at the turn of this century.[10]

The indigenous do have a lingering sense of their separateness but it hinges upon clan or lineage identity and a historic connection with their place of origin rather than upon a right to housing. It could hardly be otherwise when so many of them have chosen to live elsewhere and have themselves been instrumental in diluting the proportion of indigenous residents by selling land and houses at their village to incomers. They have found ways of expressing their identity other than by clinging to their hereditary land and its traditions. Return to the village at festivals, especially for the decennial reunion; attendance for rituals; participation in t'so t'ong affairs, if only as recipients of largesse; these are what remains of their separateness. Identification is residual and increasingly tenuous.

Certainly, there is no evidence that the small house benefit encourages native sons to remain in the village. To the contrary, most houses built in the names of indigenous males are sold at the first opportunity. Sale of new houses to outsiders both depletes the proportion of indigenes and pays for their removal to other places. There seems therefore to be no rational connection between the policy with its built-in discrimination and the aim of cohesiveness. The discrimination is disproportionate to the aim.

Gender Discrimination

The policy discriminates blatantly against women. Its discriminatory character has been implicitly acknowledged by the colonial Hong Kong government, the HKSAR government and the PRC government, each of whom have at various times excepted the policy from measures taken to combat sex discrimination.

In the 1990s the United Kingdom subscribed its colony to the United Nation's Convention on the Elimination of All Forms of Discrimination Against Women (CEDAW). By the terms of the convention a party undertakes to refrain from engaging in any practice of discrimination against women, to take measures to modify or abolish existing laws, customs and practices which constitute discrimination against women and to take measures to modify social and cultural patterns of conduct with

9. *Sandra Lovelace v Canada*, Communication No 24/1977 (UNHRC, 30 July 1981).
10. *Secretary for Justice v Chan Wah* (2000) 3 HKCFAR 459, 465 I-J.

a view to achieving the elimination of prejudices and customary and other practices which are based on the idea of inferiority or superiority of either of the sexes or on stereotyped roles for men and women.[11] But the British government entered a reservation in respect of the Small House Policy, as states which are parties to treaties such as CEDAW are entitled to do, because adoption of its provisions is voluntary.

The People's Republic of China likewise is a party to the convention. In 1997 the PRC notified the United Nations that CEDAW would apply to Hong Kong with effect from 1 July 1997 but with reservations. These included laws applicable to the New Territories which enable indigenous villagers to exercise certain rights in respect of property and which provide for rent concessions regarding property held by indigenous persons through the male line. The HKSAR government seems to think that this reservation covers the Small House Policy even though it is administrative in nature and the reservation refers to laws rather than executive policies or practices.

In 2006 the UN Committee on CEDAW urged the HKSAR to repeal all discriminatory provisions from the policy and to ensure that indigenous women have the same rights and access to property as indigenous men. Hong Kong's government played for time: it announced a review of the policy. On each occasion that it was asked about this review, the reply was to the effect that the review was ongoing and the issues were all very complicated. No details of the progress of the review were ever given. The pretence of a review was not dropped until 2016. This was done in roundabout, bureaucratic language: the government announced that it had other, more pressing priorities. An honest announcement would have said that reform of the policy is a sensitive matter and one which risked setting off another of the political storms that have been a feature of post-1997 Hong Kong.

Discrimination on grounds of gender in the Small House Policy is readily apparent. Its privileges are open to indigenous inhabitants only and indigenous inhabitants are, in the definition adopted by the government, adult males. They must be descended through the male line from an inhabitant of a listed village in 1898. Such a male qualifies for the privileges even if he no longer inhabits the village and even if he has never inhabited it. A female, even one descended through the male line until her own generation, does not so qualify. Nor does it matter that she has lived in the village all her life. She is excluded simply because of her gender.

That is seriously discriminatory because it violates a core value of equality.[12] This does not mean that differential treatment of one sex is never justifiable but it does mean that to be acceptable, any justification has to be weighty and with convincing evidence of its alleged benefits. There is no necessary connection between the avowed aim of the policy, improvement in village housing, and the exclusion of women from the benefits of the policy. Nor can their exclusion rationally be said to promote the cohesion or environment of the villages.

11. CEDAW, Arts 2(d), 2(f) and 5(a).
12. Basic Law, Art 25; Bill of Rights, Art 22.

The administration's justification for confining small house benefits to men is that the custom which preceded the policy was similarly confined. In formulating the policy, the government was not seeking to change the custom but to enable more indigenous males to exercise it. The custom was that only men built houses in the village. Men did so because they alone were the heads of household and were expected to provide shelter for the family; they remained in their village; their wives came from another village and moved to the husband's village on marriage; the house was for their new family, so the women benefited as well; the land on which it was built was part of the wealth of the man's village and should remain so, which could not happen if it belonged to someone from another village.

This is of course historical now, for Confucian and patriarchal tradition has been eroded by time. Men are no longer the sole breadwinners. Women are often treated as equals in, and may in reality dominate, the household. Wives do not have to originate from other villages. Females are allowed to own and inherit land anywhere in the New Territories.

Quaint and outdated as the custom may be, the rules of the policy were both reflecting and honouring the custom. Custom can always be criticized as old fashioned because custom is by definition long-established practice. However, it remains relevant because it was preserved as a source of law when the New Territories were brought within Hong Kong more than 120 years ago and continues to be preserved by the Basic Law of the HKSAR drafted in the late 1980s. Accordingly the justification is based on the constitution, which is about as weighty as a justification can be.

When it comes to eradication of the sex discrimination in the policy, Hong Kong's administrators are caught in a bind. Many of them do not like the policy, not so much because of its discriminatory nature but because it has proved an expensive mistake, is deeply unpopular with the wider public and has shown up embarrassing civil service incompetence. They do not wish to compound the error by extending it to women, although this would be a simple way to remove the sexually discriminatory element and has the support of the Heung Yee Kuk. At the other extreme, abolition of small house rights entirely would cause consternation amongst an assertive, well-organized, self-interested, and generally united section of the public which is used to getting its way and quite willing to cause trouble if it does not. The support of representatives of that section, the indigenous community, is important to the government's getting its business through the Legislative and Executive Councils. Abolition may anyway turn out to be unconstitutional. The third approach, reform without abolition, is likely to please no one and to cause more trouble than it is worth.

Article 40 of the Basic Law

Jurisdictions with advanced human rights laws quite often have aboriginal minorities with customs and attitudes that seem at odds with contemporary values. Those minorities are protected by legislation and exceptions in and qualifications to constitutions. Although one may question whether male descendants of those who happened to live in what became the New Territories are sufficiently distinct to be called indigenous, there is such protection in the SAR's Basic Law. This is Article 40 which preserves traditional indigenous rights.

No debate about the lawfulness and discriminatory character of the Small House Policy can ignore Article 40. The article is usually assumed to be principally about continuation and preservation of the policy, or rather the parts of the policy which are applicable to indigenes. The promoters of Article 40 undoubtedly had that in mind, but their proposal was the subject of negotiation and amendment before adoption and the eventual article is not confined to the policy and, as we shall see in the next chapter, they may not have entirely succeeded in their objective. The kuk believes it is their trump card in defending the policy from legal attacks. Preservation of the policy must have been a central concern of the kuk's leaders when they lobbied for inclusion of the article in the Basic Law.

The article preserves the lawful traditional rights and interests of the indigenous inhabitants of the New Territories. Leaders of and advisers to the kuk maintain that the policy is part of those traditional rights and interests. Their position is that prior to 1898, when the New Territories became part of Hong Kong, villagers could build on land that they owned and do so without restriction or the need for permission from anybody. That freedom was taken away by a standard clause in the Crown leases issued in 1905 and 1907 stating that government permission must be sought for erection of any building let as agricultural or garden ground, which meant most of the private land in the New Territories. One effect of Article 40, they say, is to restore the previous position. Alternatively, they say that the land policies of Hong Kong administrators after 1900 were in effect to recognize and honour the small house custom, latterly in the guise of the Small House Policy. It is the rights given by these policies, being lawful and traditional rights that existed when the Basic Law was finalized in 1990 and came into effect in 1997, which have been protected by Article 40. The purpose of the Small House Policy is to protect the right to build houses and that has been continued by Article 40.

Mismanagement of Land

Opponents of the Small House Policy sometimes claim that it breaches Article 7 of the Basic Law. This provides that land within the HKSAR is state property and that the HKSAR government is responsible for its management, use and development including its grant and leasing out. The claim rests on an assertion that the land is to be put to use for the benefit of Hong Kong people, the assertion being based on a judicial statement.[13] However, Article 7 suggests that the land is to be used for

13. By Hartmann J in *Harvest Good Development Ltd v Secretary for Justice* [2007] 4 HKC 1.

the benefit of the government rather than the people: revenues from land shall be exclusively at the disposal of the government.

The policy is assuredly an inefficient use of building land, a scarce commodity. The permitted dimensions allow houses of only three storeys and 2,100 square feet in area, covering 700 square feet of surface. The premia charged to the indigenous are either none (the free building licence) or two-thirds of the market value (private treaty grants). But to castigate this as mismanagement is an exaggeration. There are historical reasons for the concessions to indigenous villagers.

Critics are on firmer ground when they point out that the policy was intended to be temporary, an interim administrative measure pending comprehensive planning legislation for the whole of the New Territories. That legislation has been in place for the best part of three decades yet the temporary policy still exists and is largely unchanged from when it was introduced. That would suggest failure to keep the policy up-to-date, or an unannounced change of intention never publicly explained. If it should transpire that the policy which the administration has been operating is unconstitutional or otherwise illegal, that would suggest poor administration. Article 7 however does not impose a duty on the government to manage the land well, simply a duty to manage the land.

Since the uncertain scope of Article 40 is pivotal to the legality and constitutionality of the Small House Policy, it is time to examine the article more closely.

14
Article 40

Article 40 of Hong Kong's Basic Law is an unusual and contentious constitutional provision. It is in Chapter III of the Law, containing the 'Fundamental Rights and Duties of Residents'. The text of Article 40 is short and appears to be simple:

> The lawful traditional rights and interests of the indigenous inhabitants of the 'New Territories' shall be protected by the Hong Kong Special Administrative Region.

Yet the simplicity is deceptive. The wording abounds with questions. What are the traditional rights to which it refers? Is traditional the same as customary? Must a right be both traditional and lawful to fall within the article or is one of these enough? Is there a difference between a traditional right and a traditional interest and if so, what is it? Who exactly are the indigenous people to whom it refers? Is the word 'inhabitants' of significance? What precisely is meant by the New Territories and why are two of those three words in inverted commas? What duties are placed upon the Special Administrative Region by the injunction to protect these rights and interests? Does the SAR in this context mean just its administration or does it extend to its legislature? Does it extend also to its judges?

Discerning exactly what the article means therefore is not easy. Whilst many of the provisions of the Basic Law copy or reflect those found in constitutions worldwide, Article 40 is unique to Hong Kong. Consequently, there is no accumulated body of jurisprudence from elsewhere which can be consulted as to its scope and meaning. We have to rely upon local decisions about Article 40, but these are so far scanty.

Looking at the plain text of the article, two surprising matters of nomenclature stand out. One is the use of the descriptive term 'New Territories', the other is the use of 'indigenous inhabitants'. Both seem out of place in a constitutional document drafted in the late twentieth century for a small, predominantly urban, administrative region within the People's Republic of China.

'New Territories'

The terminology 'New Territories' is historical and originated from a late nineteenth-century British perspective to describe an extension of a colony by a treaty which subsequently came to be repeatedly denounced by the government of China. During the final years of British rule, the term was avoided in official usage as outdated. The origin of the term no doubt explains the quotation marks around it. Its use in Article 40 is testament to the enduring notion of the New Territories. It is also testament to the convenience of the description. A substitute such as 'indigenous inhabitants of that area of the SAR situated between the Kowloon Hills and the boundary with Shumchun' would have been unwieldy and, in the aspect of the hills, imprecise. It would also have been inaccurate in that it omits the hundreds of islands that are part of the New Territories. Two other formulations, 'indigenous inhabitants north of Kowloon' and 'indigenous inhabitants north of Boundary Street' (both were suggested during the drafting of the Basic Law), suffer from the same inaccuracy, whilst 'indigenous inhabitants of the villages' (another drafting suggestion) would have brought in those from old villages on Hong Kong island and in Kowloon as well as from newer and unrecognized villages elsewhere in the SAR. Moreover, such convoluted descriptions might have carried lurking difficulties, as might have a more accurate one such as 'the whole of the HKSAR except Hong Kong Island and Southern Kowloon'.

The drafters may have had in mind that the 'New Territories' is defined in the Interpretation and General Clauses Ordinance.[1] The state of domestic legislation at the time of the drafting of the Basic Law is indeed an aid to its interpretation. According to the ordinance it is 'all of Hong Kong except the land and sea within the boundary of Hong Kong immediately before 9 June 1898', the date of the Convention of Peking. But this applies to the phrase when used in ordinances rather than in the Basic Law and is anyway unhelpful since it moves the enquiry back to ascertainment of the boundary before 9 June 1898.

By placing the phrase in quotation marks the drafters seem to have been importing the pre-existing meaning of the New Territories. The difficulty here is that the meaning of the phrase in the late twentieth century, the time of the coming into force of the Basic Law, was not settled. There was the legalistic definition in the Interpretation Ordinance. There was the official usage which excluded New Kowloon and its built-up extensions, such as Kwun Tong, Kwai Chung and Tsuen Wan. There was one popular usage by which the New Territories came to mean the mainland portion north of the (foothills, or perhaps peaks, of the) Kowloon Hills but not the islands which were regarded as separate entities. Then there was another popular usage which discounted not just the islands but also the Sai Kung area, leaving the New Territories as just its main body to the north of the hills, the west

1. Cap 1.

of Sai Kung, and the south of the border. No doubt there are other conceptions of the New Territories, too.

'Indigenous Inhabitants'

The phrase 'indigenous inhabitants' is also borrowed nomenclature: a colonial creation, the invention of Hong Kong civil servants as a short way of describing those who had benefited from various customary practices and who would also benefit from certain of their practices, including eventually the Small House Policy. The concept is mentioned in Article 122 of the Basic Law dealing with land leases, which states that the previous government rent shall remain unchanged as long as the properties are held by certain lessees. The properties are old schedule lots, village lots, small houses, and similar rural holdings. The lessees are those descended through the male line from a person who was in 1898 a resident of an established village. The concept was no doubt copied from and is echoed in domestic legislation.[2]

As such, 'indigenous inhabitants' is a historical reference. There is no requirement that the person currently inhabit the New Territories. Only adult men can be indigenous and only those patrilineally descended from a man resident in certain villages in 1898. Given what had happened to Hong Kong, including its rural areas, over the preceding hundred years, to find this description of 'indigenous' employed in a document drafted and brought into force during the closing stages of the twentieth century seems peculiar.

The persons protected by Article 40 therefore are a minority group. Indeed, they are but a portion of a part of a minority. The article therefore protects the rights of a minority. The mainland drafters likened the protection of the traditional rights of indigenous inhabitants to the protection of minorities in China. This is an imperfect analogy however, for the descendants of males living in the New Territories in 1898 lack the classic distinctive features of a true minority and are far from being vulnerable political outsiders, quite the reverse. They are not oppressed, are not backward economically, are not primitive socially and have no culture distinctive from that of the majority.[3]

At least 'indigenous inhabitants' has a settled meaning in the eyes of the government, even if that meaning is far from natural. Not only is the phrase used in legislation, it is used in the details of the Small House Policy. There it means a male person who is at least 18 years of age who is descended through the male line from a man who lived in 1898 in a village on a list that is kept by the Director of Lands. The

2. Government Rent (Assessment and Collection) Ordinance (Cap 515).
3. Christine Chung Cheuk Kwan, *Whether the Small House Policy Is Protected by Article 40 of the Hong Kong Basic Law: A Critical View in a Legal and Historical Perspective*, unpublished independent research dissertation, Chinese University of Hong Kong, 2018–2019 (*The Small House Policy and Article 40*); Malcolm Merry, 'Indigenous Rights in Disrepute: The Curious Case of Hong Kong' (2013) 2 *Australian Property Law Review* 152.

list includes a small number of villages founded after 1898 which presumably are not established villages for purposes of Article 122 and whose inhabitants are not indigenous for purposes of Article 40. Someone who claims indigenous status has to prove it by reference to genealogies or the confirmation of a village head.

The importation of a second piece of colonial terminology into Article 40 is perhaps another indication of how out of place the whole article is, perpetuating the privileges of a certain small sub-class of Hong Kong's population long after their separate identity had ceased to be visible. But Article 40 exists and its meaning must be discerned. In order to require protection by the SAR, there must be a right or interest. That right or interest must be lawful. On the face of the text it must also be traditional and must be that of an indigenous inhabitant of the New Territories. During the process of drafting, the wording of Article 40 was amended from 'legitimate rights and interests' to 'lawful rights and interests' and then to 'lawful traditional rights and interests'. What do the last two mean?

Lawful Rights and Interests

Article 40 does not apply to all indigenous traditional rights and interests. It applies only to those which are lawful. But lawful when? If the answer is 'now', or at the time that the Basic Law was drafted and finalized in 1990 or became operative on 1 July 1997 and thereafter, to the extent that the Small House Policy violates other provisions of the Basic Law or of other laws then existing, how can Article 40 operate to preserve the policy and the rights that it gives? Article 40 could refer to other, non-discriminatory, traditional rights. If, however, the answer is 'lawful in and before 1898', it would not matter that the policy violates other provisions in the Basic Law or provisions of the Bill of Rights or other legislation because those provisions were not then in place.

Article 40 is concerned with traditional rights. These are generally taken to be those that existed by custom prior to the cession of the New Territories to Great Britain in 1898. There may however have been traditions which were illegal under Ching law although allowed by local custom. There may also have been traditions which were lawful under Ching or customary law but which became illegal under Hong Kong law in the twentieth century, such as the letting off of firecrackers at festival times. The argument against reading 'lawful' as 'lawful in 1898' is to ensure that such traditions are not resurrected after 1997.

On the other hand, Article 40 is in the Basic Law which was drafted in the 1980s, promulgated in 1990 and came into force in 1997. A law usually speaks from the date of its enactment and is generally not retrospective. Article 40 is a directive to the HKSAR and that did not come into existence until 1997. A perfectly natural reading of the words of the article is that traditional rights which are currently lawful shall be protected. Suppose that in the nineteenth century it had been the tradition in the New Territories, or in certain villages there, to forbid adultery and to punish it with torture or death. This would have become illegal when the criminal law of Hong Kong became applicable after the British takeover. Can it really be said that because it was allowed up to 1898, Article 40 restored such a tradition in 1997? Or, to take a more realistic example, prior to 1899 villages organized their own vigilantes who would apprehend thieves and other miscreants. Their practice was to mete out instant punishment, by physical beating, without trial. This seems to have been regarded as lawful, presumably because traditional. After 1899 such miscreants should have been handed to the Hong Kong police force, since assault and battery was not lawful under the new regime. Again, the 'lawful' in Article 40 would prevent resurrection of this practice.

Likewise, 'lawful' would prevent perpetuation of practices which, although customary, had become unlawful during intervening years. So, should it transpire that the policy is in breach of human rights protections and that 'lawful' in Article 40 means currently lawful, Article 40 would not have operated to protect the policy. It cannot validly be objected that this would leave Article 40 without any application, for there are a number of other traditional practices to which it might apply.

Two phrases similar to 'lawful' are contained in the Basic Law. One is 'in accordance with law', the other 'prescribed by law'. Both suggest that a provision or act which is subject to them should be sanctioned by positive law—a statute, for instance, or a decided case. Certainly anything prescribed by, or in accordance with, the law would be lawful. However, 'lawful' seems to carry a wider meaning still.

The most likely interpretation of 'lawful' in Article 40 that it means within the law or not illegal at the time that the Basic Law came into force. In other words, that it is within the framework of laws expressed to apply to the Special Administrative Region by Article 8. This would not require the policy to be based upon statute. It would be sufficient that the policy does not contravene statute or other law.

Traditional Rights and Interests

A right is something you are entitled to do. This may be because of a grant of that entitlement. Or it may simply be because there is nothing to prevent you from doing it, in other words it is an inherent power or freedom. Where the right is not allowed to others, it constitutes a privilege. The right to construct a house given by the Small House Policy is a right in the sense of a grant (of land or of licence), given by the government. It is also a privilege since it is not available to those who are not adult males of patrilineal descent from inhabitants of certain villages in 1898. Before the policy but after the block Crown leases the right was also a grant since its exercise required DO permission. Prior to the block leases, the right was customary and its limits uncertain. The traditional small house right claimed by the Heung Yee Kuk is in the nature of a power or freedom: according to the kuk, before the Crown leases indigenous villagers who owned land were free to build on that land because no-one and nothing would or could stop them. Thus they had the power to erect houses and other buildings.

The idea of an interest focuses upon the benefit or advantage of an outcome. In Chinese, the implication is of an economic benefit. However, the idea may not be separate from that of a right. In other words, 'rights and interests' is one notion, not two. It equates to a beneficial right.

The kuk argues that the purpose of placing 'traditional' into Article 40 during its drafting was to clarify that rights and interests which owed their existence to custom or customary law were included along with other lawful rights enjoyed by indigenes at the time that the Basic Law was drafted and brought into force. In other words, the kuk's interpretation is that Article 40 includes all lawful rights then enjoyed, including traditional ones. This interpretation amounts to the insertion of an imaginary conjunction between 'lawful' and 'traditional'. The conjunction would be 'or', alternatively 'and/or'. To put the kuk's contention in another way, 'traditional' does not qualify all the rights and interests to be protected by the article, it is sufficient if the right or interest is lawful, that is to say based on statute, common law and equity, or legitimate executive act.

This interpretation is inconsistent with the English text which suggests that to qualify for protection a right or interest must be both lawful and traditional, that is to say a cumulative requirement. Commentators and judges who have previously considered Article 40 have given its wording the latter meaning. In other words, they regard the text as protecting traditional rights only, and only those that are lawful. This is consistent with the background materials for Article 40 which refer to rights 'derived from hundreds of years of history', 'remnants of feudalism' and preservation of the landed rights of 1898 residents.[4]

Consequently, it seems that what is traditional is to be determined by looking at the rights and interests which existed at the time of the 1898 Convention and whether and to what extent they were retained by the Hong Kong administration thereafter. When applied to the Small House Policy this approach leads to the conclusion that Article 40 does not protect the policy as such since it dates from 1972 and is administrative, not customary, in nature. However, one can separate the traditional aspects of the policy from its twentieth-century innovations. This suggests that only the free building licence can be traditional since it can be regarded as in effect a continuation of the pre-1898 practice of an indigene building on his own land without permission. The other major aspect of the policy towards indigenous inhabitants, the organized provision of building land on the periphery of villages for sale by private treaty at a discount, would not be traditional.[5] These direct grants

4. Explanatory Note in Report of Special Group (13 April 1987); Consultation Report of Basic Law Consultative Committee, Vol 5, p 370. *Kwok Cheuk Kin v Director of Lands* [2019] 2 HKC 538.
5. *Koon Ping Leung v Director of Lands* [2012] 2 HKC 329; *Kwok Cheuk Kin v Director of Lands*, ibid; Johannes Chan and C. L. Lim (eds), *Law of the Hong Kong Constitution* (Hong Kong: Sweet and Maxwell Asia, 2nd edn, 2015), pp 1061–1062.

were introduced (or re-introduced) in 1972 as part of a wider modern housing policy.

Traditional Right to Build

On the assumption that any right or interest to be protected under Article 40 is a traditional one, what does 'traditional' import? 'Traditional' does not simply mean old. The connotation is of establishment by long repeated practice. Once a practice is established, belief in its propriety is handed down from generation to generation so that it becomes customary and part of posterity. Legitimacy is bestowed by repetition: we do it because we have always done it and we are entitled to and must continue to do it because we have always done it.

In identifying a tradition, therefore, it is relevant to be precise as to what was repeatedly done. The scope of the tradition has to be ascertained. It is all very well to claim that indigenous males were free to build on their land in their village prior to 1899. That does not tell us what type of building was traditionally erected, or what the purpose of the building was. Nor does it tell us what if any qualifications or requirements accompanied this widely formulated right.

The survey records of 1899–1903 yield a fair amount of evidence about buildings in the villages at that time and therefore about the traditional practices that gave rise to them. The great majority were houses put to predominantly domestic use to accommodate families. Some buildings though were ruined, others for agricultural use. The overwhelming majority of the houses were small, of one floor, with one room and were about 436 square feet in size. Their arrangement and interior have been described in the chapter on Small Houses. Their locations were confined to the immediate area of the established village, for practical reasons of community and security. They were not dotted about the countryside. Those outside the confines of the village were appurtenant to arable land, i.e. for use in connection with agriculture.

It seems that in fact there had been little new construction in the villages in the decades leading up to 1898 for the simple reason that the size of the rural population had been low and stable or falling. The unexplained but marked reduction in the population in the middle of the nineteenth century continued, followed by little growth, during the forty years following the British takeover. The effect of this is difficult to imagine today, so used have we become to relentless increases in population and generations of expansion and development. But one can readily appreciate that in such circumstances a villager's power to build on his own land would have been only occasionally exercised because there would have been hardly any need to do so.

There was no abstract right to build separate from the land. It was a right to build on the ding's own land. There were other constraints on the exercise of this suggested right. First, there were financial disincentives. If the villager did not own land suitable for the site of a house, he would have to buy some or use unowned ground in the vicinity with the consent of elders and leaders. There was no question of land being lent to a villager so that he could exercise the right, nor of the modern practice whereby a loan with which to buy the land is secured by mortgage over that very land. Moreover, construction of a house cost money and money was scarce in a subsistence peasant economy. Whilst the house was small and its design was simple and the villager might be able to use family labour in its construction, materials still had to be bought and transported to the village. If the villager wanted his new house to be registered with the imperial magistrate, that would be an expensive exercise.

Then there were physical restraints. The land had to be suitable for construction but much of the land around the villages consisted of terraced rice-padi and other hillside plots. Most of the lots shown on the survey plans were small and irregular in shape. Even if construction were feasible, to build would sacrifice farm land, the sale of produce from which the villager might depend upon for income.

In addition, there might have been ownership difficulties. As explained in Chapter 6, under the customary system, occupiers were not normally the sole owners of their land. Imperial grantees, often one of the great clans or their institutions, were the underlying holders who paid, or claimed to pay, imperial tax and were recorded as owners on the imperial land register, a status that gave prestige and power. The farmer or cultivator derived title from them as a tenant or similar. Often his own lineage association held the surface rights and sublet them to him. He had rights of use, but were they exclusive rights for all purposes? There is a suggestion that in traditional China the right to build on the land, whether it be a house or a grave, required both owners to consent.[6]

The understanding between the owners would surely have been that unless it was within the immediate village, the land was to be used for agriculture. One can imagine imperial grantees would not have been pleased to find a house constructed on their land without their permission. A sensible occupier intent upon putting up a house beyond the compound of existing structures would have sought the other owner's permission before doing so. He would also have sought the permission of the head of the village (tsuen cheung) and the sub-district (heung cheung) and village elders. It is conceivable that these gentlemen would have expected financial incentives for giving consent. Since the arrangements were customary, there is unlikely to have been any hard and fast rule. Enforcement of any understanding that the land should be used only for agriculture or should not be built upon without permission would have depended upon the relationship between the two owners and the influence of the subsoil owner in the locality of the land. Where the underlying owner was one of the great clans or their acolytes and the land was in or near one of their centres of influence, occupiers would have opposed them at their

6. See Ch 10.

peril. Financial consideration to allow conversion of the land to building may have been required.

It is difficult to believe that under the system of divided ownership the farmer or cultivator could simply build a house at will, as advocates of an unfettered customary right to build maintain. It is true that Cecil Clementi, one of the young civil servants seconded to the New Territories to become a member of the Land Court in which capacity he acquired knowledge of customary tenure, observed that owners might build upon their padi. That no doubt reflected the formal position, but on another occasion he observed that no development could take place without permission from the dominant local clan. The latter appears to have been based upon the realities of power in the countryside. In certain places lineages imposed rents and exactions by force. Professor Palmer has suggested that those realities would differ according to how far the land was from the clan's centre of influence: farmer tenants of one of the great clans based in the northern area would have less independence if their land were near Taipo than if it were in Sai Kung.[7]

Houses would be erected when needed for family use. There was no possibility of building them for sale or for occupation by others because of the exclusiveness of the population who made up a village. An owner was precluded by the expectations of his kin from alienating land to outsiders. He could sell only if forced to do so by extreme circumstances and then had to offer the property first to other lineage, or failing them clan, members.

There was little need for new houses because the rural populace was thinly spread and in the late nineteenth century at best steady in numbers and may have been actually falling. The commonest occasion for construction was when a son married and was expected to start his own family. This led the Hong Kong government to conclude that the custom was to build when the son married. Although contested by indigenous representatives, if custom is what has habitually been done rather than what might have been done, the government was surely correct.

Small House Tradition

So what was actually done with regard to the building of houses in rural southern San On towards the end of the nineteenth century may be summed up as follows. The surface owner was free to build a house on his land provided that the owner of the subsoil did not object or did not find out about it. The heads and elders would have to agree to the construction. If he could afford to do so, a land owner would build a house when his son married. The house would be within the bounds, or at least the vicinity, of the village. There were however practical constraints of cost, of availability of materials, and of suitability of the land. The house would be simple

7. Cecil Clementi, CSO 807/2006; Palmer, 'Surface-Subsoil', 61; Hayes, *The Hong Kong Region*, introduction, XIX.

and truly small, typically 436 square feet in area. The house would be for occupation by the owner and his family, not to rent out or to sell to others from outside the village.

That practice greatly changed during the twentieth century. The houses became larger and made of different materials. The government regulated their maximum dimensions and where they could be built. It insisted that they be for occupation by genuine villagers in need of housing. It imposed a requirement of obtaining permission to build. It, not the villager, selected new building plots and sold them by auction. So, if by 'traditional' Article 40 means traditional in 1990 (or 1997), it is difficult to discern a practice over the decades preceding that time which amounts to a tradition. The practices of the twentieth century were quite different from the custom before 1900 and the practices themselves altered as policies were refined during that century. The most consistent element was the absence of payment for permission to build on old lots and even that was not constant.

Accordingly, the only possibly traditional element in the Small House Policy was the free building licence by which indigenous males were given permission to build on their own land without being charged a premium. This accorded with the position under the Ching in that the imperial government did not levy a charge when a building was put up. It is claimed that the no-expropriation clause in the Peking Convention forbade the charging of a building premium. The British practice was however discernibly different from the imperial one in that an owner who wished to build had to request permission and, after the building had been erected, an increased Crown rent was charged.

What Was Intended?

Advocates for the kuk say that what was traditional in 1898 does not enter into the meaning of Article 40. They maintain that one purpose of the Basic Law was to ensure continuity—the much quoted 'through train'—so that the existing social, economic and legal systems would be unchanged.[8] Applied to Article 40 this means that its purpose was to guarantee the continuation of rights and interests previously enjoyed so that the traditional rights and interests recognized as lawful in the 1990s were to continue under the Basic Law. They give 'traditional' the meaning 'traditional in 1990' when the Basic Law was finalized and adopted or 'traditional in 1997' when the Law came into effect, not necessarily deriving from custom or customary law and not necessarily having existed in 1898. Accordingly, the rights which it protects can be derived from a lawful set of administrative measures such as the Small House Policy. They point out that in a case concerning payments of comprehensive social security assistance the Court of Final Appeal accepted that an administratively created right could be protected by the Basic Law and an administrative policy can

8. *HKSAR v Ma Wai Kwan David* [1997] 1 HKLRD 761, [1997] 2 HKC 315.

give rise to legitimate expectations.[9] Further, in the village elections case the Chief Justice stated that there was no dispute between the parties that rights within Article 40 included benefits relating to land granted to indigenous males under the Small House Policy and the government view is that the customary rights of indigenous males include the right to build a small house under the policy.[10] Accordingly, they say there is no need to go beyond what was intended by those who drafted the Basic Law and that if one looks at the sources contemporaneous with the drafting of the Law, it is apparent that the drafters thought that the policy was within the rights and interests embraced by Article 40.

Here it is important to appreciate that the Basic Law is a constitutional document that followed on from the Joint Declaration signed on 19 December 1984 by the governments of the UK and of the PRC and went through a deliberate process of preparation by a large drafting committee of representatives from Hong Kong and the mainland, advised by another large consultative committee similarly composed. These committees generated a wealth of background papers during their deliberations. Lawyers call such background documents extrinsic or external materials. In construing a constitutional enactment, a court not only can but must take into account extrinsic materials provided that they are relevant. They are one of the aids to interpretation. Other extrinsic aids are explanations on the draft Basic Law by the National People's Congress and (given that one of the themes of the Basic Law was to ensure continuity) the content of domestic legislation at the time of promulgation of the Basic Law in 1990 or at the time of the Joint Declaration six years earlier. The nature and contents of the Basic Law itself, including its preamble, are of course relevant too, this being an internal aid.[11]

When one looks at the extrinsic materials it becomes apparent that there was a widespread assumption that the right to build small houses was to be protected by Article 40. In anticipation of its solicitation of public opinion on the draft law, the Basic Law Consultative Committee prepared a special report on indigenous inhabitants. This emphasized the historical context, including the non-expropriation clause in the 1898 Convention by which, according to the report, 'the rights of the inhabitants of the New Territories in owning and using the land were to be explicitly protected'. A list of existing rights, statutory and non-statutory, of New Territories indigenous interests was drawn up, including the Small House Policy.[12] A draft of the Basic Law in November 1986 by the Drafting Committee stated that 'New Territories indigenous inhabitants' lawful rights and interests should be protected'.

9. *Kong Yunming v Director of Social Welfare* (2013) 16 HKCFAR 950 (Basic Law Art 145 recognizes and endorses the previous social welfare system); *Ng Siu Tung v Director of Immigration* (2002) 5 HKCFAR 1.
10. *Secretary for Justice v Chan Wah* (2000) 3 HKCFAR 459, 477 K-J; but see *Koon Ping Leung v Director of Lands* [2012] 2 HKC 329; *Tse Kwan Sang v Pat Heung Rural Committee* [1999] 3 HKLRD 267.
11. *Ng Ka Ling v Director of Immigration* (1999) 2 HKCFAR 4 at 28H; *Director of Immigration v Chong Fung Yuen* (2001) 4 HKCFAR 211 at 224 E-F.
12. *Special Reports on the Indigenous Inhabitants of the New Territories* in *The Consultation Report of the Draft Basic Law for Solicitation of Opinions*, Vol 4, para 1 (October 1988); Chung, *The Small House Policy and Article 40*, p 9.

Certain mainland members of that committee proceeded on the assumption that those rights and interests included the right of males to build small houses and not to have their rent increased. In January 1987 the Special Group on the Rights of Inhabitants and Others formed from the Consultative Committee discussed at a seminar eight sets of existing rights of indigenous inhabitants as well as further specific rights that the kuk wished to ask for. The temptation to spell out a list of rights was resisted. There was a consensus that indigenous rights and interests should be set out in general terms and the wording 'The rights and interests of New Territories indigenous inhabitants shall be respected and provided for' was recommended. The group thought that rights provided for by the current law should be preserved and could be amended in future by the SAR government according to changes in circumstances. An article annexed to the agenda for that meeting referred to free building licences and private treaty grants, as did the seminar report, the Consultative Committee's report and, naturally, the submissions of the kuk's Mr Lau Wong Fat to the drafting committee of which he was a member.

Deep and wide opposition to the entrenchment of indigenous rights was expressed by members of the public to the consultative committee. Public Consultation Reports by the committee recorded views that the draft Article 40 preserved privileges rather than human rights, privileges which were exploitative of others, inappropriate in a constitutional instrument, feudal and colonial and restrictive of development, privileges which used up scarce land and deprived the population at large of the use of land and the government of revenue. Other views were that as the New Territories urbanized, indigenes were the same as other residents and that their housing needs should be based upon a comprehensive housing policy. The Final Report of the Special Group recorded objections to stipulating the rights and interests of the indigenous in the Basic Law on grounds that they were privileges left over from history, derived from the Convention of Peking which was due to expire in 1997, a legacy of feudalism, of custom and of a policy which was incongruous once Hong Kong had returned to China, for all inhabitants should be treated equally. Retention of the privileges was said to be impractical because Hong Kong was so small. In addition, the Drafting Committee considered objections based on gender equality, discrimination between the sexes and between Hong Kong residents, inconsistency with fundamental human rights, inappropriate use of resources, abuse of rights by indigenous inhabitants who had migrated, and the wording of the article (it was said to be unclear what lawful traditional rights and interests comprised).

Despite the diversity of these criticisms, they were rejected by the drafting committee. Why? Clues were given by the mainland drafters who separately considered a similar litany of objection. They thought that what had been agreed in the Sino-British negotiations should be adhered to: the rights and interests of indigenous inhabitants should be protected, including the right of male descendants to build small houses. So the sanctity of treaty overcame the vehemence of opposition. The prescience of the kuk in lobbying in London as well as Beijing was revealed. Or was it? Neither the Small House Policy nor ding rights are mentioned in the Joint Declaration. The only indigenous right which is mentioned there is the low government rent for small houses later preserved by Article 122 of the Basic Law.[13] There would have been no breach of faith to the UK if the policy had been abandoned. There must been another reason.

That reason is hinted at in the same paragraph of the mainlanders' report. 'Protecting their rights will also contribute to the unity of Hong Kong residents' they said.[14] Given the degree of opposition to Article 40 this is at first glance a bizarre conclusion, for preservation of indigenous privileges would only exacerbate the resentment of the majority of the population. But the mainland delegates had their minds not on the reaction of the general populace: they were worried about the reaction of the rural minority. The mainlanders must have heard about that minority's notoriously vociferous intransigence. Being demanding and difficult had again paid off for the indigenous.

If the sole question in construing Article 40 is whether its drafters were thinking of small house privileges when they referred to traditional rights and interests, the answer is therefore, undoubtedly, yes. But that is not the end of the matter. In construing a provision, the courts have to look at the language used and objectively discern the intent as expressed in that language in the light of its context and purpose. The views of individual drafters are irrelevant.[15] As we have seen, the wording of Article 40 was altered during the drafting process. The adjective 'traditional' was added and in such a way that it appears to qualify the rights and interests referred to in the article. The explanation offered by the chairman of the Heung Yee Kuk is that the word was added so as to ensure that the rights to be protected included those based on custom. But this does not make sense. Custom and customary right has been part of the land law of the New Territories since 1900 and for long before then. Customary law has been part of the law of Hong Kong ever since its foundation as a colony. Article 8 of the very Basic Law of which Article 40 was to form part would expressly continue the application of customary law. There can have been no doubt that customary rights were lawful rights. If a drafter wished to put this beyond doubt, there would have been better ways to do so than by simply inserting the word 'traditional'. A more convincing explanation for inserting it is that this was a compromise brokered between committee members in response to the widespread criticisms of the protection of indigenous privileges. The rights to be preserved were to be restricted to those which were traditional, and what was traditional was left unstipulated so as to be worked out later by the HKSAR's legislature and courts.

13. Joint Declaration, Annex III, Land Leases; Chung, ibid, p 8.
14. A Compilation of the Views of Visiting Mainland Drafters on some Questions concerning the draft Basic Law for Solicitation of Opinions, para 3.7.2 (June 1988).
15. *Kwok Cheuk Kin v Director of Lands*, above, paras 25–29.

Constitutional Challenge

Arguments about the scope of Article 40 came into focus during a challenge to its constitutionality which was heard by the Court of First Instance in late 2018. A non-indigenous New Territories inhabitant complained that the policy was discriminatory, deploying many of the points which were laid out in the previous chapter. The Heung Yee Kuk was allowed to make submissions as an interested party. The government's and the kuk's cases did not dispute that the policy was discriminatory but relied upon Article 40 to justify the discrimination. The court held that an indigene's right to build on his own land without payment for permission to do so (a free building licence) is a lawful traditional right and interest protected by Article 40 but that the other types of land grant available to indigenes under the Small House Policy, the private treaty grant and grant on exchange of land, are not traditional and fall outside Article 40.[16] In assessing whether a right was traditional, the judge adopted a suggestion by the government that the question is whether the right is traceable to indigenous rights enjoyed in 1898.

But what does traceable mean? The judge decided it meant that the right must capture or reproduce the essential features of the right that existed in 1898. That said, identification of features as essential is a matter of opinion. One essential feature of the 1898 right to build was that, so far as is known, it did not require payment to the authorities. The judge must have found the absence of payment to be the only essential feature. But another essential feature of the 1898 right was that governmental permission was not required: this feature is obviously absent from the free building licence which of its very nature is a grant of permission. Moreover, whilst the free licence did not involve a premium, it did involve payment of increased rent, so payment was not completely lacking for the licence, and the colonial authorities did sometimes impose conditions and restrictions upon the grant of licence and occasionally even refuse permission, for example if there were planning or fung shui objections to the intended building. The judge thought that these considerations did not detract from the original basis of not charging for the licence. This may, however, be questioned for they show that District Officers regarded control over the use of the land as being similar, perhaps greater, in importance as honouring any promises made at the end of the nineteenth century.

There is no doubt that one reason for not extracting a premium from village landowners who wished to build on their own land was that they had not had to pay the imperial authorities for doing so. But it was not the only reason. A pragmatic political concern to placate the natives was an equal consideration. So was a desire to encourage development. Moreover, originally the incoming administrators did intend to charge villagers for permission to build on their own land and during at least two periods in the twentieth century they did indeed levy such a charge.

16. *Kwok Cheuk Kin v Director of Lands*, above, paras 50–59, 115–116 and 130. Later the judgment was amended so that certain land exchanges were also held traditional.

These could be said to have broken the link between the freedom to build without payment of imperial times and the free licence of 1997.

At root, a requirement of licence before you do something is different from freedom to do as you wish. This aspect of the judgment is likely to come under scrutiny on appeal. Equally, the kuk (and perhaps the government) may challenge the finding that private treaty grants are not a continuation of traditional practices, although this will face an uphill struggle.

Ownership of Land

Prior to 1899, the person who built the house would be the tei pei owner of the land upon which the construction would take place. That is to say, he would be in possession and control of the land: its true owner, rather than the underlying nominal owner registered as such on the imperial register. Chinese law and custom had no concept of trusteeship whereby the registered or official owner held the land for the benefit of another. This is relevant because of the modern arrangements described in Chapter 12 which dings often make with developers to sell their right to build, a right which is said to stem from the Small House Policy, or rather from the small house custom which is now incorporated into the policy. Under the arrangements, the developer buys land near the village then recruits indigenes to lend their names to applications to build a house on parts of that land. A house-sized piece of the land is purportedly sold and transferred to the ding so that he becomes its registered and legal owner. But the ding never pays for the transfer into his name. On the contrary, the developer pays the ding for use of his right to a free building licence pursuant to which a house can be put on the land. The true or beneficial owner of the land therefore remains the developer who paid for it, will build a house on it and will later sell it with the house in the expectation of profit to someone unrelated to the ding. In law, after the transfer the ding holds the piece of land on trust for the developer.

Needless to say, such an arrangement, having been devised by creative lawyers in the late 1970s, is far from traditional and is unknown to customary law. According to the custom it is the ding who builds the house and he who is the real owner of the land on which it is built and who is to live in the house with his family. Consequently, irrespective of the constitutionality of the policy, these stratagems cannot be said to be protected by Article 40.

Other Traditional Rights

If the right to be sold a piece of land for the construction of a small house is not a traditional right and interest contemplated by Article 40 and if the right to build a house does not exist separately from the land, it might be asked to what rights can the article possibly be referring? The answer is the true small house custom, that is to say the ding's right to build a house on land which he really owns in his traditional village for family occupation. In addition, there are a number of practices which can be said to give rise to rights in the broad sense and which could fall within ambit of the article.

Landholding by lineage groups, t'so and family t'ong, is undoubtedly traditional in nature and the rights and interests of members of such institutions would almost certainly fall for preservation within Article 40. So would the holding of temple land and community land by t'ongs of various descriptions. These institutions, examined earlier, are the last bastions of custom in Hong Kong.

It was and is the custom for deceased village inhabitants to be buried in the vicinity of their villages. Nearly every old village has a cemetery, usually on rising ground (of little agricultural use but with good fung shui) shrouded by trees at the back of the village. Normally the ground is government land but this is simply the consequence of no one claiming ownership of it during the survey at the turn of the twentieth century. In reality it is regarded as village communal land, as it was under the Ching, and local authorities do not interfere with this perception. Indigenous folk regard it as their entitlement to be buried in such places. Village cemeteries continue to receive fresh graves despite pressures on space due to the increase in population and despite the availability of cremation as an alternative. The practice, and the accompanying sense of entitlement, has led to acrimonious disputes between villagers.[17] Other long-standing rural agricultural practices would likewise likely fall within the ambit of Article 40. So an established right to take firewood from, and cut trees upon, slopes would be covered.

The exemption of old lots from rates and government rent at the normal charge of 3 per cent of rateable value dates back to the early nineteenth century. The Court of Final Appeal has decided that this is a traditional right and interest within Article 40, perpetuating the old low-level imperial tax.[18] It is also protected by Article 122 of the Basic Law. Privileges which appear in domestic legislation such as the exemptions of land falling within Part II of the New Territories Ordinance from rates and from the law of distress for rent would probably likewise be justified by Article 40.[19]

The village representative system is not traditional so the right to vote for a representative is not protected by Article 40. The contrary was argued by indigenous representatives when resisting the giving of the vote to non-indigenous residents of villages, but this was not sustainable because the system of election had been started by the Japanese in the 1940s. Previously, village views had been represented by unelected elders, which was more in keeping with tradition. Another reason that the village representative system is outside Article 40 is that the article applies to

17. As noted by the Court of Appeal in *Regal Shining Ltd v Secretary for Justice* [2016] 3 HKC 291 at 301A to 302A. Expert evidence of the custom was given in that case. See too Coates, *Myself a Mandarin*, p 153.
18. *Secretary of Justice v Chan Wah*, ibid.
19. Rating Ordinance (Cap 116) s 2.

rights which are exclusive to indigenes but the right to vote for a representative applies to non-indigenes too.[20]

A suggestion that the requirement that District Office permission be obtained for disposals of t'so t'ong land contained in section 15 of the New Territories Ordinance violates Article 40 because the permission was not a requirement of custom has been rejected. The judge pointed out that the requirement was for the protection of the members of customary institutions so section 15 operated to uphold traditional rights in conformity with Article 40.[21]

If the effect of Article 40 is to throw us back to 1898 and before, there is an intriguing possibility that it has restored aspects of traditional culture which did not survive the British takeover. This would call into question the arrangements which replaced customary landholding. Those arrangements relied heavily upon registration to replace customary practices: registration of documents regarding landed interests, registration of succession to property, registration of managers of t'so t'ong, registration of trustees of minors who hold land, and so forth. All these overrode the customary way of doing things and might have been made unconstitutional by Article 40. If so, the titles of a vast number of New Territories properties, not confined to present-day rural areas, would be thrown into doubt. The interests of constituents of the Heung Yee Kuk would conflict, the interests of those descended from the old subsoil owners clashing with those of the successors of topsoil owners.

The subsoil-owning 'taxlords' or fundamental owners were for the most part dispossessed of their rights by the early twentieth-century land settlement. The Land Court eliminated the majority of them from the grants under the block Crown leases and consequently from entry of their interests on the new land register. But there is no doubt that in Ching law they had legitimate claims to joint ownership of the land for which they held red deeds and they were as genuinely indigenous as the tillers of the soil whose claims were given preference over theirs. Restoration of their interests in private land at this late date would not be feasible for the land would have been sold and resold (or resumed for public purposes) over the past century, but recognition of the rights of which they had been deprived would be possible in the form of compensation from the HKSAR government. The example of the buyout of the rights of the imperial grantee which held the Crown lease of Cheung Chau would show how this might be done.

Of course the consequences of such a result would be so shocking that no sensible judge would interpret Article 40 so as to allow it. The word 'lawful' in Article 40 would probably be employed to prevent it. So would 'traditional'—interpreted to mean what was traditional in 1990 or 1997, thus restricting Article 40's scope to rights and interests which had continued throughout the years of British rule.

If Article 40 has had the effect of recognizing traditional forms of landed interests, might it not also have legitimized traditional family and personal practices

20. *Secretary for Justice v Chan Wah*, above; *Tse Kwan Sang v Pat Heung Rural Committee* [1999] 3 HKLRD 267.
21. *Man Ping Nam v Man Mei Kwai*, CACV 193/2002 (11 December 2002) (Cheung JA).

which were delegitimized by twentieth-century legislation? These would include the traditions of male-only succession to property, of primary and secondary wives and of informal modes of adoption. So protection of traditional rights and interests is not necessarily confined to preservation of picturesque practices such as the lion dance, firecrackers, lucky money and feasts at new year and of solemn rituals such as grave sweeping and veneration of ancestors during Ching Ming and Cheung Yeung.

Over-protection?

Almost thirty years have passed since the drafting of the Basic Law during which time the arguments against the entrenchment of indigenous rights have continued with force and circumstances in Hong Kong have continued to change. The Basic Law is a living instrument, designed to adapt to those changed circumstances. The rights protected by Article 40 are exceptions to and derogations from the core values enshrined in the rest of the document. The protection should not be disproportionate to those values. There must be a balance between the rights and interests of the protected group and those of the rest of the population.

It is relevant that Article 40 impacts upon a scarce and valuable commodity, building land. During the intervening years an enduring social problem, the difficulty of finding affordable housing for Hong Kong's ever-growing population, has become acute. The government has had to reserve half of the available building land to meet the anticipated demand for small houses. Those houses will be an inefficient use of the land and almost none of them will be occupied by those intended to be protected by Article 40. Instead, by dint of schemes described in Chapter 12, developers will benefit. It has therefore to be asked whether protection of the policy by Article 40 serves a clear and just purpose sufficient to justify the continuation of the constitutional exception.

15

Property Theft

It is widely believed amongst laymen, and even a few lawyers, that after occupying someone else's land for twelve years you become the owner of it in law. The belief is inaccurate for it requires qualification in several respects, but the essence is correct. Long, uninterrupted, unequivocal and exclusive control of another's land without the consent of the true owner can give an intruder a better title to the land than that of the true owner. The intruder (or interloper, or imposter) is said to acquire title by adverse possession. Time and control turns the imposter from trespasser into unofficial or de facto owner. The imposter does not acquire the title of the true owner but a separate title of his own, called a possessory title.

The existence of such a law in a small, largely built-up, jurisdiction with a comprehensive land register by which the probable owner of land may be easily ascertained may seem anomalous, even contradictory. The law seems to sanction property theft. Not surprisingly, it has been abolished or curtailed in many jurisdictions. Yet it survives in Hong Kong and actually serves some useful purposes. Those purposes are particularly apt in the New Territories which consequently have contributed most of the cases which have shaped and which illustrate the law on the subject in Hong Kong. The assertive nature of many of the population must also have played a role in this, for it takes a certain self-confidence to take and hold something as prominent and valuable as land which you know is not yours.

During the late twentieth century the peculiar history and social circumstances of the New Territories gave rise to a number of cases in which unsanctioned occupiers of pieces of ground defied demands by their registered owners (often a developer) that the occupiers vacate it. The basis of the occupiers' defence invariably included that they had acquired title to the land by long possession of it. The developers responded with clever arguments, thought up by their lawyers, based on considerations unique to the New Territories and which tested the abilities of the judges who decided the cases. These cases attracted publicity which broadened awareness of the law, gave ideas to unauthorized occupiers and in turn gave rise to more cases. In the new century the rash of adverse possession cases has continued and the flow of clever arguments has not diminished. A high proportion of those cases have concerned land, mostly unbuilt upon, in rural areas. So the New Territories continues to cause difficulties.

Small landowners, especially indigenous ones, have no patience with clever arguments and no need of expensive lawyers. They tend to favour more direct methods of regaining their land. So, one interloper who was on the sharp end of threats of violence from people claiming that they were indigenous to the village and to represent the landowner obtained an injunction pending trial against the owner.[1] In another case, from the Pat Heung, there was evidence of what the judge called 'inappropriate action' to retake the land from a squatter by members of a t'ong which owned the land.[2] In a third case, a man who had squatted on land for many years had signed a tenancy agreement with the owner (thereby losing rights acquired by adverse possession) but alleged that he had done so under duress.

Types of Dispute

The predominance of rural disputes is hardly surprising because adverse possession claims tend to fall into common patterns that are prone to involve unbuilt land. One such is the boundary dispute in which one neighbour's fence or buildings have encroached upon another's land. Sometimes the boundary of each of the parties' land is marked inaccurately and trespasses upon the other's. This may be the result of unclear or inaccurate plans or of builders' disregard for the plans. Since properties in urban districts usually have well-defined borders consisting of walls, floors and ceilings, and rarely have gardens, the scope for such disputes there is extremely limited. By contrast, the great survey of the New Territories soon after their acquisition was carried out in a hurry and under difficult conditions and is acknowledged to contain numerous errors.[3] The encroachment in these cases is often unwitting and a result of following the inaccurate survey plan. In the case of buildings which existed at the time of the survey (1899–1904) or which have been rebuilt on the site of such buildings, invariably it is the survey plans rather than the builders which are to blame.

A second common scenario is that of the outright squatter, that is to say a person who takes over vacant or abandoned land knowing that it does not belong to him. The land may be next or near to other land which the squatter lawfully occupies. An example of this sort of case came before the court in 2017 concerning abandoned land at Castle Peak Road, Ping Shan, near Yuen Long. The applicant, finding the land unused, had (she said) entered and fenced it in 1992. She moved her vehicle maintenance business to the land. She cut the grass and paved the surface. She put a

1. *Wong Fu Ying v Yuen King Hay*, HCA 2612/2014 (7 September 2015).
2. *Wealth Hill International Investment v Wong Kwan Siu*, HCA 828/2008 (29 May 2013).
3. See Ch 4.

container there for storage and office use. She kept dogs there for security. She had keys to the gates. She paid no rent and had never seen the owner.[4]

A similar case of an unknown owner occurred on Lamma Island. The applicant's father had gone into occupation of land there in 1962. Nothing had been heard from the registered owner, who did not appear at the hearing. Adverse possession was therefore established and land which was effectively without an owner now had one.[5]

The conscious taking over of adjacent or nearby land is often gradual. The neighbour starts by making occasional and tentative incursions onto the apparently abandoned land, putting it to temporary or spasmodic use in connection with his business. Perhaps the boundaries between that land and his are unclear. Later, when no one interferes with the occasional use, the incursions become greater and bolder, perhaps as a result of the expansion of the business. Then the land, together with his own land, is enclosed by the squatter. Eventually the squatter may let the land out to a tenant. What was once vacant is now used for parking, or repairs or container storage. Meanwhile registered ownership of the land has come into the hands of a developer, who eventually sues for vacant possession or is sued by the squatter for a declaration that the owner has lost title.[6]

Land Vacancy and Takeover

Abandonment of land, especially in Hong Kong where it is so valuable, is not normal behaviour. Yet instances of disappeared registered owners are quite common. The social trends and population movements recounted in Chapter 4 have had an impact on the law of adverse possession. The 1940s and 1950s were decades of dislocation, with large movements of people initially out of, and later into, the colony, rapid change in agriculture with the decline in the growing of rice in favour of livestock and vegetable farming, and great growth in Hong Kong's industrial sector. The last lured people (mainly young women) from the land. Emigration to work overseas continued to be popular with rural residents.

During that era there was also an influx of people from elsewhere, especially farmers from Chiu Chau, who rented or simply occupied vacant land. If the latter, the occupiers may not have known or cared who the owner was but they did know that here was land that ought to be put to use. That indeed is one of the justifications for the legal sanctioning of the takeover of unused land by a long-term trespasser: it encourages efficient use of a scarce resource. It is more likely in the rural setting than in the urban that the claimant entered without any permission, in other words that the case is an instance of plain squatting.[7]

4. *Wong Pui Ling v Leung Kit Fun Beatrice Benedict* [2017] 3 HKLRD 700.
5. *Ying Fai v Chan Bo Cheung*, HCA 891/2012 (28 January 2015).
6. Eg, *Wu Yim Kwong Kindwind v Manhood Development Ltd*, DCCJ 3839/2012 (31 December 2014).
7. Rural examples: *Tsang Cho Kiu v Lam Tsat Fuk*, HCMP 1077/2013 (10 December 2013); *Ying Fai v Chan Bo*

As for rented land, a common scenario with uncontested applications by squatters for declarations of title is that the claimants or their forbears had been tenants of the property. They or their family had simply stayed on after the landlord had died or otherwise ceased to collect rent.[8] This is more likely to be the case with urban property such as flats than with rural property.

Famine, economic dislocation and social upheavals in China ensured that the flood of refugees and migrants continued throughout the 1960s with consequent pressure upon housing and land in Hong Kong. The vicissitudes of farming during the middle years of the twentieth century and their impact upon squatters' ability to show sufficiently long possession (in those days twenty years) are illustrated by the facts of a case that came before the District Court in 2013. The land in issue was at Mui Wu on Lantau Island, an area made more accessible by road improvements, and was registered in the name of a developer. On part of the land stood a house and a building used as a store which had been occupied, along with the land, by the defendant's parents in about 1954. After Typhoon Wanda had ruined the house in 1962 the family had converted the other building to domestic use and moved into it. The defendant had been in adverse possession of the building ever since, the judge held, but farming activities on the rest of the land had been given up by 1973 when the defendant's mother fell ill (his father had died years before). Any use of the land by the defendant and his family from then until 1982 had been insufficient to amount to exclusive control. Farming had been restarted by a friend of the claimant in 1982 but again ceased in 1986. After that, the defendant's activity on the unfenced land, gardening and picking fruit, had not been enough to constitute control of it. However, he had retained sufficient control of the building because, although he had moved to town in 1978, he occasionally returned and had kept personal items including ancestral tablets at the building which he had renovated in the early 2000s.[9]

In many claims to adverse possession of agricultural (or formerly agricultural) land, the squatter says that he or she came to the lots in the 1950s, 1960s or 1970s. At that time the land was either found vacant or the claimant rented it from the then owner who had since ceased to collect the rent and had not been seen for many years. The story tends to be different with more recent takeovers: here there is more commonly encroachment or opportunistic use by a neighbour, at first tentative and slight, but later burgeoning into full ouster with enclosure, and the land being put to non-agricultural uses such as open storage. In the latter sort of case, opposition by registered owners or their heirs is more likely but absence of opposition is far from unknown.

Cheung, above; *Chan Michael v PR of Tam Siu Fung, dec'd*, HCMP 745/2015 (7 April 2017); *Wong Pui Ling v Leung Kit Fun Beatrice Benedict*, above.

8. Overstaying tenants obtaining possessory title: *Wong Wing Man v Wong Chung On*, DCMP 1009/2013 (4 April 2014); *Shue Huei Yue v Tan Chung Meng*, DCCJ 2294/2013 (1 August 2014); *Ip Ying Kung v Louie Hong Sue Gay*, DCCJ 4719/2015 (17 August 2016).
9. *On Yip Property Development Co Ltd v Kwok Tai Kuen Alan*, DCCJ 1154/2010 (23 August 2013).

Evidence from Cases

Changes in the population of the New Territories would suggest that a prime period for abandonment of land by owners and intrusion onto that land by squatters would have been the twenty years from the late 1940s. In other words, squatters would disproportionately claim to have entered vacant land in or around the years 1949 to 1968. Is that suggestion borne out by the facts of applications which reached the courts in subsequent years?

There is certainly correlation between the social history and the background of the cases related in the judgments. During the 1990s there was an upsurge in adverse possession disputes as a result of legislation, enacted in 1969, for the renewal of New Territories Crown leases in 1973.[10] Most of the 300,000 or so lots granted by block Crown leases in 1905 and 1907 following the British takeover were for seventy-five years from 1 July 1898 with an option to the lessee of a further term which, if exercised, would take the term to June 1997 and almost the end of British sovereignty. The legislation deemed the options to have been exercised so that the leases were automatically renewed on 1 July 1973. The main question in the disputes concerned the effect of the renewal upon squatters who had been in possession of the relevant land for more than the limitation period of twenty years: were their rights unaffected by the automatic renewal or was it in effect a fresh grant to the Crown lessee? If the latter, time would start to run afresh against the squatter so that the owner would have another twenty years, until July 1993, in which to take action despite the squatter by then having been in possession for much longer than twenty years.

A clutch of cases worked their way through the Hong Kong courts in which the registered owner, usually a developer which had acquired the land for future use from absent or careless owners or their heirs, sought to recover the land from long-established interlopers. In two, the squatter claimed to have taken possession in 1949.[11] In four others, it was a decade later.[12] In only one had the intruder come to the land in the late 1960s.[13] In the five actions, all concerning land at Sheung Shui, which reached the Privy Council and resolved the issue in favour of the occupiers, all the defendants had taken possession (they said) between 1 July 1953 and 10 June 1973.[14]

The argument was re-run several years later in connection with the extension by legislation of New Territories government leases to 2047.[15] Again the courts

10. New Territories (Renewable Crown Leases) Ordinance (Cap 152), now the New Territories (Renewable Government Leases) Ordinance (Cap 152).
11. *Lam Kee On v Lam Hing* [1992] 2 HKC 317; *Yeung Kong v Fu Mei Ling Mary* [1994] 2 HKC 1.
12. *Cheuk Chau Co Ltd v Chau Kwan Nam*, HCMP 274/1982 (6 July 1983): 1960; *Tang Shu Tin v Tang Kin Kwok* [1994] 2 HKC 727: 1959; *Ho Yee Ming Theresa v Chung Loi Tai* [1994] 1 HKC 618: 1960; *Tang Tak Hong v Cheung Yat Fuk* [2002] 4 HKC 475: 1960.
13. *Chui Shui On v Tang Koon Yung* [1992] 2 HKC 323.
14. *Lam Island Development Co Ltd v Lai Moon Hang* [1994] 1 HKC 613 (HC); [1994] 2 HKC 11 (CA); also *Sze To Chun Keung v Kung Kwok Wai David* [1997] 1 WLR 1232 (PC); 1955.
15. By New Territories Leases (Extension) Ordinance (Cap 150).

ultimately decided that the extension did not affect squatters' rights. The facts of the cases showed the defendants' possession starting during the two decades after 1948.[16] The background to interlopers' claims against absentee or disappeared owners reveals a similar pattern. A number of claimants alleged that they or their predecessors came to the land in or before 1949.[17] There is a concentration of cases in which possession began in the 1950s.[18] In quite a number it began in the 1960s.[19] But the incidence of possession beginning in later decades is low.

Return of the Owner

It is difficult for the real owner entirely to lose possession to an intruder. Any small activity (act of dominion) by the owner on the land, such as parking cars there, is enough to show some continued possession and will prevent a squatter's possession from being exclusive. It is conversely difficult for an owner who has undoubtedly been dispossessed to gain back possession from the intruder. The owner has to do more than merely return to the land; he must perform an effective act taking back exclusive possession and bringing the squatter's factual possession to an end.[20] A symbolic or ephemeral act such as putting up a notice or a flag would not be enough. So when an owner, whose land next to a poultry farm had been enclosed, improved and rented out by the farmer and his predecessors, returned occasionally to the land to prune trees there, that did not amount to retaking possession.[21] But what is sufficient can be difficult to assess. A former tenant farmer who continued to cultivate the land for more than twenty years after his lease had expired initially was held to have established adverse possession even though the owner showed that his representatives had gone on the land during that time to put up notices, iron staves and wires. These had been taken down by the farmer after eight to ten days so the trial judge thought there had not been sufficient interruption of his possession. The Court of Appeal, however, thought otherwise.[22]

16. *Chan Tin Shi v Li Tin Sung* [2005] 1 HKC 1: 1954; *Unijet Ltd v Yiu Kwai Hoi*, HCA 13637/1998 (21 June 2002): 1962; *Mutual Luck Investment Ltd v Yeung Chi Kuen (No 2)* [2003] 1 HKC 90: 1966; *China Overseas Grand Gain Property Development Ltd v Wong Chi Sum*, HCMP 969/1999 (18 July 2003): 1959; *Chan Suk Yin v Harvest Good Development Ltd*, CACV 101/2009 (10 March 2005): 1961, originally tenant 1951.
17. *Law Yuk Cheung v Loa Ku Tai*, DCCJ 4/2012 (9 January 2014): 1940s.
18. *Lai Wai Kuen v Wong Shau Kwong* [2004] 4 HKC 528: after 1949; *Tsang Cho Kiu v Lam Tsat Fuk*, HCMP 1077/2013 (10 December 2013): 1954; *On Yip Property Development Co Ltd v Kwok Tai Kuen Alan*, DCCJ 1154/2010 (23 August 2013): 1954; *Choy Yuk Por v Chan Kam Muk* [2013] 1 HKC 505: 1958; *Law Yuk Fong v Man Chung Wai*, HCA 2195/2015 (16 January 2017): originally as tenant 1954.
19. *Ying Fai v Chan Bo Cheung*, HCA 891/2012 (28 January 2015): 1962; *Grand Wayfair Investment Co Ltd v Chan Yung Kan*, HCA 558/2007 (18 October 2013): 1960; *Cheung Yat Fuk v Tang Tak Hong* (2004) 7 HKCFAR 70: 1960; *Winpo Development Ltd v Wong Kar Fu*, HCA 2228/2011 (26 May 2017): 1968.
20. *Zarb v Parry* [2012] 1 P & CR 10.
21. *Law Bing Kee v Persons in Occupation of RP*, HCMP 2270/2009 (8 March 2013).
22. *Kan Yau Shan v Mo Yiu Mut* [2018] 2 HKC 492.

Repairing the Title

Mistakes concerning the registration of ownership of land can be remedied by the law of adverse possession. The land registration system introduced to the New Territories in the early twentieth century was superior to that which it replaced. Like the old imperial register, the Hong Kong land register was (and is) not a register of title but of documents affecting land.[23] It was, however, more efficiently kept. But irrespective of its type, no registration system is infallible for it depends upon people. The system requires those who tender deeds for registration to have the correct documents and to fill the forms in accurately. There have been instances of one piece of land mistakenly being registered as having two different owners. In one, the manager of t'so (lineage) property during the 1930s had overlooked that in 1914 his predecessor had sold a piece of the t'so's land near Hiram's Highway at Sai Kung town. When he became the manager he mistakenly registered that piece in the t'so's name. The purchaser from the t'so had also registered it as his and years later his successor attempted to take possession. Under the impression that it still belonged to the t'so, the successor manager had been using the piece, which bordered upon other land which was undoubtedly owned by the t'so, for many years. The courts resolved the difficulty by accepting the elderly manager's evidence of continued exclusive use and finding that the t'so had adverse possession.[24]

Then there is the case of the tenant with a disappearing landlord, the third common pattern. Land is let by the owner to the tenant, perhaps under successive leases each of a few years. The owner may be represented by a relative or other agent who collects the rent in cash in person. Eventually that agent does not appear, perhaps because of illness or death or because of a disagreement with the owner. The tenant continues in occupation, expecting to pay rent but unable to do so. The owner has probably died or emigrated. He may have no successors, or they may be ignorant of his title or not interested in it. The tenant starts to treat the land as his own but cannot sell it because he is not the registered owner. What is to be done?

After a suitable period of exclusive control with intention to possess the land, the erstwhile tenant may seek a court declaration that he has a squatter's title. Provided that the court is satisfied with the evidence, the title of the true owner will thereupon become extinguished, by virtue of statute.[25] There is a procedure by which the squatter can obtain such a declaration relatively speedily. If it is apparent that the true owner will not be contesting the case, the squatter can apply for judgment without trial on the basis simply of allegations made in his pleadings rather than by giving written or oral evidence.[26] Normally a court will not make a declara-

23. An intended title registration scheme in the New Territories had to be abandoned because of complexities of land holding there. Title registration legislation for the whole SAR was enacted in 2004 but has yet to be brought into force.
24. *Chow Tin Sang v Citihero International Ltd*, HCA 2315/2009 (4 May 2012); CACV 121/2012 (20 June 2013).
25. Section 17 of the Limitation Ordinance (Cap 347).
26. For judgment by default under Order 19 rule 7 of the Rules of the High Court (Cap 4A); *Lam Shing Shou v*

tion that title has been extinguished (or about anything else) without a trial because it wishes to be certain that the factual basis for what it declares is correct. However, this is a rule of practice only, not of law. Accordingly, there is an exception: the practice will not be followed where the applicant has genuine need and justice would not be done without the relief requested.[27] This exception is supposedly to be exercised sparingly and with caution. Yet the courts have frequently accepted that a squatter who is seeking to establish entitlement to land against an absent true owner has such a need and that justice requires summary disposal of the case. It might have been thought that, after so many years of occupation of the land, there is no immediate threat to the squatter's use of it and no pressing need in the case and that accordingly the squatter's story should be told, and tested by the judge, in live testimony before the court. There seems no injustice in requiring this for, although the application is unopposed, squatters still have to prove by compelling evidence that they have occupied the land in question for the statutory period without consent of the owner, that the occupation has been exclusive, that the use has been of sufficient intensity to amount to possession and that they intended to possess the land. The most persuasive evidence of all this is not what the squatter says but what objective circumstances show. Those circumstances ought to be investigated. It is by no means a foregone conclusion that the case will be found proven: there have been instances in which the squatter's claim has not been established at trial despite the absence of opposition.[28]

The need for circumspection in accepting a squatter's claim is fortified by the gravity of the declarations that the court is asked to make: in effect, the court will be awarding title to valuable property, perhaps worth tens of millions of dollars as developable land, to an interloper. The courts' ready resort to the exception seems to be based on the convenience of avoiding a trial which appears likely to lead to only one outcome rather than upon the genuine need of the applicant, the dictates of justice or the importance of the subject-matter.[29]

This exception was applied in the Ping Shan case dealt with above. Attempts to trace the defendant owners had been unsuccessful; a search at the register of births and deaths found no record of the defendants' death; the court had ordered that the papers be served by sending them to the last known address of the owners and by advertisement in a Chinese newspaper rather than by the normal handing of the documents to the defendants (personal service); there had been no acknowledgment of that service by the owners or any representative; they did not turn up at the

---

Lam Hon Man, HCA 361/2001 (15 January 2002). Alternatively, for judgment under the originating summons procedure in Order 28.

27. *Tsui Ming Sin v Tsui Chi Ping*, HCA 2550/2014 (2 February 2016); *Leung Pak Ki v The Estate of Pang Kau, dec'd*, HCA 624/2009 (1 March 2016); *Law Yuk Fong v Man Chung Wai*, HCA 2195/2015 (16 January 2017); *Wu Chi Kwong v Estate of Cheung Man Yau, dec'd* [2008] 3 HKLRD 503.
28. Eg, *Yeung Shuk Ching v PR of Yong Mung, dec'd*, HCMP 2224/2016 (24 August 2017) and *Tsui Kwong On v Koo Ling Sung*, DCCJ 4550/2009 (9 November 2011).
29. Malcolm Merry, 'Adverse Possession, Default Judgment and the Disappeared Owner' (2018) 48 HKLJ 511.

court hearing. The judge made the declaration that the defendants' title had been extinguished. He also, mistakenly and to the benefit of the squatter, declared that the squatter was entitled to be registered as the holder of the land. There have been other instances of a court making such an order, although not where the point that it would be wrong to do so has been raised.[30]

The reason that it is wrong to treat the intruder as the new registered or true owner is that the status of registered owner arises by virtue of the grant from the government of a long lease of the land. The court cannot force the government to treat the squatter as a replacement for or the successor to its lessee. Nor can the court force the Land Registrar to register documents. Neither the government's lease authority (the Lands Department) nor the Land Registrar are parties to the litigation, so they cannot be subject to any injunction issued as a result of its outcome.

Judges who order that registration of the true owner be vacated and that the squatter become the registered owner may be under the mistaken impression that the Land Register is a register of title, i.e. that the registered owner is the person with the best title, and that once the owner's title is extinguished by operation of section 17 of the Limitation Ordinance, the person with the best title is the intruder. It is legally incorrect that the squatter has good title and it is also doubtful whether the court even has power to vacate the registration of the government lessee as owner.[31]

The exception which allows default judgment for a declaration has been applied in a number of New Territories squatter cases. In them the court has made a declaration that the registered owner's title has been extinguished and that the squatter has a possessory title but not that the squatter is to be registered as the owner instead. Often the registered owners were last heard of so long ago that it is a reasonable assumption that they are deceased, although in one, the exception was applied even though the registered owners were thought to be in the United Kingdom.[32]

One judge at least has been more difficult to convince that cases of disappeared owners merit summary disposal. In one application brought before that judge the owner, who was the grandfather of the alleged squatter, had bought the land lots in 1959 but subsequently abandoned them; the grandson, had come from Shanghai in 1976, located the lots and cultivated them ever since. A house stood on one of the lots. The house had been given as the grandfather's address by the grandson, which raised doubt as to whether the grandfather really was untraceable. The judge felt that it was unlikely that the owner would simply abandon the house and ordered a trial.[33] It might have been added that the relationship raised the question of whether the grandson's occupation of the land had been with consent and so was not a trespass.

30. Eg, *Ng Lai Sim v Lam Yip Shing*, HCA 2963/1995 (22 November 1999); *Fan Kui v Li Kwai Wan*, HCA 3860/1998 (25 February 2002).
31. *Tsang Cho Kiu v Lam Tsat Fuk*, HCMP 1077/2013 (10 December 2013) (Jat SC Dep-J); *Lai Wai Kuen v Wong Shau Kwong* [2004] 4 HKC 528.
32. *Law Yuk Fong v Man Chung Wai*, HCA 2195/2015 (16 January 2017).
33. *Tsui Ming Sin v Tsui Chi Ping*, HCA 2550/2014 (Kenneth Kwok SC Dep-J, 2 February 2016); see too *Yeung Shuk Ching v Psui Chi Ping*, HCA 2550/2014 (2 July 2016).

In such cases, adverse possession is being employed as a substitute for the laws of succession. Instead of going through the complexity and expense of winding up the owner's estate and following the rules of intestacy or probate for distribution of the property, the occupying relatives are claiming a right to the land by virtue of their long occupation of it.[34] The attractions to relatives of using adverse possession for this purpose were increased by the abolition in 1994 of the simple procedure for succession to rural land formerly available under section 17 of the New Territories Ordinance.

If the claim is contested, the evidence must be presented at trial and must be sufficient for the claimant squatter to prove his case. Where the claimant has been the tenant, he first entered the land with consent of the owner, so the possession as tenant will not have been adverse. It will remain so during any subsequent tenancies and probably for a period afterwards because expiry of the tenancy does not necessarily mean that the landlord wishes the tenant to leave. The Limitation Ordinance provides that the consent ends with expiry of the period to which the last payment of rent relates.[35] However, in those circumstances the tenant is naturally expecting to negotiate a further tenancy and is willing to continue to pay for occupying the premises but is unable to do so because the landlord or the agent is uncontactable. That willingness will, for an interval at least, prevent the running of time in favour of the tenant (as lawyers put it) and so will delay the establishing of adverse possession, for he will lack the intention to possess the land adversely—or so the Hong Kong Court of Final Appeal has held.[36] At some point, however, that attitude may change and, instead of regarding himself as potential tenant, the occupier will start to regard himself as the owner. When the tenant makes this manifest, time starts to run against the true owner. The difficulty lies in identifying that point.

In the past, the rustic life was simple and informal and country folk may well have felt that buying and selling land ought to be as straightforward as buying and selling a bag of rice or a pair of boots. The property was inspected, the price agreed, the money paid and the property handed over. The money is however greater when buying land than when buying rice or boots, so perhaps the agreement to buy and to sell should be written down and signed. The transaction might be carried out in a hurry or in an emergency, so there is no time for niceties and lawyers. The buyer has possession of the property and no apparent cause for concern. If the seller is trustworthy and does not try to sell the land to someone else as well, the lack of registration of the informal sale will cause no difficulty until the buyer or his heirs wish to sell the land, perhaps to a developer, or to receive compensation where the land is required for some public works project. In those circumstances the absence of deeds will prevent them from proving title to the land.

34. An illustration from the urban area is *Hun Jay Nam Johnson v Hun Tai Sun*, DCMP 921/2014 (24 November 2016).
35. Limitation Ordinance (Cap 347) s 12 (2).
36. *Wong Tak Yue v Kung Kwok Wai David (No 2)* (1998) 1 HKCFAR 55.

Adverse possession has a role in giving effect to these informal sales, at least where a sale of land has not been recorded in signed writing or where the sale is not explicitly of the land. Where there is no signed writing, a sale of land is unenforceable as a matter of law.[37] Where the sale is of a mere right to occupy or of just a structure upon the land or of a business operated from the land, no interest in the land passes to the buyer. The buyer has at best a licence to occupy the land binding as a contract upon the seller, only. The buyer's right is personal rather than proprietary. The buyer has nothing to sell to a later purchaser that the law will recognize as effective against others. However, after the statutory period of possession, the buyer can fortify his position by invoking adverse possession against the true owner of the land.[38]

The position is different if the seller is the true owner and the sale has been recorded in a proper written, signed sale and purchase agreement. Then the agreement is enforceable so a purchaser who has gone into possession under the agreement but who has not received a formal transfer of the property into his name (an assignment) can sue for an order that the vendor complete the contract: a decree of specific performance of the contract. There is no room for the application of the law of adverse possession because the purchaser has possession by consent of the vendor, the true owner.[39] That consent may be stated in the contract of sale, where the purchaser is expressly let into possession prior to completion, or it may be by prior oral permission. Pending completion the purchaser will have paid a proportion of the price as a deposit. Once the purchaser has paid the full price to the vendor, the latter becomes a trustee of the property for the purchaser who is entitled to possess it as beneficiary under the trust. Either way, the purchaser occupies the property with consent. It is only if the contract is for some reason not completed and the vendor's consent is regarded as withdrawn that the purchaser's possession becomes a trespass and thus adverse.[40]

It may be that the title problem is deeper seated than an absence of formality. The buyer in such an informal purchase will not have checked the seller's entitlement to the land. The seller may himself be a squatter. He might have mortgaged the property for a loan. The buyer's title is defective. This is where adverse possession comes in useful again. After the appropriate number of years of exclusive occupation, the law of adverse possession washes the buyer's title clean. Even if there should be a mortgagee or another claimant to the land, twelve (or before July

---

37. Conveyancing and Property Ordinance (Cap 219) s 3.
38. As in *Chow Yuen Ling v Kwan Lau Ying*, DCMP 1203/2013 (30 July 2014), right to reside in portion of flat.
39. *Hyde v Pearce* [1982] 1 WLR 560; *Country Rich Development Ltd v Ma Chan Fuk Kiu* [1995] 1 HKLR 265; *Long Best Development Ltd v Sham Shun Tsing*, HCA 1399/2012 (11 February 2015); *Soong Sou Fun v Yew Man Hum*, DCMP 715/2014 (12 May 2015).
40. *Chiu Si Hon v Estate of Chan Shui Kiu, dec'd*, HCMP 1849/2011 (3 May 2012), *Lam Chi Keung v PR of Choi Chung Fun*, HCMP 1202/2011 (15 July 2013), *Lok Siu Fei v Estate of Chung Wan Kung, dec'd*, DCMP 1056/2015 (1 September 2017): sales subject to condition which was not fulfilled; *Cheung Chi Kui v Li Siu Kwong*, HCMP 2990/2014 (18 May 2015): sale terminated by repudiation of vendor accepted by purchaser; *Yu Fung Co Ltd v Olympic City Properties Ltd*, HCMP 1084/2008 (30 July 2015).

1991, twenty) years since assuming exclusive control, the buyer's title will become unassailable.

So adverse possession has its purposes. The law is not as outrageous as may appear at first sight. That is why the Law Reform Commission has recommended that the law be retained.[41] The law is based on the notion that ownership of land stems from possession of that land, a notion rooted in the common law and reflected in the old saying 'possession is nine-tenths of the law'.

Safeguards

The law, as developed by the courts, has certain safeguards against injustice to the real owner built in. These are obstacles which the intruder must overcome or requirements that he must satisfy. The first is that the intruder must have actual possession of the land. Possession is a legal concept which is deduced from acts and facts. Actual possession means more than just using the land: it means physical control and physical control requires continuous and exclusive possession. So occasional, trivial, or accidental acts are not sufficient to constitute actual possession. A farmer who grazes his cows on or lets his poultry onto an unoccupied piece of nearby ground does not have actual possession of it. Nor does he do so if he lays out his grain to dry on it or if he cuts the grass there. A family that picks fruit from an abandoned orchard, even if they do so every season, does not have actual possession of the orchard. A woman who enters a grove of trees and cuts branches for firewood or goes to a field and cuts grass for goats, does not have possession of the grove or field. Merely symbolic acts or declarations, such as putting up a notice saying 'private' or 'keep out' are likewise insufficient.

All these acts are at best ambiguous. They might have been performed as acts of possession, but then again they might not. None of the acts is inconsistent with continued enjoyment of the land by the real owner. Something deeper is required if that is to be achieved and actual possession is to be demonstrated.

The possession required of a squatter not only must be actual, it also must be exclusive. Here the squatter faces the obstacle that, since the owner has title to the land, he is presumed to have possession of it. It is difficult to counteract this presumption. Even quite trivial acts by the owner, such as things which had they been done by a squatter would have been insufficient to constitute possession, are sufficient to show that the owner has not been dispossessed. In one case, the owner of land called Lychee Garden near Yuen Long and his family and friends occasionally visited it for picnics and to gather fruit. They also stored goods and allowed others to park vehicles there. However, their use of the land was much less than that of the claimant squatter. Nevertheless, the owner's occasional use was enough to defeat

41. Law Reform Commission of Hong Kong, Report on *Adverse Possession* (20.10.2014).

the squatter.[42] In another, similar, instance the then owner and his family who held keys to two gates to the land in question had paid weekly visits with his children during the period in which a squatter had also been using the land. Later the land was sold to a developer which then faced a claim from the squatter. The occasional use by the developer's predecessor was enough to fend off the claim.[43] In fact the owners' use in those cases was quite substantial compared with that relied upon by a minority co-owner of some hereditary land which had been let out as a car park by his fellow clansman and co-owner, who held a majority interest in their land. The majority owner had denied the minority owner a share of the rental income, on the basis that he now had sole ownership by virtue of adverse possession. It is unusual for one co-owner to assert adverse possession against another for to succeed he must show that the other, and every other, co-owner has been ousted, that is to say completely excluded from the land. There was no ouster in this case because the minority owner was able to show that he had once parked his car at the car park and had done so without payment to the tenant. His doing so was attributable to his co-ownership of the land so he had not been completely excluded by the majority owner.[44]

Acts of Possession

What does an interloper have to do in order to establish exclusive possession against the true owner? He must demonstrate that he has performed acts which make plain to the whole world that he intends to exclude the owner from possession.[45] Those acts must be unequivocal and unconcealed.

Actual occupation of the land by the intruder, accompanied by its enclosure by wall or fence, is the usual and clearest way of asserting exclusive control over it.[46] However, enclosure is not always enough. As lawyers like to say, it depends upon the facts of the case. This means that the trial judge, who hears the evidence and finds the facts, usually determines the outcome. Judges' views may turn on an impression of the witnesses, resulting in apparently inconsistent conclusions on apparently similar facts. In one case the claimant used land adjacent to his own in Sai Kung, planting trees, gathering branches, and harvesting fruit. The judge found him to be acting as an occupying owner might, so he was in exclusive possession. The Court of Appeal accepted this finding.[47] Yet in another case, decided soon after, a judge reached a different conclusion on facts which were ostensibly more favourable to the intruder: a villager, who had a flat in a three-storey house, took over a neighbouring

42. *Chu Kwok Wai v Tang Wing Tung Anthony*, DCCJ 3267/2011 (16 April 2013).
43. *Hong Kong Kam Lan Koon Ltd v Realray Investment Ltd*, CACV 79/2008 (18 February 2009).
44. *Tang Tak Sum v Tang Kai Fong* [2015] 1 HKLRD 286.
45. *Powell v MacFarlane* [1979] 38 P & CR 452 at 468, per Slade J.
46. *Leigh v Jack* (1879) 5 Ex D 264.
47. *Chow Tin Sang v Citihero International Ltd*, CACV 121/2012 (20 June 2013).

piece of empty ground; he had partly enclosed the land, renovated and locked a shed that stood on it, erected other structures on it, and planted trees on it; he told the judge that he slept in the shed. The judge disbelieved him: why would he sleep there if he had a flat next door? This affected the judge's assessment of the rest of the claimant's evidence. The Court of Appeal refused to intervene.[48]

Indeed enclosure is not always necessary, again depending upon the facts of the case. Mere cultivation, paving or other use of the land may be enough, without closing it off.[49] This is especially so in the case of land surrounded by large open spaces. Those, however, are rare in Hong Kong. More likely is that the land needs no fences or walls because it has natural boundaries such as streams and hillsides, or that putting them up is impracticable. Where some land in the Yuen Long district was remote and isolated but defined by natural features, the judge found in the squatter's favour despite the absence of fencing. There was only one path leading to the land. The squatter had lived there, continuously and openly, since 1968. He had buried his parents and his grandparents in the land, a consideration which, given that treatment of ancestors' remains are important to traditional farmers, the judge thought showed the requisite intention to possess.[50]

The difficulty of establishing possession of land open to all is shown by a squatter's claim to fish ponds at Mai Po. A farmer had been raising fish and ducks at ponds on the owners' land for many years but the owners (including a television company) had access to the land, as did others because there were no barriers to entry. The evidence showed that the owners had been using it from time to time: among other things, the television company had recorded costume dramas there. So although the farmer's use had been substantial, it had not been exclusive. The court concluded that his occupation and use had fallen short of possession, had not been exclusive and furthermore that he had not had the requisite intention to possess.[51]

Since he has possession of the land, a squatter may let it to a tenant and give the tenant possession during the period in which time is running. When this happens, the squatter does not lose possession, for he has possession through the tenant. The same happens when the squatter allows someone else to occupy the land under licence. So, where a villager and his wife in 1995 had taken over land the registered owner of which had died in 1977, and had allowed other villagers to use it, that did not prevent them acquiring squatters' rights.[52]

48. *To Wai Sing v To Hung Tai*, CACV 48/2014 (5 August 2014).
49. *Seddon v Smith* (1877) 36 LT 168 (CA, Eng).
50. *Winpo Development Ltd v Wong Kar Fu*, HCA 2228/2011 (26 May 2017).
51. *Gotland Enterprises Ltd v Kwok Chi Yau*, CACV 260/2014 (19 January 2016).
52. *Chan Michael v PR of Tam Siu Fung, dec'd*, HCMP 745/2015 (7 April 2017).

Permission to Occupy

If there is any indication that the true owner gave the intruder permission to occupy the land, that will prevent the occupation from being adverse and becoming exclusive possession. Permission from the owner gives the intruder licence to occupy the land with the result that he ceases to be a trespasser and time ceases to run against the owner. The permission can be before or during the period of occupation.[53] The permission may be express, implied or inferred. It must however be communicated to the intruder either explicitly or by inference from the circumstances.

Express consent is the reason that a co-owner of a building cannot acquire exclusive rights to use the common parts of the building over his fellow owners, even if he has enjoyed those parts in practice to the exclusion of the other owners. This is the result of the nature of the co-ownership used in most buildings and estates in the HKSAR. The co-ownership is by tenancy-in-common under which each of the joint owners has unity of possession with all the others. Each of them holds undivided shares in the land with the right (through covenants in a deed of mutual covenant) to occupy exclusively a particular unit and to enjoy the common parts with the co-owners. This scheme of ownership is binding on all of them since they are each bound by the provisions of the deed. As a result, each has consented to the arrangement, including the joint use of the common parts. Any owner who takes over some of the common parts may be in breach of covenant but all the owners have consented to that owner having some use of those parts by virtue of their tenancy in common. Consequently, no co-owner can successfully claim to have adverse possession of any of the common parts. High-rise buildings are unknown in the villages but some three-storey village houses are divided on a floor basis with each floor allocated to shares in the land and relationships between the owners of the house being governed by a deed of mutual covenant. Also, certain developments of village houses have common parts which may be co-owned even though the houses stand on separate lots and so are individually owned. In such places adverse possession of the common parts by one owner would not be possible.

Express consent is also the reason that adverse possession is not available where the owner as vendor has sold the property unconditionally to the occupier. If the vendor allows the purchaser to take possession before the sale has been completed, the purchaser's possession is not adverse for the vendor has given licence to occupy. It is only if the sale is not completed and circumstances show that the licence was withdrawn that the purchaser can say that his possession is adverse.[54] Once the price has been paid in full, the vendor holds the land as trustee for the purchaser, so the purchaser's possession can be attributed to his being a beneficiary under a

53. *Ho Hang-wan v Ma Ting-cheung* [1990] 1 HKLR 649 applying *BP Properties Ltd v Buckler* [1988] 55 P & CR 337.
54. *Yu Fung Co Ltd v Olympic City Properties Ltd*, HCMP 1084/2008 (30 July 2015).

trust with an equitable right to possess the property. Accordingly, adversity does not arise.[55]

Not infrequently, especially in the complicated setting of the sale of ding houses, the ultimate purchaser goes into possession after paying all or part of the price but before the sale is completed. If for some reason completion does not take place, the purchaser's remedy is an action for specific performance of the contract against the vendor who in law is a trustee holding the bare legal title for the purchaser. The ostensible vendor is usually a villager holding the legal title which has been transferred to him by a developer who was the real owner of the land. Provided that he has been paid for giving the developer his right to build a house, the villager will have no motivation to oppose the purchaser's action. If, instead, the occupying purchaser waits, enjoys the property for twelve (or, depending upon when possession began, twenty) years and then relies upon adverse possession for a declaration that the villagers' rights have been extinguished, the application should be refused because the villager, having agreed to sell the house and consented to the purchaser's taking possession of it, has no entitlement to an order for possession and thus has no action for possession to be barred by the Limitation Ordinance.[56] That said, there have been cases of uncompleted sales of land in which the court has granted declarations to the occupying purchaser on the basis of adverse possession, including one concerning one of three ding houses in Sai Kung built by a developer who went into liquidation after selling one to the plaintiff in the name of an indigenous vendor (resident in the United Kingdom) but before paying the premium for relaxation of the condition against assignment to the government. However, in that case the corporate purchaser had not paid the full price and had successfully sued for rescission of the contract and return of its deposits, so there was no contract to be enforced. Despite the rescission, the purchaser remained in possession, living in and letting out the house over many years without any entitlement to do so.[57]

The discerning of implied or inferred permission to occupy the property causes difficulty. If the courts insisted that the owner's consent be explicit (for example, in writing), that would introduce inflexibility and rule out permission being given by act rather than words. But equally judges have to guard against promoting to permission mere acquiescence in, or toleration of, the intrusion. Such promotion seems to have occurred in two controversial decisions by the English Court of Appeal in which a squatter was denied possessory title after occupying land for the statutory period because the squatter's use did not contravene the owner's postponed plans for the land. The court reasoned that an implied licence could in these

55. *Hyde v Pearce* [1982] 1 WLR 560 (CA, Eng), applied in *Country Rich Development Ltd v Ma Chan Fuk Kiu* [1995] 1 HKLR 265; *Long Best Development Ltd v Sham Shun Tsing*, HCA 1399/2012 (11 February 2015); *Soong Sou Fun v Yew Man Hum*, DCMP 715/2014 (12 May 2015); cf *Bridges v Mees* [1957] Ch 475.

56. *Lam Chi Keung v PR of Choi Chung Fun*, HCMP 1202/2011 (15 July 2013), where Leung Dep-J discussed the point and the authorities and was able to rely on adverse possession because the sale and purchase agreement was conditional. Also, *Soong Sou Fun v Yew Man Hum*, ibid.

57. *Cheung Chi Kui v Li Siu Kwong*, HCMP 2990/2014 (18 May 2015).

circumstances be presumed to have been given by the owner to the squatter.[58] The effect of the decisions was reversed by legislation in England and in 1984 a Hong Kong judge refused to follow them, almost twenty years before they were criticized by the highest court in England.[59] The position is that consent can be implicit or inferred from the acts as well as the words of the owner but the acts must be overt or there must be some demonstrable circumstance from which it can be inferred that permission was given. If the squatter is not aware of the acts or circumstance, they must be such that a reasonable person would have appreciated that the use was with permission.[60]

Implied permission was one of the reasons for the court's rejection of the adverse possession claim of the occupier in *Yu Kit Chiu v Chan Shek Woo*.[61] There the occupier had used land and buildings at Yuen Long exclusively since the 1960s. The plaintiff owner of the land held it under a government tenancy. A permit was issued to the owner by the government in 1970 granting a modification of the tenancy to allow addition of a porch, kitchen and lavatory. The occupier signed the permit 'on behalf of the registered owner'. In 1986 a short-term waiver had been issued by the government to the owner, copied to the occupier, permitting non-agricultural use by the owner who accepted the waiver and paid the fee charged for it. The judge inferred from these facts that a licence to occupy must have been given by the owner, that the occupier had acknowledged the plaintiff's ownership and that the occupier had no intention to possess, as opposed to occupy, the land.[62]

Acknowledgement of Title

An acknowledgement of the owner's title by the trespasser will end the period of adverse possession or, as lawyers say, stop time from running in favour of the trespasser. Since it is all too easy for an owner to allege that the squatter acknowledged that he was not the real owner and that the owner is, the Limitation Act requires that any acknowledgement of title be in writing, addressed to the owner or his representative and signed by the person acknowledging title, i.e. the squatter.[63] Any act which freely and unequivocally acknowledges that the real owner is the true owner is sufficient. So a written, signed offer to buy or rent the land signed by the trespasser and addressed to the owner or his agent would be acknowledgement of title.[64]

---

58. *Williams Brothers Direct Supply Ltd v Raftery* [1958] 1 QB 159; *Wallis & Cayton Bay Holiday Camp Ltd v Shell-Mex and BP Ltd* [1975] QB 94.
59. The criticism was by the House of Lords in *JA Pye (Oxford) Ltd v Graham* [2003] 1 AC 419. The Hong Kong decision is that of Hunter J in *Man Kam Tong v Man Lin Tai* [1984] HKLR 181, [1985] 2 HKC 299.
60. The formula by Etherton J in *London Borough of Lambeth v Rumbelow* (unreported) approved by the English Court of Appeal in *Zarb v Parry*, above. Cf *J. Alston & Sons Ltd v BOCM Panels Ltd* [2008] EWHC 3310.
61. *Yu Kit Chiu v Chan Shek Woo*, CACV 137/2010 (18 February 2011). There was no overt act in *Yu Kit Chiu v Lam Ming Kwong*, DCMP 2706/2011 (13 July 2017).
62. The Court of Appeal agreed though expressed no view regarding the licence: ibid.
63. Limitation Ordinance (Cap 347) s 24(1).
64. *Edginton v Clark* [1964] 1 QB 367. Whether the wording amounts to acknowledgement of title is a matter of

Informal acknowledgement lacking the statutory prerequisites may amount to evidence of the squatter's lacking the intention to possess the land, although this would depend upon the circumstances. Where the wife of a neighbour who had intruded onto a land lot at Ta Kwu Ling in the far north of the SAR signed a preliminary agreement to purchase the lot from the owner and paid a deposit which was later followed by further discussion of purchase, there was no acknowledgement because the agreement had not been signed by the intruder himself. However, the judge concluded that the intruder had no intention to possess the lot. The intruder had bought a neighbouring lot and built a house there, then had fenced off most of the disputed lot with wire. The owner said also that he had given the neighbour permission to occupy the lot.[65]

The squatter's signing a tenancy agreement with the owner would ordinarily be an acknowledgement of the owner's title. However, the act must be voluntary. An agreement signed by an occupier, who was illiterate, only after threats of violence and misrepresentations by the owner, was held void and not a true acknowledgement.[66] It is tempting for an owner who knows that the interloper has been in possession for more than the statutory period to try threats and tricks in order to gain possession, especially when the owner is lured into wanting the land by a generous offer from a developer or large compensation for resumption, but it is quite wrongful and counter-productive to do so.

Title can also be acknowledged by payment of part of the principal or interest due on a debt. So a tenant who continues in possession after the end of the lease (holds over) and sends payment to the landlord as rent or compensation for his unauthorized occupation (mesne profits) would be acknowledging the landlord's title.[67] Similarly, an interloper who paid the government rent on behalf of the registered owner would be acknowledging the latter's title.[68] However, acknowledgment or payment after expiry of the limitation period has no effect upon the squatter's rights since they have already accrued: the owner has already lost the right to recover the land and his title has been extinguished.

Proof of Possession

A further protection for the real owner is that the onus of proof is upon the squatter. This means that the squatter has to bring forward evidence showing that, more probably than not, he has been in control of the premises, that the control is exclusive, that the owner has not been in possession even slightly and that this state of affairs has continued for the required period, which is twelve years since the

construction of the document in context: *Allen v Matthews* [2009] EWCA Civ 216.

65. *Chan Kwai Choi v Tsang Yuen Kin*, DCCJ 3889/2011 (6 January 2014).
66. *Chong Yuk Por v Chan Kam Mak* [2013] 1 HKC 505.
67. Limitation Ordinance (Cap 347) s 23(1); time runs again after acknowledgement.
68. *Tang Kai Tung v Tang Wai Lun*, HCA 2411/2012 (30 June 2015).

owner went out of, and the squatter went into, possession.[69] Many disputes turn on whether the judge believes the squatter's claims as to when he first took control of the land and his allegations as to continuing use of the land throughout the required period. This usually involves extended cross-examination of the claimant, scrutiny of documents such as electricity bills and family photographs, and oral evidence from relatives, neighbours and other local residents. Opportunistic claims have failed because the claimant has found town life more attractive than living in the country and has abandoned the land for a period or has not occupied it with the intensity sufficient to constitute possession.[70]

Invariably, much time is spent on aerial photographs. Since 1945 the government has kept an archive of regular and comprehensive photographs of Hong Kong from the air. During the first few decades these were in black and white and their resolution left something to be desired, so minute and sometimes inconclusive examination of them is required to discern, for instance, whether a particular patch of ground was under cultivation, whether a particular structure was present, or whether the squatter's use was exclusive. Each side may put forward experts in the interpretation of the photographs to assist (or confuse) the judge and take up hours of court time. Yet usually the judge is in as good a position to interpret the contents of the photographs as the so-called experts and the judge may reject their views, even if they are unanimous.[71] In one case the judge relied upon his impressions from a succession of aerial photographs to deduce that the claimant had not enjoyed exclusive possession of land at Fanling for any significant period. In another the judge simply rejected the views of both experts.[72]

Surveyors may be called upon to report on the condition of the land as they found it at various dates. This is especially likely where one party is a development company. In such circumstances, however, the surveyor is not acting as an expert giving specialist opinion to assist the court but as a witness of fact and so is prone to become a promoter of the interests of the client who engaged him rather than maintaining the independence of a true expert.[73]

Intention

One last safeguard for the true owner is that the intruder has to show that he intended to possess the land. The intention is objectively assessed, that is to say it is an inference drawn from the facts and circumstances. This means that intention is bound up with the acts of the intruder: 'acts of the mind can be, and sometimes can

69. Assuming that occurred after 1 July 1992. If the squatter took possession before then, the period is twenty years.
70. As in, eg, *Chan Kan Mun v Sanyear Investments Ltd*, DCCJ 520/2014 (18 September 2017).
71. *Grand Wayfair Investment Co Ltd v Chan Yung Kan t/a Luk Yau Yau Organic Vegetable*, CACV 238/2013 (26 September 2014).
72. *Worldpart Industrial Ltd v All Occupiers*, HCMP 53/2005 (20 June 2014).
73. *Wong Shing Tit v Fuk Wah Lam*, DCCJ 1385/2010 (27 January 2015).

only be, demonstrated by acts of the body'.[74] What the intruder says about his intentions is usually disregarded because that is inevitably self-serving. However, the Court of Final Appeal has created an exception or qualification to this where what the intruder says is an admission against interest. This occurred in a long-running case that proceeded through the courts during a period in which the state of the law was in flux. In an affidavit made for an earlier procedural hearing the intruder, who for many years had been farming land near Taipo that she had found vacant, had said that she would have paid rent had the owner appeared and asked for it.[75] This apparently natural and innocent statement condemned her to fail to establish adverse possession because, in the eyes of the court, it showed that she lacked the necessary intention to possess the land. The decision seems questionable because a tenant possesses land for the duration of the lease so an intention to be a tenant is an intention to possess. Another reason that the decision is questionable is that the court purported to rely on a decision of the English Court of Appeal which was subsequently disapproved by a higher court, and that higher court was the Judicial Committee of the Privy Council which used to be Hong Kong's ultimate court. The Court of Appeal decision was also subsequently criticized by the House of Lords.[76]

The Court of Final Appeal did not mention the Privy Council decision and may not have been aware of it. To the Privy Council, a statement by a squatter that he would have paid rent if the owner had come along and asked for it was just the sort of thing one would expect a squatter to say and did not prove absence of intention to possess the land. Indeed, someone who wishes to be a tenant intends to possess the land, for a tenant has possession during the term of the lease. The difference is that a tenant, unlike a squatter, intends to possess the land with permission, hence the tenant has no intention to possess the land adversely. However, the limitation statutes do not refer to possession having to be adverse before an action for possession is barred, they require only possession for the appropriate period. The requirement of adversity comes from the law of trespass, in other words the landlord's cause of action at common law. It is a defence to an action in trespass to land that the occupier was given permission to occupy it.

Lower courts in Hong Kong have to apply the Court of Final Appeal judgment, even though the reasoning has been criticized, and have done so in a number of cases.[77] This means that Hong Kong law differs from that elsewhere. It also leads to apparent inconsistencies. A squatter who mistakenly believes that he is a tenant

74. Lord Hope, *JA Pye (Oxford) Ltd v Graham* [2003] 1 AC 419, 446A.
75. *Wong Tak Yue v Kung Kwok Wai David (No 2)* (1998) 1 HKCFAR 55.
76. The Court of Appeal decision is *Ex p Davies*, the PC decision is *Ocean Estates v Pinder* and the HL decision is *JA Pye (Oxford) Ltd v Graham*, above.
77. *Lau Wing Hong v Wong Wor Hung* [2006] 4 HKLRD 671, [2006] 4 HKC 221; *Hong Kong Kam Lan Koon Ltd v Realray Investment Ltd (No 5)* [2007] 5 HKC 122; *Tsui Kwong On v Koo Ling Sung*, DCCJ 4550/2009 (9 November 2011); *Chu Po Ling v Chung Chun Shing*, DCCJ 32/2012 (28 March 2014); *Fung Ka Wing v The Kok Lok Tung Benevolent Society Ltd*, DCCJ 2293/2015 (31 July 2017).

of the true owner has intention to possess the land. Yet a squatter who would have been willing to pay rent if asked has no intention to possess the land.

This shows that the requirement of intention to possess, or *animus possidendi*, is difficult to apply. An owner occupying his own land of course intends to possess it. Since we are concerned with a state of mind, it is sufficient that the occupier believes that he owns the land, for that belief is consistent with intent to possess the land. So even if the belief is mistaken, he is not precluded from establishing the necessary intent.[78] This can easily happen in rural areas where boundaries are inexact and informal transfer of ownership occurs. It happened in a family dispute that arose in Sha Kok Mei village, Sai Kung. The son had occupied some land for years and, believing that he owned it exclusively, was building a house there, though the land was in fact owned by him and two relatives equally. When one of the relatives sought a share of the house, the son successfully relied on adverse possession to resist the claim.[79] It happened also in the case of a nunnery in Sai Kung. The founder orally gave the land on which it stood to one of her followers, the claimant's husband, in 1979 when she was very ill. A gift made in contemplation of death (or *donatio mortis causa*) can be effective as a conditional gift, the conditions being that the donor does soon die and that the donee does not die first, but in this instance the court could not be certain that the founder wanted to transfer the land as opposed to wanting the husband to manage the nunnery and the founder had survived for a considerable period after the attempted gift. The husband and the claimant had lived at the nunnery thereafter, the husband passing away in 2012 and the claimant continuing to live there after that. Although the gift was not established, more than twenty years' possession was. The fact that the husband believed the land had been given to him did not prevent him from being in possession. In effect adverse possession completed the supposed gift. It also performed the function of the law of succession, effecting a transfer of the land to the husband as if by the founder's will and then by husband to wife as if by will or on intestacy.[80] Although the result seems to have been in accordance with the intentions of those involved, there is difficulty with the use of adverse possession to achieve this. The husband and wife must have been in occupation of the nunnery with the founder's consent so their possession was not adverse, at least not initially.

If the occupier believes he is the owner of the land but knows or suspects that there may be doubt as to the extent of what he owns, that may prevent him from having the requisite intent with regard to possession of the parts that he does not own. This occurred in respect of two lots at Ho Chung, Sai Kung, which the owner of neighbouring land had trespassed upon since (he said) 1994. The neighbour's solicitors had written to the owner of the lots questioning the accuracy of boundary

78. *Cheung Kwong Yuen v Sun Hui Fang* [2017] 2 HKC 171, applying *Wong Luen Chun v Secretary for Justice* [1998] 4 HKC 122, 129C. Also, *Wong Kar Sue v Sun Hung Kai Properties Ltd* [2006] 2 HKC 600.
79. *Cheung Lai Mui v Cheung Wai Shing*, HCA 1652B/2012 (10 April 2017).
80. *Wang Hanzhen v PR of Li Kuen*, DCMP 3269/2014 (17 February 2016).

fences. This, the judge decided, implied that the neighbour would move out of the lots if the fence was not in the correct place and therefore showed that he lacked intention to possess the land.[81]

Offers or suggestions by the squatter can count against him, as a claimant who with his family had occupied as tenant since 1959 the first floor of a two-storey house at Kam Shan Village, Taipo, discovered. The landlord had passed away in 1988, leaving the lot to his daughter, the defendant. The claimant ceased paying rent in 1996. More than twelve years passed before the daughter took legal action. However, members of the claimant's family had told the daughter that they would pay rent once the daughter became the registered owner. This was an informal acknowledgement of title. Later, the claimant told the daughter that he wanted to purchase the house. The judge decided that the claimant lacked intention to possess.[82]

Where the squatter claims that he made an agreement with the owner to use the land, that will prevent him from having the necessary intent. If there was such an agreement, his possession is not adverse, but even if the court finds that there was no such agreement, the squatter will not have intent to possess. The grant of a tenancy to the occupier by the owner is an example of the giving of express consent to use the land. So is the grant of a licence to occupy the land. Both grants prevent the occupier's actual possession from being adverse during the period of grant. The difficulty arises when that period comes to an end: any continued occupation after that period is adverse but does the continuing occupier have intent to occupy adversely during that continuing occupation? The intent may not be to use the land without permission but to recognize the rights of the true owner by seeking fresh permission to occupy.[83] This is particularly likely to be the case where the occupation has continued for many years under successive grants and the owner is known to have died and especially if the owner previously shared the premises with the licensee.

The requirement of intent to possess is in reality a control device which enables the court to refuse unmeritorious claims over land by opportunistic squatters. It is usually possible for a judge to discern from some aspect of the evidence doubt as to the squatter's intentions and that is all that is required to conclude that the case has not been established.

81. *Wu Yim Kwong Kindwind v Manhood Development Ltd*, DCCJ 3839/2012 (31 December 2014).
82. *Hui Fu Keung Christopher v Wong Sui Sum*, DCCJ 4358/2013 (29 January 2016).
83. *Jin Yu Chia v PR of Lee Ah Hsin, dec'd*, HCA 1121/2011 (24 April 2017).

16
Illegal Structures

Buildings legislation has existed in Hong Kong for more than 125 years.[1] The original concern was to ensure the safety of buildings and the health of their inhabitants in the crowded parts of the then colony. The legislation was not extended to the New Territories when they were acquired in 1898. Until the middle of the twentieth century the bulk of the New Territories were predominantly countryside with relatively spacious low-rise buildings even in the market towns. In the rural parts the custom was that an indigenous male could build in his village a small house for himself or his son upon marriage. What little control over these and other constructions was exercised by the District Office through the terms of the Crown lease which forbade the erection of buildings except with government permission. However, the process of creeping urbanization and suburbanization rendered this approach inadequate so the administration determined to extend statutory controls to the New Territories.

On 1 January 1961 the Buildings Ordinance and associated regulations were first applied to the whole of the New Territories.[2] Previously, the only part of the territory ceded in 1898 to which they had applied was New Kowloon. Until then, what control the administration had exercised over construction work outside the urban areas had been through the provisions of Crown leases which required that government permission be obtained before any new building was constructed but did not lay down any requirement for the drawing up and approval of plans or compliance with quality controls.

The application of building controls to the whole of the territory meant that, in principle, country areas had to comply with the same rules as everyone else. But this was in principle only, for, as we have seen, the construction of village houses was excluded from the rules and in respect of other buildings there is much laxer enforcement of the rules. Illegal structures, or as administrators call them, unauthorized building works, have proliferated throughout the New Territories. What are those rules?

1. The earliest legislation dealing solely with buildings was the Buildings Ordinance 1889, No 15 of 1889.
2. Buildings Ordinance (Application to the New Territories) Ordinance, effective 1 January 1961; originally Cap 322, replaced in 1987 by Cap 121.

The Law

The underlying law concerning illegal structures is simple. Anyone who wishes to carry out building works must obtain permission from the Building Authority. It is an offence to carry out such works without that permission. The principal provision is section 14(1) of the Buildings Ordinance, the relevant part of which reads:

> no person shall commence or carry out any building works . . . without having first obtained from the Building Authority –
> (a) his approval in writing of documents submitted to him in accordance with the regulations; and
> (b) his consent in writing for the commencement of the buildings . . .

The Building Authority (or BA) is the government's Director of Buildings and Lands who is in charge of the Buildings Department.[3]

Building works are very widely defined. They include repairs, demolition, alterations, and additions. They embrace any kind of building construction and every kind of building operation.[4] There is very little judicial guidance as to the limits of this definition and as to what does or does not constitute building works. Unhelpfully, this is said to be a matter of fact and degree in every case. It is safe to say that the Buildings Department's view of what is building works is wider than most people's conception of them.

Grammatically, the description 'building works' suggests a process rather than a result. Works start, are carried out and eventually finish. The result of the works is a building, or a changed building, a wall, a wharf, a bridge, or whatever: all are structures. This result cannot sensibly be described as works, yet the statutory definition says otherwise.

There are exceptions to the requirement of permission for works. Those that take place inside a building, which do not involve the structure of the building and which do not contravene any regulations are exempt.[5] Under a relatively recent and long overdue amendment, minor works, such as canvas canopies and air-conditioner supports, can be erected without prior permission provided that an authorized contractor is used.[6] There is however no exception for works done in traditional village houses or by indigenous villagers.

Building works or their consequences which take place without the required permission are known as unauthorized building works: UBWs in the Buildings Department's jargon. The terminology 'illegal structure', although commonly used and convenient, is inaccurate. It is not the structure which is forbidden so much as the works that lead to its making. Also, unauthorized works may not lead to a structure: demolition of a building would require permission just as much as

3. Buildings Ordinance (Cap 123) (hereinafter BO) s 2.
4. BO s 2.
5. BO s 41(3).
6. BO s 14AA.

would erection of a building. Moreover, it is an offence to build without permission but not, without more, to keep or have the building that results. Consequently, a person who buys and uses property which contains an unauthorized structure does not commit an offence. That person would, however, be guilty of an offence if the Building Authority were later to order him, as owner, to remove the structure and he did not comply.[7]

Documents and Permissions Required

Regulations made under the Buildings Ordinance require that plans of the proposed works (other than minor works, which have a separate procedure) be lodged with the Buildings Department for approval. Those plans must be drawn up by an architect, engineer or other authorized person. Standards regarding design, planning and construction with which the plans must comply are set out in regulations. The plan is to be approved and consent to commencement of works given by the Building Authority. A permit must be sought and granted before a building can be occupied. Any drainage works or street access must be separately approved.[8]

When the Buildings Ordinance and regulations were applied to the New Territories, it was recognized that the complex and expensive business of lodging plans for approval, complying with regulations and applying for permissions was undesirable and unnecessary for small village houses. So an exemption was written into the ordinance which extended the law to the New Territories. Provided that a house was within set dimensions and met certain other requirements, the controls would not apply to it. This is the New Territories Exempted House, or NTEH, introduced in Chapter 10.

The dimensions of an NTEH have changed from time to time but currently and for many years exempted houses have no more than three storeys, do not exceed 27 feet (8.3 metres) in height, and have a flat roof and a roofed-over area not exceeding 700 square feet (65.03 square metres). There are also restrictions upon the size of balconies, canopies and roof-top structures and upon the thickness of walls.

Houses of this size, typically a three-storey, flat-roofed, 2,100 square-foot, so-called Spanish-style villa, proliferated in the rural New Territories during the final quarter of the last century. They were built mainly on the periphery of villages on land made available by the government under the Small House Policy or provided by developers and transferred temporarily into the names of indigenous males. The intention of the policy to alleviate a perceived shortage of affordable housing for indigenous men and their families in the rural areas has been frustrated by the continued migration of native villagers to the city and overseas and by the sale of their rights to developers and of their completed houses to 'outsiders'. This has led

7. BO s 24.
8. BO ss 4, 21, 28 and 30.

to tensions between new residents and old in the villages. It has also led to suburbanization, with developers building clusters of expensive 'small' houses on the periphery of villages.

Nevertheless, a proportion of 'small' houses, particularly those at the centre of the villages built on land which was used for housing long before 1972, continue to be occupied by original villagers. Typically the occupants are several generations of a family or are members of one extended family. A few of these houses have more than three storeys and have had more than three since the time that they were built. However, the great majority were built within the scheduled dimensions and have three storeys or fewer.

Construction of this type of house is therefore not subject to the Buildings Ordinance and is outside the jurisdiction of the Building Authority. Responsibility for ensuring that the rules regarding construction of exempted houses are obeyed is solely upon the government's Lands Department operating through its District Land Offices (DLOs) which took over responsibility for land matters from the District Offices in 1982. Control is exercised through the terms of the government lease and the policies adopted by the DLOs with respect to the giving of permissions under that lease. The DLO is responsible for issuing the requisite documentation: a certificate that the building is exempt from the Buildings Ordinance, a certificate that the terms of the government lease have been complied with and a letter that there is no objection to the occupation of the house. Once the house has been finished and occupied, changes to the house fall under the jurisdiction of the Building Authority.

Construction of other types of buildings in the New Territories is subject to the Buildings Ordinance and is therefore the responsibility of the BA throughout. These include high-rise constructions and commercial centres found in the new towns and estates of modern luxury villas. Only houses within the dimensions of a NTEH fall outside building controls; such a house ceases to be exempted if for some reason it exceeds those dimensions. So if, during construction, an extra floor or half floor is added, or a ground-floor extension is built, or a balcony is widened, the house will not be exempt and will become subject to the Buildings Ordinance and regulations thereunder, enforcement of which is the responsibility of the BA. Should such adaptations occur after the house has been completed, the works require BA permission as with any other building in the SAR.

In law, therefore, every piece of building construction or demolition which requires Building Authority consent and does not have it, is a breach of the law and ought to be stopped or removed. The requirement of consent is however roundly ignored throughout the Special Administrative Region. The reasons for this are a matter of speculation, but one reason must be that the law is a paper tiger: the chances of 'getting away with it', at least for a considerable period, are large. The chances are, however, significantly greater in the rural areas than in town.

Practice

Enforcement action against unauthorized structures is primarily carried out by the Buildings Department. Many years ago the department recognized the inevitable—that it could not inspect every building for UBWs and that disobedience of the law was widespread. The department also recognized another reality: that the removal of every unauthorized structure is not equally pressing. Accordingly, a policy of distinguishing between UBWs for enforcement purposes was adopted. This was called 'prioritized enforcement'. A statement of this policy was released to the public in 1995. That statement has been modified, but only slightly, over the years. It is published in leaflet form and on the department's website.

According to the statement the highest priority was to be given to the removal of structures that posed an obvious or imminent danger to life or property and those that were newly completed or in the course of construction.[9] In theory, structures for which the case for removal was less pressing would be dealt with later. In practice such structures would not be the subject of a removal order, even if discovered in the course of taking action against high-priority structures in the same building or vicinity. Instead, the owner of the building would be given a warning, in the form of a letter advising that the structure was unauthorized and the owner might like to consider removing it.

In 2002 a small but significant revision of the policy took place. As a result of reconsideration by a working group of representatives from various government land divisions, it was decided that action would be taken at NTEHs against dangerous structures and work in progress only. So, in the case of village houses, recently completed unauthorized works would not be acted against. When does work cease to be in progress and become simply new? The dividing line adopted by administrators in 2006 was that work is regarded as new but not in progress if it is 'practically completed', which means that the main structure is completed. This is to be judged as at the date of first detection of the structure.[10]

The manpower limitations of the Buildings Department have necessitated this approach. They have also necessitated that the department use enforcement weapons of lower potency than a removal order. So the department issues advisory letters to owners, suggesting that the UBW at the owner's property ought to be removed (or 'purged'). It also issues letters to owners demanding removal of UBWs, these letters being registered on the Land Register if the structure is not removed so as to warn potential purchasers of the property. The thought was that this registration would blight the title and force the owner to remove the structure if he really wanted to sell the property. Anecdotal evidence however suggests that

9. Other high priority targets were UBWs which had been the subject of complaint by public bodies and UBWs in buildings or districts which were the subject of 'blitz' operations for comprehensive enforcement action.
10. Office of the Ombudsman, *Enforcement against Unauthorised Building Works in New Territories Exempted Houses*, April 2011.

the registration does not prevent the property from being sold or even lead purchasers to bargain for a reduced price. At most, the purchaser's intending mortgagee lender will reduce the amount of the loan that it offers to the purchaser by the estimated cost of the removal of the structure. Sometimes an owner will comply and the Building Department's inspector will ascertain that the offending structure has gone but the owner will later re-instate the structure. The department's power to carry out works itself or through contractors to remove unauthorized works, the cost to be met by the owner, has been used in cases of persistent breach. However, shortage of funds, staff and technical expertise has limited the use of this power.[11]

Enforcement action has increased somewhat as a result of the Buildings Department contracting out the inspection of premises to professional consultants. These are typically firms of building surveyors. Nevertheless, statutory notices and orders issued as a result of such inspections have to go out under the name of the Building Authority.

The Buildings Department therefore concentrates upon eliminating UBWs which are dangerous or in course of construction. It has enforcement teams and action units ready to intervene when unauthorized changes to a building are taking place. They issue letters advising the owner to stop the work and remove whatever has so far been built. If that is not done, a removal order will follow, requiring the works to be removed within a certain period of time. If that is not done, prosecution may follow.

Whilst the occasion for enforcement action by the Buildings Department is the carrying out of unauthorized works, the occasion for enforcement action by the District Lands Office is the carrying out of works which are, or which result in, what the office regards as a breach of the government lease. These are not necessarily the same. However, in the case of village houses the most common kinds of unauthorized structure, such as those on roofs and balconies, would usually lead to the dimensions of the house permitted by the government lease being exceeded so the DLO would have grounds for action for breach of the lease.

The DLOs' practice is to distinguish between blatant (i.e. obvious and major) breaches and minor breaches of the government lease. Many alterations to exempted houses constitute minor breaches. These can be tolerated on payment of a penalty. The policy adopted in 2002 of not taking action against completed new works at exempted houses and concentrating upon work in progress and dangerous structures was applied to lease enforcement as well as Buildings Ordinance enforcement.

The jurisdiction of the Buildings Department does extend to building works added to village houses. The exemption from building controls applies only to the initial construction of such houses. Any later additions, or indeed any initial construction beyond the scheduled dimensions, would be required to comply with the buildings legislation. Nevertheless, the notion has taken root that exempted houses

11. BO s 24. *Enforcement against Unauthorised Building Works in New Territories Exempted Houses*, April 2011, p 5.

are completely outside building controls and are entirely the responsibility of the District Lands Office. This is partly a matter of convenience: the BD is so stretched by looking after UBWs on multi-storey buildings in the urban areas that it has no desire or capacity to take on UBWs in the rural areas as well. So in practice enforcement there has been left to the various DLOs.

This pragmatic division of responsibility has contributed to the perception that there is uneven enforcement of the law; or that there is in reality one law for unauthorized structures on village houses and another for unauthorized structures on all other buildings. The perception is essentially correct, as the reports of the Office of the Ombudsman reveal. The DLOs give priority to action against the use of residential buildings for dangerous industrial undertakings. The DLOs also keep an eye open for work in progress at NTEHs but have a different interpretation from the BD as to what constitutes work in progress and consequently a more tolerant attitude towards illegal structures.

There is, however, more to it than a matter of interpretation. It turns out that the nine District Land Offices have different procedures for dealing with illegal structures. As with the Buildings Department, the DLOs have limited resources. Low priority is given to lease enforcement. In 2004 the Ombudsman examined the practices of the DLOs with regard to lease enforcement in the villages and reported that DLOs lacked a positive attitude towards tackling the UBW problem.

One consideration barely touched upon in the report but which must be a major consideration for land officers is the attitude of indigenous villagers. They are very protective of their property and of what they consider to be their rights. They are suspicious and confrontational towards officialdom. Accordingly, they tend to adopt an aggressive, fierce attitude towards outsiders and officials. The attitude is epitomized by the reply of one village wife when she was asked about action being taken against illegal structures in their extended house. 'This is village land. No policeman dares to come in here, let alone any official from the Lands Department. You saw the signs.' The signs said, in Chinese, 'strangers are not welcome'.[12]

The closed, exclusionary nature of villages has survived a century of change. Despite immigration and emigration, despite advances in education and communication, traces of a tribal attitude subsist. The family, ancestors, and local customs remain important as part of the indigenous identity and what it means to be Chinese. The right to extend a family home is seen as a natural adjunct to the right to build one.

The taking of action against unauthorized works requires proof of the work and of the breach which often involves entry to and inspection of property. Offenders are often obstructionist and confrontational. They refuse entry to officials. They stall and are uncooperative. Government staff are naturally cautious and diffident. Some of them may live in villagers and be sympathetic to the claims of indigenous

12. Evan Fowler, 'Two Systems, One Colony: The Small House Policy Is a Reminder of the Duality of Hong Kong's Past', *Hong Kong Free Press*, 13 January 2018.

people; they may even be indigenous themselves. In many cases no action is taken for want of evidence.

After inspection, a letter is sent to the house owner and may be registered. In cases in which the unauthorized structure is removed as a result of the letter and the removal verified by inspectors from the DLO, a replacement may be erected after the inspectors have gone. Often the letter is ignored, especially if the owner has no desire to sell the house. No further action is taken in most instances. If the breach of the lease is minor, it will be tolerated, a waiver being given on payment of a penalty, for the life of the house. The ultimate sanction is re-entry (termination of the government grant by forfeiture) which can be effected by an entry on the land register.[13] But this is used very rarely indeed since it is grossly disproportionate to the breach. The Ombudsman's investigations showed that the proportion of cases in which a satisfactory result was achieved has been estimated at just 5 per cent.[14]

Proliferation of Rural Illegal Structures

In consequence of these factors, unauthorized additions and alterations to village houses are rife. Attention has focused upon roof structures: covers of aluminium and glass, metal framework, additional rooms or half floors, even complete extra storeys. But new, extended and enclosed balconies are common, too, as are concrete or framed retractable canvas canopies and other projections, grilles and gates, also window and door grilles. In the case of houses standing in their own grounds, extensions, out-houses and car ports can be constructed.

No systematic statistics are collected but the total number of unauthorized structures at village houses is estimated to be in the tens of thousands. A survey by the DLO in Tuen Mun in 2003 found that the number of detected UBWs there was five times that of two years earlier. A visual survey conducted by the Lands Department in 2004–2005 concluded that the UBW problem at NTEHs was serious. The northern and western parts of the New Territories are particularly affected.[15] On average there are about 500 complaints a year concerning UBWs on village houses. But of course not all UBWs are the subject of complaint. The Lands Department estimated that, as at February 2004, about 13,000 of the unauthorized structures resulted in a breach of lease conditions.[16]

The number of removal orders and prosecutions relating to UBWs on village houses is modest. There were 217 orders in 2010, 155 in 2009 and 220 in 2008. Prosecutions were 129 in 2010, 132 in 2009 and 66 in 2008. Compare those figures with the corresponding ones for urban areas where the number of removal orders

13. Government Rights (Re-entry and Vesting Remedies) Ordinance (Cap 126) s 4.
14. *Enforcement against Unauthorised Building Works in New Territories Exempted Houses*, April 2011.
15. Carrie Lam, Secretary for Development, in answer to an oral question from LegCo member Lee Wing-tat, 18 May 2011.
16. Ombudsman's Report, 2011.

is usually in excess of 20,000 per annum and the number of prosecutions is usually more than 2,000 per annum.[17]

When asked to estimate how long it would take to complete action against existing UBWs in their district, one DLO answered fifty years and another ninety-seven years. The Ombudsman concluded in 2004 that the problem of illegal structures in the New Territories was widespread and that it would not be possible for the government to eliminate it in the foreseeable future: the best that could be aimed for was containment by stopping new UBWs being completed and having a realistic enforcement policy which was widely known.[18]

Conclusions

What lessons can we learn from the above? There seems to be a number but they can be grouped under three general propositions. The first is that the law is generally misunderstood and is confused with its application and enforcement. The law itself casts a wide net. It requires prior permission for nearly all building work. The definition of building work is very broad, taking in items which sensible people would not regard as building work and requiring permission for doing things which ordinary property owners regard as part of their rights. In consequence the law is unrealistic and has been brought into disrepute. The requirement of permission, if understood, is roundly ignored. Full enforcement of the law is impossible. The administration has tacitly recognized this with its policy of prioritized enforcement.

The policy of prioritization has given a false impression of the law. It is widely believed, even among professionals such as architects and estate agents, that certain types of work do not require permission or at least are tolerated and therefore within the law. The severity of the Buildings Ordinance is therefore generally not appreciated: perhaps this is as well, for there might otherwise have been civil discontent.

The second proposition is that the impression that there is one law of building works for village houses and another for all other property is false. The Buildings Ordinance applies to all buildings throughout the territory. The only qualification to that concerns the initial construction of village houses. These are subject to separate controls. However, once completed, the Buildings Ordinance applies to them, too.

The idea that there are no controls for village houses stems from a confluence of factors. One is that initial construction of village houses is exempted from statutory controls. Another is that indigenous villagers enjoy privileges and that those privileges relate most notably to housing. Their lawful traditional rights are enshrined in the Basic Law and jealously guarded by the Heung Yee Kuk. The courts are empowered to apply customary law in the rural New Territories. The major supposed custom is that male villagers may build a house on their own land in

17. Reply of the Secretary of Security to a written question raised in LegCo by Wong Yuk-man, 15 June 2011.
18. Office of the Ombudsman, *Report on Enforcement Action on UBWs in NTEHs*, 2004.

their ancestral village. For almost fifty years the government has facilitated this by creating and maintaining the Small House Policy under which building land near villages is made available to indigenous males at low cost. This privilege has been roundly exploited with non-resident, and even non-native, male descendants of indigenous males claiming (often through developers) the right to a house which they promptly re-sell. The government has done little to stop the practice. Given the number and scale of their land privileges, indigenous immunity from building controls is only to be expected.

Indeed some villagers and their representatives claim just such an immunity. They assert that custom permits small houses to be enlarged if indigenous people require the living space. They say that before the Small House Policy was instituted, or at least before the British took over in 1899, there was no limit to the size of such houses. That is why on some old house lots in the centre of certain villages you find houses with more than three storeys. The claims are exaggerated, if not entirely specious, but they add to the perception that the law does not apply to village properties.

However, the biggest contribution to the false impression is administrative inaction. The Buildings Department and the District Land Offices are over-stretched so they have adopted a practice of not acting against new UBWs in rural areas. They concentrate instead upon dangerous structures and work in progress. This difference in approach to enforcement between urban and rural parts has been exacerbated by the adoption of a very narrow interpretation by DLOs of what constitutes work in progress. Add to this the reluctance of government officers to incur the wrath of villagers and the result is that there is a markedly lower degree of enforcement of the law in the New Territories. This is not confined to village houses. Other types of residence in rural areas enjoy the same tolerant treatment.

The final proposition is a deeper one: the law is badly in need of reform. This is not addressed by the Ombudsman's reports—unsurprisingly, since they are concerned with administrative practice in the enforcement of the existing law. However, the reports unwittingly bring out the weaknesses, indeed the absurdity, of the current law. By forbidding land owners from altering their properties in any substantial way without first going through a debilitating bureaucratic process with no certainty of receiving permission, the government is setting itself against normal expectations. A law which may have been appropriate when Hong Kong had a much smaller population, many fewer buildings and far fewer property owners, and when building standards were much lower, is not appropriate now. A law which does not provide for retrospective consent to be given, so that an owner is obliged to remove perfectly safe unauthorized structures before applying to re-build them, is seriously flawed. When the administration itself does not expect its legislation to be obeyed, as is apparent from the prioritization policy and the starving of the Buildings Department and the District Land Offices of resources to enforce the legislation, how can the public be expected to respect the law?

17
Despoliation

A journey around the areas of the contemporary New Territories outside the new towns and villages gives the visitor the sense that large parts of it have been laid waste. Particularly in the flat lands of the north and west, great stretches have seemingly been covered with concrete or hardcore and turned over to dirty, unsightly uses such as builders' yards, used car dumps and container depots. Other parts have been fenced off and left to the weeds. Former wetlands and fish ponds have been filled in with building material. Planners call these brown field sites.

This is the consequence of the administration's loss of control over the use of the land at the beginning of a vital stage in Hong Kong's development, the final two decades of the twentieth century. During that time land values were booming, agriculture was continuing to decline and cross-border trade was growing greatly. How did the loss of control happen?

At root, the cause was the incompleteness of the land settlement imposed upon the New Territories in the years after 1899. The survey, block Crown leases and registration of land documents were not aimed at regulating use of land but at raising revenue. It was assumed that land would continue to be utilized for the purposes for which it had traditionally been put. The only restrictions imposed by the leases were that agricultural land could not be built upon without government permission and that offensive trades could not be carried on there. The first was as much a revenue-raising device as a control of use (a premium could be levied for granting permission to build) and the latter was a standard restriction in leases of the era aimed at preventing nuisance.

It was also assumed that the schedule to the block leases contained restrictions. The individual lots were listed there, together with columns giving details, one of which described what it was being used for. The uses recorded were predominantly agricultural in nature, as might be expected. 'Padi' was the commonest description, for the land surrounding the villages was largely devoted to wet cultivation of rice. Some was employed for beating out grain ('threshing floor') and others for growing vegetables and the like ('dry cultivation').

The only explicit restrictions in the body of the lease forbad erection of buildings without prior government consent. Perhaps the drafters thought that the descriptions listed in the schedule were restrictions. Almost certainly they would not have envisaged that the peasant farmers of this backward and inaccessible new territory would have wanted, or been able, to do anything with their land except cultivate it. They could not have foreseen the demand for developable land that was to arise before the seventy-five-year terms had expired.

For decades the attitude prevailed that 'old schedule' Crown leases permitted only farming on those lots devoted to agriculture at the time of grant. If someone wanted to build on such land, they would have to ask the District Officer for permission. If other use which did not require building construction was contemplated, again a licence would be required and a premium might be demanded. The uses listed in the schedules were assumed to be prescriptive rather than descriptive.

The post-war rise in manufacturing and simultaneous decline in agriculture altered these considerations. Well before the 1970s rice farming had ceased to be profitable. Occupations ancillary to manufacturing, such as storage of construction materials and parking of vehicles, had risen. Industry required a back yard in which such occupations could be carried out. Communications between urban and rural areas had improved. The only obstacles to the recruitment of vacant rural land for such purposes were the contents of the Crown leases.

Melhado

The assumption that the uses listed in the lease schedules were prescriptive was exploded when a company which had become Crown lessee of thirteen pieces of ground applied successfully to court for a declaration that it was not inhibited from using them for storage purposes. The company had entered into a two-year sub-lease with a tenant for the purpose of storage of steel. In fact, photographs exhibited before the court showed steel girders and drums, suggesting storage of building materials. The hearing took place before Mr Justice Jackson-Lipkin on 18 May 1982. There was no doubt as to the importance of the issues at stake for the company was represented by eminent Queen's Counsel and the government by one of the attorney-general's chambers' strongest advocates. In his judgment, delivered immediately and orally (ex tempore), Jackson-Lipkin J referred twice to the case going on appeal to the Privy Council, which was then Hong Kong's ultimate court.

The judge pointed out that nowhere in the lease was there a provision that the lessee must use the land for agricultural purposes. As a matter of construction and common sense it could not have been intended that land described in the lease schedule as 'waste' was to be kept as waste (which is what the government's argument, if correct, would have required). The descriptions in the schedules were just that, descriptions.[1]

1. *Melhado Investment Ltd v Attorney General*, HCMP 1982/1981.

The government appealed. In March 1983 the appeal was dismissed. 'In our view' said the Vice President Sir Alan Huggins delivering the court's judgment, 'the contention on behalf of the Attorney General that the words in the schedule are something more than descriptive is completely untenable.' The purpose of the schedule, he went on, was to identify the lands and the parties to which the lease related and then to particularize the terms and the rents which had been reserved in the body of the lease. Sir Alan pointed out that the covenant against building without government permission in the lease would have been unnecessary if the lessee of every plot expressed to have been demised as 'padi' had been obliged to maintain it as padi throughout the term. In another Crown lease which had been shown to the court, one lot of land had been described as 'broken latrine': it would be absurd to suggest (as the government argument inevitably did) that it must be maintained as such.

The Attorney General's fallback contention was that a covenant against using the lots for any purpose other than those stated in the schedule was to be implied. The court dismissed this even more easily than the first argument. Terms were to be implied in leases and contracts only as a matter of necessity and it was not necessary in this instance to restrict a lessee's use of his land. The lease was to be construed as at the time that it had been made, in January 1905. 'The reality' explained the Vice President, 'is that in 1905 no one ever imagined that land in the New Territories might be wanted otherwise than for cultivation and building.'[2]

The decision was a disaster for the rural environment. Some thought that the three expatriate judges who decided the case knew little and cared less about the countryside and its beauty. But the judges had no choice: the express descriptions were so clearly not prescriptive that the government barely argued the point on appeal, relying instead on implications. The judge's prediction that his decision would be considered by the Privy Council turned out not to be accurate. However, the decision was confirmed as correct in a different case the following year by the Privy Council.[3]

Furthermore, the uncomfortable truth is that it is the locals, the indigenous themselves and their representatives, who are insensitive to preservation of their own places. They prefer to make a good living from letting land to tenants for uses such as the builder's yard in the Melhado case, as the rapid expansion of such uses showed. Brown field sites in the rural and semi-rural areas became so common that they were soon known as 'Melhado land'.

There were no statutory planning controls applicable to the New Territories except with regard to Country Parks. The Buildings Ordinance had given the Building Authority powers over rural buildings but not until 1961 and not in regard the construction of new small houses. Crown leases could still be used to control buildings but administrators were now powerless to stop every other use.

2. *Attorney General v Melhado Investment Ltd* [1983] 2 HKLR 327.
3. *Winfat Enterprises (HK) Co Ltd v Attorney General* [1988] 1 HKLR 5.

From an environmental point of view, the timing could not have been worse. Hong Kong's economy was booming, the mainland was opening up. Manufacturing was still a big driver of employment, commerce was healthy, new towns were under construction. Like every prosperous major metropolis, Hong Kong needed a hinterland to accommodate less salubrious supporting activities. Undeveloped rural areas, now served by new or improved roads linking them to the city, provided this. The container port, situated in the south-west of the New Territories, had become the busiest in the world. Many of the containers carried goods from new Chinese factories through rural areas to the port, destined for abroad. The empty containers, their transporters and cabs needed somewhere to park: flat areas of the northern districts were ideal.

By contrast, the timing of the legal clarification was fortunate for rural landholders. After *Melhado*, the way was open to devote unbuilt old schedule lots to lucrative commercial purposes provided that they did not involve permanent buildings. More than anything this meant open storage, a use which was both unsightly and inefficient.

Degradation

The Melhado decision gave a decided boost to the exploitation of rural land but it would be wrong to think that there had been no degradation of that land before 1982. The expansion of development and the decline in farming had already led landholders to seek new tenants and new uses.

The spectacular effect of the decision is shown by the evidence of changes presented to the court in a case in 2011 concerning land at Tai Tong, an extensive, largely flat district to the south of Yuen Long. For many years it had been difficult to access and the subject of regular flooding. In 1950 the land in question had been part of 'a large and lush area of trees', mainly lychee orchards, with cultivated farmland on one side. A system of deep nullahs or drains new in the 1960s had alleviated the flooding. Aerial photographs showed that by 1993 there were non-agricultural activities upon the land: workshops and garages, parked vehicles, a welding business. These were operated by tenants and licensees and brought an annual income of more than HK$1m, not for the owner but for an enterprising squatter. The area covered by trees began to shrink and was steadily reduced until less than half the original remained. The rest of the land had been either dug up or eroded by motor vehicles and machinery. Major new roads had opened up the area in the early 1990s. By 2008 more than half the land was bare and used only 'for storage of cargo containers, vehicles and other structures of similar aesthetic appeal'.[4]

The judge reflected sadly: 'This has now become the typical evolution of land in the New Territories'. However, it turns out that Tai Tong is no longer typical of

4. *Wai Wah Traders Ltd v Wong Yim*, HCMP 965/2000 (Mimmie Chan DJ, 8 December 2011).

degraded rural land because the area became the subject of extensive residential development in the second decade of the twenty-first century. It is now the home of several luxurious tower blocks and villa estates. This is the result of its infrastructure—not just drains and roads but railways too—suggesting that degradation can be but a stage on the way from rural to urban if the conditions are right. The difficulty is that many brown field sites are on back roads which are unsuitable for the heavy vehicles which they now have to bear and which do not make for a convenient and attractive living environment.

Planning at Last

It took more than seven years for the government's land experts to re-impose the control lost to *Melhado*. The delay was disastrous. Failure to enact statutory restrictions on the use of land 'resulted in the tragic misuse in both economic and environmental terms of the limited land resources of the New Territories'.[5] During that time, container yards, vehicle parking lots, building supply depots, car repair shops, scrap metal and spare parts pounds, waste tips and used vehicle dumps appeared throughout the countryside. As the Court of Final Appeal observed, this was the despoliation of the New Territories.[6]

Amendments to the Town Planning Ordinance which imposed restrictions upon development in rural parts were finally announced with a bill in July 1990 and enacted in January 1991.[7] The amendments authorized the Director of Planning to prepare plans designating most of the New Territories outside new towns and country parks as Development Permission Areas (DPAs), showing zones in which various types of use would be permitted and in which development or further development required government permission. The DPAs were to be effective for an initial period of three years (extendable) whilst more detailed permanent Outline Zoning Plans were drawn up by the Town Planning Board. The intention was to prevent changes in the use of the land from that for which it had been used when the bill was first published.

However, final plans for DPAs were not ready in the summer of 1990. So the Director of Planning was empowered to prepare temporary plans designating any area of Hong Kong as an Interim Development Permission Area (IDPA).[8] This has been described as 'an emergency stop-gap measure' to preserve the status quo in rural parts. But one can hardly call an seven-year delay in responding to *Melhado* an emergency. The Planning Department had taken its time in drawing up the plans and legislation. IDPAs were indeed temporary: their purpose was to prevent development and changes in use after the new law had been announced and before DPA

5. Cruden DJ in *Niceboard Development Ltd v China Light and Power Co Ltd* [1994] HKDCLR 69.
6. *Secretary for Transport v Delight World Ltd* (2006) 9 HKCFAR 720.
7. Town Planning (Amendment) Ordinance 1991.
8. Town Planning Ordinance (Cap 131) (hereinafter TPO) s 26.

plans were ready so that the government's intentions as regards use of land within the area were not jeopardized by alterations on the land. The bill amending the Town Planning Ordinance was not passed into law until the following January. In order to prevent rural landowners from rushing through changes on their land during preceding months, IDPAs were prepared and the amendments were made retroactive to the date of gazettal of the bill, 27 July 1990. Retroactive legislation is unusual. Normally the courts presume that a statute speaks from the date of its passing but in this instance the intention to make the controls retrospective had been announced when the bill had been gazetted and 'the legislature firmly set its face against further environmental harm' to those rural areas covered by IDPA plans.[9]

By the new law, no one was allowed to undertake or continue development unless the development was an existing use or permission for the development had been obtained.[10] Development was broadly defined to mean the carrying out of operations (including building, engineering and mining) in, on, over, or under land or the making of a material change in use of land or buildings. A material change in use was in turn defined to include the depositing of matter on land if the area, height, or amount of the deposit was increased, notwithstanding that the land was already used for depositing matter. So intensification of present uses as well as changes from present use would require permission.

The plans, notes and explanatory statement for a DPA prepared by the Planning Department designated the uses which would or might be allowed in the various zones within the Area. This was a practice already familiar from Outline Zoning Plans (OZPs) used in urban Hong Kong. However, the amendments broadened the categories of use permitted. The zones which might be indicated in a plan were supplemented to include those for village-type development, for open storage and for country parks, areas of scientific interest and green belts.[11]

The replacement of DPAs with OZPs was a slow process. It had not been completed by the year 2000. But twenty years on, all but the most remote parts of the territory (mainly country parks) have their own OZP. The plans for both OZPs and DPAs designate certain zones and uses, including green belt and village zones. In 'the V zone', village-type development including small houses would always be permitted. Small houses might also be specially permitted on the green belt.

Land Owners' Reaction

The response to the new law of rural landowners and their spokesmen was unusually muted. This may have been because most of those who wished to turn their land into brown fields had already done so, and therefore would not be disturbed by the

9. TPO ss 26 and 1(2); *Tse Kwei King v Attorney General*, HCMP 1509/1993 (Rhind J, 21 December 1993); *R v Power Straight Ltd* [1995] 3 HKC 402.
10. TPO s 20(7).
11. TPO s 4 as amended by s 6(b) of the 1991 Amendment Ordinance.

controls unless there was a demonstrable increase in such use. Or it may have been because the legislation would not forbid changes, merely require that permission for them be obtained and the permission would not be charged for. But the likeliest explanation is that owners did not know of, or did not care about, the new law. They carried on as if nothing had happened. Those who intended to alter the use of their land calculated that enforcement of any restrictions would be difficult: they could go ahead with their changes and see what happened. Over-stretched and under-resourced inspectors might never find out or, if they did, might not act quickly.

On paper, however, the planners had considerable enforcement options. It was an offence to undertake or continue development in a DPA in contravention of the ordinance. The Planning Authority could serve notices upon owners and occupiers requiring them to stop or reinstate any changes and it was an offence not to comply. The Director of Planning could enter the land and carry out reinstatement work at the expense of the owner or occupier.[12]

One business caught out by the new retrospective controls sold construction materials at Pak Kong in Sai Kung. The village, located some distance from the main road beneath the hills of a water catchment area, was still predominantly rural. The business was run by a Madam Tse and her husband on two pieces of previously vacant agricultural land which they had bought in September 1990, just two months after the amendment bill had been announced. One piece was to the east, the other to the west, of a water reserve access road. There they stored cement, sand, bricks, gravel, pipes, grids and other material for retail sale and kept lifting machinery for stacking goods. On 12 October 1990 the IDPA plan for Pak Kong was gazetted, prohibiting development without permission. The couple claimed that on that date they were already using both sides of the road to store materials. Site inspections were carried out by departmental staff, warnings and notices were issued and, when they were ignored, enforcement proceedings were brought in March 1993 alleging unauthorized development and requiring discontinuance of the development within three months. Madam Tse sought judicial review of the enforcement notice, claiming the Planning Authority had made an error. She was defeated by aerial photographs which had been taken on the day of publication of the plan. Although one side was shown to contain materials, all that could be seen on the other side was one parked van.

The judge, Mr Justice Rhind, had some sympathy for Madam Tse and her husband. When they had bought the land, the Town Planning Ordinance had not yet come into operation at Pak Kong and storage was allowed. They had much at stake, he noted, for their livelihood would be affected by the new rules. But, the judge pointed out, their neighbours in the nearby old village also had much at stake. Their view of farmland had been affected by the yard which produced dust, noise

12. TPO ss 21 and 23.

and, during summer rain, polluting run-off and was attended by heavy lorries on the small road.

Enforcement

In a series of prosecutions in magistrates' courts during the mid-1990s, the Director showed determination to enforce the new law. A handful of the cases were appealed to the High Court where they were heard by Mr Justice Litton, an appellate judge sitting specially in the lower court to decide them. As Henry Litton QC he had made something of a name as an environmental campaigner, but also had played a role in the background to the new law, having been counsel for the successful landowner Melhado in the case which had made the amendments necessary.

The facts of these prosecutions suggest that extension of planning controls had made little impact on owners' behaviour. One, concerning a site at Lin Tong Mei, a village in Kwu Tung south-west of Sheung Shui, until about October 1991—months after the Amendment Ordinance had been passed—had been essentially vacant, a collection of bushes, trees, shrubs and weeds with a few vehicles parked on it, a track to the village running through it and sporadic storage of spillover goods from a neighbouring warehouse. Then the site had been cleared, surfaced with hard material, and provided with drains, fencing and a gate. It was turned into a container storage depot, the North District's spoliation of choice. Containers were brought in, stacked up and topped with iron sheets to form a roof. The company that carried this out no doubt thought that it was a sensible use of derelict land, providing valuable services to cross-border container traffic. But the site fell within a new DPA, the plan for which had been published in July 1991. The work done to the site was unauthorized development and a material change of use. An enforcement notice was issued requiring the site to be restored to its previous use. When that was ignored, prosecution and conviction followed. Since the proceedings, including the futile appeal, lasted until March 1995, the company had been able to run the unauthorized depot for almost three-and-a-half years.[13]

On the same day Litton JA gave judgment in another container storage case in which an enforcement notice had been ignored. The defendants were two members of the Tang clan who owned five lots at Ha Tsuen, Ping Shan, which in 1992 they had cleared of vegetation, levelled and let for five years as a container terminal. By November 1992 containers were stacked and cranes were operating on the lots. A draft DPA plan had been published for the area in July 1991. The lots had been placed in an 'unspecified use' zone on the plan. This meant that any new use had to be specifically authorized by the Town Planning Board. The tenant applied to the Board for permission to change the use but this was refused. Enforcement notices demanding discontinuance of the unauthorized use were issued at the end of 1992.

13. *R v Way Luck Industrial Ltd* [1995] 2 HKC 290.

The lot owners were convicted of failure to comply with the notices. On appeal, their lawyer deployed a variety of arguments including that there was no unauthorized development because no use had been specified on the plan and that the land owner could not be liable unless shown to be responsible for the unauthorized development. All failed.[14]

Impetus for debasement of abandoned agricultural land had been provided by the improvement of transport links during and after the 1980s. Three-lane dual carriageways were built to replace the principal single-lane arterial roads that had been put in immediately after the territory had come under British administration. Construction of the New Territories Circular Road, the replacement for the old Castle Peak Road, had almost reached Yuen Long in 1990. The owners of some fish-ponds at the side of the new highway at Ngau Tam Mei saw the opportunities that this presented. They filled the ponds in, levelled, fenced and gated the site and cut a path to the highway then under construction. Before they could start operations, an IDPA for Ngau Tam Mei was instituted in September 1990. This did not discourage the owners. By July 1991 the site was being used for the dismantling of vehicles and the storage of vehicles and their parts. In that month the draft DPA plan was gazetted showing the site zoned for unspecified uses. Enforcement notices were issued alleging unauthorized development and a material change in use since publication of the IDPA. Although the owners' legal representatives argued that the condition of the land as at the time of the DPA was the basis for assessing what was the existing use and whether there had been a change in use, Litton JA concluded that it was the condition as at the coming into effect of the IDPA in July 1990 that was the true basis. Consequently, the work done in forming the site was irrelevant because by then it had already taken place but the work subsequently done there upon the vehicles was a change in use which could and should have been discontinued.[15]

The influence of main roads is again seen in the case of a yard on the way from Sheung Shui to the border checkpoint at Man Kam To. The site had been formed, again by the in-filling of fish ponds and the building up of the surface with sand and soil, in 1989. Later that year the then owner had started a small business there for the parking of commercial vehicles and repairing of tyres with an office in a small container. In late 1990 he surfaced the land with asphalt. The scale of the business increased markedly from January 1991 when the defendant Helen Transportation took over. Gates and access to Man Kam To Road were put in. The land was used progressively as a depot for containers and a yard for trailers and tractors, with repair facilities. The relevant IDPA plan had been published on 7 September 1990, followed by a DPA plan in July 1991, both showing the site as within an 'unspecified use' zone. Aerial photographs from that time showed the land mostly covered in vegetation with just one container-like object. By August 1993 containers were stacked two-storeys high with storage space on the ground floor, air-conditioned

14. *R v Tang Ying Yip* [1995] 2 HKC 277.
15. *R v Power Straight Ltd*, above.

accommodation on the first floor and iron girders forming a cover for a vehicle repair shop. Old tyres and drums were stacked on the ground. Trailers and a mobile crane were parked there.

An enforcement notice was issued in August 1993 based upon unauthorized development by material change of use. When there was no compliance (except for removal of the repair shop) after three months, prosecution followed, with conviction in February 1995. The appeal was heard in June the same year. The question of whether there had been a change of use was, Litton JA explained, one of fact and degree. But the facts in this case were overwhelming. In September 1990 there had been no container or trailer park. Unquestionably there had been unauthorized development. The transportation company had been rightly convicted. But it had managed to operate its unauthorized yard for four-and-a-half years.[16]

The Price of Development

Welcome as the imposition and tightening of statutory controls over the use of rural land were, they could not reverse the damage already done, nor could they intervene where no change of use was involved or where the abuse was not evident or reported to the authorities. Furthermore, the degradation might be the result of an approved change of use. Economic development and employment opportunities desired by government and people within a modern economy dictate that space be made available for industrial and commercial projects, including dirty ones. Infrastructure beneficial to the community likewise demands space. The likeliest place in which to find or make that space remains the remoter reaches of the New Territories.

Nothing illustrates this better than the fate of Lung Kwu Tan, a district beyond Tuen Mun at Castle Peak in the far south-west of the mainland part of the SAR. It has been described, with little exaggeration, as the 'dumping ground' of Hong Kong. Long ago it became the host of two power stations, one fuelled by coal, the other by gas. An associated ash lagoon was formed. The district's remote location attracted a site for storage of aviation fuel. These have been joined by a cement works, a steel factory and a sludge incinerator plant. Most recently was added a columbarium for 160,000 niches. The coast has been extended and built up by construction waste and other land fill. More reclamation is proposed. Yet this abused corner contains five traditional villages which house more than a thousand people.[17]

Moreover, elsewhere the conversion of fallow agricultural land and unwanted fish ponds to Melhado uses continues. The lure of the greater rent which such uses can command is too great, even if it is for a year or two until the authorities catch

16. *R v Helen Transportation Co Ltd*, HCMA 303/1995 (14 June 1995).

17. Shirley Zhao, 'Villagers in Lung Kwu Tan, "Hong Kong's dumping ground", fear the environmental consequences of 250-hectare reclamation plan', *South China Morning Post*, 27 August 2018.

up. Once the use has been discontinued, the site remains converted to brown field status and thus more likely eventually to be developed.

Threats to the Environment

Lung Kwu Tan is of course an extreme instance of despoliation. Little heavy industry and few power stations are needed in Hong Kong. Open storage and smaller polluting operations such as car repairs are much more frequently encountered. Yet they are not the only threats to the rural environment. The intensity of development, particularly the expansion in the number of small houses, has caused difficulties of its own.

The belated application of planning controls accounts for rural sprawl, the irregular arrangement of houses that disfigures many villages. Typically, a ragged string of individual houses of varying age and design rubs shoulders with cramped developments of a few identical houses. More and more land on the outer reaches of the village has been levelled, reclaimed from water or converted from waste ready for new houses.

Unsightly development is only the start of the problems. Construction of the houses produces building waste, often casually dumped nearby along with fly-tipped detritus from redecoration. Each house produces sewage but, except for those villages adjacent to new towns, there is no sewer. The houses rely upon septic tanks with soakaway pits for waste disposal. Where a house has many residents or visitors (such as when used as restaurants or holiday homes) the pipes and tanks simply cannot take the demand. The tanks are emptied or de-sludged infrequently or not at all. They are rarely inspected, let alone maintained. Once full, their contents leak into the surrounding land. During heavy rain, the soakaways are inundated and spill over to foul nearby watercourses. Waste water from baths, showers and sinks (greywater) only adds to the overuse if connected to the septic tank. Where there are pipes and drains, they discharge this water untreated into waterways nearby.

New village houses need vehicular access and parking. This means more roads, authorized and unauthorized. Unauthorized roads, which are estimated to comprise more than half of rural roads, tend to be roughly made with inadequate surfaces, underpinning and drainage. Roads and parking spaces may be cut into hillsides or built over ponds and ditches; trees may be cut down or uprooted to make way for them. Green space becomes brown, grass turns to mud. Wildlife habitat is lost and streams polluted.[18]

A phenomenon which came into public focus in 2016, the deliberate piling of refuse of all descriptions upon vacant land, is an unintended consequence of the imposition of planning laws. These 'waste mountains' are unsightly and can become dangerous through instability, particularly after heavy rain. It seems that

18. Hopkinson and Lao, *Rethinking the Small House Policy*, pp 22–23.

landowners allow such accumulations in order to improve the chances of the land being re-zoned for building.

Where villages have not been built out so as to merge with the next settlement, the space between has often become unsightly. Ever since the authorities gave up restricting the number of vehicles by increasing the cost of a licence, every verge that has not been marked off by bollards or other obstructions has been apt to become a parking area. In the northern and western districts, lay-bys and passing places have become free storage sites for used car traders, the police and transport department having seemingly given up the unequal struggle to control this.

Even the heart of the traditional New Territories has succumbed to degeneration. At Ping Shan, once the proud centre of the Tang clan, one can follow a heritage trail which starts a short distance to the south of the Tin Shui Wai railway station. Close by is a pagoda and, tucked down a lane behind the inevitable yards, the renovated grey-brick Tai Tak Communal Hall completed in 1857. The hall was once in the middle of a village market but there is no trace of that now. Here the Tangs and others plotted to resist the British in 1899. The trail curves round beside a nullah towards the ancient villages but the uninitiated are soon lost in an immense parking lot, rough surfaced and full of buses and lorries. This used to be open fields and ponds which old photographs tell us afforded a pleasant aspect of the settlements of Hang Cheung Wai, Hang Tau Tsuen and Hang Mei Tsuen with their temples, study halls and ancestral halls. These venerable buildings are still there, hidden behind the vehicles, but they are overshadowed by a variety of close-packed houses.

The Hong Kong authorities so distrusted the Tangs that in 1905 they built a police station on the hill dominating the Ping Shan villages. The station long ago moved to modern facilities at Yuen Long. The old building was transformed in the 1990s to a visitor centre and gallery commemorating the Tangs. The clan may believe that this symbolizes their survival under passing rulers. Yet what they have done below the hill surely questions whether their heritage really survives.

The story is similar at two other ancient village clusters, Santin and Ho Sheung Heung, home to the Mans and the Haus respectively. Their temples and halls, much renovated, still stand. But for the most part houses of varying vintages and sizes are packed closely up against them and the ponds and padis of the periphery are now filled and levelled to provide parking.

The temptation to despair seems overwhelming. But then one remembers that this is the villagers' choice, and that this is not the well-ordered city. This is the unruly New Territories.

Acknowledgements

The author gratefully acknowledges help and support received in the research and preparation of the text from the following people:

John Chan, solicitor, Yuen Long; Cheng Gau Hung, indigenous villager; Elaine Chow; Professor Johannes Chan SC (Hon); Cheung Tsuen Cheung, village representative; Cliff Chow, solicitor; Brendan Clift; the late Anthony Dicks SC; Louis Fung, solicitor; Dr Danny Gittings; Dr James Hayes; Dr Devin Lin; Ng Wing Kit; Professor Michael Palmer; Felix Tsang; Teresa Wong; Clarissa Wu; Michael Yeung, village representative.

Index

General

Persons

Places

www.ingramcontent.com/pod-product-compliance
Ingram Content Group UK Ltd.
Pitfield, Milton Keynes, MK11 3LW, UK
UKHW021836100926
8556IPUK00004B/379

9 789888 528325